EDITED BY WAYNE AU

RETHINKING MULTICULTURAL EDUCATION

Teaching for Racial and Cultural Justice

A RETHINKING SCHOOLS PUBLICATION

SECOND EDITION

Rethinking Multicultural Education: Teaching for Racial and Cultural Justice
Second Edition
Edited by Wayne Au

A Rethinking Schools Publication

Rethinking Schools, Ltd., is a nonprofit educational publisher of books, booklets, and a quarterly magazine on school reform, with a focus on issues of equity and social justice. To request additional copies of this book or a catalog of other publications, or to subscribe to *Rethinking Schools* magazine, contact:
Rethinking Schools
6737 W. Washington St. Suite 3249
Milwaukee, Wisconsin 53214
800-669-4192
www.rethinkingschools.org

© 2014 Rethinking Schools, Ltd.
Second edition

Cover Design: Nancy Zucker
Cover Illustration: Favianna Rodriguez
Managing Editor: Jody Sokolower
Curriculum Editor: Bill Bigelow
Production Editor: Mike Trokan
Book Design: Nancy Zucker
Proofreading: Lawrence Sanfilippo
Business Manager: Mike Trokan

Second Edition ISBN: 978-0-942961-53-9

The Library of Congress has cataloged the first edition as follows:
Rethinking multicultural education : teaching for racial and cultural justice /
edited by Wayne Au. -- 1st ed.
p. cm.
ISBN 978-0-942961-42-3 (pbk.)
1. Multicultural education--United States. 2. Discrimination in education--United States. 3. Minorities--Education--United States. 4. Social justice--United States. I. Au, Wayne, 1972-
LC1099.3.R494 2009
370.1170973--dc22
            2009001983

ACKNOWLEDGMENTS

All writing is a collective process, and none more so than with Rethinking Schools. This book would have not been possible without the collective efforts of many people. This second edition would not have happened without the tremendous efforts of Rethinking Schools Business Manager Mike Trokan pushing the project along, Nancy Zucker providing layout and art direction, and Lawrence Sanfilippo's proofing. These folks provided the nuts and bolts of making this book happen. Special thanks goes to all the artists who contributed images and to the contributors for doing the work that they do. As always, the Rethinking Schools editorial collective and staff provided support for this project. So continued thanks goes to Linda Christensen, Dyan Watson, Bill Bigelow, David Levine, Stan Karp, Larry Miller, Bob Peterson, Stephanie Walters, Melissa Bollow Tempel, Grace Cornell Gonzales, Helen Gym, Jesse Hagopian, Adam Sanchez, Jody Sokolower, Kathy Xiong, Kris Collett, and Tegan Dowling. Finally, thanks to my family, Mira Shimabukuro and Mako Shimabukuro-Au, for always supporting me in my work.

—Wayne Au

CONTENTS

INTRODUCTION
TO THE SECOND EDITION

By Wayne Au

Rethinking Multicultural Education: Teaching for Racial and Cultural Justice, second edition, has been a long time coming. Over its almost 30 years of existence, *Rethinking Schools* has published more than 200 articles that dealt explicitly with issues of race and culture. Even though *Rethinking Schools* has always kept racial and cultural justice amongst our main focal points, until the first edition of *Rethinking Multicultural Education* in 2009, we had never published a book that specifically focused on race and culture in education in their own right. This book does just that: provide a *Rethinking Schools* vision of anti-racist, social justice education that is both practical for teachers and sharp in analysis.

It is my hope that the selections included in the second edition of *Rethinking Multicultural Education: Teaching for Racial and Cultural Justice* offer a more robust and powerful definition of multicultural education than we see so often used. For instance, some educators and teacher educators say they teach multicultural education, but do it under the guise of "global education." This form of multiculturalism feels safer to some because it uses the veneer of international cultures to avoid more serious and painful realities of issues like racism. Similarly, "diversity education" and "cultural pluralism" get used with the singular intent of promoting heroes and holidays and celebrate individual differences, again circumventing issues of power and privilege.

The terms "diverse students" and "urban students," two more stand-ins for "multicultural" students, have devolved into meaning "poor African American and Latino students" or "students who aren't white." This is particularly ironic given that in some school districts in the United States, schools might be approaching 100 percent African American or Latino students, as is the case in Detroit and Santa Ana, California, respectively, and are regularly referred to as "diverse" by professors, teachers, and politicians alike.

The right wing has also developed its own, sometimes contradictory definitions of multicultural education. While some conservatives have vehemently attacked multicultural education as representative of the downfall of Western Civilization, others such as E. D. Hirsch (founder of the Core Knowledge curriculum) have developed a different definition of multicultural education. As Kristen Buras, professor of education at Georgia State University, talks about in her book, *Rightist Multiculturalism,* Hirsch's Core Knowledge curriculum has recently taken up the banner of multicultural education by defining the United States as a multicultural nation of diverse immigrants—while simultaneously covering up systematic oppression based on class, race, and nation status.

Multicultural education is also being narrowly defined as a path students can take to "higher" status literature. Teachers use Tupac's lyrics to move students to Shakespeare; students can unpack hip-hop lyrics as a way to learn literary language like stanza and rhyme, but they need to study Frost and Yeats to be considered well read. Students in regular classes can read "thug" literature, but AP classes need to read the classics. (Does anyone read Morrison as a precursor to Chaucer? She's harder than the *Canterbury Tales*). This version of multicultural education focuses on access to the canon of high-status knowledge. In doing so, such a definition not only keeps the Eurocentric canon of knowledge at the heart of "real" education, it also communicates to students the idea that the diversity of their identities, lives, and communities do not really matter when it comes to learning.

The second edition of *Rethinking Multicultural Education* is an attempt to reclaim multicultural education as part of a larger, more serious struggle for social justice, a struggle that recognizes the need to fight against systematic racism, colonization, and cultural oppression that takes place through our schools. In the chapters included here, multicultural education:
- is grounded in the lives of our students.
- draws on the voices and perspectives of those "being studied."
- teaches through dialogue.
- critically supports students' identities.
- embraces and recognizes the value of students' home languages.
- critiques school knowledge, knowledge that has historically been Eurocentric.
- invites students to engage in real social and political issues.
- creates classroom environments where students can meaningfully engage with each other.
- is rigorous, and recognizes that academic rigor is impossible without it.
- connects to the entire curriculum.
- is rooted in an anti-racist struggle about which knowledge and experiences should be included in the curriculum.
- celebrates social movements and the fight against nativism, xenophobia, and white supremacy.
- explores how social, economic, and cultural institutions contribute to inequality.

It is critical that I take a moment here to address an issue regarding how I am defining "multicultural" in this book. Some friends and allies, for instance, critiqued the first edition of *Rethinking Multicultural Education* for focusing too narrowly on typical categories of race, ethnicity, and culture, to the exclusion of more expansive definitions of "multiculturalism" that might include, for instance, an attention to the identities of LGBTQ youth in our classrooms and curriculum, or to the religious diversity of our students and communities. I understand and appreciate these concerns. The identities of our students and their communities are diverse and exceedingly complex, and certainly one approach is to define "multiculturalism" in ways to match every aspect of those identities—every aspect of "difference."

My answer in conversation with these friends and allies has been along two lines. First I attend to the context of *Rethinking Schools* itself. Two of our earlier, widely used books, *Rethinking Our Classrooms Volumes 1 & 2*, take up a broad definition of teaching for social justice, and in doing so, both volumes seek to embrace an expansive definition of culture, and also span grade levels and subject areas. Granted these two volumes are not perfect, but in many ways, my choice of focusing on more typically defined notions of race, culture, and ethnicity was a conscious one within the context of *Rethinking Schools*. We had already worked with the more expansive notion of culture in those two volumes, but had yet to take up a book that focused on race, racism, and the ways culture intertwines with them.

The second part of my decision to define "multiculturalism" in the manner that I have for *Rethinking Multicultural Education* is connected to my experience teaching multicultural education and diversity courses at the university level. As I discussed earlier in this introduction, I worry that multiculturalism has been equated with "diversity" and has become the "everyone else" category. Teacher education credential coursework at many universities, for instance, require some sort of "diversity" class as a part of their core sequence of courses. Although I generally believe in the importance of requiring such courses and certainly do not want them taken out of teacher credential programs, the "every aspect of difference" nature of these classes oftentimes means that students—future teachers in this case—may talk about race, privilege, and myriad issues associated with diversity but give short shrift to the painful and powerful systemic racism, the legacies of colonization, and the realities of cultural oppression.

To be clear, I'm not opposed to more expansive definitions of multiculturalism and diversity, and I'm open to hearing the critiques of my friends, colleagues, and allies regarding the definition of multiculturalism I've chosen within the context of *Rethinking Schools* as a whole and the field of multicultural education as it currently exists. But this book represents the need to defend the conscious and explicit attention to race and ethnicity, and the aspects of culture that extend from them, as I have done here in this second edition of *Rethinking Multicultural Education*.

Changes and Organization of the Second Edition

This second edition of *Rethinking Multicultural Education* is significantly different from the first edition. There are more than 15 new chapters included here, drawn from the strong articles about race and culture printed in the pages of *Rethinking Schools* since the first edition was published in 2009, and I removed some chapters that I felt became redundant in the context of the new edition. This second edition of *Rethinking Multicultural Education* also has been reorganized to include a new section, "The Fight for Multicultural Education." This new section came about because the last five years have seen immense struggles over state standards, especially the banning of the Mexican American Studies program in the Tucson Unified School District.

The first section is "Anti-Racist Orientations," and it examines the importance of recognizing the role of race and culture in education in our schools today. Here, chapters focus on general anti-racist orientations that are important for teachers to carry into the classroom, on dispositions that take justice seriously and examine privileges as they exist in practice. This exploration includes understanding the relationships among teaching, culture, and privilege, as well as recognizing the more historical and institutional inequalities that we see today.

Section two, "The Fight for Multicultural Education," is new for the second edition of *Rethinking Multicultural Education*. This section highlights how the establishment and maintenance of anti-racist, multicultural curriculum is always steeped in struggle over the politics of curriculum and what knowledge is deemed important and worthwhile for students to learn. These chapters document the fights about what should or should not be included in state-level standards for history, as well as the banning of the Mexican American Studies program in Tucson, Arizona, that have taken place. Further, it highlights how regimes of high-stakes, standardized testing pose a constant threat to multicultural education.

Language is central to culture, and how we understand and treat language in our classrooms speaks to issues of power both inside and outside of education. The chapters in section three, entitled "Language, Culture, and Power," look at the relationship between language and culture, finding connections between the cultural politics of Black English, Bilingual Education, and the cultural norms for communication. It also addresses the ways in which we deal with culture and language in the classroom that speak specifically to student identities.

Section four, "Transnational Identities, Multicultural Classrooms," includes chapters that look at what it means to be an anti-racist, social justice educator within the context of immigration, globalization, and colonization—where our students' identities are transnational, both rooted in the United States and not rooted in the United States. This section attempts to stretch our normal categories for students, many of whom are immigrants, and many of whom, while not immigrants themselves, hail from immigrant communities. The transnational, even globalized, identities of our students sometimes make issues of cultural identity relative to the U.S. and "home" countries mixed up and even contradictory, forcing educators to recognize the dynamic nature of cultures and communities.

Although concrete examples exist throughout the book, the final section, "Confronting Race in the Classroom," focuses specifically on examples of anti-racist teaching at the elementary and secondary levels, in multiple grades and across multiple subject areas. Even though other chapters in other sections are clearly grounded in classroom practice, here the focus is on how elementary and secondary teachers have critically considered issues of race and culture in their curriculum—oftentimes experiencing both success and difficulty in raising such important and complex issues.

In these times of high-stakes testing, the standards movement, shrinking budgets, and increased workloads, teachers are continuously being pushed to leave justice and equality behind. Instead, they find themselves having to focus on test scores, pacing guides, and scripted instruction. But, as W. E. B. Du Bois once said, "Education must keep broad ideals before it, and never forget that it is dealing with Souls and not with Dollars." Teaching for racial and cultural justice is one of those "broad ideals" that we can't lose sight of if we are to live up to our commitments to teach all children. *Rethinking Multicultural Education* is a tool for educators to address these ideals in their classrooms, to take a stand against the dollarization of education and for the soul of our students, communities, and world.

SECTION 1
ANTI-RACIST ORIENTATIONS

FAVIANNA RODRIGUEZ

Chapter One

TAKING MULTICULTURAL, ANTI-RACIST EDUCATION SERIOUSLY:

An interview with Enid Lee

Enid Lee is the director of Enidlee Consultants Inc., a Toronto-based consultancy dedicated to anti-racist education and organizational change. She has more than 35 years' experience in the classroom and is the former supervisor of race/ethnic relations for the North York Board of Education in metropolitan Toronto. Her publications include Letters to Marcia: A Teacher's Guide to Anti-Racist Education, *and* Beyond Heroes and Holidays: A Practical Guide to K–12, Anti-Racist, Multicultural Education and Staff Development, *which she co-edited. She is currently a visiting scholar with Teaching for Change in Washington, D.C., and formerly held the same position at the University of California, Santa Cruz's New Teacher Center. She was interviewed by Barbara Miner.*

RICK REINHARD

What do you mean by a multicultural education?

The term "multicultural education" has a lot of different meanings. The term I use most often is "anti-racist education."

Multicultural or anti-racist education is fundamentally a perspective. It's a point of view that cuts across all subject areas, and addresses the histories and experiences of people who have been left out of the curriculum. Its purpose is to help us deal equitably with all the cultural and racial differences that you find in the human family. It's also a perspective that allows us to get at explanations for why things are the way they are in terms of power relationships, in terms of equality issues.

> **If you don't take multicultural education or anti-racist education seriously, you are actually promoting a monocultural or racist education.**

So when I say multicultural or anti-racist education, I am talking about equipping students, parents, and teachers with the tools needed to combat racism and ethnic discrimination, and to find ways to build a society that includes all people on an equal footing.

It also has to do with how the school is run in terms of who gets to be involved with decisions. It has to do with parents and how their voices are heard or not heard. It has to do with who gets hired in the school.

If you don't take multicultural education or anti-racist education seriously, you are actually promoting a monocultural or racist education. There is no neutral ground on this issue.

Why do you use the term "anti-racist education" instead of "multicultural education"?

Partly because, in Canada, multicultural education often has come to mean something that is quite superficial: the dances, the dress, the dialect, the dinners. And it does so without focusing on what those expressions of culture mean: the values, the power relationships that shape the culture.

I also use the term anti-racist education because a lot of multicultural education hasn't looked at discrimination. It has the view "People are different and isn't that nice," as opposed to looking at how some people's differences are looked upon as deficits and disadvantages. In anti-racist education, we attempt to look at—and change—those things in school and society that prevent some differences from being valued.

Oftentimes, whatever is white is treated as normal. So when teachers choose literature that they say will deal with a universal theme or story, like childhood, all the people in the stories are of European origin; it's basically white culture and civilization. That culture is different from others, but it doesn't get named as different. It gets named as normal.

Anti-racist education helps us move that European perspective over to the side to make room for other cultural perspectives that must be included.

What are some ways your perspective might manifest itself in a kindergarten classroom, for example?

It might manifest itself in something as basic as the kinds of toys and games that you select. If all the toys and games reflect the dominant culture and race and language, then that's what I call a monocultural classroom even if you have kids of different backgrounds in the class.

I have met some teachers who think that just because they have kids from different races and backgrounds, they have a multicultural classroom. Bodies of kids are not enough.

It also gets into issues such as what kind of pictures are up on the wall? What kinds of festivals are celebrated? What are the rules and expectations in the classroom in terms of what kinds of language are acceptable? What kinds of interactions are encouraged? How are the kids grouped? These are just some of the concrete ways in which a multicultural perspective affects a classroom.

How does one implement a multicultural or anti-racist education?

It usually happens in stages. Because there's a lot of resistance to change in schools, I don't think it's reasonable to expect to move straight from a monocultural school to a multiracial school.

First there is this surface stage in which people change a few expressions of culture in the school. They make welcome signs in several languages and have a variety of foods and festivals. My problem is not that they start there. My concern is that they often stop there. Instead, what they have to do is move very quickly and steadily to transform the entire curriculum. For example, when we say classical music, whose classical music are we talking about? European? Japanese? And what items are on the tests? Whose culture do they reflect? Who is getting equal access to knowledge in the school? Whose perspective is heard; whose is ignored?

I have met some teachers who think that just because they have kids from different races and backgrounds, they have a multicultural classroom. Bodies of kids are not enough.

The second stage is transitional and involves creating units of study. Teachers might develop a unit on Native Americans, or Native Canadians, or people of African background. And they have a whole unit that they study from one period to the next. But it's a separate unit and what remains intact is the main curriculum, the main menu. One of the ways to assess multicultural education in your school is to look at the school organization. Look at how much time you spend on which subjects. When you are in the second stage you usually have a two- or three-week unit on a group of people or an area that's been omitted in the main curriculum.

You're moving into the next stage of structural change when you have elements of that unit integrated into existing units. Ultimately, what is at the center of the curriculum gets changed in its prominence. For example, civilizations. Instead of just talking about Western civilization, you begin to draw on what we need to know about India, Africa, China. We also begin to ask different questions about why and what we are doing. Whose interest is it in that we study what we study? Why is it that certain kinds of knowledge get hidden? In mathematics, instead of studying statistics with sports and weather numbers, why not look at employment in light of ethnicity?

Then there is the social change stage, when the curriculum helps lead to changes outside of the school. We actually go out and change the nature of the community we live in. For example, kids might become involved in how the media portray people, and start a letter-writing campaign about news that is negatively biased. Kids begin to see this as a responsibility that they have to change the world.

I think about a group of elementary school kids who wrote to the manager of the store about the kinds of games and dolls that they had. That's a long way from having some dinner and dances that represent an "exotic" form of life.

In essence, in anti-racist education we use knowledge to empower people and to change their lives.

Teachers have limited money to buy new materials. How can they begin to incorporate a multicultural education even if they don't have a lot of money?

We do need money and it is a pattern to underfund anti-racist initiatives so that they fail. We must push for funding for new resources because some of the information we have is downright inaccurate. But if you have a perspective, which is really a set of questions that you ask about your life, and you have the kids ask, then you can begin to fill in the gaps.

In anti-racist education we use knowledge to empower people and to change their lives.

Columbus is a good example. It turns the whole story on its head when you have the children try to find out what the people who were on this continent might have been thinking and doing and feeling when they were being "discovered," tricked, robbed, and murdered. You might not have that information on hand, because that kind of knowledge is deliberately suppressed. But if nothing else happens, at least you shift your teaching, to recognize the native peoples as human beings, to look at things from their view.

There are other things you can do without new resources. You can include, in a sensitive way, children's backgrounds and life experiences. One way is through interviews with parents and with community people, in which they can recount their own stories, especially their interactions with institutions like schools, hospitals, and employment agencies. These are things that often don't get heard.

I've seen schools inviting grandparents who can tell stories about their own lives, and these stories get to be part of the curriculum later in the year. It allows excluded people, it allows humanity back into the schools. One of the ways that discrimination works is that it treats some people's experiences, lives, and points of view as though they don't count, as though they are less valuable than other people's.

I know we need to look at materials. But we can also take some of the existing curriculum and ask kids questions about what is missing, and whose interest is being served when things are written in the way they are. Both teachers and students must alter that material.

How can a teacher who knows little about multiculturalism be expected to teach multiculturally?

I think the teachers need to have the time and encouragement to do some reading, and to see the necessity to do so. A lot has been written about multiculturalism. It's not like there's no information. If you want to get specific, a good place to start is *Beyond Heroes and Holidays: A Practical Guide to K–12, Anti-Racist, Multicultural Education and Staff Development.*

You also have to look around at what people of color are saying about their lives, and draw from those sources. You can't truly teach this until you reeducate yourself from a multicultural perspective. But you can begin. It's an ongoing process.

> **I think the teachers need to have the time and encouragement to do some reading, and to see the necessity to do so.**

Most of all, you have to get in touch with the fact that your current education has a cultural bias, that it is an exclusionary, racist bias, and that it needs to be purged. A lot of times people say, "I just need to learn more about those other groups." And I say, "No, you need to look at how the dominant culture and biases affect your view of nondominant groups in society." You don't have to fill your head with little details about what other cultural groups eat and dance. You need to take a look at your culture, what your idea of normal is, and realize it is quite limited and is in fact just reflecting a particular experience. You have to realize that what you recognize as universal is, quite often, exclusionary. To be really universal, you must begin to learn what Africans, Asians, Latin Americans, the aboriginal peoples, and all silenced groups of Americans have had to say about the topic.

How can one teach multiculturally without making white children feel guilty or threatened?

Perhaps a sense of being threatened or feeling guilty will occur. But I think it is possible to have kids move beyond that.

First of all, recognize that there have always been white people who have fought against racism and social injustice. White children can proudly identify with these people and join in that tradition of fighting for social justice.

Second, it is in their interest to be opening their minds and finding out how things really are. Otherwise, they will constantly have an incomplete picture of the human family.

The other thing is, if we don't make it clear that some people benefit from racism, then we are being dishonest. What we have to do is talk about how young people can use that from which they benefit to change the order of things so that more people will benefit.

If we say that we are all equally discriminated against on the basis of racism or sexism, that's not accurate. We don't need to be caught up in the guilt of our benefit, but should use our privilege to help change things.

I remember a teacher telling me last summer that after she listened to me on the issue of racism, she felt ashamed of who she was. And I remember wondering if her sense of self was founded on a sense of superiority. Because if that's true, then she is going to feel shaken. But if her sense of self is founded on working with people of different colors to change things, then there is no need to feel guilt or shame.

What are some things to look for in choosing good literature and resources?

I encourage people to look for the voice of people who are frequently silenced, people we haven't heard from: people of color, women, poor people, working-class people, people with disabilities, and gays and lesbians.

> **I encourage people to look for the voice of people who are frequently silenced, people we haven't heard from.**

I also think that you look for materials that invite kids to seek explanations beyond the information that is before them, materials that give back to people the ideas they have developed, the music they have composed, and all those things which have been stolen from them and attributed to other folks. Jazz and rap music are two examples that come to mind.

I encourage teachers to select materials that reflect people who are trying and have tried to change things to bring dignity to their lives, for example Africans helping other Africans in the face of famine and war. This gives students a sense of empowerment and some strategies for making a difference in their lives.

I encourage them to select materials that visually give a sense of the variety in the world.

Teachers also need to avoid materials that blame the victims of racism and other "isms."

In particular, I encourage them to look for materials that are relevant. And relevance has two points: not only where you are, but also where you want to go. In all of this we need to ask what's the purpose, what are we trying to teach, what are we trying to develop?

What can school districts do to further multicultural education?

Many teachers will not change curriculum if they have no administrative support. Sometimes, making these changes can be scary. You can have parents on your back and kids who can be resentful. You can be told you are making the curriculum too political.

What we are talking about here is pretty radical; multicultural education is about challenging the status quo and the basis of power. You need administrative support to do that.

Multicultural education is about challenging the status quo and the basis of power.

In the final analysis, multicultural or anti-racist education is about allowing educators to do the things they have wanted to do in the name of their profession: to broaden the horizons of the young people they teach, to give them skills to change a world in which the color of a person's skin defines their opportunities, where some human beings are treated as if they are just junior children.

Maybe teachers don't have this big vision all the time. But I think those are the things that a democratic society is supposed to be about.

Chapter Two

"MULTIPLICATION IS FOR WHITE PEOPLE"

An interview with Lisa Delpit

By Jody Sokolower

In the introduction to her new book, *"Multiplication Is for White People": Raising Expectations for Other People's Children,* Lisa Delpit describes her response when Diane Ravitch asked her why she hasn't spoken out against the devastation of public schools in her home state of Louisiana and the efforts to make New Orleans the national model. She explained to Ravitch that she has been concentrating her efforts where she feels she can make a difference: working with teachers and children in an African American school. She says her "sense of futility in the battle for rational education policy for African American children had gone on for so long . . . that I needed to give my 'anger muscles' a rest."

GLORIA O'CONNELL

But that interchange made her realize that she is still angry, and that anger fuels and defines *Multiplication Is for White People.* "I am angry," she begins, "that public schools, once a beacon of democracy, have been overrun by the anti-democratic forces of extreme wealth." As she continues to enumerate the sources of her anger, the introduction comprises a focused and comprehensive indictment of the neo-liberal attack on public education.

Two themes drive *Multiplication Is for White People:* Delpit infuses the interplay between her role as a scholar/activist and as the mother of a child with a unique learning style. And she organizes her text around 10 factors she believes "foster excellence in urban classrooms." Because children who don't fit the white middle-class norms, especially those with real and/or perceived learning differences, are among the most marginalized by the scourges of corporate education reform, I chose to start my interview with Delpit there.

Jody Sokolower for Rethinking Schools: You say in your new book that middle-class children come to school with different—although not more important—skills from children from low-income families. What do you mean? And is this a class difference or a cultural difference?

Lisa Delpit: It is difficult to disaggregate class and culture. Children who have to take on more responsibility in real life will know and be able to do those types of things earlier. The specific responsibilities they take on are cultural—that would be different for Alaskan children as opposed to African American children or Appalachian children. We in middle-class families tend to keep our children young longer, to infantilize them.

> **If we are going to ensure that all children learn to read, I believe we have to turn our notion of 'basic skills' on its head. ... What we call basic skills are only 'basic' because they are one aspect of the cultural capital of the middle class.**

This difference has great significance when we think about schools. If we are going to ensure that all children learn to read, I believe we have to turn our notion of "basic skills" on its head. What we call basic literacy skills are typically the linguistic conventions of middle-class society—for example, punctuation, grammar, specialized subject vocabulary, and five-paragraph essays. All children need to know these things. Some learn them from being read to at home. What we call basic skills are only "basic" because they are one aspect of the cultural capital of the middle class.

What we call advanced or higher-order skills—analyzing new information, evaluating the relative merits of concepts and other problem-solving skills—are those that middle-class children learn later in life. But many children from low-income families learn them much earlier because their parents place a high value on independence and real-life problem-solving skills.

So children come to us having learned different things in their four-to-five years at home, prior to formal schooling. For those who come to us knowing how to count to 100 and to read, we need to teach them problem-solving and how to tie their shoes. And for those who already know how to clean up spilled paint, tie their shoes, prepare meals, and comfort a crying sibling, we need to make sure that we teach them the school knowledge that they haven't learned at home.

JS: How does this relate to children who are seen as having learning disabilities or special needs?
LD: The biggest issue for all children is not that we don't see what they don't know, but we don't see what they do know, what they do come to school with. They learned something in those years since they entered the world.

JS: You quote a young woman who struggled with learning in school who wonders why learning differences are classified as negative attributes—"Can we not focus on strengths and positive attributes?" she asks. How could it be different?
LD: I am not a special education teacher, nor am I a specialist in special education research, so I don't want to position myself as an expert. But I do sometimes ask teachers to identify the students who are considered the most problematic in their class for whatever reason, be it behavior or be it in academic areas, and to write down 10 ways in which they are exhibiting difficulty or challenges. Then I ask the teachers to look at those challenges and see if they can be redefined as strengths, or if they can find other strengths in those children.

What we call basic skills are only 'basic' because they are one aspect of the cultural capital of the middle class.

One teacher said, "I'm looking at this child who is disruptive and all the other children do what he or she does." She was able to translate that into "This is a leader. I need to give this child leadership roles so that she can assist me rather than detract from what I'm doing." Another child was always tattling: "So and so did such and such." So she reinterpreted that as a way of looking out for others—getting into a fuss with somebody because they did something to another child. So then she was able to translate that into nurturing behavior and to give the child roles that would allow her to nurture without creating a problem.

No matter what the child brings, be they special needs or learning disabilities or whatever label we want to put on them, instead of looking at the label and the problem that the label might represent, we can look at the person and see what strengths are there and what we can build on.

JS: Why do you think there are so many African American children in special ed programs?
LD: I think there are a multitude of answers. The larger society has a view of Af-

rican American people as being less intellectually capable. It's not something that anybody designed or set out to do, but it's almost in the air that we breathe. And as a result of that, when African American children do poorly, the first explanation is that there's something inherent in them that's keeping them from performing well. In fact, as Beth Harry and Janette Klingner say in their book *Why Are So Many Minority Children in Special Education? Understanding Race and Disability in Schools,* much of the time the reason is external to the child—for example, poor instruction, or maybe something happening in the family or community that caused trauma. But the official explanation tends to be that there's something wrong with the child.

Another piece is that the behavior of many boys, particularly African American boys, is seen as pathological. Some white female teachers from middle-class families (who are, of course, most of our teachers) are not accustomed to seeing this behavior and so they tend to think of it as something that is abnormal. There may be a higher tolerance for movement within some cultures that teachers again may not be accustomed to.

Another thing we run into a lot is young African American students who have learned what some people refer to as street sense, but their language might seem more mature in many ways. Teachers who are not familiar with the culture of the children actually get fearful and their fear pushes them to direct more African American kids to special education.

JS: With all the pressure on "seat time" and standardized tests, schools have less tolerance for movement than they used to.

LD: Yes, the norms of regular classrooms are often so restrictive that any deviation suggests a pathology. So you get more African American children whose cultural norms may be a little different being directed into special education. Often teachers just don't know how to best reach these kids, how to connect to what they know, how to connect to what their interests are, and that plays a part in it, too. So there are numerous reasons, but I think the largest one is the underlying belief system—and not just among white people, among all Americans, often including black people—that African American students are less capable.

JS: Many of the factors you mention aren't about learning, they are about behavior. So part of what you're saying is that kids are being treated as having learning disabilities when it is actually a question of behavior.

LD: Well, there is a category called behavior disorders. It changes from state to state exactly what the wording is, but there's actually a category for behavior issues. And that's the one that many black boys particularly are referred into.

Even among African American children who are labeled as having learning disabilities, they face the psychological trauma of not having those learning problems specifically defined. When you have a specific learning difference, you can understand that you have strengths and weaknesses as a learner. You can receive help to overcome that specific issue. But many African American children are labeled "slow learners" or "educable mentally retarded/behavior disordered." It's very difficult as a student to see what your strengths are in that context, and many times they don't get the specific help that they might need.

JS: Do you think there is enough emphasis on critical thinking and social justice education in special ed classes?
LD: Critical thinking and social justice issues are factors that everyone in the United States needs to tackle. I also think that the more disconnected the content we teach—the more teachers try to teach skills out of context—the less likely students are to make sense of it. So we have to talk about the big picture, then use aspects of that discussion to look at specific skills. When we isolate or decontextualize skills or facts, they are just meaningless little pieces that don't make any sense.

In my book, I talk about the work of Petra Munro Hendry, who did oral history with a group of low-performing black kids at a high school in Baton Rouge, Louisiana. The students researched the history of their school, which turned out to be one of the first public high schools for black students in the entire southern region of the country. In the context of doing that, they interviewed people, they recorded interviews. If you think about what you have to do when you take an interview and transcribe it, you have to learn spelling, you have to learn punctuation, you have to learn capitalization, you have to learn how to create a real sentence out of what somebody said who may not have spoken distinctly and clearly, or who has had some "um's" and "uh's." In other words, you have to learn what is taught in a remedial class, but it's put in the context of something much bigger and much more important. The students said to themselves: "We are researchers. We are people who are doing the kind of work that one might find college students doing." Not: "We are remedial learners."

> **The more teachers try to teach skills out of context, the less likely students are to make sense of it.**

And that is the way that we need to go to teach the small pieces like grammar, punctuation, capitalization, and spelling, rather than just keep those in isolation.

JS: How important is it to have a diversity of teachers in a school? How important is it for students to have a teacher who looks like them, who comes from their culture?
LD: I think what we need is people who represent the culture of the kids in the school, not necessarily in every classroom, because I think teachers of other cultures also have something to offer. However, I think that the piece that is often missing in our schools is the opportunity for professional learning communities where teachers can share what they know and collectively resolve issues relating to culture as well as other factors. If we can do that and ensure that the people who are most familiar with the culture of the children have the opportunity and the responsibility to share some of that knowledge with other teachers, then we will

be doing OK. If the culture of the school is set up so that sharing is important and collaborating is important, the children will be the beneficiaries.

Jennifer Obidah and Karen Manheim Teel wrote a book, *Because of the Kids: Facing Racial and Cultural Differences in Schools,* about a white teacher who was having some difficulty in class and approached an African American teacher for help. The African American teacher spent some time in the classroom, they worked collaboratively and had some arguments about different kinds of things. At the end they were able to figure out what each could learn from the other and the culture piece came to the forefront.

Black kids need black teachers' presence in the school, and white teachers need black teachers' presence in the school.

They were able to resolve the issues and create a better situation for the children. I don't want to make the claim that all black teachers are better or that every black teacher is good for every black child because, as I mentioned before, many of us have also internalized negative notions about black children. We really have to look at the specific teacher and what the teacher's beliefs are and how the teacher sees the culture of the children, regardless of the teacher's ethnicity. But black kids need black teachers' presence in the school, and white teachers need black teachers' presence in the school.

JS: You talk about the need to neutralize, educate, or get rid of bad teachers. Can we do that without standardized tests?
LD: There are a lot of pieces to that question. We do need to neutralize, educate, or get rid of bad teachers—that is true. But I think we need to take another look at assessment. If we can create professional learning communities where everyone is responsible to everyone else and we have a joint responsibility for these children in the school, then we can create a situation where teachers can do a lot of peer assessment of other teachers.

Many teachers are not using a quarter of what they know because the school environment is so foul. And we know that the culture of the school very much affects the teaching that goes on in classrooms. So my question becomes not so much whether the teachers at a specific school are good or bad but what is it in this setting that's not allowing them to teach to their full potential. And many times it is the question of trust.

Charles Payne has a great book, *So Much Reform, So Little Change: The Persistence of Failure in Urban Schools.* One of the things that he brings out is that the level of disorganization and mistrust in a school affects how well a teacher teaches. I don't think we can just look at the individual teaching level. We have to look at the school: What about the school is not allowing teachers to teach to their potential? So the problem may be the environment, or it may be some skills that teachers are lacking, or it may be that it's time for some teachers to look into other areas of work.

One time, I went to visit a teacher's classroom for the first time. He didn't know who I was or where I was coming from. He proceeded—in front of the children—to tell me how terrible these students were. He told me that he had wanted to be a lawyer but he fell into teaching, and now he thought these kids were not worth the effort. I was in shock. Finally I said to him, "Well, I think it is time for you to pursue your dreams. You need to go to law school."

So sometimes it is important to help folks find where their talents will best be used so as not to destroy children. But most of the current notions of accountability are wrongheaded and will never improve what's going on with teachers and what happens in classrooms.

Lisa Delpit is the Felton G. Clark Distinguished Professor of Education at Southern University in Baton Rouge, Louisiana. Jody Sokolower is a teacher educator in the Bay Area and co-coordinator of the Teach Palestine Project at the Middle East Children's Alliance. She is a former Rethinking Schools *managing editor and author of a new book,* Determined to Stay: Palestinian Youth Fight for Their Village.

Chapter Three

WHAT DO WE NEED TO KNOW NOW?

By Asa G. Hilliard III

The following is condensed from a speech in the spring of 1999 to a conference on Race, Research, and Education, held in Chicago at an African American symposium sponsored by the Chicago Urban League and the Spencer Foundation.

S ome say that the contemporary concept of "race" is grounded in Nazi Germany. Adolph Hitler was surely aware of the "race" matter and was the person who most clearly saw its full political potential. Scholar Max Weinreich quotes Hitler as admitting to an associate that "in the scientific sense, there is no such thing as race." But Hitler goes on to note that as a politician he needs

JEAN-CLAUDE LEJEUNE

a conception "which enables the order which has hitherto existed on [a] historic basis to be abolished and an entirely new and anti-historical order enforced and given such an intellectual basis. . . . With [the] conception of race, national socialism will carry its revolution abroad and recast the world."

Hitler was very clear about "race" as a fabrication, as anti-historical, and as a tool of political power.

We must tie together the issues of 'race,' identity, hegemony, and education.

In preparing for this [speech] on race, education, and research, I found that it is premature to discuss research needs until the "race" dialogue is clarified. Otherwise, we could spin our wheels by using the same popular language, definitions, constructs, paradigms, and problem definitions that have been typical of past work.

Most important, we must tie together the issues of "race," identity, hegemony, and education. Fundamentally, the question of "race" is not a matter of skin color, anatomy, or phenotype, but a matter of the domination of one group of people by another. Any consideration of "race" is useless unless it also considers racism, white supremacy, and any other form of racial supremacy—and considers them as a hegemonic system. The real problem is hegemony, not "race!"

Naming Africans

During my lifetime, I have witnessed several transitions in the ethnic group name used by people of African ancestry. I was born during the time when it was popular to use "colored" when referring to African people. "Negro" was also used. During the 1960s, many people felt a major shift had been made when "black" became popular, with the predictable addition that the "b" in black be capitalized, just as the Spanish version of the word for black (negro), had gradually evolved to the status of capitalization. We even became "Black and proud," i.e. we made black a positive instead of a negative name.

These changes represented struggles within the African community to take control of our naming and self-definition from our oppressors, and to imbue our collective ethnic name with positive meaning. Yet we wrestled with the ascribed terms, "colored," "negro," and "black," as if we had no other choices.

Yet historically, "African" was often the preferred term, especially up until the early 1900s. The term was also used by some in the 1960s, following the publication of the book by Richard Moore, *The Name "Negro": Its Origin and Evil Use*. At a national conference in New Orleans led by the Rev. Jesse Jackson and Dr. Ramona Edlin Hodge, the name "African American" was advocated—followed by widespread acceptance of that designation within the African community. This happened even as many Europeans opposed the action, as if they had any right to enter dialogue about an African family matter.

In my opinion, few of us in the 1980s were prepared to deal properly with this matter of naming, because few of us were well informed about the history of our people before our enslavement by Europeans. We did not understand our history as a whole and healthy ethnic people, as not merely a pigmented people. We did not understand how and why we were coerced by Europeans to change our ethnic names to names that caused us to become preoccupied with aspects of our phenotype, mainly our skin color, hair texture, and facial features. The Europeans were looking for names that dehumanized and subordinated us, that contained us in our physical being, separating us from our minds, souls, and spirits. We did not understand how they, the authors of this specious system, were using their "race" construction in irrational and pseudoscientific but calculated political ways.

The names "colored," "negro," "black," "African," "African American," are more or less terms that have been accepted within the African family. My own strong preference is for African. Nationality and ethnicity are not always the same. The term "African" fits our actual historical, cultural, and even political circumstances more precisely than any other name. As Sterling Stuckey has shown, the Western experience has fused Africans from all over the diaspora into a new family that still shares the African

Nationality and ethnicity are not always the same.

root culture at the core, in the same way that diverse ethnic groups from Europe are tending toward a common European ethnic identity after having spent so many years believing that they had no ethnicity or that they were just Americans. The African continental name reflects that reality of a common cultural heritage and a common political need. Naturally, we recognize that the influences in the diaspora among other ethnic groups are reciprocal. We also recognize that cultural change in response to new environments will continue to happen.

External to the African community, other terms have been used as euphemistic designators to refer primarily to people of African ancestry. Nonethnic terms, such as "minority," "the disadvantaged," "culturally deprived," "culturally disadvantaged," "inner-city," and "at-risk," are ascribed, fostering amorphous identities that detach Africans from time, space, and the flow of human history. Note that these terms emphasize numerical status, social class, and political status, e.g., how many we are, how wealthy we are, how powerful we are. But they do not denote ethnic identity; they do not tell us who we are. In fact, these names apply easily, potentially, to any ethnic group.

Almost without exception, the group names ascribed by Europeans to Africans are adjectives, never proper nouns as names. Significantly, they are adjectives that suggest no respect for who we are or for our uniqueness as an ethnic family. In fact, they suggest nothing but something of minimal or even negative import. In the case of African people, this demeaning language was part of a strategy to commit "cultural genocide," a strategy to destroy ethnic family solidarity, a strategy to place emphasis on individual rather than family behavior, a strategy to confuse Africans about their ethnic identity, to destroy our consciousness. Why? As Dr. John Henrik Clarke has so often said, "It is impossible to continue to oppress a consciously historical people."

I do not believe that there can be a resolution of this matter of ethnic designation or group identity until the question of identity is situated in its historical, cultural, and sociopolitical context. We must understand how the idea of "race" emerged. We must also admit that the poison of "race" and hegemony, or white supremacy, is now a part of global ideology and structure. And our response to the problem ultimately must be to target ideology and structure, not merely everyday individual behavior.

The ideology of 'race' drives much of what happens in the world and in education.

The ideology of "race" drives much of what happens in the world and in education. It is like a computer software program that "runs in the background," invisible and inaudible. However, our silent and invisible "racial" software is not benign. It is linked to issues of power and hegemony, the domination of a given group by another. "Race" thinking has no reason for being except for the establishment of hegemony.

We must look beyond "race" as our criteria for identity. We need to ask questions such as: What was the historical nature of group identity when "race" was not in the picture? What is the normal basis for group identity in world history? What were the criteria for ethnic family identity prior to the invention of the race construct?

The History of 'Race' and Hegemony

Color prejudice associated with white supremacy appears to be quite old, as old as several thousands of years ago in India, resulting in the dehumanizing caste system. However, "race" as a "scientific" construct or concept is quite recent. (By "race" I mean the allegedly scientific view that the human race can be divided into varieties distinguished by physical traits such as color, hair type, body shape, etc.) This concept of "race" is the product of Europe's colonization of Africa and other parts of the world, of its enslavement of Africans, and of the development of apartheid, segregation and the supporting ideology of white supremacy. Other ethnic groups such as Indians and Asians, indeed groups of color around the whole world, came under the umbrella of the construct of "race" and experienced the dehumanizing colonial treatment.

'Race' must also be situated in its global political context.

Hegemony was also at the root of the creation and adoption of the construct as it was applied to these other groups. Even European ethnic groups were divided into "races" and ranked, to establish domination of the "superior European race." In Germany the ultimate realization was the fabrication of the "Master Race."

It's important to realize that the concepts of race and racism are a Western idea.

But it's more important to understand that, more specifically, race and racism are tools that Western civilization used to split and dominate the world. A society's racism is not defined by its degree of racial segregation or how racially prejudiced the population may be. These are manifestations of racism. The racism itself is the tendency of a society to degrade and do violence to people on the basis of race, and by whatever mediations may exist for this purpose.

Ashley Montague, who has written extensively on the problem of the validity of the concept of "race," notes:

> The modern conception of 'race' owes its widespread diffusion to the white man. Wherever he has gone, he has carried it with him. . . . This is not to say that discrimination against [personal] groups on the basis of skin color or difference did not exist in the ancient world; there is plenty of evidence that it did. But it is to say that such views never became the officially established doctrine, upon any large scale, of any ancient society. . . .
>
> While the concept of race can be described as both an oversimplified theory and an outmoded methodological approach to the solution of a highly complex problem, it has become these things only for a small number of thinkers, and when the history of the concept of race finally comes to be written, it is unlikely that it will figure prominently, if at all, among the fruitful [ideas]. The probabilities are high that the concept will be afforded a status similar to that now occupied by the nonexistent substance known as "phlogiston."
>
> Race is the phlogiston of our time. (Montague, 1970 p. xii.)

According to Montague, phlogiston was a substance supposed to be present in all materials given off by burning. Phlogiston was advanced in the late 17th century by the chemist J. J. Becher, and was accepted as a demonstrable reality by all intellectuals until the true nature of combustion was experimentally demonstrated by Lavoisier 100 years later. It is an illuminating commentary on the obfuscating effect of erroneous ideas that Joseph Priestley, who stoutly defended the phlogiston theory all his life, was unable to perceive that he had discovered a new gas in 1774, which according to the (Fall) theory he thought to be "dephlogisticated air," but which Lavoisier correctly recognized and named "oxygen."

"Race" must also be situated in its global political context. As Mills notes:

> One could say that the Racial Contract creates a transnational white polity, a virtual community of people linked by their citizenship in Europe, at home and abroad (Europe Proper, the Colonial Greater Europe, and the "fragments" of Euro-America, Euro-Australia, etc.), and constituted an opposition to their indigenous subjects. . . .
>
> Economic structures have been set in place, causal processes established, whose outcome is to pump wealth from one side of the globe to another,

and which will continue to work largely independently of the ill will/good will, racist/anti-racist feelings of particular individuals. This globally color-coded distribution of wealth and poverty has been produced by the racial contract and in turn reinforces adherence to it in its signatories and beneficiaries.

Kotkin and Huntington make a similar point. They argue that while large parts of the world's population are becoming more diffused, a few ethnic groups rule the world, groups they refer to as "global tribes or civilizations." According to Kotkin and Huntington, these tribes or civilizations are able to dominate because they preserve a strong sense of ethnic identity. This is the basis of the trust within that permits collaboration in economic and political arenas.

Some scholars, I among them, argue that greed and/or fear are the elemental sources of the drive to dominate others. Scholars such as Hodge, Struckmann, and Trost further argue that the greedy and fearful actions lead to the creation of definitions, assumptions, and paradigms that are embedded in the belief system, which then dictates domination or hegemonic behavior. They write:

> A common Western notion, occasionally expressed, usually implied, is that Western culture is superior to other cultures. Western culture is generally considered to be identical with 'civilization,' and the non-Western world is considered to be in varying states of development, moving toward civilization. "Primitive" and "uncivilized" are terms frequently used by Westerners to refer to people in cultures which are unlike the West.
>
> That the people of a culture should view themselves as culturally superior is certainly common. But not so common is the feature contained in Western cultural thinking, that the superior should control the inferior. It is this kind of thinking which emphasizes the value placed on control, that produces the missionary imperialism. The notion of "white man's burden" is also derived from this type of thinking. Western control over non-Western people is thereby often considered morally defensible. (Hodge, Struckmann, and Trost, 1975, p. 3)

Changing Ethnicity to Phenotype

Prior to the 1700s, identity was fundamentally an ethnic identity based upon cultural traditions, linguistic traditions, historical traditions, and so forth. This does not mean that physical features or phenotypical diversity went unnoticed. It simply means that phenotype was not the core of ethnic identity!

"Race," or phenotypical diversity, did not become the core of ethnic identity, or more accurately, a substitute for ethnic identity, until there was a political necessity to make it so. Why? Because one of the most significant forces for the expansion of racism and white supremacy was the successful attempt by Europeans to shift the basis of group designation from its traditional cultural and ethnic base to an exclusively physiological one. They treated phenotype as if it were "race," and they treated "race" as if it were the primary explanatory factor in human social behavior.

What is the purpose of the use of this invalid construct of "race"? What are the consequences of the use of the construct? How is society structured to project and to legitimize the construct? These are the fundamental questions that we should be following with research.

Unfortunately, we have been following the detour of "race" rather than the ideology that propels it. Some of my most respected friends have made the study of "racial identity" a core of their academic work. Implicit in the study of "black racial identity" is the idea that "race" is real, that it is valid and meaningful, and that we should strive to have a "healthy 'racial' identity." Of course, when this work is conducted as an anti-hegemonic exercise, in other words to counter European defamation, I would be the first to defend it. I also suspect that these scholars tend to use "racial" categories as if they were ethnic categories.

We have been following the detour of 'race' rather than the ideology that propels it.

However, I do not believe that the appropriate response to the use of invalid "racial categories" is to reify the categories by having the victims create a better use of the categories. I believe that the search for a "racial identity" leads us in the wrong direction. It is not a matter of research methodology, of assessment instruments, of educational theory. It is simply the wrong question! The right question is: "How do we restore a healthy ethnic identity?"

This does not mean that problems with respect to our perception of our phenotypical characteristics do not exist. The centuries of propaganda and defamation have definitely taken their toll. The continuing brisk sales of Nadinola and Porcelana skin lightening or bleaching creams in the United States and even in Africa itself tell us that something is wrong.

I believe that our goal should not be to search for "racial identity," but to decolonize our minds and purge them of images of white supremacy—and to restore the African family. This must include a move to restore our ethnic base and nurture a healthy ethnic identity. Then the question of our obvious phenotype will take care of itself.

We do not need an oppositional ethnic identity. We are not a "civil rights" people, even though we have fought to the death in heroic struggles for our rights. We do not exist merely because we are oppressed. The essence of our identity does not depend upon our oppressors. Who would we be if they did not exist? Our condition may find disproportionate numbers of us in poverty; however, our identity is not "the poor." Genuine identity is based upon collective culture and traditions, not on opposition to white supremacy, no matter how necessary that struggle is.

The Current Agenda in Education

Where does this bring us in terms of research and education? I believe that we must know the history, purposes, consequences, and structure of the racial paradigm. And we must dismantle that evil paradigm brick by brick. Then it is our obligation to go about the process of healing ourselves.

We cannot make ourselves whole merely by studying problems of "human relations," "stereotypes," "prejudice," "bigotry," and so forth. That vocabulary tends to trivialize the hegemony problem, to misdirect attention from the root problem. The real problem will never be remedied by capitalizing the word "black," making Africans the only group in the world's list of ethnic groups that is an adjective instead of a proper noun.

We need to do whatever is necessary so that our children and our people accept themselves, with all our magnificent phenotypes, as people of beauty. But to stop there is a gross mistake. To use phenotypical features as the essence of identity is literally to remove the bearer, or the bearer's ethnic family, from time and space, from the human historical and cultural process. That is the ultimate in dehumanization and cultural genocide.

Ethnicity implies history, culture, location, creativity. Color does not. To become pathologically preoccupied with phenotype, to the exclusion of an understanding of one's place in the cosmos, to an understanding of the evolution of the ethnic family, to creating stronger bonds among ethnic family members, will lead our people down the wrong path.

Ethnicity implies history, culture, location, creativity. Color does not.

After serious study and debate, the Harlem scholars led by Richard B. Moore concluded that we should be referred to as African Americans. They understood the cultural criteria for designating family membership. But it is the family that the hegemonic oppressor sought to destroy! They wanted to destroy any bond, any unity, any solidarity. It is family that the current systems of neo-white supremacy still seek to destroy. And, therefore, it is family and its preservation that is the issue, not phenotype. Family, independent and conscious, is the opposite of hegemonic victim.

The fundamental question, as I have stated elsewhere, for people of African ancestry, is: "To be African or not to be?"

In my work, I have looked at common elements in structures of domination throughout history. Specifically, dominating populations suppress the history of their victims, destroy the practice of the culture of their victims, prevent the victims from coming to understand themselves as a part of a cultural family, teach systematically the ideology of white supremacy, control the socialization process, control the accumulation of wealth, and perform segregation and apartheid.

It is very important to realize that these are matters of structure, and matters of systematic practices founded upon ideology. No attempt to remedy problems in education can occur apart from an understanding of these things. In fact, one of the reasons that we have been so unsuccessful in producing educational equity is that our understanding of the structure of hegemony was focused on a single element, that of segregation of "the races." This left the other elements largely untouched since they were not prominent in our understanding of segregation.

Race, Identity, and Hegemony in Education

Education, like "race," is situated in a context. There should be no need to go into great detail about the history of the education of Africans under slavery, colonization, apartheid, and white supremacy ideology. The record is clear. The treatment of Africans was not a matter of negligence or accident. It was not benign. Massive and strategic attempts were made to use educational structures to destroy "critical consciousness," to alienate Africans from tradition and from each other, to teach African inferiority and European superiority.

We have two major concerns. First, there is the need to access and to dismantle a tremendous array of aggressive negative beliefs, behaviors, and strategies. Second, there is the need to construct normal nurturing.

Appropriate research will contribute to our understanding of what is going on with race, hegemony, and education. Except for simple and overt factors, much of what we need to know is now "silent and invisible." Obviously, there are thousands of studies that could be done, producing interesting information, even useful information. However, I will limit myself here to examples of categories of needed research. The following brief list is suggestive only.

Abandoning the Race Construct. The continued use of the race construct is an issue. Racial comparisons, especially biological aspects, are prominent in educational research and in public policy. For example, I have pointed out to the American Psychological Association that our field of psychology is saturated with studies of racial comparisons in spite of the absence of construct validity for race. And yet there is a dearth of information on hegemony. For example, the words racism and white supremacy do not appear in the *Diagnostic and Statistical Manual of Mental Disorders* that defines mental illness, yet I believe they both belong there.

What might be the consequences if we continue to focus on "race" rather than hegemony?

Interestingly, the policy chapter in the popular *Bell Curve* book, which appears to seek to scientifically bolster the white supremacist view that the African "race" is genetically and intellectually inferior, speaks about those in the bottom 25 percent of IQ test scores as being "expendable." In the authors' own words:

> What happens to the child of low intelligence who survives childhood and reaches adulthood trying to do his best to be a productive citizen? Out of the many problems we have just sketched this is the one we have chosen to italicize. All of the problems that these children experience will become

worse rather than better as they grow older, for the labor market they will confront a few decades down the road is going to be much harder for them to cope with than the labor market is now. . . . People in the bottom quartile of intelligence are becoming not just increasingly expendable in economic terms: they will sometime in the not-too-distant future become a net drag. In economic terms and barring a profound change in direction for our society, many people will be unable to perform that function so basic to human dignity: putting more into the world than they take out. . . . For many people, there is nothing they can learn that will repay the cost of the teaching. (Murray and Herrnstein, 1994, pp. 519–520.)

Equitable Treatment. One of the most common errors in educational research is to operate on the assumption that when children fail to perform, the problem is with the child, the family, the community—in short the child or the child's non-school environment. Furthermore, within the child's environment, we emphasize the problems of poverty, crime, gangs, and so forth. Although these and other potent forces are important and may impact teaching and learning, it is also true that the school's treatment of the child is potent, and under some circumstances more potent than almost anything else. Therefore, we must have detailed and valid information about how the child is treated in school. These are intervening variables. Rarely do we control for them, especially in comparative studies involving "race."

The absence of sufficient studies on these factors within school foster the belief that African children tend to fail in school primarily because of internal and non-school factors. This belief system is a part of the structure of domination.

Alien and/or Invalid Curriculum. African children are subjected to massive doses of misinformation and neglect in the school curriculum. Many of these messages are "silent and invisible." Studies must be done to reveal more precisely what goes on under the name of curriculum. Anthropologist Sheila Walker, for example, did a study of library holdings in the Oakland Unified School District. Her study showed vast gaps between the content offered about African people and what is true, valid, and important. We may also wish to do research on the beneficial effects on students when valid and affirming curriculum is offered.

Schools and African Academic Excellence Without Excuse. Few things are more important than to document that not only can all children learn, but that children are learning in many schools with ordinary teachers and no special programs. Yet most of these schools, or classes, are "silent and invisible." As a result, educators and policy makers become unsure about what we can "expect" from poor African children.

The Effects of Special Treatment. The structure of services, such as special education, more often stratify students rather than benefit them. Tracking and "special" services, in the main, label and stigmatize students, disproportionately by "race," with minimal to negative benefits. We need many sophisticated studies on the alleged benefits of such services, especially when there is disproportionate impact by "race."

Culture as Context. The great error in behavioral research, now acknowledged by prestigious scholars, is that in most cases there has been a failure to take context into account. Research tends to proceed as if constructs, methods, instruments, and interpretations in culturally embedded studies are universal. Nothing could be further from the truth. Most researchers are ill-prepared to do research in a culturally plural environment or to deal with hegemony as it relates to culture.

So what needs to be done in terms of research and education? What do we need to know now?

We have an enormous task before us. We must forego our preoccupation with the false construct of "race" and focus instead on our African ethnic identity. We must support a healing process for damaged ethnic families. And we must focus the spotlight on hegemony so that we can take actions against it.

Scholarship is a double-edged sword. It can cut two ways, for good or for evil.

Asa Hilliard, now deceased, was the author of numerous books and articles on education, particularly the education of African American children.

References and Selected Bibliography

Anderson, J. D. (1988). *The Education of Blacks in the South, 1860-1935.* Chapel Hill: The University of North Carolina Press.

Alba, R. D. (1990). *Ethnic Identity: The Transformation of White America.* New Haven: Yale University Press.

Ani, M. (1994). *Yurugu: An African-centered Critique of European Thought and Behavior.* New York: Africa World Press.

Barzun, J. (1965). *Race: A Study in Superstition.* New York: Harper Torchbooks.

Bell, D. (1992). *Faces at the Bottom of the Well: The Permanence of Racism.* New York: Basic Books.

Bell, D. (1973). *Race, Racism and American Law.* Boston: Little, Brown and Company.

Benedict, R. (1959). *Race: Science and Politics.* New York: Viking Press.

Ben Jochannan, Y. (1972). *Cultural Genocide in the Black and African Studies Curriculum.* New York: Alkebu-Lan.

Bernal, M. (1987). *Black Athena: The Afroasiatic Roots of Classical Civilization: Volume I, The Fabrication of Ancient Greece 1785–1985,* Piscataway, NJ: Rutgers University Press. (See especially chapter 4, "Hostilities to Egypt in the 18th Century," pp. 189-223.)

Biddis, M. D. (1970). *Father of Racist Ideology: The Social and Political Thought of Count DeGobineau.* New York: Weybright and Talley.

Blauner, R. (1972). *Racial Oppression in America.* New York: Harper and Rowe.

Carruthers, J. (1995). Science and Oppression. In *D.* Azibo (ed.), *African Psychology in Historical Perspective and Related Commentary.* Trenton, NJ: Africa World Press.

Chase, A. (1977). *The Legacy of Malthus: The Social Costs of the New Scientific Racism* New York: Alfred A. Knopf.

Crick, B. (1996). *Race: The History of an Idea in the West.* Baltimore: Johns Hopkins University.

Cross, W., Parham, T., & Helms, J. (1998). Nigrescence revisited. In R. Jones (ed.). *Advances in Black Psychology.* Oakland, CA: Cobb and Henry.

Cruse, H. (1967). *The Crisis of the Negro Intellectual: From Its Origins to the Present.* New York: Morrow.

Diop, C. A. (1955). *The African Origin of Civilization: Myth or Reality.* Westport, CT: Lawrence-Hill and Co.

Edwards, L. (1997). *The Power of Ideas: The Heritage Foundation at 25 Years.* Ottowa, IL: Jameson Books Inc.

Erny, P. (1976). *Childhood and Cosmos.* New York: Black Orpheus Press.

Erny, P. (1981). *The Child and His Environment in Black Africa.* New York: Oxford University Press.

Fairchild, H. H. (1991). Scientific Racism: The Cloak of Objectivity. In *Journal of Social Issues,* 47(3), 101–115.

Fanon, F. (1967). *Black Skin, White Masks.* New York: Grove.

Felder, C. H. (1991). Race, Racism, and the Biblical narratives. In C. H. Felder (ed.), *Stony the Road We Trod: African American Biblical Interpretation* (pp. 127-145). Minneapolis: Fortress Press.

Gould, S. J. (1981). *The Mismeasure of Man.* New York: Norton.

Greene, E. (1998). *Planet of the Apes as American Myth: Race, Politics, and Popular Culture.* Hanover, NH: Wesleyan University Press.

Guthrie, R. (1998). *Even the Rat Was White.* New York: Harper and Row.

Hegel, G. W. F. (1991). *The Philosophy of History.* New York: Prometheus Books.

Herrnstein, R. & Murray, C. (1994). *The Bell Curve: Intelligence and Class Structure in American Life.* New York: The Free Press, 1994.

Hilliard III, A. G., Jenkins, Y., & Scott, M. (1979). *Behavioral Criteria in Research and the Study of Racism: Performing the Jackal Function. Technical Reports I and II.* (Contract No. N00014-177-C0183). Washington, DC: Office of Naval Research.

Hilliard III, A. G. (1995). Either a Paradigm Shift or No Mental Measurement: The Nonscience and Nonsense of *The Bell Curve. Psych Discourse,* 76(10), 6–20.

Hilliard III, A. G. (1990). Fabrication: The Politics and Sociology of Knowledge in the Study of Ancient Kemet (Egypt) and Greek and Roman World. Paper presented at Temple University, Symposium on Martin Bernal's *Black Athena,* Department of African American Studies and Department of Classics. Philadelphia: Temple University.

Hilliard III, A. G. (1995). *The Maroon Within Us: Essays on African American Community Socialization.* Baltimore: Black Classic Press.

Hilliard III, A. G. (1998). *SBA: The Reawakening of the African Mind.* Gainesville, FL: Makare Publishers.

Hilliard III, A. G. (1998). Psychology as Political Science and as a Double-Edged Sword: Racism and Counter-Racism in Psychology. *Psych Discourse,* 2(5&6).

Hilliard III, A. G. (1994). What Good Is This Thing Called Intelligence and Why Bother to Measure It? *The Journal of Black Psychology,* 20(4).

Hodge, J. L., Struckmann, D. K., & Trost, L. D. (1975). *Cultural Bases of Racism and Group Oppression: An Examination of Traditional "Western" Concepts, Values and Institutional Structures Which Support Racism, Sexism and Elitism.* Berkeley: Two Riders Press.

Huntington, S. P. (1996). *The Clash of Civilizations and the Remaking of World Order.* New York: Simon & Schuster.

Jordan, W. (1968). *White Over Black: American Attitudes Toward the Negro, 1550–1812.* New York: W. W. Norton & Company Inc.

Kly, Y. N. (1990). *International Law and the Black Minority in the U.S.* Windsor, Canada: Clarity International.

Kotkin, J. (1993). *Tribes: How Race, Religion, and Identity Determine Success in the New Global Economy.* New York: Random House.

Leary, W. E. (November 10, 1992). Exhibition Examines Scientists' Complicity in Nazi-Era Atrocities: *The New York Times.* Medical Science Section, B-8.

Lewis, D. (1973). Anthropology and Colonialism. *Current Anthropology,* 14(5), 581–602.

Lieberman, L., Hampton, R. E., Littlefield, A., & Hallead, G. (1992). Race in Biology and Anthropology: A Study of College Texts and Professors. *Journal of Research in Science Teaching,* 29(3), 301–321.

Lutz, C. A. & Collins, J. L. (1993). *Reading National Geographic.* Chicago: University of Chicago Press.

Maxwell, F. J. (1975). *Slavery and the Catholic Church: The History of Catholic Teaching Concerning the Moral Legitimacy of the Institution of Slavery.* Barry Rose Publishers.

Mills, C. W. (1997). *The Racial Contract.* Ithaca, NY: Cornell University Press.

Montague, A. (1970). *The Concept of Race.* London: Cathier Books.

Montague, A. (1968). *The Concept of the Primitive.* New York: The Free Press.

Montague, A. (1974). *Man's Most Dangerous Myth: The Fallacy of Race.* New York: Oxford University Press.

Moore, R. B. (1960). *The Name "Negro": Its Origin and Evil Use.* Baltimore: Black Classic Press.

Muller-Hill, B. (1988). *Murderous Science: Elimination by Scientific Selection of Jews, Gypsies and Others, Germany 1933–1945.* New York: Oxford University Press.

Nunn, K. B. (1997). Law as a Eurocentric Enterprise. *Law and Inequality Journal of Theory and Practice.* IV(2), 323–71.

Obenga, T. (1988). Who Am I? In J. Carruther, H. Jacob, & L. Harris (eds.). *African World History Project: The Preliminary Challenge* (pp. 31–46). Los Angeles: Association for the Study of Classical African Civilizations.

Osborne, N. G., & Feit, M .D. (1992). The Use of Race in Medical Research. *Journal of the American Medical Association.* 267(2), 275–279.

Patterson, W. L. (1970). *We Charge Genocide: The Historic Petition to the United Nations for Relief from a Crime of the United States Government Against the Negro People.* New York: International Publishers.

Poliakov, L. (1974). *The Aryan Myth: A History of Racial and Nationalistic Ideas in Europe.* New York: Meridian.

Quigley, C. (1981). *The Anglo-American Establishment: From Rhodes to Cliven.* New York: Books in Focus.

Schwartz, B. N. & Disch, R. (1970). *White Racism: Its History, Pathology, and Practice.* New York: Dell.

Selden, S. (1991). Selective Traditions and the Science Curriculum: Eugenics and the Biology Textbook, 1914–1949. *Science Education,* 75(5), 493–512.

Spindler, G. & Spindler, L. (1998). Cultural Politics of the White Ethniclass in the Mid-Nineties. In Y. Zou & E. T. Trueba (eds.), *Ethnic Identity and Power: Cultural Contexts of Political Action in School and Society.* Albany: State University of New York Press.

Spivey, D. (1978). *Schooling for the New Slavery: Black Industrial Education 1868–1915.* Westport, CT: Greenwood.

Stuckey, S. (1987). *Slave Culture: Nationalist Theory and the Foundations of Black America.* New York: Oxford University Press.

Tatum, B. D. (1997). *"Why Are All the Black Kids Sitting Together in the Cafeteria?" and Other Conversations About Race."* New York: Basic Books.

Thompson, A. (1998). Developing an African Historiography in Carruthers. In H. Jacob & L. Harris (eds.), *African World History Project: The Preliminary Challenge.* Los Angeles: Association for the Study of Classical African Civilizations.

Tucker, W. H. (1994). *The Science of Politics of Racial Research* Chicago: University of Illinois Press.

Van Dijk, T. A. (1993). *Elite Discourse and Racism. Sage Series on Race and Ethnic Relations* (vol. 6). London: Sage Publications.

Wa Thiong'o, N. (1987). *Decolonizing the Mind: The Politics of Language in African Literature.* London: Heinemann.

Walker, S., Spohn, C., & DeLonc, M. (1996). *The Color of Justice: Race, Ethnicity, and Crime.* New York: Wadsworth Publishing Company.

Weinberg, M. (1977). *A Chance to Learn: The History of Race and Education in the United States.* New York: Cambridge University Press.

Weinreich, M. (1946). *Hitler's Professors: The Part of Scholarship in Germany's Crimes Against the*

Jewish People. New York: Yiddish Scientific Institute.

Welsing, F. C. (1991). *The Isis Papers: The Keys to the Colors.* Chicago: Third World Press.

Willhelm, S. (1983). *Black in White America.* Cambridge: Schenkman.

Willhelm, S. (1971). *Who Needs the Negro?* New York: Anchor.

Wobogo, V. (1995). *The Prehistoric Origins of White Racism* San Francisco: Unpublished manuscript.

Wynter, S. (1992). *Do Not Call Us Negroes: "Multicultural" Textbooks Perpetuate Racism.* San Francisco: Aspire.

Yee, A. H. (1983). Ethnicity and Race: Psychological Perspectives. *Educational Psychologist,* 18(1), 14–24.

Zou, Y. & Trueba, E. T. (1998). *Ethnic Identity and Power: Cultural Contexts of Political Action in School and Society.* Albany: State University of New York Press.

Chapter Four

DIVERSITY VS. WHITE PRIVILEGE
An interview with Christine Sleeter

The following is condensed from an interview with Christine Sleeter, a professor emerita at California State University–Monterey Bay and co-editor of Multicultural Education, Critical Pedagogy, and the Politics of Difference. *Sleeter was interviewed by Barbara Miner and Bob Peterson of* Rethinking Schools.

Q: You stress the importance of multicultural education as a struggle against white racism, rather than multiculturalism as a way to appreciate diversity. Why?

JEAN-CLAUDE LEJEUNE

Both historically and in contemporary society, the relationships between racial and ethnic groups in this country are framed within a context of unequal power. People of European descent generally assume the power to claim the land, claim the resources, claim the language. They even claim the right to frame the culture and identity of who we are as Americans. That has been the case ever since Columbus landed on the North American continent.

Generally, people of European descent still claim white privileges. This is particularly true of wealthy people of European descent. I know a lot of poor people who, while they reap the benefits of looking white, are certainly disenfranchised in many ways.

I keep going back to the fact that multicultural education came out of the Civil Rights Movement. It wasn't just about, "Let me get to know something about your food and I'll share some of my food." The primary issue was one of access to a quality education. If we're not dealing with questions of why access is continually important, and if we're not dealing with issues like why we have so much poverty amid so much wealth, we're not dealing with the core issues of multiculturalism.

I know it may sound trite, but the central issue remains one of justice.

Q. You talk a lot about white privilege. Why do you use that term and how do you explain it to white teachers?
If I do well at something, nobody is going to say, "You're a credit to your race." Saying that presumes that the race that the person is a member of ordinarily doesn't do very well.

Because I am white, nobody says that about me. Yet such statements frequently surround kids of color. People make assumptions about their intellectual ability, about their family support, simply on the basis of their skin color.

That's what I mean by reaping privileges of white racism, just on a personal level. At a more institutional level, I sometimes use this example.

I know it may sound trite, but the central issue remains one of justice.

My grandfather was a painter and wallpaper hanger who did fairly well in his life by buying property, renovating it, and then selling it. I grew up with the family story that he only had a 2nd-grade education and look how well he did. Yet he was buying property at a time in which property ownership was much easier for white people. As a part of New Deal legislation, Franklin Delano Roosevelt made a deal with Southern senators that the money for low-cost federal subsidized housing loans would be made available to white families and not to families of color, because the Southern senators wanted to keep African Americans working as sharecroppers.

Part of that New Deal legislation was specifically crafted so that people like my grandfather could buy property. I have inherited then, the benefits of that piece of systemic, historic white racism. Even today, I can walk into a real estate office and will more likely be shown places in "better" neighborhoods. I am also more likely to be given a better mortgage deal.

Those are examples of how white racism keeps reaping me benefits. Sometimes I am aware of it and sometimes I am not.

Q. A lot of white people resist using terms such as white racism, white supremacy, white privilege. How do you break through that defensiveness where they might argue, "I am where I am because I worked hard, not because I am white."

One tactic is to look at family stories and situate those stories in a historical context. Let's use my grandfather as an example again. My grandfather worked very hard and I can't say that he didn't. But I can't just individualize his success. I have to look at it in the historical context of who had access to what. This allows me to say that yes, my grandfather worked hard, but in a situation in which the doors were closed to people who may have worked equally hard but who were not white.

Q. A lot of teachers might respond, "That was 80 years ago. Today, we're in a colorblind society and it is illegal to discriminate on the basis of race. How can you say white privilege still exists?"

Often, I have my students go out and do mini-investigations in the community. Here's an exercise that helps. One of the investigations involves students pairing up—one white student and one student of color. Sometimes they've looked at places to rent and one will go in and then the other, and they later compare notes. I have a colleague who's done a similar exercise with the students applying for the same job. Sometimes my students will go shopping together—that seems to be a popular one—and they will compare their treatment by store clerks. With that one, inevitably they come back with biased differential treatment.

> If the white students are allowed to think of the differing treatment only in terms of one particular instance, they can still minimize and individualize the phenomenon.

After these investigations, the students will try to interpret what happened. Students of color aren't surprised by the differing treatment, but the white students tend to be surprised. And some will say, "Well, that was just that store clerk, who was having a bad day."

If the white students are allowed to think of the differing treatment only in terms of one particular instance, they can still minimize and individualize the phenomenon. But in classes where I have been teaching about institutional racism, I'll have groups of students come in and report what they've found. If eight of 10 students report incidents of racism, it becomes much harder to say that racism doesn't happen today. And when they report that data in conjunction with information I bring to class—statistical data about racism and home mortgages, and racism in educational tracking, and racism in racial profiling by police—it makes a powerful statement.

Q. Multicultural education is more than a self-help movement for racist whites. What does this have to do with schools and multicultural education?

> **Teachers will often frame multicultural education in terms of merely teaching about cultural differences.**

Teachers will often frame multicultural education in terms of merely teaching about cultural differences. This is a sort of a stereotypical way that often happens. I remember talking with a kindergarten teacher who had this lesson around Thanksgiving about the Pilgrims and the Indians sitting down together at the first Thanksgiving. She wanted to use that as a tool for teaching about the cultures of indigenous people.

"But that isn't the story," I said. "From the perspective of indigenous people, the real story has been one of genocide and of taking land away. It's important for kids to understand that story. From the perspective of indigenous people today, what's important is reclaiming land, reclaiming sovereignty, rebuilding economies, reclaiming and rebuilding cultures that have been devastated. If kids today really want to understand relationships between whites and indigenous peoples, we need to understand that within an accurate historical context."

She responded, "Kids are too young for that." I disagree. I've seen teachers of young children teach a much more accurate version of history. I don't think kids are too young if you frame matters properly and in a way they can understand.

For example, I watched a combination 4th/5th-grade teacher teach a lesson about discrimination as part of a unit on immigration. She told the students that schools used to let only boys play sports, and asked the students if they thought that was fair. Of course the students said it wasn't and some of them giggled at what a silly idea that was.

Then she applied the same idea to the kind of discrimination that immigrants experienced historically. One of the ideas she taught was about the discrimination Asian immigrants experienced coming through Angel Island. Once students got the idea of what discrimination is, she then tried to help them understand that not everyone experienced the same discrimination all the time. She told me that helping students understand nuances was difficult, as they tended to want to apply an idea uniformly to everyone, once they grasped it.

Q. You have written about the difference between psychological explanations of racism that focus on individual prejudice, and institutional racism that is manifested in social, economic, and political structures. Why is it important to move toward an understanding of institutional racism?

Let's look at a particular school issue such as tracking. As a teacher, if I am individualizing racism then I am going to be figuring out how to make myself a less prejudiced, more accepting person. I think it's very good for people to do that kind of work. But if that's the only thing, it can lead to a point where the person is saying, "Now I'm a good white. I've expunged myself of racism and I am accepting of all people."

But you can be a "good white" and still be in a school in which kids are being rank-ordered based on estimates of their learning ability and where lower tracks are predominantly kids of color and/or low-income kids. So the tracking system becomes an example of institutional racism, a way of sorting kids on the basis of both race and social class. It's essential that multiculturalism address these institutional inequities.

Q. What if a teacher says, "I'm not sorting kids on the basis of race. I hate to say it, but some kids work harder and have more support at home."

If you go into classrooms that are taught at the different track levels, very often you will see qualitatively different kinds of instruction, and that tends to perpetuate tracking. I have seen schools that have eliminated the bottom track and the teachers have said, "My gosh, when you start expecting more out of the kids, the kids tend to rise to the level of expectation."

Let me give you a classic example.

In the city of Salinas, there were some 8th-grade kids who were not promoted to high school because they weren't achieving. The presumption was that they weren't ready to survive academically in high school.

These kids were aware that the system doesn't do a very good job of keeping track of where kids go, so they enrolled in the high school anyway. They cut back on some of the behavior that caused them to be noticed in the first place and kind of blended in. Halfway through the school year, some of their previous 8th-grade teachers asked, "Hey what happened to these kids, they're not still in the 8th-grade." And they discovered them in the high school, doing fine academically. The kids had the capability to learn well and they knew that if they went on to a more challenging environment, that they would do OK.

> The tracking system becomes an example of institutional racism, a way of sorting kids on the basis of both race and social class.

Oftentimes, we hold kids back by not expecting much out of them. I say that partly from having been a learning disabilities teacher in Seattle. I was trained to focus on what the kids couldn't do, rather than on what the kids could do. As I realized that the kids had a whole lot of capabilities that I wasn't aware of, my expectations went up markedly. My approach changed from trying to remediate what they didn't have to teaching to what they could do, which was actually quite considerable.

From that I started questioning the expectations we have for kids and how we teach to those expectations. The tracking system is built on presumptions about kids from low-income backgrounds and kids of color, that their parents don't care, that they have language deficits, that nobody is around to push them with their homework, that they lack a lot of those things. Then we build teaching around that presumption.

Q. Some white teachers say they are sensitive to students of color because they adopt a colorblind approach. They'll say, "I don't deal with this kid as a black kid, I see a kid. I treat everyone equally." How would you respond?

In a colorblind approach, there is a whole lot about a student that you are not seeing.

In a colorblind approach, there is a whole lot about a student that you are not seeing. For example, if you take a kid who is of Mexican descent and you say, "I don't see a Mexican kid, I just see a kid." you are preventing yourself from knowing something about that student's culture and community—and an important part of the student. Do you know much about where the kid's family came from? Do you know much about Mexican holidays and Mexican festivals that the kid may be participating in? Do you know much about church traditions or family celebrations that the kid is a part of? Do you know much about Mexican American literature and stories that the kid is learning at home?

If a teacher is insisting on being colorblind, then the teacher is putting herself in a position of saying, "I don't know about the kid's background, I don't believe that's really important, and I'm not going to learn about it."

Q. You have argued that one can educate white teachers to death but that in the long run it's more important to increase the number of teachers of color so that schools do not remain institutions dominated by white people. Why?

I argue this on the basis of several different things. First, if you look at research on who are the best teachers of kids of color, generally they have come from the kids' communities. The study that shows this extremely well is Gloria Ladson-Billings' work, *The Dreamkeepers: Successful Teachers of African-American Kids.* That's one of my arguments.

The second piece of my argument involves my work as a teacher/educator over the last 25 years, of trying to prepare predominantly white groups of students to teach in culturally diverse schools. Even though I think there is a lot that can be done to educate white teachers, when I see where they start and where they finish by the end of their teacher training, most end up with a superficial understanding of the issues—unless they go into settings where people are continuing to extensively work with them. I do not want to populate urban schools with people who are coming in with superficial understandings of multicultural education and of progressive education.

The third thing I draw on is my experience working in multiracial groups of adults. At California State University–Monterey Bay, where I teach, half the faculty are faculty of color. The discussions we have, the issues that are brought to the table, the connections to the community, the breadth of wisdom that comes into the discussions—these are all qualitatively different from when I have worked with predominantly white groups of educators.

Q. You deal mostly with teacher education, where would-be teachers tend to have at least some support for multiculturalism. Do you have any advice for a classroom teacher concerned about anti-racist education but who knows they can't do all this by themselves—and may feel isolated in their school or district?

I tell people to join a network or organization in which there are people who will give them support. I also tell people to subscribe to *Rethinking Schools* so they won't feel like they're out there by themselves, and I give them the "Teaching for Change" catalog. I encourage them to join groups such as the National Association for Bilingual Education or the National Association for Multicultural Education. You need to also look around for local grassroots organizations, or local chapters of national groups. Feeling like you have to take on these issues all by yourself can be self-defeating.

Q. Some people argue that multicultural education is being undermined by standardized testing, which rewards superficial knowledge about conventional aspects of the curriculum. On the other hand, some community groups, particularly in communities of color, argue that we need much more accountability because obviously the schools have underserved their children. How might people committed to multicultural curriculum and academic equity balance those two perspectives?

That's a very important question. I don't advocate just simply throwing out testing. Testing that's used to guide instruction is extremely important. We need to monitor how kids are doing because kids of color and low-income white kids have been underschooled historically. So I believe in testing to improve instruction.

But I don't believe in testing to rank-order kids and schools, and to give some schools a lot of money while other schools get less. With the extreme emphasis now on high-stakes testing, so much is getting lost in the process. Teachers are telling me that due to the amount of testing, science is going by the wayside, social studies is going by the wayside—so there's a certain amount of devastation that's being done even to the traditional curriculum.

> I do not want to populate urban schools with people who are coming in with superficial understandings of multicultural education and of progressive education.

We're also defining what kids learn in ways that leave out important forms of knowledge. Just take the question of reading. In California, it's the English reading score that counts, even for kids whose first language is Spanish or any other language except English. They're not even thinking in terms of a child's reading ability, but only in terms of their ability to read in English. It's those kinds of issues that get lost in some of the discussion about raising test scores.

Q. In many urban areas, there is a lack of concern with segregation. How might that affect multicultural education, and what might be some strategies for moving forward?

School segregation is clearly linked to housing segregation. As long as housing segregation isn't actively on the agenda and we're only talking about school segregation, I don't know where you go with that. Back in the 1960s, we were addressing housing segregation. I don't hear much about that now.

With the extreme emphasis now on high-stakes testing, so much is getting lost in the process.

There is nothing inherent in a predominantly black or predominantly Latino school that makes it a bad school. The issue is access to resources. And that's clearly what is happening when you look at the resources gap between urban and suburban schools.

Chapter Five

YOU'RE ASIAN.
HOW COULD YOU FAIL MATH?
Unmasking the myth of the model minority

By Benji Chang and Wayne Au

Have you ever sat next to an Asian student in class and wondered how she managed to consistently get straight A's while you struggled to maintain a B-minus average?
—*from* Top of the Class: How Asian Parents Raise High Achievers—and How You Can Too

In January 1966, William Petersen penned an article for *The New York Times Magazine* titled "Success Story: Japanese-American Style." In it, he praised the Japanese American community for its apparent ability to successfully assimilate into mainstream American culture, and literally dubbed Japanese Americans a "model minority"—the first popular usage of the term.

By the 1980s, *Newsweek, The New Republic, Fortune, Parade, U.S. News & World Report,* and *Time* all had run articles on the subject of Asian American success in

JORDIN ISIP

schools and society, and the Myth of the Model Minority was born. The Myth of the Model Minority asserts that, due to their adherence to traditional Asian cultural values, Asian American students are supposed to be devoted, obedient to authority, respectful of teachers, smart, good at math and science, diligent, hard workers, cooperative, well behaved, docile, college-bound, quiet, and opportunistic.

Top of the Class (quoted above) is a perfect modern example. Published in 2005, the authors claim to offer readers 17 "secrets" that Asian parents supposedly use to develop high school graduates who earn A pluses and head to Ivy League colleges. It's a marketing concept built purely on the popular belief in the Myth of the Model Minority.

However, in both of our experiences as public school teachers and education activists, we've seen our share of Asian American students do poorly in school, get actively involved in gangs, drop out, or exhibit any number of other indicators of school failure not usually associated with "model minorities."

A critical unmasking of this racist myth is needed because it both negatively affects the classroom lives of Asian American students and contributes to the justification of race and class inequality in schools and society.

Masking Diversity

On the most basic level, the Myth of the Model Minority masks the diversity that exists within the Asian American community. The racial category of "Asian" is itself emblematic of the problem. Asia contains nearly four billion people and more than 50 countries, including those as diverse as Turkey, Japan, India, the Philippines, and Indonesia.

> **On the most basic level, the Myth of the Model Minority masks the diversity that exists within the Asian American community.**

The racial category of "Asian" is also historically problematic. Similar to those categories used to name peoples from Africa and the Americas, the definition of Asia as a continent (and race) and division of Asians into various nations was developed to serve the needs of European and U.S. colonialism and imperialism.

The category of Asian gets even fuzzier in the context of the United States, since there are more than 50 ways to officially qualify as an Asian American according to government standards. Pacific Islanders and "mixed race" Asians are also regularly squished together under the banner of Asian or Asian Pacific Islander (which, out of respect for the sovereignty of Pacific peoples, we refuse to do here).

Masking the Class Divide

The Myth of the Model Minority, however, masks another form of diversity—that of economic class division. As Jamie Lew explains in her 2007 book, *Asian Ameri-*

cans in Class, there are increasing numbers of working-class Korean American students in New York City performing more poorly in schools than their middle-class counterparts.

Similarly, Vivian Louie found class-based differences in her study of Chinese American students. Her research indicated that middle-class Chinese American mothers tended to have more time, resources, and educational experience to help their children through school and into college than mothers from working-class Chinese American families, who had longer work hours, lower-paying jobs, and lower levels of education.

The Myth of the Model Minority, however, masks another form of diversity—that of economic class division.

These class differences are sometimes rooted in specific immigrant histories and are connected to the 1965 Immigration Act. The act not only opened up the United States to large numbers of Asian immigrants, but, among a handful of other criteria, it granted preference to educated professionals and those committing to invest at least $40,000 in a business once they arrived.

As a consequence, some Asian immigrants, even those within the same ethnic community, enter the United States with high levels of education and/or with economic capital attained in their countries of origin. Others enter the United States with little or no education or money at all. These educational and financial heritages make an important difference in how well children gain access to educational resources in the United States.

In other words, whether we are talking about African American, white, Latina/o, indigenous, or "model minority" Asian American students, the first rule of educational inequality still applies: Class matters.

Masking Ethnic Inequity

To add to the complexity of Asian American diversity, many of the class differences amongst Asian Americans also correlate with ethnic differences. According to the 2000 census, 53.3 percent of Cambodians, 59.6 percent of Hmong, 49.6 percent of Laotians, and 38.1 percent of Vietnamese over 25 years of age have less than a high school education. In contrast, 13.3 percent of Asian Indians, 12.7 percent of Pilipinos,[1] 8.9 percent of Japanese, and 13.7 percent of Koreans over 25 years of age have less than a high school education.

These educational disparities are particularly striking considering that, for instance, 37.8 percent of Hmong, almost 30 percent of Cambodians, and 18.5 percent of Laotians have incomes below the poverty line (compared to 12.4 percent of the total U.S. population). Indeed, the 2000 census reveals relatively consistent high education rates and income amongst South Asian, Korean, and Chinese Americans, and relatively low education rates and low income amongst Cambodian, Lao, and Hmong Americans. Hence, the Myth of the Model Minority serves to obscure the struggles of poor or "undereducated" families working to gain a decent education for their children.

Masking Economic Circumstance

One of the most cited statistics proving the Myth of the Model Minority is that Asian Americans even outearn whites in income. What is obscured in this "fact" is that it is only true when we compare Asian American household income to white household income, and the reality is that Asian Americans make less per person compared to whites. Statistically, the average household size for Asian Americans is 3.3 people, while for whites it is 2.5 people.

Consequently, Asian American households are more likely than white households to have more than one income earner, and almost twice as likely to have three income earners. When we take these issues into account, Asian American individuals earn $2,000 on average less than white individuals.

The statistics on Asian American income are further skewed upward when we look at the economies of the states where the majority live. The three states with the highest proportion of Asian Americans, Hawai'i, California, and New York, all have median income levels in the top third of states. This means that, regardless of statistically higher household incomes, the high cost of living in states with large Asian American populations guarantees that Asian Americans, on average, are more likely to have less disposable income and lower living standards than whites.

Masking Racism

Although the above statistics may be remarkable in the face of the Myth of the Model Minority, they also point to another serious problem: The myth is regularly used as a social and political wedge against blacks, Latina/os, and other racial groups in the United States.

The myth is regularly used as a social and political wedge against blacks, Latina/os, and other racial groups in the United States.

The racist logic of the model minority wedge is simple. If, according to the myth, Asian Americans are academically and socially successful due to particular cultural or racial strengths, then lower test scores, lower GPAs, and lower graduation rates of other groups like African Americans and Latina/os can be attributed to their cultural or racial weaknesses.

Or, as one high school guidance counselor in Stacey J. Lee's book, *Unraveling the Model Minority Stereotype,* puts it, "Asians like. . . M. I. T., Princeton. They tend to go to good schools. . . . I wish our blacks would take advantage of things instead of sticking to sports and entertainment."

The Myth of the Model Minority also causes Asian American students to struggle with the racist expectations the myth imposes upon them. An Asian American high school student in Lee's book explains, "When you get bad grades, people look at you really strangely because you are sort of distorting the way they see an Asian."

Unfortunately, some East and South Asian Americans uphold the myth because it allows them to justify their own relative educational and social success in terms of individual or cultural drive, while simultaneously allowing them to distance themselves from what they see as African American, Latina/o, indigenous, and Southeast Asian American educational failure.

The Myth of the Model Minority also causes Asian American students to struggle with the racist expectations the myth imposes upon them.

As Jamie Lew observes, the Myth of the Model Minority "attributes academic success and failure to individual merit and cultural orientation, while underestimating important structural and institutional resources that all children need in order to achieve academically." In doing so, the Myth of the Model Minority upholds notions of racial and cultural inferiority of other lower achieving groups, as it masks the existence of racism and class exploitation in this country.

The Challenge of Educating Asian America

One of the difficulties of unmasking the Myth of the Model Minority is that the diversity of the Asian American experience poses substantial challenges, particularly in relation to how race, culture, and ethnicity are typically considered by educators.

For instance, Asian American students challenge the categories commonly associated with the black-brown-white spectrum of race. Many Asian American students follow educational pathways usually attributed to white, middle-class, suburban students, while many others follow pathways usually attributed to black and Latina/o, working-class, urban students.

Other Asian American groups challenge typical racial categories in their own identities. Pilipinos, for instance, don't quite fit into the typical categories of South, East, or Southeast Asian, nor do they quite fit the category of Pacific Islander. Further, some argue that Pilipinos have a lineage that is more closely related to Latina/os because they were in fact colonized by Spain. Consequently, because of their particular circumstances, many Pilipinos more strongly identify with being brown than anything else. As another example, many high-achieving, middle-class South Asians consider themselves "brown," especially after the discrimination endured after 9/11.

Asian American students also challenge typical notions of immigration and language by blurring the typical dichotomies of native language vs. English and immigrant vs. American-born. Some Southeast Asian refugees, like those from Laos, may develop fluency in multiple languages and attend universities, even as their

Asian American students also challenge typical notions of immigration and language by blurring the typical dichotomies of native language vs. English and immigrant vs. American-born.

parents are low-income and do not speak English. On the other hand, there are groups of Pilipinos who grow up highly Americanized, who have been taught English their whole lives, but who have some of the highest dropout and suicide rates.

Asian American students also challenge popularly accepted multicultural teaching strategies because they are often a numerical minority in classrooms, and multicultural teaching strategies designed to meet the needs of classroom majorities can leave out the culturally specific needs of Asian American students. These can include the language acquisition needs of students who come from character-based languages (e.g., Chinese, Japanese), social and ideological differences of students from majority Muslim nations (e.g., Pakistan, Indonesia), and psychological issues that emerge from student families traumatized by U.S. intervention/war policies (e.g., Korea, Vietnam, Thailand).

From the Fukienese Chinese student in an urban Philadelphia classroom with mostly black or Latina/o students, to the Hmong student who sits with two or three peers in a mostly white school in rural Wisconsin, to the Pilipino student in a San Diego suburb with predominantly Pilipino classmates and some white peers, Asian American youth do not fit neatly into the typical boxes of our educational system.

Unmasking the Myth in Our Classrooms

Bring the lives of all of your students, Asian Americans included, into your classroom.

Despite the diversity and complexity inherent in working with Asian American populations, there are many things that educators can do to challenge the Myth of the Model Minority. Similar to other communities of color, effective steps include recruiting more educators from Asian American backgrounds, promoting multilingual communication in instruction and parent involvement, and developing relationships between parents, community groups, and schools.

Within the classroom, teachers can make use of several strategies to counter the Myth of the Model Minority in their own classrooms. The following list offers a starting point to address the realities of Asian American students' lives.

Don't automatically assume that your Asian American students are "good" students (or "bad," for that matter), and get to know them.

Personally get to know students and their family's practices, which widely vary from home to home, despite their "membership" in specific ethnic or linguistic groups. Start by researching the specific histories and cultures of the students in your classroom to better understand the historical and political contexts of their communities. Also, bring the lives of all of your students, Asian Americans included, into your classroom. Have them consider, reflect, and write about how their home lives and experiences intersect with their school lives and experiences.

Develop strategies to personally engage with students and their communities, whether through lunchtime interactions or visits to their homes, community centers, and cultural or political events. Although we recognize the limited resources of all teachers, learning about your Asian American students and their communities takes the same energy and commitment as learning to work with any specific group of students.

Rethink how you interpret and act upon the silence of Asian American students in your classroom.

Asian American student silence can mean many things, from resistance to teachers, to disengagement from work, to a lack of understanding of concepts, to thoughtful engagement and consideration, to insecurity speaking English, to insecurity in their grasp of classroom content. Rather than assume that Asian American student silence means any one thing, assess the meaning of silence by personally checking in with the student individually.

Teach about unsung Asian American heroes.

Teachers might include the stories of real-life woman warriors Yuri Kochiyama and Grace Lee Boggs, for instance. Kochiyama has been involved in a range of efforts, from working closely with Malcolm X in Harlem, to Puerto Rican sovereignty, to freeing political prisoners like Mumia Abu Jamal. Boggs' efforts have included work with famed Marxist humanist Raya Dunayevskaya, organized labor, and the Detroit Freedom Summer schools.

Or perhaps teach about Ehren Watada, the first commissioned officer to publicly refuse to go to war in Iraq because he believes the war is illegal and would make him a party to war crimes. Learning about heroes like these can help students broaden the range of what it means to be Asian American.

Highlight ways in which Asian Americans challenge racism and stereotypes.

Schools should challenge racist caricatures of Asians and Asian Americans, including viewing them as penny-pinching convenience store owners, religious terrorists, kung fu fighting mobsters, academic super-nerds, and exotic, submissive women.

One way to do this is to introduce students to stereotype-defying examples, such as Kochiyama, Boggs, and Watada. There are also many youth and multigenerational organizations of Asian Americans fighting for social jus-

Schools should challenge racist caricatures of Asians and Asian Americans.

tice in the U.S. These include Khmer Girls in Action (KGA, Long Beach), and the Committee Against Anti-Asian Violence/Organizing Asian Communities (CAAAV, New York).

These organizations are extremely important examples of how youth can be proactive in challenging some of the issues that affect our communities, and their work challenges the stereotypes of Asian Americans as silent and obedient.

Illustrate historical, political, and cultural intersections between Asian Americans and other groups.

There are historical and current examples of shared experiences between Asian Americans and other communities. For instance, teachers could highlight the key role of Asian Americans in collective struggles for social justice in the United States. Possible examples include Philip Vera Cruz and other Pilipino farmworkers who were the backbone and catalyst for the labor campaigns of Cesar Chavez and the United Farm Workers in the late 1960s and early 1970s; Chinese students and families who challenged the racism of public schools in the Lau v. Nichols case of the 1970s that provided the legal basis for guaranteeing the rights of English language learners and bilingual education; Asian American college students who in 1967–69 organized with blacks, Latina/os, and Native Americans at San Francisco State University in a multi-ethnic struggle to establish the first ethnic studies program in the nation, united under the banner of "Third World Liberation."

Weave the historical struggles, culture, and art of Asian American communities into your classroom.

By believing in a 'positive' stereotype we ultimately give credence to an entire way of thinking about race and culture, one that upholds the stereotypic racial and cultural inferiority of African Americans and Latina/os and maintains white supremacy.

As part of a curriculum that is grounded in the lives of all of our students, teachers can highlight Asian American history, culture, and art in their classroom practices to help Asian American students develop not only positive self-identity, but also empathy between Asian Americans and other racial, cultural, or ethnic groups. Teachers might use novels by Carlos Bulosan, John Okada, Nora Okja Keller, Lê Thi Diem Thúy, Jessica Hagedorn, Jhumpa Lahiri, or Shawn Wong; poetry by Lawson Inada, Li-Young Li, Marilyn Chin, Nick Carbó, or Sesshu Foster; spoken word by Reggie Cabico, Ishle Park, Beau Sia, or I Was Born With Two Tongues; hip-hop music by Blue Scholars, Skim, Native Guns, Himalayan Project, or Kuttin Kandi; and history texts by Ron Takaki, Sucheng Chan, Peter Kwong, or Gary Okihiro.

When it comes to dealing with Asian Americans in education, it is all too common for people to ask, "What's wrong with the Myth of the Model Minority? Isn't it a positive stereotype?" What many miss is that there are no "positive" stereotypes, because by believing in a "positive" stereotype, as, admittedly, even many Asian Americans do, we ultimately give credence to an entire way of thinking about race and culture, one that upholds the stereotypic racial and cultural inferiority of African Americans and Latina/os and maintains white supremacy.

The Myth of the Model Minority not only does a disservice to Asian American diversity and identity, it serves to justify an entire system of race and class inequality. It is perhaps for this reason, above all else, that the Myth of the Model Minority needs to be unmasked in our classrooms and used to challenge the legacies of racism and other forms of inequality that exist in our schools and society today.

Wayne Au, a former public high school teacher and current editor of Rethinking Schools, *is an Associate Professor in the Education Program at the University of Washington, Bothell Campus.*

Benji Chang, a former teacher in the Los Angeles Unified School District, is an Adjunct Assistant Professor in the Institute for Urban & Minority Education, Teacher College, Columbia University.

Endnote

1. Pilipino is a term used by some activists in the Pilipino American community as means of challenging the way that Spanish and U.S. colonization of the islands also colonized the language by renaming them the Philippines after King Phillip, and introducing the anglicized "f" sound that did not exist in the indigenous languages there.

Chapter Six

SCHOOLS AND
THE NEW JIM CROW
An interview
with Michelle Alexander

By Jody Sokolower

Michelle Alexander is author of *The New Jim Crow: Mass Incarceration in the Age of Colorblindness*. In her book, Alexander poses a thought-provoking and insightful thesis: Mass incarceration, justified and organized around the war on drugs, has become the new face of racial discrimination in the United States. Since 1970, the number of people behind bars in this country has increased 600 percent. What is most striking about these numbers is the racial dimension. The United States imprisons a larger percentage of its black population than South Africa did at the height of apartheid. In Washington, D.C., for example, it

is estimated that 75 percent of young black men can expect to serve time in prison.

Equally disturbing is Alexander's description of the lifelong civil and human rights implications of being arrested and serving time in prison, and the implications for what many call our "post-racial" society. As she explains in her introduction:

> "What has changed since the collapse of Jim Crow has less to do with the basic structure of our society than with the language we use to justify it. In the era of colorblindness, it is no longer socially permissible to use race, explicitly, as a justification for discrimination, exclusion, and social contempt. So we don't. Rather than rely on race, we use our criminal justice system to label people of color "criminals" and then engage in all the practices we supposedly left behind. Today it is perfectly legal to discriminate against criminals in nearly all the ways that it was once legal to discriminate against African Americans. Once you're labeled a felon, the old forms of discrimination—employment discrimination, housing discrimination, denial of the right to vote, denial of educational opportunity, denial of food stamps and other public benefits, and exclusion from jury service—are suddenly legal. As a criminal you have scarcely more rights, and arguably less respect, than a black man living in Alabama at the height of Jim Crow. We have not ended racial caste in America; we have merely redesigned it."

We asked Alexander to share her thoughts about the implications of her work when applied to education and the lives of children and youth. She spoke with *Rethinking Schools* editor Jody Sokolower on Sept. 1, 2011.

RS: What is the impact of mass incarceration on African American children and youth?

MA: There is an extraordinary impact. For African American children, in particular, the odds are extremely high that they will have a parent or loved one, a relative, who has either spent time behind bars or who has acquired a criminal record and thus is part of the under-caste—the group of people who can be legally discriminated against for the rest of their lives. For many African American children, their fathers, and increasingly their mothers, are behind bars. It is very difficult for them to visit. Many people are held hundreds or even thousands of miles away from home. There is a tremendous amount of shame with having a parent or other family member incarcerated. There can be fear of having it revealed to others at school.

But also, for these children, their life chances are greatly diminished. They are more likely to be raised in severe poverty; their parents are unlikely to be able to find work or housing and are often ineligible even for food stamps.

For children, the era of mass incarceration has meant a tremendous amount of family separation, broken homes, poverty, and a far, far greater level of hopelessness as they see so many of their loved ones cycling in and out of prison. Children who have incarcerated parents are far more likely themselves to be incarcerated.

When young black men reach a certain age—whether or not there is incarceration in their families—they themselves are the target of police stops, interrogations, frisks, often for no reason other than their race. And, of course, this level of harassment sends a message to them, often at an early age: No matter who you are or what you do, you're going to find yourself behind bars one way or the other. This reinforces the sense that prison is part of their destiny, rather than a choice one makes.

A Birdcage as a Metaphor

RS: At one point in *The New Jim Crow,* you refer to the metaphor of a birdcage as a way to describe structural racism and apply that to mass incarceration. How does what is happening to African American youth in our schools fit into that picture?

MA: The idea of the metaphor is there can be many bars, wires that keep a person trapped. All of them don't have to have been created for the purpose of harming or caging the bird, but they still serve that function. Certainly youth of color, particularly those in ghetto communities, find themselves born into the cage. They are born into a community in which the rules, laws, policies, structures of their lives virtually guarantee that they will remain trapped for life. It begins at a very early age when their parents themselves are either behind bars or locked in a permanent second-class status and cannot afford them the opportunities they otherwise could. For example, those with felony convictions are denied access to public housing, hundreds of professions that require certification, financial support for education, and often the right to vote. Thousands of people are unable even to get food stamps because they were once caught with drugs.

The cage itself is manifested by the ghetto, which is racially segregated, isolated, cut off from social and economic opportunities. The cage is the unequal educational opportunities these children are provided at a very early age coupled with the constant police surveillance they're likely to encounter, making it very likely that they're going to serve time and be caught for committing the various types of minor crimes—particularly drug crimes—that occur with roughly equal frequency in middle-class white communities but go largely ignored.

So, for many, whether they go to prison or not is far less about the choices they make and far more about what kind of cage they're born into. Middle-class white children, children of privilege, are afforded the opportunity to make a lot of mistakes and still go on to college, still dream big dreams. But for kids who are born in the ghetto in the era of mass incarceration, the system is designed in such a way that it traps them, often for life.

RS: How do you define and analyze the school-to-prison pipeline?

MA: It's really part of the large cage or caste that I was describing earlier. The school-to-prison pipeline is another metaphor—a good one for explaining how children are funneled directly from schools into prison. Instead of schools being a pipeline to opportunity, schools are feeding our prisons.

It's important for us to understand how school discipline policies have been influenced by the war on drugs and the "get tough" movement. Many people imagine that zero tolerance rhetoric emerged within the school environment, but it's not true. In fact, the Advancement Project published a report showing that one of the earliest examples of zero tolerance language in school discipline manuals was a cut-and-paste job from a U.S. Drug Enforcement Administration manual. The wave of punitiveness that washed over the United States with the rise of the drug war and the get tough movement really flooded our schools. Schools, caught up in this maelstrom, began viewing children as criminals or suspects, rather than as young people with an enormous amount of potential struggling in their own ways and their own difficult context to make it and hopefully thrive. We began viewing the youth in schools as potential violators rather than as children needing our guidance.

The Mythology of Colorblindness

RS: In your book, you explain that the policies of mass incarceration are technically "colorblind" but lead to starkly racialized results. How do you see this specifically affecting children and young people of color?

MA: The mythology around colorblindness leads people to imagine that if poor kids of color are failing or getting locked up in large numbers, it must be something wrong with them. It leads young kids of color to look around and say: "There must be something wrong with me, there must be something wrong with us. Is there something inherent, something different about me, about us as a people, that leads us to fail so often, that leads us to live in these miserable conditions, that leads us to go in and out of prison?"

The mythology of colorblindness takes the race question off the table. It makes it difficult for people to even formulate the question: Could this be about something more than individual choices? Maybe there is something going on that's linked to the history of race in our country and the way race is reproducing itself in modern times.

I think this mythology—that of course we're all beyond race, of course our police officers aren't racist, of course our politicians don't mean any harm to people of color—this idea that we're beyond all that (so it must be something else) makes it difficult for young people as well as the grown-ups to be able to see clearly and honestly the truth of what's going on. It makes it difficult to see that the backlash against the

> The mythology of colorblindness takes the race question off the table. ... It makes it difficult to see that the backlash against the Civil Rights Movement manifested itself in the form of mass incarceration, in the form of defunding and devaluing schools serving kids of color.

Civil Rights Movement manifested itself in the form of mass incarceration, in the form of defunding and devaluing schools serving kids of color and all the rest. We have avoided in recent years talking openly and honestly about race out of fear that it will alienate and polarize. In my own view, it's our refusal to deal openly and honestly with race that leads us to keep repeating these cycles of exclusion and division, and rebirthing a caste-like system that we claim we've left behind.

RS: We are in the midst of a huge attack on public education—privatization through charters and vouchers; increased standardization, regimentation, and testing; and the destruction of teachers' unions. Much of it is justified by what appears to be anti-racist rhetoric: Schools aren't meeting the needs of inner-city children, so their parents need choices. How do you see this?

MA: People who focus solely on what do we do given the current context are avoiding the big why. Why is it that these schools aren't meeting these kids' needs? Why is it that such a large percentage of the African American population today is trapped in these ghettos? What is the bigger picture?

The bigger picture is that over the last 30 years, we have spent $1 trillion waging a drug war that has failed in any meaningful way to reduce drug addiction or abuse, and yet has siphoned an enormous amount of resources away from other public services, especially education. We are in a social and political context in which the norm is to punish poor folks of color rather than to educate and empower them with economic opportunity. It is that political context that leads some people to ask: Don't children need to be able to escape poorly performing schools? Of course, no one should be trapped in bad schools or bad neighborhoods. No one. But I think we need to be asking a larger question: How do we change the norm, the larger context that people seem to accept as a given? Are we so thoroughly resigned to what "is" that we cannot even begin a serious conversation about how to create what ought to be?

The education justice movement and the prison justice movement have been operating separately in many places as though they're in silos. But the reality is we're not going to provide meaningful education opportunities to poor kids, kids of color, until and unless we recognize that we're wasting trillions of dollars on a failed criminal justice system. Kids are growing up in communities in which they see their loved ones cycling in and out of prison and in which they are sent the message in countless ways that they, too, are going to prison one way or another. We cannot build healthy, functioning schools within a context where there is no funding available because it's going to building prisons and police forces.

RS: And fighting wars?

MA: Yes, and fighting wars. And where there is so much hopelessness because of the prevalence of mass incarceration.

At the same time, we're foolish if we think we're going to end mass incarceration

We're not going to provide meaningful education opportunities to poor kids, kids of color, until and unless we recognize that we're wasting trillions of dollars on a failed criminal justice system.

unless we are willing to deal with the reality that huge percentages of poor people are going to remain jobless, locked out of the mainstream economy, unless and until they have a quality education that prepares them well for the new economy. There has got to be much more collaboration between the two movements and a greater appreciation for the work of the advocates in each community. It's got to be a movement that's about education, not incarceration—about jobs, not jails. A movement that integrates the work in these various camps from, in my view, a human rights perspective.

Fighting Back

RS: What is the role of teachers in responding to this crisis? What should we be doing in our classrooms? What should we be doing as education activists?

MA: That is a wonderful question and one I'm wrestling with myself now. I am in the process of working with others trying to develop curriculum and materials that will make it easier to talk to young people about these issues in ways that won't lead to paralysis, fear, or resignation, but instead will enlighten and inspire action and critical thinking in the future. It's very difficult but it must be done.

We have to be willing to take some risks. In my experience, there is a lot of hesitancy to approach these issues in the classroom out of fear that students will become emotional or angry, or that the information will reinforce their sense of futility about their own lives and experience. It's important to teach them about the reality of the system, that it is in fact the case that they are being targeted unfairly, that the rules have been set up in a way that authorize unfair treatment of them, and how difficult it is to challenge these laws in the courts. We need to teach them how our politics have changed in recent years, how there has been, in fact, a backlash. But we need to couple that information with stories of how people in the past have challenged these kinds of injustices, and the role that youth have played historically in those struggles.

I think it's important to encourage young people to tell their own stories and to speak openly about their own experiences with the criminal justice system and the experiences of their family. We need to ensure that the classroom environment is a supportive one so that the shame and stigma can be dispelled. Then teachers can use those stories of what students have witnessed and experienced as the opportunity to begin asking questions: How did we get here? Why is this happening? How are things different in other communities? How is this linked to what has gone on in prior periods of our nation's history? And what, then, can we do about it?

Just providing information about how bad things are, or the statistics and data on incarceration by themselves, does lead to more depression and resignation and is not empowering. The information has to be presented in a way that's linked to the piece about encouraging students to think critically and creatively about how they might respond to injustice, and how young people have responded to injustice in the past.

RS: What specifically?

MA: There's a range of possibilities. I was inspired by what students have done in some schools organizing walkouts protesting the lack of funding and that sort of thing. There are opportunities for students to engage in those types of protests—taking to the streets—but there is also writing poetry, writing music, beginning to express themselves, holding forums, educating each other, the whole range. For example, for a period of time the Ella Baker Center in Oakland, Calif., was focused on youth engagement and advocacy to challenge mass incarceration. They launched a number of youth campaigns to close youth incarceration facilities in Northern California. They demonstrated that it is really possible to blend hip-hop culture with very creative and specific advocacy and to develop young leaders. Young people today are very creative in using social media and there is a wide range of ways that they can get involved.

The most important thing at this stage is inspiring an awakening. There is a tremendous amount of confusion and denial that exists about mass incarceration today, and that is the biggest barrier to movement building. As long as we remain in denial about this system, movement building will be impossible. Exposing youth in classrooms to the truth about this system and developing their critical capacities will, I believe, open the door to meaningful engagement and collective, inspired action.

Jody Sokolower is a teacher educator in the Bay Area and co-coordinator of the Teach Palestine Project at the Middle East Children's Alliance. She is a former Rethinking Schools *managing editor and author of a new book,* Determined to Stay: Palestinian Youth Fight for Their Village.

Chapter Seven

ONCE UPON A GENOCIDE
Columbus in children's literature

By Bill Bigelow

Children's biographies of Christopher Columbus function as primers on racism and colonialism. They teach youngsters to accept the right of white people to rule over people of color, of powerful nations to dominate weaker nations. And because the Columbus myth is so pervasive—Columbus' "discovery" is probably the only historical episode with which all my students are familiar—it inhibits children from developing democratic, multicultural, and anti-racist attitudes.

Almost without exception, children's biographies of Columbus depict the journey to the New World as a "great adventure" led by "probably the greatest sailor of his time." It's a story of courage and superhuman tenacity. Columbus is depict-

ed as brave, smart, and determined. But behind this romanticized portrayal is a gruesome reality. For Columbus, land was real estate and it didn't matter that other people were already living there; if he "discovered" it, he took it. If he needed guides or translators, he kidnapped them. If his men wanted women, he captured sex slaves. If the indigenous people resisted, he countered with vicious attack dogs, hangings, and mutilations.

On his second voyage, desperate to show his royal patrons a return on their investment, Columbus rounded up some 1,500 Taínos on the island of Hispaniola and chose 500 as slaves to be sold in Spain. Slavery did not show a profit as almost all the slaves died en route to Spain or soon after their arrival. Nonetheless, he wrote, "Let us in the name of the Holy Trinity go on sending all the slaves that can be sold."

Columbus decided to concentrate on the search for gold. He ordered every Taíno on Hispaniola 14 years and older to deliver a regular quota of gold. Those who failed had their hands chopped off. In two years of the Columbus regime, perhaps a quarter of a million people died.

This article examines eight children's biographies of Columbus[1], comparing the books with the historical record and analyzing how these accounts may influence young readers.

Portrait of Columbus

Why did Columbus want to sail west to get to the Indies? The answer offered to children in today's books hasn't changed much since I was in 4th grade. I remember my teacher, Mrs. O'Neill, asking our class this question. As usual, I didn't have a clue, but up went Jimmy Martin's hand. "Why do men want to go to the moon?" he said triumphantly. Mrs. O'Neill was delighted and told us all how smart Jimmy was because he answered a question with a question. In other words: just because—because he was curious, because he loved adventure, because he wanted to prove he could do it—just because. And for years I accepted this explanation (and envied Jimmy Martin).

In reality, Columbus wanted to become rich.

In reality, Columbus wanted to become rich. It was no easy task convincing Queen Isabella and King Ferdinand to finance this highly questionable journey to the Indies, partly because his terms were outrageous. Columbus demanded 10 percent of all the wealth returned to Europe along the new trade route to Asia (where Columbus thought he was headed)—that's 10 percent of the riches brought back by everyone, not just by himself. And he wanted this guaranteed forever, for him, for his children, for their children, in perpetuity. He demanded that he be granted the titles "Viceroy" and "Admiral of the Ocean Sea." He was to be governor of all new territories found; the "Admiral" title was hereditary and would give him a share in proceeds from naval booty.

As for Queen Isabella and King Ferdinand, curiosity, adventure, and "exploration" were the last things on their minds. They wanted the tremendous profits that could be secured by finding a western passage to the Indies. The books acknowledge—and even endorse—Columbus' demands and readily admit that securing "gold and spices" was an objective of the enterprise. "Of course [Columbus] wanted a lot! What was wrong with that?" James de Kay's *Meet Christopher Columbus* tells 2nd graders. But this quest for wealth is downplayed in favor of adventure. "Exploration" meant going to "strange cities" where "many wonderful things" could be seen [de Kay]. Travel was exciting: Columbus "felt the heady call of the open sea. 'I love the taste of salt spray in my face,' he told a friend, 'and the feel of a deck rising and falling under my feet.'" [Monchieri]. According to these eight biographies, a major reason Columbus wanted to sail west was because of his deep faith in God. Columbus thought "that the Lord had chosen him to sail west across the sea to find the riches of the East for himself and to carry the Christian faith to the heathens. His name was Christopher. Had not the Lord chosen his namesake, Saint Christopher, to carry the Christ Child across the dark water of a river?" [D'Aulaire]. Religion, curiosity, adventure—all those motives are given preference in the Columbus biographies. But each of these supposed motives pales before the Spanish empire's quest for wealth and power. In burying these more fundamental material forces, the Columbus books encourage students to misunderstand the roots of today's foreign policy exploits. Thus students are more likely to accept platitudes—"We're involved in the Middle East for freedom and democracy"—than to look for less altruistic explanations.

Religion, curiosity, adventure—all those motives are given preference in the Columbus biographies.

The Kind and Noble Columbus

None of the biographies I evaluated—all still on the shelves of school and public libraries and widely available—disputes the ugly facts about Columbus and the Spanish conquest of the Caribbean. Yet the sad irony is that all encourage children to root for Columbus and empathize with him, using phrases such as "It was lucky that Christopher Columbus was born where he was or he might never have gone to sea," [Fritz] or "There once was a boy who loved the salty sea" [D'Aulaire]. Some of the books, particularly those for younger readers, refer to Columbus affectionately, using his first name. Unlike the people he will later exterminate, Columbus is treated as a real human being, one with thoughts and feelings: "When Christopher Columbus was a child, he always wanted to be like Saint Christopher. He wanted to sail to faraway places and spread the word of Christianity" [Osborne].

The series title of Robert Young's *Christopher Columbus and His Voyage to the New World* sums up the stance of most biographies: "Let's Celebrate." The books cheer Columbus on toward the Indies. Each step on the road to "discovery" is told from his point of view. When Columbus is delayed, this is the "most unhappy part of his great adventure" [de Kay]. Every successful step is rewarded with exclamation marks: "Yes, [the queen] would help Columbus!" [Osborne]. "After all these years, Columbus would get his ships!" [de Kay].

Unlike the people he will later exterminate, Columbus is treated as a real human being.

Columbus' devout Christianity is a theme in all the books—and is never questioned. The most insistent of these—and the worst of the lot in almost every respect—is Sean J. Dolan's *Christopher Columbus: The Intrepid Mariner.*

By the second page in Dolan's reverent volume, we're reading about Columbus' attachment to his leather-bound Bible. Dolan is constantly dipping us into the admiral's thoughts. Usually these meditations run deep and pious: "[He] believed that the awe-inspiring beauty that surrounded him could only be the handiwork of the one true God, and he felt secure in his Lord and Savior's protection. 'If only my crewmen shared my belief,' Columbus thought." And this is only on the third page—Dolan's narrative goes on like this for 114 more. The reader is practically strangled by Columbus' halo.

Jean Fritz's *Where Do You Think You're Going, Christopher Columbus?* is the only book somewhat skeptical about religion as a motive. Fritz tells her readers that Queen Isabella "was such an enthusiastic Christian that she insisted everyone in Spain be a Christian too. . . . Indeed, she was so religious that if she even found Christians who were not sincere Christians, she had them burned at the stake. (Choir boys sang during the burnings so Isabella wouldn't have to hear the screams.)"

This is pretty strong stuff, but the implied critique would likely be lost on upper elementary students, the book's targeted readers. The close association between God and Columbus in all the books, with the possible exception of Fritz's, discourages children from criticizing Columbus. "Columbus marveled at how God had arranged everything for the best," the D'Aulaires write. Well, if God arranged everything, who are we, the insignificant readers, to question?

No book even hints that the Indians believed in their own god or gods who also watched over and cared about them. The Columbus expedition may be the first encounter between two peoples—Us and Them—where children will learn that "God is on our side."

Evils? Blame the Workers

Columbus' journey across the Atlantic was not easy, according to most of the books, because his crew was such a wretched bunch. The sailors were stupid, superstitious, cowardly, and sometimes scheming. Columbus, on the other hand, is portrayed as brave, wise, and godly. These characterizations, repeated frequently in many of the books, protect the Columbus myth. Anything bad that happens, like murder and slavery, can always be blamed on the men. Columbus, the leader, is pure of heart. Taken together, the books' portrayals serve as a kind of anti-working class, pro-boss polemic: "Soon [Columbus] rose above his shipmates, for he was clever and capable and could make others carry out his orders" [D'Aulaire]. Evidently, ordinary seamen are not "clever and capable," and thus are good merely for carrying out the instructions of others. "Soon [Columbus] forgot that he was only the son of a humble weaver," the D'Aulaires write, as if a background as a worker were a source of shame. The books encourage children to identify with Columbus' hardships, even though his men worked and slept in horrible conditions while the future admiral slept under a canopy bed in his private cabin. The lives of those who labored for Columbus are either ignored or held in contempt.

> **The lives of those who labored for Columbus are either ignored or held in contempt. Columbus is treated as a real human being.**

The 'Discovery'

At the core of the Columbus myth—and repeated by all eight books—is the notion that Columbus "discovered" America. Indeed, it's almost as if the same writer churned out one ever-so-slightly different version after another.

De Kay describes the scene this way in *Meet Christopher Columbus:*

> The sailors rowed Columbus to the shore. He stepped on the beach. He got on his knees and said a prayer of thanks. Columbus named the island San Salvador. He said it now belonged to Ferdinand and Isabella. He tried to talk to the people on San Salvador. But they could not understand him.

Of course he couldn't understand them, either. But de Kay attributes the inability to understand solely to the Indians. Is it these Indians' implied ignorance that justifies heavily armed men coming onto their land and claiming it in the name of a kingdom thousands of miles away? In *Christopher Columbus and His Voyage to the New World,* Robert Young doesn't even tell his young readers of the people on these islands. Young's Columbus found "lands" but no people: In illustrations we see only palm trees and empty beaches.

Why don't any of the books ask students to think about the assumptions that underpinned this land grab? Naively, I kept waiting for some book to insert just a trace of doubt: "Why do you think Columbus felt he could claim land for Spain when there were already people living there?" or "Columbus doesn't write in his journal why he felt entitled to steal other people's property. What do you think?"

This scene of Columbus' first encounter with the Indians—read in school by virtually every child—is a powerful metaphor about relations between different countries and races. It is a lesson not just about the world 500 years ago, but about the world today: Clothed, armed, Christian white men from a more technological-ly "advanced" nation arrive in a land peopled by darker-skinned, naked, unarmed, non-Christians—and take over. Because no book indicates which characteristic of either group necessitates or excuses this kind of bullying, students are left alone to puzzle it out: Might makes right. Whites should rule over people who aren't white. Christians should control non-Christians. "Advanced" nations should dominate "backward" nations. Each and every answer a student might glean from the books' text and images invariably justifies colonialism and racism.

In Columbus' New World "adventures," the lives of the Indians are a kind of "muzak"—insignificant background noise. Only one book, *Where Do You Think You're Going, Christopher Columbus?*, tries to imagine what the Indians might have been thinking about the arrival of the Spaniards. Still, the point here seems more to gently poke fun at Columbus and crew than to seriously consider the Indians' point of view: "[I]f the Spaniards were surprised to see naked natives, the natives were even more surprised to see dressed Spaniards. All that cloth over their bodies! What were they trying to hide? Tails, perhaps?" Jean Fritz's interior monologue for the Indians makes fun of the explorers but in the process trivializes the Indians' concerns.

Each and every answer a student might glean from the books' text and images invariably justifies colonialism and racism.

Not a single Columbus biography ever asks children: "What might the Indians have thought about the actions of Columbus and his men?" The silent Indians in Columbus stories have a contemporary consequence. The message is that white people in "developed" societies have conscious-ness and voice, but Third World people are thoughtless and voiceless objects. The books rehearse students in a way of looking at the world that begins from the assumption: They are not like us. A corollary is that we are more competent to determine the conditions of their lives: their social and economic systems, their political alliances, and so on. As shown by interventions in Iraq and Vietnam, sub-version of the government headed by Salvador Allende in Chile, the invasions of Grenada and Panama, the attempted overthrow by proxy of the Nicaraguan and Angolan governments, our right to decide what's best for them is basic to the con-duct of this nation's foreign policy. As most children's first exposure to "foreign policy," the Columbus myth helps condition young people to accept the unequal distribution of power in the world.

Theft, Slavery, and Murder

Columbus' genocidal policies toward the Indians were initiated during his second journey. The three books aimed at children in early elementary grades, Gleiter and Thompson's *Christopher Columbus*, de Kay's *Meet Christopher Columbus*, and Young's *Christopher Columbus and His Voyage to the New World*, all conveniently stop the story after his first journey. The Columbus myth can take root in young minds without the complications of the slavery and mass murder to come.

After his first trip, Columbus returned to a hero's welcome in Spain. He also arrived telling all kinds of lies about gold mines and spices and unlimited amounts of wealth. The admiral needed royal backing for a second trip, and had to convince his sponsors that the islands contained more than parrots and naked natives.

During his second voyage, in February of 1495, Columbus launched the slave raids against the Taínos of Hispaniola. Four of the eight books I reviewed—the ones aimed at older children—admit that Columbus took Indians as slaves [Monchieri, Fritz, Osborne, and Dolan]. Their critique, however, is muted. No account tells children what slavery meant for its victims. One of the books, Monchieri's *Christopher Columbus,* says that taking slaves was "a great failing of Columbus. ... He saw nothing wrong with enslaving the American Indians and making them work for Spanish masters. ... Missionaries protested against this policy, but they were not listened to."

Mary Pope Osborne in *Christopher Columbus: Admiral of the Ocean Sea* writes that "this terrible treatment of the Indians was Columbus' real downfall." Still, Osborne is unable to offer even this minimal critique of the admiral without at the same time justifying his actions: "Since Columbus felt despair and disappointment about not finding gold in the Indies, he decided to be like the African explorers and try to sell these Indians as slaves." Neither book ever describes the character of slave life—or slave death.

As most children's first exposure to 'foreign policy,' the Columbus myth helps condition young people to accept the unequal distribution of power in the world.

The other two biographies offer Columbus' justifications for taking slaves: "African explorers were always sending Africans back to Spanish slave markets, Columbus told himself. Besides, the natives were all heathens. It wasn't as if he were selling Christians into slavery" [Fritz]. Dolan at one point blames it all on the men: "Given the attitude of the men at large, however, [Columbus] had little choice but to give his approval to the slaving sorties."

Imagine, if you will, Nazi war crimes described in this way—nothing about the suffering of the victims, tepid criticism of the perpetrators, the horrendous crimes explained by the rationalizations of Hitler and his generals. How long would these books last in our schools?

From the beginning, locating gold was Columbus' primary objective. In one passage, not included in any of the children's books, Columbus wrote: "Gold is a wonderful thing! Whoever owns it is lord of all he wants. With gold it is even possible to open for souls the way to paradise." Two of the eight authors, Fritz and Dolan, describe Columbus' system for attempting to extract gold from the Indians. Dolan writes that Columbus instituted "a system of forced tribute: Each Indian was to provide a certain amount of gold each year. Penalties for failure to comply with this rule included flogging, enslavement, or death." Nothing here about cutting people's hands off, which is what Columbus did, but still it's pretty explicit. Fritz writes simply that Indians who didn't deliver enough gold "were punished." She concludes that "between 1494 and 1496 one third of the native population of Hispaniola was killed, sold, or scared away." The passive voice in Fritz's version—"was killed, sold, or scared away"—protects the perpetrators: Exactly who caused these deaths?

More significantly, these accounts fail to recognize the Indians' humanity. The books' descriptions are clinical and factual, like those of a coroner. What kind of suffering must these people have gone through? How did it feel to have their civilization completely destroyed in just a few years? What of the children who watched their parents butchered by the Spanish gold-seekers? These books show no passion or outrage—at Columbus or at the social and economic system he represented. This devastation happened to several hundred thousand human beings, maybe more. Why don't the writers of these books get angry?

These books show no passion or outrage—at Columbus or at the social and economic system he represented.

I find the most "honest" books about Columbus' enterprise—those that admit slavery and other crimes—the most distressing. They lay out the facts, describe the deaths, and then move on to the next paragraph with no look back. These books foster a callousness toward human suffering—or is it simply a callousness toward people of color? Apparently students are supposed to value bravery, cunning, and perseverance over a people's right to life and self-determination.

Contempt for Native Resistance

Given that Columbus biographies scarcely consider Indians as human beings, it's not surprising that native resistance to the Spaniards' atrocities is either barely acknowledged or treated with hostility. Gleiter and Thompson's *Christopher Columbus* notes that in future trips Columbus "fought with the natives." In a single sentence, Lino Monchieri writes: "The Indians became rebellious because [Columbus] compelled them to hand over their gold." At least here the author credits the Indians with what might be a legitimate cause for revolt, though offers no further details. Mary Pope Osborne buries the cause of resistance in nonexplanatory, victimless prose: "But the settlers had run into trouble with the Indians, and there had been a lot of fighting."

Some writers choose to portray Indian resistance not as self-defense, but as originating from the indigenous people's inherently violent nature. In *Meet Christopher Columbus,* "unfriendly Indians" surprise the innocent Spaniards: "Suddenly more than 50 Indians jumped out from behind the trees. They had bows and arrows. They attacked the men. The men fought back." Thus, Indian resistance to the Spaniards' invasion and land grab is not termed "freedom fighting," but instead is considered "unfriendly." The violence of the Spaniards is described as self-defense. Note that in this quote, the Spaniards are "men" and the Indians are, well, just Indians. The books that bother to differentiate between groups of Indians single out the Caribs for special contempt. Caribs are presented as cannibals, even though no historical evidence exists to corroborate such a claim. The Caribs lived on islands "so wild and steep, it seemed as if the waterfalls came tumbling out of the clouds. The Indians who lived there were wild too. They were cannibals who ate their enemies" [D'Aulaire]. In Dolan's *Christopher Columbus: The Intrepid Mariner,* Columbus sends an armed contingent to "explore" the island that today is St. Croix. Because Caribs attack the Spaniards, Dolan considers this resistance sufficient to label the Caribs as ferocious. In fact, according to the eyewitness account of Dr. Diego Alvarez Chanca, the Indians attacked only when the Spaniards trapped them in a cove. In today's parlance, the Caribs were "radicals" and "extremists"—in other words, they tenaciously defended their land and freedom.

The books condition young people to reject the right of the oppressed to rebel. We have a right to own their land, and they should not protest—at least not violently. Those who do resist will be slapped with a pejorative descriptor—cannibal, savage, communist, militant, radical, hard-liner, extremist—and subdued. The Columbus biographies implicitly lead students to have contempt for contemporary movements for social justice. Obviously, they leave children ill-prepared to respect current Indian struggles for land and fishing rights.

Columbus' Legacy

I expected each book to end with at least some reflection on the meaning of Columbus' voyages. None did. In fact, only one book, *Meet Christopher Columbus,* even suggests that today's world has anything to do with Columbus: Thanks to the admiral, "Thousands of people crossed the ocean to America. This 'new world' became new countries: the United States, Canada, Mexico, Brazil, and many others."

It's much simpler for the authors to ignore both short- and long-term consequences of Columbus' enterprise. Instead of linking the nature of Columbus' Spain to 20th-century America, each book functions as a kind of secular Book of Genesis: In the beginning there was Columbus—he was good and so are we.

This is a grave omission. In addition to the genocide of native peoples in the Caribbean, the most immediate effect of Columbus' voyages was the initiation of the Atlantic slave trade between Africa and America.[2] Colonialism and slavery: This was the "new world" Columbus did not so much discover as help to invent. In the emerging commercial ethos of his society, human beings were commodities whose value was measured largely in monetary terms. The natural environment was likewise

Colonialism and slavery: This was the 'new world' Columbus did not so much discover as help to invent.

cherished not for its beauty but for the wealth that could be extracted. Columbus' enterprise and the plunder that ensued contributed mightily to the growth of the nascent mercantile capitalism of Europe. His lasting contribution was to augment a social order that confronts the world in commercial terms—how much is it worth?—and which appreciates markets rather than cultures.

Asking 'Why?'

Why are Columbus biographies characterized by such bias and omission? I doubt any writers, publishers, or teachers consciously set out to poison the minds of the young. The Columbus story teaches important values, some would argue. Here was a young man who, despite tremendous adversity, maintained and finally achieved his objectives. Fear and narrow-mindedness kept others from that which he finally accomplished.

But in the Columbus biographies, these decent values intermingle seamlessly with deep biases against working-class people, people of color, and Third World nations. The blindness of writers and educators to these biases is simply an indication of how pervasive they are in the broader society. The seeds of imperialism, exploitation, and racism were planted with Columbus' first transatlantic enterprise—and these seeds have taken root.

Without doubt, ours is a very different world from Spanish America in the 15th and 16th centuries, but there is a lingering inheritance: the tendency for powerful groups to value profit over humanity; racial and cultural differences used to justify exploitation and inequality; vast disparities in living conditions for different social classes; economically and militarily strong nations attempting to control the fates of weaker nations. Hence, life amidst injustice in today's United States inures many of us to the injustice of 500 years earlier. Characteristics that appear to someone as natural and inevitable in the 21st century will likely appear as natural and inevitable in the descriptions of the world five centuries ago.

The Biographies' Pedagogy

The Columbus stories encourage passive reading and never pose questions for children to think about. Did Columbus have a right to claim Indian land in the name of the Spanish crown? Were those Indians who resisted violently justified in doing so? Why does the United States commemorate a Columbus Day instead of a Genocide Day? The narratives require readers merely to listen, not to think. The text is everything, the reader nothing. Not only are young readers conditioned to accept social hierarchy—colonialism and racism—they are also rehearsed in an authoritarian mode of learning.

By implication, in this review essay I suggest the outlines of a more truthful history of Columbus and the "discovery" of America. First, the indigenous peoples of America must be accorded the status of full human beings with inalienable rights to self-determination. The tale of "discovery" needs to be told from their perspective as well as from the Europeans'. Although there is little documentation of how the Indians interpreted the Spaniards' arrival and conquest, readers could be encouraged to think about these events from the native point of view. Columbus' interior monologue should not be the only set of thoughts represented in the story. A more accurate tale of Columbus would not simply probe his personal history but would also analyze the social and economic system he represented. And children might be asked to think about how today's world was shaped by the events of 1492. Above all, young readers must be invited to think and critique, not simply required to passively absorb others' historical interpretations.

> **The Columbus stories encourage passive reading and never pose questions for children to think about.**

Until we create humane and truthful materials, teachers may decide to boycott the entire Columbus canon. The problem with this approach is that the distortions and inadequacies characterizing this literature are also found in other children's books.

A better solution is to equip students to read critically these and other stories—inviting children to become detectives, investigating their biographies, novels, and textbooks for bias. In fact, because the Columbus books are so bad, they make perfect classroom resources to learn how to read for social as well as for literal meaning. After students have been introduced to a critical history of Columbus, they could probe materials for accuracy. Do the books lie outright? What is omitted from the accounts that would be necessary for a more complete understanding of Columbus and his encounters with native cultures? What motives are ascribed to Columbus, and how do those compare with the actual objectives of the admiral and the Spanish monarchs? Whom does the book "root" for and how is this accomplished? What role do illustrations play in shaping the view of Columbus? Why do the books tell the story as they do? Who in our society benefits and who is hurt by these presentations?

Teachers could assign children to write their own Columbus biographies—and some of these could be told from Indians' points of view. Or youngsters might take issues from their own lives suggested by the European invasion of America—fighting, fairness, stealing, racism—and write stories drawn from these themes.

Significantly, to invite students to question the injustices embedded in text material is implicitly to invite them to question the injustices embedded in the society itself. Isn't it about time we used the Columbus myth to allow students to begin discovering the truth?

Bill Bigelow is curriculum editor of Rethinking Schools *and co-director of the Zinn Education Project. He co-edited* A People's Curriculum for the Earth: Teaching Climate Change and the Environmental Crisis.

For Further Reading

Zinn, H. (1980). *A People's History of the United States.* New York: Harper and Row.
Sale, K. (1990). *The Conquest of Paradise: Christopher Columbus and the Columbian Legacy.*
New York: Knopf.
Davidson, B. (1961). *The African Slave Trade: Precolonial History 1450–1850.* Boston: Little, Brown.

1. Books reviewed in this article:
   Young, R. (1990). *Christopher Columbus and His Voyage to the New World.* Englewood Cliffs,
   NJ: Silver Press.
de Kay, J.T. (1989). *Meet Christopher Columbus.* New York: Random House.
Gleiter, J. & Thompson, K. (1995). *Christopher Columbus.* Orlando, FL: Steck-Vaughn.
   Parin D'Aulaire, I. & Parin D'Aulaire, E. (1987). *Columbus.* New York: Doubleday.
   Fritz, J. (1997). *Where Do You Think You're Going, Christopher Columbus?* New York: G. P. Put-
   nam's Sons.
   Monchieri, L. (1985) Christopher Columbus (Mary Lee Grisanti trans.). Englewood Cliffs, NJ:
   Silver Burdett Press.
   Osborne, M. P. (1997). *Christopher Columbus: Admiral of the Ocean Sea.* Strongville, OH: Gareth
   Stevens Publishing.
   Dolan, S. J. (1989). *Christopher Columbus: The Intrepid Mariner.* New York: Fawcett Columbine.

2. For more information, see Bigelow, B. & Peterson, B. (eds.) (1998). *Rethinking Columbus: The Next
   500 Years.* Milwaukee, WI: *Rethinking Schools.*

Chapter Eight

WHAT DO YOU MEAN WHEN YOU SAY URBAN?

Speaking honestly about race and students

By Dyan Watson

Ethnic, inner city, urban. What do these terms mean in education?

I am a teacher educator who studies how people use language to talk about race. One word that I've examined over the past five years is *urban*. A quick look in the dictionary, and there is no surprise: Urban means related to the city, characteristic of a city or city life. So what does that mean when we say urban education? What is unique about city schools or city education? That depends on the city you're talking about. In large, densely populated cities, such as Boston, New York, and Los Angeles, city schools are often characterized by large, diverse populations, many poor students, budget shortfalls, and bureaucracy. So why, then, do we use the term *urban* when what we really mean are schools with majority black and Latina/o populations?

Take for example my city: Portland, Ore. Downtown there is a high school named Lincoln. It is less than a mile from the Pearl District, a hip place that boasts unique food, shops, new condos, and the best of urban renewal. It is a stone's throw from a soccer stadium and surrounded by tall buildings, people biking to work in

PETE RAILAND

suits, folks who routinely beg, and the hub of the public transit system.

Across the river in North Portland, there is a high school named Jefferson. It is surrounded by family dwellings, mom-and-pop shops, and wide streets for biking, walking, and playing. There is a community college across the street.

Which one of these schools is urban? Lincoln? Jefferson? Both?

Before you decide, let me give you a bit more information. At Lincoln, the downtown school, the population is more than 75 percent white, 4.5 percent of the students are black, 8.6 percent are Asian, and 6.6 percent are Latina/o; 10.5 percent are on free/reduced lunch; and the school does not receive Title 1 funding. At Jefferson, the school across the river, 59 percent of the students are black, 8 percent are Asian/Pacific Islanders, and 17 percent are Latina/o; 70 percent are on free/reduced lunch; and the school does receive Title 1 funding.

Made up your mind yet?

A few years ago I interviewed 17 teachers who attended an "urban education" program. I asked them what was the difference, if any, between urban teaching and non-urban teaching. Ruth remarked: "To me, urban students come from an environment where they can't see the value of education. They can't see why it matters, because everyone that they know, everything that they do, has nothing to do with having an education."

Thinking about the definition of urban—related to the city—I can't help but wonder: What is it about city kids that makes this teacher think they don't value education? It wasn't until after three interviews of each teacher that the whole picture emerged, one in which urban was constructed as a code word for *race*—specifically black and Latina/o—and often for poor. Teachers equated urban with students of color and the characteristics they perceived as belonging to students of color.

At one point I asked these teachers what *urban* meant and the most often cited response was "racially diverse students." Now taken as is, this would mean students of a multitude of races—including whites. But it was clear from these interviews that "racially diverse" excluded white students and often left Asian Americans and Native Americans on the side as well.

As Molly noted: "My teacher education program definitely prepared me to be a teacher. I think my school placement prepared me to be an urban teacher. Had I been in the exact same university classes, but had a school placement in Lake Genesis [a majority white high school], I wouldn't have been prepared to be an urban teacher."

I wonder, which parts of good teaching translate into all types of schools and which parts don't? What's urban about urban teaching?

Two years ago I presented some of my research to preservice teachers. One of them challenged me. "But that is how they act. Urban kids don't want to learn as much as the other students in class. Their parents don't care as much, they don't arrive at school on time, and they don't get their homework done. So these teachers are just responding to reality. I see it at North High School all the time."

Reflecting on this, I thought about how he separated his students—all of whom were from the local neighborhood—into two categories: urban and normal. Then I thought, oh yeah, urban means *less than*. The kids who are doing well, the kids who know how to do school, are normal. And the kids who don't know how to do school are urban.

Does it matter what language we use? It only matters if you are going to use it to mask your feelings—overly positive or negative—about a certain race or economic group. This is no time for euphemisms and unexamined beliefs about race. Our schools are deeply divided along racial and class lines. We need teachers who will examine themselves as racial beings who teach other racial beings and figure out what they are doing wrong and what they are doing right.

We need teachers who will examine themselves as racial beings who teach other racial beings and figure out what they are doing wrong and what they are doing right.

What would it look like to use race words (e.g., African American, European American, Korean American) when thinking about your classroom and curriculum? You might test yourself by starting to use "black" when you really mean it instead of low achieving, underserved, at-risk, our kids, those kids, inner city—or urban.

So what do you mean when you say urban?

Dyan Watson (watsond@oes.edu), a former high school teacher, is the Director for Inclusion at Oregon Episcopal School in Portland, Oregon, and an editor of Rethinking Schools.

SECTION II
THE FIGHT FOR MULTICULTURAL EDUCATION

FAVIANNA RODRIGUEZ

Chapter Nine

DECOLONIZING THE CLASSROOM
Lessons in multicultural education

By Wayne Au

When I was in 9th grade, I had Mr. Anderson for honors World History. Mr. Anderson was one of those teachers that all the honors-and AP-track parents wanted their kids to have. He had a reputation for academic rigor, of preparing teenagers for their stratospheric climb toward being a National Merit Scholar slated to attend an Ivy League college.

Like many history teachers, Mr. Anderson talked about his trips to places we studied. During our unit on China, I remember him telling us stories about his trip there, including the exciting fruit he ate, something he called "lee-chee."

I knew what he was talking about. I loved lychee. Available only about six

JORDIN ISIP

weeks a year and costing up to $8 a pound, lychees were a rare treat in my family. After my parents divorced, my father would take me to San Francisco's Chinatown during summer visits, where we bought bunches of the syrupy sweet fruit with translucent flesh. Sitting in the park, cracking the lychee's rough, deep red skin and feeling its juices drip down our chins and fingers, my father told me stories of his childhood in Hawaii, about how he would sneak into the lychee groves to get the precious fruit at the risk of getting shot by farmers guarding their crops.

> **Sitting in the park, cracking the lychee's rough, deep red skin and feeling its juices drip down our chins and fingers, my father told me stories of his childhood in Hawaii.**

But in my family, we said it differently. We called it "LIE-chee." Knowing that the translation between Chinese and English is difficult and imprecise, I raised my hand and tried to tell Mr. Anderson how my family pronounced it. He wasn't having it. This white teacher had been to China and knew better. So he told me (and the class) that I was simply wrong, that I didn't know what I was talking about. Never mind my memories of lychee, never mind my father's stories, and never mind that my Chinese grandmother, aunts, uncles, and cousins all pronounced it LIE-chee.

Now that I have been both a high school teacher and a teacher of teachers, when I reflect back on his class, I see that Mr. Anderson taught us some basic lessons about multicultural education, albeit by negative example. For instance, in Mr. Anderson's class, student knowledge about communities, cultures, and diversity didn't matter, especially if it contradicted his own. Further, Mr. Anderson's contempt for student knowledge revealed no sense of curiosity about the experiences and stories that might lead to a different perspective from his. The lesson to learn here is that multicultural education should be grounded in the lives of students, not only because such a perspective provides a diversity of viewpoints, but also because it honors students' identities and experiences.

Another related lesson to take away from Mr. Anderson's negative example is that multicultural education should seek to draw on the knowledge, perspectives, and voices of the actual communities being studied. In Mr. Anderson's class, my own authentic cultural knowledge and perspective as a Chinese American had no value, and he actively disregarded my own lived experiences. Again, Mr. Anderson was contemptuous of student knowledge and he disregarded the importance of building from kids' lives and prior experiences.

Mr. Anderson's example also teaches us that, because it is connected to students' lives, multicultural education has to be based on dialogue—both amongst students and between students and teachers. As students in Mr. Anderson's class we were always on the outside looking in, and he and the textbooks were the sole authorities. There was no dialogue, only monologue.

The final lesson to draw from Mr. Anderson is that, when classes are not grounded in the lives of students, do not include the voices and knowledge of communities being studied, and are not based in dialogue, they create environments where not only are white students miseducated, but students of color feel as if their very identities are under attack.

Multicultural Education on the Down Low

I had to get my real multicultural education on the down low, outside of classes like Mr. Anderson's. I went to Garfield High School, located in Seattle's historically African American neighborhood, the Central District. Garfield has been known for many years as Seattle's "black high school," and back in the 1970s there was a strong Black Panther Party presence both in the neighborhood and in the school itself. Garfield, always a basketball powerhouse, also boasts a rich connection to African American culture and music, with names like Quincy Jones and Jimi Hendrix still haunting the hallways.

By the time I got there in the late 1980s, Garfield had become a flagship for the Seattle Public Schools. It housed the district's AP program, maintained a world-renowned jazz band, was the district's science magnet high school, and provided a model of Seattle's desegregation busing system (of which I was a part). Totaling around 1,600 students, Garfield's student body hovered at about 50 percent African American and 50 percent white, with a few Latinos and Asian Americans like myself sprinkled in.

Given Garfield's history, position in the community, and commitment to racially integrated education, you might think that real multicultural education took place in most classes. Sadly, it didn't. There was one teacher, Mr. Davis, who taught two "secret" classes at my school: one section of Harlem Renaissance and one section of African Studies.

To get into Mr. Davis' classes, you first had to learn (by word of mouth) the true content of his classes, which were listed plainly in the schedule as Language Arts 10b and Social Studies elective. Second you had to convince your counselor that yes, you really did want to be in Mr. Davis' class, that yes, you really knew what you were getting into.

> **For the first time in my schooling experience, I was one of only two non-African American students in a class.**

For the first time in my schooling experience, I was one of only two non-African American students in a class. In Mr. Davis' classes we looked at the politics of Blackness through the poetry and literature of the Harlem Renaissance and hashed through segregation, desegregation, and African American identity in U.S. history. We read about how Greek civilization was built upon a legacy of knowledge that had already existed in Egypt. And then we learned that Egypt wasn't really "Egypt." From an African-centric standpoint it was actually called Kemet, with its own rich cultural worldview, symbolism, and creation stories.

I sat in this decidedly African-centric, predominantly African American cultural space, trying to sort through my own cultural identity as a mixed white and

Chinese American young man, my own connection with African American culture, and my own sense of education and the politics of race. And I'm sure my presence also left many of my African American classmates questioning. I mean, what was this half-Asian kid doing in the black studies classes anyway? Why does he care? Isn't race and racism mainly about black and white? Do Chinese Americans, let alone half-bloods, even count as people of color? Struggling with these questions (and many more), all of us were asked to stretch.

To be sure, an African-centric course cannot be "multicultural" in and of itself. African-centered is just that, African-centered. But in the real-life context of a school like Garfield, Mr. Davis' classes embodied multicultural education: It was grounded in the lives, identities, and histories of students; it provided critical and alternative perspectives on history that we were not getting in our other classes; and it openly addressed the issue of racism.

Again, now having worked with very diverse populations of students, I see that Mr. Davis' classes also taught me about multicultural education. For instance, his class illustrated how multicultural education is fundamentally based in a critique of school knowledge that has historically been Eurocentric. For example, it was in his class that we learned that "civilization" did not start in Europe, that other nations and cultures had great civilizations that predated their Western counterpart. Challenging such Eurocentrism also spoke to the cultural and political imperative to resist Eurocentric curriculum, as Mr. Davis saw his course as a positive and supportive intervention in the identity development and self-esteem for the students in his classes. Finally, inherent in Mr. Davis' instruction is the lesson that it is important to critically question what textbooks and teachers say about the world.

Mr. Davis' classes also offer a lesson on how multicultural education invites students to engage with real social issues. In his courses my classmates and I connected our burgeoning historical understandings of race and racism to contemporary issues. We argued about interracial dating, black nationalism, racism, and education. In this way, multicultural education inherently connects learning to the world outside of our classrooms.

Another lesson to be gained from Mr. Davis' example is that multicultural education creates a space for students to meaningfully engage with each other. It was through such struggle over social and political issues that I developed substantive relationships with my African American classmates—relationships that I do not think could have developed in my other, more Eurocentric classes that were either populated predominantly by white kids or simply did not create the space to really engage students of color.

Finally, it is crucial to acknowledge that Mr. Davis' classes helped me learn that multicultural education is rigorous. In African Studies and Harlem Renaissance we read serious texts like George G. M. James' *Stolen Legacy* to learn about ancient Egypt's effect on ancient Greek civilization, or Joel Augustus Rogers' *From "Superman" to Man* to gain historical perspectives of U.S. race relations.

Multicultural Education and Rigor

The connection between multicultural education and rigor is important because one of the consistent critiques against multicultural education is that it isn't "real" education, that it isn't rigorous. However, the idea that multicultural education represents a lowering of standards or represents a neglect of academic rigor is false.

Let's compare Mr. Davis' and Mr. Anderson's classes. As with most "rigorous," upper-track classes, the central pieces of rigor I remember from Mr. Anderson's "honors" World History class consisted of an immense amount of textbook reading, chapter questions, and a research paper. And such courses are rigorous in particular ways. Certainly they have formal and strict requirements, and Mr. Anderson's class, like most others of its kind, was demanding in terms of workload. We were always kept busy.

Now as a professor of education, when I critically reflect on these types of "honors" or "advanced" classes, I think that, although they require significant amounts of work, they are not necessarily *intellectually* rigorous. Instead, it often asks for memorization and textbook reading comprehension, not critical analysis. Knowledge is multifaceted and simply reading tough books does not mean that students are engaged in understanding the complexities of any particular historical episode or time period.

Take teaching about the U.S. war with Mexico, for instance. A typical class would focus solely on the actions of governments—U.S. and Mexican alike. A multicultural perspective asks about the Irish American soldiers, Mexican women in conquered territories, black and white abolitionists who opposed the war, soldiers who embraced and also rejected the war, Mexican cadets who jumped to their death rather than surrender to invading U.S. troops, etc. A multicultural perspective is not only inherently more interesting, it is also more complex—and more fully truthful, if we dare use that word. Further, academic rigor is impossible without the multiple perspectives that multicultural education provides because without it, we miss huge pieces of history, culture, and society—leaving huge gaps in our knowledge about the world.

> **The idea that multicultural education represents a lowering of standards or represents a neglect of academic rigor is false.**

Mr. Anderson's class miseducated us about the world too. For instance, in addition to the textbook readings for our unit on Africa, Mr. Anderson had us watch the movie *The Gods Must Be Crazy*. In this movie an African San is befuddled by Western technology and makes a buffoon of himself. Through my 9th-grade eyes, I saw the colonizers' view of the African-native-as-primitive, of darker peoples as idiotic and childlike.

Mr. Anderson didn't really teach about this film. He just showed it as an "entertaining" way for 14-year-olds to learn about Africa. So we never learned about how such a film could justify the system of apartheid in South Africa by portraying the San people as incompetent and unable to be incorporated into a democratic society. We never learned how such a film might rationalize the idea that the San needed "benevolent" white rulers to take care of them.

My African Studies course with Mr. Davis, however, was different, and despite its tag as being "regular," its perspective made it more intellectually rigorous than my "honors" history classes because, as all good multicultural education should do, we were asked to consider the variety of our own experiences and relate them to the complexities of history and society.

I remember struggling to write a paper for Mr. Davis that explained the relationship between race, poverty, and education in the United States. Although in many ways this topic was probably beyond my mid-teen reach, in many ways it wasn't: The relationship between race, poverty, and education was something I was trying to understand (and still am), and writing a paper about it pushed me in my writing and my thinking. Assignments like this made me think hard in my "regular" African Studies class, whereas my "honors" World History class asked for very little thinking at all—just lots of work. More importantly, this assignment illustrates how a multicultural curriculum honors the experiences and curiosity of students so that their own questions about these issues are encouraged and honored as a way of fueling their academic inquiry.

A multicultural perspective is not only inherently more interesting, it is also more complex—and more fully truthful, if we dare use that word.

This rigorous need for multicultural perspectives raises another critical lesson: Multicultural education cannot be relegated to individual classes. Mr. Davis' classes were important because they existed within a context where most other classes were Eurocentric, so they became spaces of multicultural resistance. But ideally all classes at Garfield—social studies, language arts, math, science, art, etc.—should have taken multicultural education seriously if they really wanted to be rigorous and if they really wanted to engage all students in learning. For that matter, all classes for all students, from prekindergarten on, should take multicultural education seriously. Then, students would generally be in a position to more actively and collectively resist classroom colonization and smarter in that they could take up a more critical analysis of all course content.

The Struggle for Multicultural Education

Sadly, college-bound students at Garfield certainly didn't fight to get Mr. Davis' classes on their transcripts. Instead, they would forego Harlem Renaissance and African Studies in order to stay in AP and on the honors track. Things haven't changed all that much since I was in high school, because in today's context of high-stakes education, multicultural education is still viewed as not academically rigorous, not "real" education, and not worthy of being included in the curriculum in its own right.

The lowly status of multicultural curriculum has also meant a constant fight to justify its existence. Take again for instance the African Studies class at Garfield. Ten years after I had walked the halls as a student, I returned to Garfield as a teacher. To my great pleasure, African Studies was given to me as part of my teaching load.

Not surprisingly, I found that many teachers in the social studies department openly sneered at the African Studies course, and the department chair—seeing that Mr. Davis had left to become a principal—thought it would be a good chance to get rid of the class. In his mind, it had no value. What the department chair couldn't see, and what I knew as a legacy student of that very same class, was that African Studies created an irreplaceable space to engage in the politics of Blackness that existed nowhere else at Garfield. Further, African Studies was an irreplaceable space where students' cultures were respected, where students learned to think in terms of multiple social experiences, where traditional narratives and explanations were complicated by race and culture. After a protracted and sometimes nasty fight, the African Studies course survived (and I enjoyed teaching it), but there shouldn't have been a fight to begin with. My experience fighting for African Studies taught me another lesson: Multicultural education is rooted in an anti-racist struggle over whose knowledge and experiences should be included in the curriculum.

The Need for Multicultural Education

I think the biggest lesson in multicultural education I've learned from my experiences as a student, teacher, and teacher educator is that it is a valuable and necessary orientation toward teaching and learning that needs to be embraced by all educators. Every institution I've ever worked in has been resistant to multicultural education in some way, shape, or form, and I'm tired of having to justify it, tired of having to prove its worth. As a person of color I take offense at the idea that my history, my perspective on the world as an individual and a representative member of a community does not matter.

As a teacher educator I encounter on a daily basis the consequences of schooling that is not multicultural. Many of my students know little of the histories and cultures of the students that they will end up teaching. What's more, they don't know that they don't know, and I fear that many of them will enter communities of color as an army of Mr. Andersons, damaging the young people they're trusted to educate. Hopefully, the lessons in multicultural education they learn in my classes will help them become more like Mr. Davis, teachers who can lead a struggle against racism in their classrooms.

Wayne Au, a former public high school teacher and current editor of Rethinking Schools, *is an Associate Professor in the Education Program at the University of Washington, Bothell Campus.*

Chapter Ten

WHY THE BEST KIDS' BOOKS ARE WRITTEN IN BLOOD

By Sherman Alexie

In 2011, I was the surprise commencement speaker at the promotion ceremony for a Seattle alternative high school. I spoke to 60 students, who'd come from 16 different districts, and had survived depression, attempted suicide, gang warfare, sexual and physical abuse, absentee parents, poverty, racism, and learning disabilities in order to graduate.

HENRIK DRESCHER

These students had read my young adult novel, *The Absolutely True Diary of a Part-Time Indian,* and had been inspired by my autobiographical story of a poor reservation Indian boy and his desperate and humorous attempts to find a better life.

I spoke about resilience—about my personal struggles with addiction and mental illness—but it was the student speakers who told the most important stories about survival.

A young woman recalled the terrible moment when indifferent school administrators told her that she couldn't possibly be a teen mother and finish high school. So they suggested she get a general education degree (GED) and move on with her life. But, after taking a practice test, she realized that the GED was far too easy for her, so she transferred to that alternative high school, and is now the mother of a 3-year-old and a high school graduate soon to attend college.

After the ceremony, many of the graduates shook my hand, hugged me, took photos with me, and asked me questions about my book and my life. Other students hovered on the edges and eyed me with suspicion and/or shyness.

It was a beautiful and painful ceremony. But it was not unique. I have visited dozens of high schools—rich and poor, private and public, integrated and segregated, absolutely safe and fearfully dangerous—and have heard hundreds of stories that are individually tragic and collectively agonizing.

Almost every day, my mailbox is filled with handwritten letters from students—teens and preteens—who have read my YA book and loved it. I have yet to receive a letter from a child somehow debilitated by the domestic violence, drug abuse, racism, poverty, sexuality, and murder contained in my book. To the contrary, kids as young as 10 have sent me autobiographical letters written in crayon, complete with drawings inspired by my book, that are just as dark, terrifying, and redemptive as anything I've ever read.

And, often, kids have told me that my YA novel is the only book they've ever read in its entirety.

So when I read Meghan Cox Gurdon's complaints about the "depravity" and "hideously distorted portrayals" of contemporary young adult literature, I laughed at her condescension.

Does Ms. Gurdon honestly believe that a sexually explicit YA novel might somehow traumatize a teen mother? Does she believe that a YA novel about murder and rape will somehow shock a teenager whose life has been damaged by murder and rape? Does she believe a dystopian novel will frighten a kid who already lives in hell?

When I think of the poverty-stricken, sexually and physically abused, self-loathing Native American teenager that I was, I can only wish, immodestly, that I'd been given the opportunity to read *The Absolutely True Diary of a Part-Time Indian.* Or Laurie Halse Anderson's *Speak.* Or Chris Lynch's *Inexcusable.* Or any of the books that Ms. Gurdon believes to be irredeemable. I can't speak for other writers, but I think I wrote my YA novel as a way of speaking to my younger, irredeemable self.

Of course, all during my childhood, would-be saviors tried to rescue my fellow tribal members. They wanted to rescue me. But, even then, I could only laugh at their platitudes. In those days, the cultural conservatives thought that KISS and Black Sabbath were going to impede my moral development. They wanted to protect me from sex when I had already been raped. They wanted to protect me from evil though a future serial killer had already abused me. They wanted me to profess my love for God without considering that I was the child and grandchild of men and women who'd been sexually and physically abused by generations of clergy.

What was my immature, childish response to those would-be saviors?

"Wow, you are way, way too late."

And now, as an adult looking back, I wonder why those saviors tried to warn me about the crimes that were already being committed against me.

When some cultural critics fret about the "ever-more-appalling" YA books, they aren't trying to protect African American teens forced to walk through metal detectors on their way into school. Or Mexican American teens enduring the culturally schizophrenic life of being American citizens and the children of illegal immigrants. Or Native American teens growing up on Third World reservations. Or poor white kids trying to survive the meth-hazed trailer parks. They aren't trying to protect the poor from poverty. Or victims from rapists.

He was old enough to die and kill for his country. And old enough to experience the infinite horrors of war. But according to Ms. Gurdon, he might be too young to read a YA novel that vividly portrays those very same horrors.

No, they are simply trying to protect their privileged notions of what literature is and should be. They are trying to protect privileged children. Or the seemingly privileged.

Two years ago, I met a young man attending one of the most elite private high schools in the country. He quietly spoke to me of his agony. What kind of pain could a millionaire's child be suffering? He hadn't been physically or sexually abused. He hadn't ever been hungry. He'd never seen one person strike another in anger. He'd never even been to a funeral.

So what was his problem?

"I want to be a writer," he said. "But my father won't let me. He wants me to be a soldier. Like he was."

He was 17 and destined to join the military. Yes, he was old enough to die and kill for his country. And old enough to experience the infinite horrors of war. But according to Ms. Gurdon, he might be too young to read a YA novel that vividly portrays those very same horrors.

"I don't want to be like my father," that young man said. "I want to be myself. Just like in your book."

I felt powerless in that moment. I could offer that young man nothing but my empathy and the promise of more books about teenagers rescuing themselves from the adults who seek to control and diminish them.

Teenagers read millions of books every year. They read for entertainment and for education. They read because of school assignments and pop culture fads.

And there are millions of teens who read because they are sad and lonely and enraged. They read because they live in an often terrible world. They read because they believe, despite the callow protestations of certain adults, that books—especially the dark and dangerous ones—will save them.

> **I don't write to protect teenagers. It's far too late for that. I write to give them weapons—in the form of words and ideas—that will help them fight their monsters.**

As a child, I read because books—violent and not, blasphemous and not, terrifying and not—were the most loving and trustworthy things in my life. I read widely and loved plenty of the classics, so yes, I recognized the domestic terrors faced by Louisa May Alcott's March sisters. But I became the kid chased by werewolves, vampires, and evil clowns in Stephen King's books. I read books about monsters and monstrous things, often written with monstrous language, because they taught me how to battle the real monsters in my life.

And now I write books for teenagers because I vividly remember what it felt like to be a teen facing everyday and epic dangers. I don't write to protect them. It's far too late for that. I write to give them weapons—in the form of words and ideas—that will help them fight their monsters. I write in blood because I remember what it felt like to bleed.

Chapter Eleven

THOSE AWFUL TEXAS SOCIAL STUDIES STANDARDS

And what about yours?

By Bill Bigelow

I n March of 2010, the Texas board of education gave preliminary approval to new standards that, according to the *New York Times*, "will put a conservative stamp on history and economics textbooks, stressing the superiority of American capitalism, questioning the Founding Fathers' commitment to a purely secular government, and presenting Republican political philosophies in a more positive light." The Texas board of education has rehabilitated Sen. Joe McCarthy, erased mention of the 1848 Seneca Falls women's rights declaration, and required that the inaugural address of Confederate President Jefferson Davis be taught alongside Lincoln's inaugural. And that's just a taste of more than 100 amendments that Re-

DAVID MCLIMANS

publicans have made to the 120-page social studies curriculum standards.

No doubt, the victory of conservative ideologues on the Texas board of education is troubling and worth the attention it's getting. With 4.7 million students, the Texas market is huge and exerts a powerful influence on the whole textbook industry. As Fritz Fischer, chair of the National Council for History Education, told the *Washington Post,* "The books that are altered to fit the standards become the bestselling books, and therefore within the next two years they'll end up in other classrooms."

But all this Texas bashing implies that standards everywhere else are good and fair and true. In fact, other states' social studies standards have their own conservative biases (and occasional silliness) and deserve the same critical scrutiny that Texas' new standards are receiving. Other states may not celebrate Jefferson Davis, but neither do they encourage teachers to equip students with the historical background and analytical tools that they'll need to understand and address today's social and environmental crises.

But all this Texas bashing implies that standards everywhere else are good and fair and true.

Take my own blue state of Oregon. This is no bastion of conservatism. We have a Democratic governor and a Democratic legislature; both U.S. senators are Democrats, as are four of our five U.S. representatives. But our social studies standards are profoundly conservative—in big and little ways. There is no recognition of the social emergency that we confront: a deeply unequal and unsustainable world, hurtling toward an ecological crisis without parallel in human history. The standards portray U.S. society as fundamentally harmonious, with laws designed to promote fairness and progress. Today's wars don't exist. Nor does hunger or poverty.

Political Bias

The first social studies benchmark in Oregon's standards requires that 3rd graders begin a nationalistic curricular journey as they learn to "identify essential ideas and values expressed in national symbols, heroes, and patriotic songs of the United States." By the time these 3rd graders reach high school they'll "understand how laws are developed and applied to provide order, set limits, protect basic rights, and promote the common good." Capitalism is a well-oiled machine.

Eighth graders learn "how supply and demand respond predictably to changes in economic circumstances." The 8th-grade economics standards include not a single mention of social class. Instead, everyone is smashed together as "a consumer, producer, saver, and investor in a market economy." No owners and workers who might have conflicting interests—we're all *producers.*

And what about the inequality that so many students can observe on their way to school? Eighth graders should: "Understand that people's incomes, in part, reflect choices they have made about education, training, skill development, and careers." No mention of the other factors that determine income: race, gender, social class, nationality, immigration status.

Labor unions make only one parenthetical appearance. But unions are irrelevant, because in Standardsland, wages and salaries are "usually determined by the supply and demand for labor"; organizing has nothing to do with wages.

In fact, in most instances, the standards do not ask teachers or texts to alert students to the power of collective action, of working in concert with others to enhance their economic circumstances—which, in the real world, is when people's lives actually get better. Instead, students are told to get ahead by making smarter individual choices.

And that's the message of the standards in a nutshell: In the United States we wend our way through society as individual choice makers. Grade 5: "Identify and give examples of how individuals can influence the actions of government." And then in grade 8: "Identify the responsibilities of citizens of the United States and understand what an individual can do to meet these responsibilities." In the standards, individuals may have social efficacy, but for the most part only as individuals, not as members of organizations or social movements. Not surprisingly, the standards' pull-yourself-up-by-the-bootstraps message is never complicated by concepts like race or racism, which make no appearance in the standards.

And, in these times of ecological crisis, the standards include no mention of human-caused climate change—only a line about how climate change can affect human activity. The standards encourage students to view the earth as a playground and a source of wealth. By grade 5, students will: "Understand how the physical environment presents opportunities for economic and recreational activity."

Pedagogical Bias

There is also a crucial pedagogical bias in social studies standards that was evident as far back as 1994, with the publication of the first *National Standards for United States History* by the National Center for History in the Schools. Those standards required coverage of such an enormous amount of material that teachers could succeed only if they adopted a stand-and-deliver rush through the ages. This academic weightlifting lives on. For example, Oregon's high school world history standards require students to learn about: how the agricultural revolution contributed to and accompanied the Industrial Revolution; the concepts of imperialism and nationalism; "how European colonizers interacted with indigenous populations of Africa, India, and Southeast Asia and how the native populations responded"; Japanese expansion and the consequences for Japan and Asia during the 20th century; the impact of the Chinese revolution of 1911 and the cause of China's Communist Revolution of 1949; the causes and consequences of the Russian Revolution of 1917; the causes and consequences of the Mexican Revolution of 1911–17; the causes of World War I and why the United States entered it; World War II; the

Holocaust; the Cold War; the causes and impact of the Korean and Vietnam wars.

I'm not joking. In one year. And that's only a sampling of what students are expected to learn. There's more. Obviously, the only way a conscientious—well, obedient—teacher could handle such a curricular task is to start talking fast in September and not stop until sometime in June. And rely on a huge textbook. Sorry, kids, no time for role plays, trials, simulations, imaginative writing, small group discussions, short stories, poetry, or anything else that will slow us down. It's December, and we haven't even gotten to Mao's Long March.

Social studies should help students grasp knowledge and tools of analysis so as to make the world a better place. Social studies should help students name and explain obstacles to justice, peace, equality, and sustainability. Instead, social studies standards like Oregon's are simply about covering material.

What Do Your State Standards Say?

These are merely my own state's standards. In the fall of 2004, Christine Sleeter wrote a fine article for *Rethinking Schools,* "Standardizing Imperialism" analyzing how the California state social studies standards endorsed a curricular Manifest Destiny that celebrates "explorers" and "newcomers" who "visit" and "settle." Sleeter found that "California's curriculum folds students into a 'we' that is Western, Judeo-Christian, and has a democratic government with a capitalist market economy. These are juxtaposed to 'them': non-Western, not Judeo-Christian, and totalitarian (or not free). . . . The standards have difficulty incorporating as 'we' those whom the United States had previously colonized."

The real Texas standards story is not that the state has become some curricular outlaw. Yes, Texas has adopted some especially obnoxious standards—e.g., celebrating right-wing icon Phyllis Schlafly while scrapping United Farm Workers leader Dolores Huerta. But, as historian Eric Foner pointed out in a recent article in the *Nation,* Texas harms its students not so much by inserting or erasing particular facts or individuals, but in its overall framework—one that uncritically endorses "free enterprise" as it "ignores those who have struggled to make this a fairer, more equal society." And in this respect, the Texas standards more likely resemble than depart from other states' social studies standards. So by all means, let's monitor, critique, and organize against Texas' reactionary standards. But let's also revisit our own state social studies standards and not just shake a scolding finger at Texas.

Bill Bigelow is curriculum editor of Rethinking Schools *and co-director of the Zinn Education Project. He co-edited* A People's Curriculum for the Earth: Teaching Climate Change and the Environmental Crisis.

Chapter Twelve

'GRECO-ROMAN KNOWLEDGE ONLY' IN ARIZONA SCHOOLS

Indigenous wisdom outlawed once again

By Roberto Cintli Rodriguez

In Lak Ech—
Tu eres mi otro yo—
You are my other self.
I am you and you are me.
If I hurt you, I hurt myself.
If I hate you, I hate myself.
If I love and respect you,
I love and respect myself.

This is how Maria Federico Brummer's class begins at Tucson High School in Arizona. Students here, part of Tucson Unified School District's highly successful Mexican American Studies (MAS) K-12 program, the largest in the nation, are taught this and other Indigenous concepts, including Panche Be (seek the root of the truth), and the Aztec and Maya calendars.

JORDIN ISIP

I am here to speak to the students about the relationship among In Lak Ech, Panche Be, and Hunab Ku. Hunab Ku is a beautiful Maya philosophy and human rights ethos based on maize. It affirms, contrary to what is taught in most schools, that the ancient peoples of this continent were not savage, that they clearly understood how the universe functions and what it means to be a human being.

Not coincidentally, MAS students, many of whom were doing poorly in school prior to entering this program, consistently outperform their peers academically. The program claims a high rate of college-bound graduates.

Hunab Ku affirms, contrary to what is taught in most schools, that the ancient peoples of this continent were not savage, that they clearly understood how the universe functions and what it means to be a human being.

In a parallel universe, across Highway 10 at the state capitol in Phoenix, 518 years after Columbus initiated the theft of a continent, Arizona's State Superintendent of Schools Tom Horne has declared, via the passage of HB 2281, that Indigenous peoples and Indigenous knowledge are (still) not part of Western civilization.

In his relentless campaign against ethnic studies, the would-be governor engineered the passage of a state law that seeks to ban the teaching of ethnic studies by withdrawing its funding. (In a separate but clearly related ruling, the Arizona Department of Education recently banned teachers with heavy accents from teaching English classes.) This is the same state that just passed and signed into law SB 1070, racial profiling legislation that primarily targets those who appear to be Mexicans or Central Americans and are thus suspected of being "illegal aliens."

Despite the success of the MAS program, Horne has long expressed the view that the only facts and ideas that should be taught in Arizona schools are those that originated in "Western or Greco-Roman" civilization. Although his bill affects the whole state, his actual target has long been Tucson's program.

In 2009, progressive education activists (mostly young students) defeated a similar bill by running from Tucson to Phoenix in 115-degree heat. The author of the 2009 bill, Jonathan Paton, withdrew it at that time, but vowed that he and his allies would kill ethnic studies in 2010.

The 2010 bill caused the geographic dislocation of the continent. Acting as royal cosmographer, Horne has ruled that maize (Mesoamerican) knowledge—indigenous to this continent and the philosophical foundation for MAS—is subversive and not part of Western civilization. Horne also mischaracterized the program by claiming that its teachers preach hate, segregation, anti-Americanism, and the violent overthrow of the government. The bill sets up an inquisitorial mechanism that will monitor books and curriculum. Horne has been especially critical of Rudy Acuña's *Occupied America* and Paulo Freire's *Pedagogy of the Oppressed*.

According to the language of HB 2281, American Indian courses are exempt from the legislation in order to comply with federal law, but there are no federal laws that compel the teaching of American Indian Studies. The bill also exempts

African American studies courses as long as they are open to everyone. This, too, is a canard because all ethnic studies courses are open to everyone. The exemption language in the bill is an effort to divide us from each other and a clear signal that it is Mexican American studies that is the immediate target.

By targeting Mexican American studies, Horne also sets himself up as the chief arbiter of what is and is not Indigenous knowledge. In fact, maize knowledge, which is the foundation of Mexican American studies, is also the foundation of much of Indigenous knowledge throughout North, Central, and South America. Apparently Horne has decided that Mesoamerican knowledge is not part of American Indian studies.

Apartheid Arizona

Apartheid Arizona? Consider the Tucson federal courthouse: Like clockwork, at 1:30 p.m., 70 short, brown men (sometimes a few women) occupy the left side of the courtroom, shackled at the ankles, waist, and wrists. Within one hour, they are charged, tried, and convicted en masse of being present illegally in the United States. After this dehumanizing process, they are paraded out of the courtroom. Most have either served time already or are sentenced to a private detention facility operated by the Corrections Corporation of America (CCA). This drama unfolds here every weekday of the year.

Welcome to Operation Streamline. Its goal is to criminalize every migrant who steps into this kangaroo court, while enriching CCA to the tune of some $15 million per month.

Meanwhile, in Southside Tucson in 2010, several days before the state legislature passed the anti-immigrant SB 1070, a massive raid involving 800 military-clad U.S. federal agents swooped into this primarily Mexican-Indigenous community, occupying and terrorizing its residents, all for the purpose of arresting 48 suspects in a human smuggling operation. Shortly thereafter, in Maricopa County, Sheriff Joe Arpaio showcased his 15th major "crime sweep" since early 2008. The sweeps—which targeted Mexican-Indigenous communities—may have actually backfired. They provided a glimpse to the world of how the entire state and nation could look if SB 1070 is affirmed by the courts and spreads beyond Arizona. To conduct these sweeps, Arpaio utilizes the state's smuggling law, which provides for the arrest and conviction of migrants as accomplices in their own smuggling. Such a use of the legal system smacks of official kidnapping and terror.

The Arizona/Mexico Border

In the realm of violence, Arizona is no South Africa, but we do have our own killing fields. For the past dozen years, some 5,000 migrants have been found dead in the inhospitable desert; medical reports confirm that many have died due to violence, including blunt trauma to the head (see www.derechoshumanosaz.net). Funneling thousands of migrants through the desert annually has long been official policy by U.S. immigration officials. Under international law, this could be construed as negligent homicide.

Arizona's smuggling law provides for the arrest and conviction of migrants as accomplices in their own smuggling.

Ironically, in response to these draconian laws and human rights abuses, Democrats have joined Republicans in pushing for more apartheid measures (walls, more agents, and the further militarization of the border) as the solution.

Just solutions for these problems require international agreements that place human beings at the center, solutions that don't force individuals to lose their citizenship, culture, rights, or humanity.

Teaching youth In Lak Ech (you are my other self) and Panche Be (seek the root of the truth) seems a good place to begin.

Roberto Rodriguez is an assistant professor at the University of Arizona. He was arrested on May 21, 2010, with 14 others as they protested the signing of HB 2281 by Arizona Gov. Jan Brewer

Chapter Thirteen

PRECIOUS KNOWLEDGE:
Teaching solidarity with Tucson

By Devin Carberry

The class huddled around my laptop. Their efforts to be silent made the anticipation palpable. We had been invited to speak on NPR's *Call-In Radio* and the broadcast was under way. Omar and Diana, elected to be our spokespeople, sat together on the other side of the room, waiting to be brought on the air to discuss HB 2281, Arizona's controversial ethnic studies ban. Talking points had been discussed and collectively decided upon.

"This is perfect timing," the radio host said, "because Devin Carberry is calling in right now. Devin is a teacher at ARISE high school over in Oakland and is calling in with his class. Devin, how are you talking about this with your students?"

"Good morning," I answered, tensing at the awkward 15-second delay before we heard my voice coming out of a laptop speaker. "I am trying to cultivate my

ROBERTO LEVINS MORALES

students as leaders, so I'm going to pass the phone to them."

Omar picked up the phone and introduced himself. "We are really engaged by this topic because we see what's happening in Arizona is wrong—that they are going into schools and taking away people's history."

"What was your reaction?" the host asked.

"I was shocked. They are treating books and knowledge like weapons by confiscating them from students and suspending classes having to do with Mexican American Studies."

Omar passed the phone to Diana, who was visibly nervous. "It reminds me of the movie *Walkout*. History is repeating itself. Back then they didn't let Latino students use the bathrooms or speak Spanish in their classrooms. The banning of books made me mad because they are obviously trying to . . . hide the truth that for 500 years we have been oppressed. I feel like it's time to fight back."

The host thanked us for joining the show, we logged off, and the students applauded. Then, energized, we went back to our study of the attack on Tucson's Mexican American Studies (MAS) program.

"Our Education Is Under Attack!"

Although the physical distance is great, there is a thin membrane of cultural and ideological distance between Oakland and Tucson. Ninety-five percent of my students are Latina/o, mostly first generation, mostly Mexican. Our charter school is located in the heart of the Fruitvale District of Oakland, a largely Latina/o barrio with a history of community organizing.

> **Although the physical distance is great, there is a thin membrane of cultural and ideological distance between Oakland and Tucson.**

While I anchored my junior/senior humanities class on contemporary social movements in skill development, critical analysis, and assessment, I included students in the process of deciding which movements to study. For each topic we discussed, we considered what would foster growth while keeping students engaged. We had decided to begin with the Zapatistas in the context of Mexican history but, before long, current events burst into the classroom as events in Tucson heated up.

I showed the class a film clip of youth taking over a Tucson Unified School Board (TUSD) meeting—chaining themselves to the chairs of school board members. They were fighting to defend the MAS program in the district, which Arizona's HB 2281 had targeted the previous spring. The dramatic imagery of students pushing past security guards and police, while unfurling the chains hidden beneath their shirts, was a definite conversation starter. And when we watched the video of Tucson youth chanting "Our education is under attack. What do we do? Fight back!" my students were provoked and full of questions: What happened to the arrested students? What if students weren't documented? Did the TUSD

School Board still cancel the MAS program? I asked if this was something we wanted to investigate further. The response of my class was a resounding yes.

We began with some background reading. Our school uses a "five levels of critical analysis" framework across classes and subject areas:

- Explicit: what is being directly said or done
- Implicit: the message behind the statement or action
- Interpretive: connection to yourself and your surroundings
- Theoretical: what theoretical concepts apply and how they help explain the
  issues (e.g., white supremacy, capitalism)
- Applied: what course of actions you are going to take once you have acquired
  this knowledge

Using this framework, I prepared two articles for them to read about the Tucson ethnic studies debacle: one on the passage of HB 2281 and one on the impact
on the MAS program. I provided additional background information myself since
I was involved in Arizona local and state educational politics during my five-year
stint attending college and then teaching there from 2003
to 2008.

I created three columns on the board: explicit, implicit, and interpretive. As we read the articles together,
students wrote facts and important quotes in the explicit section, including the percent of TUSD's budget
that would be withheld if the MAS program continued,
quotes from Arizona State Superintendent of Schools John Huppenthal and Attorney General Tom Horne, and key components of HB 2281.

In the implicit section students wrote what they thought were the implications
of the information in the explicit column. For instance, they saw the withholding
of funds as a tactic to turn the rest of the district against MAS.

In the interpretive column, they wrote their personal reactions to the articles.
Joaquin observed that books were being treated like contraband: "Does that mean
that the school can search you for those books . . . as if you were carrying a weapon?" That implies, he went on, that "knowledge is a weapon. It's no wonder they
want to shut down MAS."

'Knowledge is a weapon. It's no wonder they want to shut down MAS.'

'Precious Knowledge'

Once we knew the broad strokes, I screened the film *Precious Knowledge,* a powerful documentary on the history and impact of the MAS program in Tucson, and
the struggle to defend it. I distributed a graphic organizer with two columns on
one side—Explicit and Implicit—and a larger square on the back for Interpretive.
The explicit column was for important quotes, facts, laws, and characters in the
documentary. The implicit section asked students to read between the lines of each
of the explicit column entries—examining the intent of the director, the underlying
message, and the larger context. The interpretive section was homework. Students

were asked to reflect on their personal reactions to the movie as well as draw connections to other texts, their own lives, and other coursework.

As we watched, I paused the video after the first few scenes to ask what they had written in the explicit section. The students focused on the establishment of MAS as a continuation of the walkouts that happened in Tucson decades prior. Then I asked, "So what are the implications of those facts? Why did Tucson educators feel the need to create MAS?"

Edgar responded: "The United States makes Latinos believe that their culture isn't important or needed. It's as if Latinos had nothing to do with the development of the United States. Students don't learn to appreciate their culture's struggles, therefore they follow the system's expectations, which involves dropping out. They begin to work for the rich class and stay poor."

Janeth added: "Without our history there really isn't an us."

Other students talked about the absence of ethnic studies in their previous schooling and how refreshing it was to learn about nonwhite people upon their arrival at ARISE.

At the next pause, students noted central facts about HB 2281. "It basically makes ethnic studies illegal in Arizona," one student volunteered.

"What is the implication?" I probed. "Why would the state of Arizona want to pass a law banning ethnic studies?"

"Tom Horne is disallowing students from learning about their own Raza because he is afraid those students would take action based on their knowledge of their past history and present oppression," answered Janeth.

"So why are they doing this?" I asked. "What do you think their motivations are?"

Diana responded that Arizona politicians are afraid that students learning about oppression "would direct anger toward the government. People like Tom Horne are afraid of being overthrown. But it's not about that; it's about the right to learn about your own culture. They must fear that too, though. It's like Frederick Douglass said: A slave is no longer a slave after gaining knowledge about himself. I think it's that and, like we've talked about, it's divide and conquer."

"I don't get what you mean," I said. "They are trying to keep us divided and uneducated so we won't fight for what's ours," Diana continued. "They want us to just stay Americanized and whitewashed. They benefit when we don't know ourselves and our purpose, when we are divided as a community. The classes in Tucson teach people to unite."

For homework, Edgar wrote in the interpretive section: "Ethnic studies wasn't just any class for students, it inspired them to succeed in high school so they can go into college and further on. Students learned what society expects them to do as they grow, so they decided to stay in school and prove society wrong—that not all people of color end up being criminals or janitors."

To follow up on the film and readings, we held a Socratic seminar based on these questions:

- Why is ethnic studies important?
- What theories help us explain the ban on ethnic studies?
- How should we apply our knowledge?

On a graphic organizer, each question had three corresponding boxes:

- What is my opinion?
- What evidence supports this opinion?
- What questions do I have related to this question?

Students spent an hour working individually and in small groups to review and develop their ideas.

When the Socratic discussion began, students were charged with indignation that the majority of their teachers prior to high school had failed to teach them about their own history. Amabel mentioned her involvement in a Raza education program that started in 6th grade, and how it helped her to develop a positive self-identity grounded in the historical context of her ancestors. I pushed back: If ethnic studies is such a necessity, and worth fighting for, then why is it many of you don't do your homework related to ethnic studies, don't show up to school on time, cut class, and are resistant to reading outside of class? No one had an answer, but for many, this unit was the most engaged they had been in class.

Talking to UNIDOS

Whenever possible, I like to arrange for people to speak with my class who are directly involved with the topic of study. In this case, I already had connections in Tucson, so it wasn't difficult to arrange a Skype date with Elisa Meza, a University of Arizona student and alumna of MAS who works with UNIDOS, the youth-led grassroots organization fighting against HB 2281. To prep for the interview, we filled out a KWL chart reviewing what we knew already, creating questions about what we wanted to know and, after the discussion with Elisa, filling in what we had learned.

With Elisa projected onto the screen and all my students huddled around my webcam, we spoke for nearly an hour. Elisa painted a vivid picture of the political climate in Arizona and updated us on UNIDOS' organizing efforts. She described their strategy: garner local and national community support to oppose HB 2281 through direct action, protest, and litigation. In addition, UNIDOS was working to continue ethnic studies outside of school. Someone had donated a small house to UNIDOS, which they were using as their headquarters as well as a space to continue ethnic studies classes. My students were impressed by the level of commitment and organization of UNIDOS, a group run by people approximately their age. They wanted to help.

"What can we do?" they asked Elisa. She asked us to educate our community about the struggle in Arizona. She also asked us to take a photo demonstrating our solidarity, one that would alert Arizona politicians to growing national anger at the attack on the MAS program.

Martina reflected in her journal afterward: "Today's experience has been amazing. I am thankful we were able to speak with people who are being affected by other people's bad choices. Those choices affect us even though we are miles away. It is our Raza and we can help them out and show them our support by sending them books that they are not able to access in school anymore. We can also help them spread the word and call for attention and support towards them."

In response to Elisa's request for solidarity, students decided to use our all-school weekly meeting for an informational skit depicting students watching banned books packed up and taken from their classes. Five students volunteered to plan and act in the skit, while others created a banner that read "Tucson: You hella shady!" We took an all-school photo in front of the banner. Our photo went out across social media and was included in UNIDOS' newsletter.

Then we got an even better opportunity to help spread the word. We were invited to the Bay Area Urban Schools Student Leadership Conference at Berkeley High School, and the students were asked to present workshops.

Students separated into two groups based on the topic they were most passionate about; one group chose Tucson. The Tucson group began by outlining what they thought was the most important content to convey. Students excavated all the materials I'd given them and reviewed their notes. Once the outlines were made, they delegated responsibility for pieces of the presentation to one another. Diana described the process:

If someone had more notes about one part or more understanding about one part of what was going on in Arizona, we let that person plan that part. We started by dividing the lesson. We knew we needed to explain this, this, and this, so we asked: What do you know how to explain the best? We assigned it accordingly and then had one person put it together as a PowerPoint presentation. Whoever created a slide for the PowerPoint also taught it.

As I watched from the sidelines, it didn't seem like they needed much help. I interjected occasionally to help them see where they might need to better develop connections and background knowledge; otherwise I gave them space. Once the slideshow was finished, I encouraged them to practice it.

Each One, Teach One

We were unaware until we got to Berkeley High that we would be the only high school students presenting. I reminded my suddenly nervous students that they were prepared, that youth love youth presenters, and when they first heard about Tucson they were thirsty to learn more.

Once the first group of students had settled into their chairs, Amabel asked if they had heard about the banning of ethnic studies. There were a few nods and a young woman from Berkeley High summarized HB 2281. Then they asked all the students to join them in reciting the poem *In Lak 'Ech,* which we had begun reciting every morning after watching Tucson students do the same in *Precious Knowledge*. Diana explained more about HB 2281, followed by Janeth, who read excerpts from the law. Next, Edgar talked about the key proponents of the law. Kevin introduced the *Precious Knowledge* trailer.

After the trailer, Roxanna asked students: "How do you relate to the movie?" One student said: "I can identify with what the students are talking about because this is the first year I've taken an African American class. . . . The Europeans asserted their greatness and that's what you learn about in 'U.S. history', but all of us are U.S. history. We are forced to learn about Caucasian people who did these great things but seldom do we learn about ourselves, so then our image of ourselves isn't the best. I don't see myself in history books, in these people."

Everyone applauded. Roxanna then asked: "What would you do to fight against it if they passed a similar law in California?" The participants discussed occupying schools, boycotting "American History," walking out, and distributing fliers. A young man offered: "Before a bill like that passes we should try to promote other cultures to sort of show how cool some things are, passing knowledge, so that you don't have to take [an ethnic studies] class to know about it." A young woman suggested that all the students at the conference should come together again to help Tucson and help themselves. Another student asked, "What did Tucson say they want us to do?" In unison four of my students said: "Inform others."

At the end of the workshop, the participants joined together for a photo to send to UNIDOS.

The next day we reflected on what worked and what needed improvement. Everyone agreed that the workshops were a success. Diana thought that her group should have more explicitly used the five levels of analysis. "[The participants] could have used the five levels to see what's behind things, and not just for what we are teaching; they can apply it other aspects of life and the world."

A couple of weeks after the workshops, we were invited back to Berkeley High School to screen *Precious Knowledge* and facilitate breakout conversations with 175 students, mostly students learning English. Janeth reflected later: "The students were very engaged . . . because they are all from different ethnicities and understand completely how the students in Arizona feel about their history being taken away from them."

Each year, we hold an exhibition night for families during the last week of school. My students wanted to teach their parents about HB 2281 and ask them what sort of Raza education they wanted for their children. The conversation was electric. Parents talked about the contradiction that their children wanting ethnic studies in school, but they never asked their parents about their family history. Parents also praised the school for integrating ethnic studies into our curriculum, since many of them never had such opportunities. The conversation caused me to lament the fact that I had not involved parents more during the semester. We should have invited them in as teachers, experts, and participants.

Diana, in her reflection on the course, said: "I gained a lot of skills, especially in learning how to teach what we had learned. It was able to get stuck in our heads that way.... We all felt motivated because it was something we chose to learn about and that affected our community."

Resources

Billeaud, Jacques. "Arizona Schools' Ethnic Studies Program Ruled Illegal," Associated Press, Dec. 27, 2011.

Rodriguez, Luis J. "Arizona's Attack on Chicano History and Culture Is Against Everyone," *Huffington Post,* Jan. 18, 2012. *Precious Knowledge,* A Dos Vatos Production, 2012.

Devin Carberry is an English and social studies teacher at ARISE High School in Oakland, California.

Chapter Fourteen

YOUR STRUGGLE IS MY STRUGGLE

By Marcela Itzel Ortega

You have to know where you are coming from to know where you are going.

t's funny how a single lucid moment can change so many things; a single video can light a spark for justice. That reality hit me when my teacher, Devin Carberry, played a YouTube clip of UNIDOS, a group of students fighting to keep ethnic studies alive in Arizona (See "Precious Knowledge: Teaching Solidarity with Tucson"). I was befuddled as to why these students were chaining themselves to chairs in a courtroom when the police force was clearly evident. I kept asking myself: Why are these students running the risk of incarceration? I had trouble analyzing the video's hidden messages, yet I still felt a tug inside of me. The people chaining

SCOTT BRALEY

themselves looked like me; they were students of color trying to make a statement, and whatever statement they were making, it seemed it was worth finding out about.

Devin brought in the documentary *Precious Knowledge,* an intimate look into ethnic studies classes in Tucson high schools and the community battle to defend the program. As we analyzed the video, I made connections between the students in the film and myself. For example, in the beginning, Gilbert, Crystal, and Priscilla, the three students who are the focus of the film's narrative, are looking off into the distance. The look in their eyes reflects their need to get away from the injustice in the world. I remember I did the same thing every day in the car going to and from school. When I looked out the window, I saw how vast and unfair the world is. There was always the reflection of a familiar pair of eyes looking back at me saying, "You'll never be able to change it."

Growing up, I always had a tough time understanding why life wasn't fair. Other people had more privileges and a better life, yet a kid never thinks, "Oh, maybe it's because my ancestors were killed and made slaves as a means of profit and gain." My classes have taught me the real history that pertains to my background. I saw how Gilbert, Crystal, and Pricilla all had difficult circumstances and struggles they had to overcome in their daily lives so that they could focus on school. It made me wonder how my life and theirs would have been different if colonization never took place, if our civilizations had been left unharmed, if our people had not been murdered and enslaved.

I made many connections from the film to the theory of white supremacy, which is the belief that white people or Anglos are the superior race and therefore they should be the ones in power. They didn't say so explicitly, but I think many of the politicians in the film were against the Mexican American Studies (MAS) program because it gave students a way out of the roles society has created for them. It meant those students would go to college and get higher paying jobs, taking the place of "deserving" Americans. I will be the first in my family to attend college. I am going against the role society has created for me. I am not taking anyone's place, but the one that rightfully belongs to me.

> **When I looked out the window, I saw how vast and unfair the world is. There was always the reflection of a familiar pair of eyes looking back at me saying, 'You'll never be able to change it.'**

I understand why Arizona lawmakers think that knowledge is a dangerous weapon. When we know our history, we no longer are lost souls, roaming and looking for our self-identity; we become confident individuals united for a cause. In class, I saw how my peers had grown spiritually because of the movie. A young man in the video made the same point: "For someone that's felt so out of place for the majority of their life, it feels good to have a home [in MAS]."

I was inspired by the MAS students because of the sheer audacity they showed: They marched, ran, and protested because education was a right they were being denied. I was able to imagine being in the same situation and reflecting on what

I would do: Would I march for hours in the hot Arizona sun? Would I run miles across the desert? Would I put myself in danger for my history? Before the film, my answer would have been a nonchalant maybe, now my answer is a definite yes, because seeing those students take the struggle in their own hands was a beautiful sight. And it gave me, as a student, the confidence that I could do the same.

If I had watched the film alone it would have been a very different situation. Without the guidance of the five levels (see Carberry, Precious Knowledge), I would not have developed a deeper understanding of why these students were fighting so ardently for their education, or the slightest idea how big-picture ideas like white supremacy are connected to the banning of ethnic studies.

> **I will be the first in my family to attend college. I am going against the role society has created for me. I am not taking anyone's place, but the one that rightfully belongs to me.**

It's devastating to know that history has a face to it, and that any history that is different runs the risk of being untaught. Many times we ask ourselves why success is so difficult to find. We don't realize that our past intertwines with our future, and not knowing we end up following someone else's history, not our own. If it wasn't for Raza studies, I wouldn't be able to lift my head up and think to myself that I actually belong, that I have a right to make my dreams a reality as much as any other person does.

When I got assignments to learn about my family tree and my personal history, there were many things I found out that still affect me today: My father grew up in extreme poverty because of his skin color, while my mother, who is lighter skinned, had it a tad easier. That led me to research my parents' hometown, where the same thing is still happening. When I visited, people made it seem as if being darker was a curse. My father growing up in poverty because of his color makes me want to work harder and get a degree so that I can give my family the life they deserve, not the one that was given. After our class watched the film, there was a No History Should Be Illegal meeting at Mission High School in San Francisco. The speakers included Sean Arce, director of the MAS program in Tucson; Flor Burruel, a member of UNIDOS (who was skyped in); and Roger Alvarado, who co-founded the Third World Liberation Front at San Francisco State in 1968. Our class was asked to send a spokesperson and I volunteered.

I was hesitant at first but then I remembered Crystal's words from *Precious Knowledge:* "I can't be another Latina woman, just sitting down at home. I want my voice to be heard." She inspired me to let my voice be heard. It was difficult for me to discuss ethnic studies, which I care about deeply, while not letting my nerves overtake me. I had not imagined that I would be sitting with people who had helped create radical movements, and that I would be considered of that same caliber. That small school library felt magical because everyone had an aura of equality and togetherness that made speaking easier. I spoke about how I was learning not to be just another face in the crowd. Raza studies made it possible for me to stand up not only for myself but for all the women in my life as well. It gave me the confidence to believe in my history without feeling ashamed of where or whom I come from. It made me see that there is no shame in being a woman of color; gender and race are just categories into which I was placed, and to me these categories are no longer a curse but a blessing. At least for now, they have closed down the MAS program in Tucson, but I know that the struggle for ethnic studies continues. In the words of César Chávez, "When social change begins, it cannot be reversed, you cannot un-educate a person who has learned to read, you cannot humiliate the person who feels pride, and you cannot oppress the people who are not afraid anymore." I am not afraid, are you?

Marcela Itzel Ortega was a senior at ARISE High School in Oakland, California, when she wrote this piece.

Chapter Fifteen

FROM JOHANNESBURG TO TUCSON

By Bill Bigelow

On Jan. 13, journalist Jeff Biggers contacted me with the news that the book I co-edited with Bob Peterson, *Rethinking Columbus,* had been banned in the schools of Tucson, Arizona, as part of that state's suppression of the Mexican American Studies program. The state superintendent of schools, John Huppenthal, had found the acclaimed Tucson program out of compliance with House Bill 2281, which outlaws courses that teach "ethnic solidarity" or promote "resentment toward a race or class of people." On Jan. 10, the Tucson school board had voted to end the program rather than lose 10 percent of its state funding. Biggers was working on a piece for salon.com and wanted a quote about the banning.

RICARDO LEVINS MORALES

I had a stew of emotions: Sadness that, in some cases, the books had been boxed up during class time, with students present. As one student said, "It was very heart-breaking to see that happening in the middle of class." Pride that our book had been honored in this way, alongside revered texts like Paulo Freire's *Pedagogy of the Oppressed,* Elizabeth Martínez's *500 Years of Chicano History in Pictures,* and the granddaddy of Mexican American Studies texts, Rodolfo Acuña's *Occupied America: The Chicano's Struggle Toward Liberation*—all books that I've had in my collection for decades. But mostly I felt anger: that our book had been caught in the conservative dragnet that led to the termination of the Mexican American Studies program; that students were being victimized by the anti-immigrant, anti-Latina/o racism that characterized Arizona's infamous racial profiling law, Senate Bill 1070; that yet one more attack on multicultural, social justice education in the country seemed to be winning.

The only other time I'd had a book outlawed was my curriculum on teaching about South Africa, *Strangers in Their Own Country* (Africa World Press, 1985), which had been banned in South Africa in 1986, no doubt because it featured a speech by then imprisoned Nelson Mandela, quotes from other officially banned individuals, and lessons on the movement to demand corporate divestment from apartheid South Africa.

More than 25 years separates the banning of each of these books, but as events in Tucson have unfolded, I've found myself making comparisons between South Africa and Arizona.

Student Courage and Determination

The first similarity to come to mind is the courage and dedication of the students involved in struggles to make education more meaningful, more connected to addressing issues of racial and economic inequality. I traveled throughout South Africa in July and August of 1986, during the State of Emergency, and young people—high school and even younger—saw the struggle to improve schooling as inextricably tied to the broader struggle to improve society. I sat in on a student representative council meeting at a school in Mitchell's Plain, a so-called "colored" township of Cape Town. These were illegal gatherings of elected student representatives, and South African army troop carriers sat about 100 yards away at the end of the block as a visible warning to youngsters. But the high school kids met together anyway. As one determined teenage girl there told me: "It's tough for us—such small people making such big decisions." And big decisions they were: Students inside South African schools risked expulsion for their activism, and students in demonstrations in the streets outside risked their lives.

I have not spent time with students in Tucson, but I've talked with their teachers, watched their videos, and read their interviews. Students like Mayra Feliciano, one of the founders of the student activist organization UNIDOS, became politically aware through high school coursework in the Mexican American Studies program, and learned to think deeply about their place in the world. As Feliciano told Biggers in an interview at wordstrike.net:

> Before I took these classes I was ashamed of my culture. Born in Tapachula, Chiapas, Mexico, I felt very different—I was darker than a lot of my friends and I felt like people were always prettier than me. I didn't care about learning more about my culture; I didn't even pay attention to what was going on around me. I took the Mexican American Studies course and my life turned around for the better. I was struggling to graduate, but this class taught me that we all live in a society where we all struggle and that knowledge and facts are what help to get you through.

In April 2011, Feliciano participated in an "occupation" of a Tucson school board meeting to prevent consideration of a resolution that would have undermined the Mexican American Studies program before there had been a full public debate. Students chained themselves to board members' chairs, chanting, "Our education is under attack! What do we do? Fight back!"

Students featured in the celebrated film *Precious Knowledge* offer eloquent testimony to the power of education that is grounded in young people's lives and cultures, is about issues in society that matter, and that expects that students can and will achieve. One student describes the impact of Mexican American Studies classes: "You know, I started thinking, oh I'm a Chicana, I ain't going to be able to graduate, I'm going to have kids young, I'm . . . you know, like that. And then I started coming to these classes and I started seeing, like, why am I believing all this? Instead of believing it I should change it."

Contempt for Students

Another similarity between apartheid South Africa and HB 2281 Arizona is the contempt with which those in positions of authority regard students. Tucson Superintendent John Pedicone refused to believe that students could organize the April 2011 school board takeover and articulate demands. In an op-ed in the *Arizona Daily Star,* Pedicone wrote that the students "have been exploited and are being used as pawns to serve a political agenda." He claimed that Tucson students "are being used to lead the charge for those who wish to make this a civil rights issue"—as if it required some specialized adult perspective to recognize that the abolition of ethnic studies is a civil rights issue.

Student-as-puppet is a familiar canard, also used in South Africa by a white elite confronting a massive uprising by students of color.

Student-as-puppet is a familiar canard, also used in South Africa by a white elite confronting a massive uprising by students of color. During the 1986 State of Emergency, the (white) minister in charge of black education, Gerrit Viljoen, complained about "outside agitators," and instituted a policy of ID cards that all students were forced to carry—on the presumption that if only *students* were on school grounds, and not their nonstudent allies, the protests would stop. The students responded with bonfires of burning ID cards.

Throughout my teaching career, I've encountered this same adult contempt for student political initiative. One year at Portland's Jefferson High School, where for many years I taught an 11th-grade block history-language arts class with Linda Christensen, our students were required to take the Armed Services Vocational Aptitude Battery Test (ASVAB), administered by uniformed military personnel. In order to have the tests scored, students had to sign a statement agreeing to be contacted by military recruiters. We had not even talked about the ASVAB in class, but a group of our students organized a "question-in"—refusing to take the test until all of their questions were answered. An enraged school official arrived at Linda's and my classroom door with the demand "Call your dogs off."

The common denominator in these instances is the disrespect of those in power for students' capacity to think critically and to take action based on their beliefs. When educational authorities consistently display such slight regard for students' academic and moral capacities, is it any wonder that they match this contempt with an intellectually thin, idea-poor curriculum?

In South Africa, students' overarching demand was for an end to what they called "gutter education." Theirs was a critique of an education system that prepared them for menial labor—the gutter. As Hendrik Verwoerd, then minister of native affairs, had baldly declared in 1953, "The purpose of Bantu education is to ensure that the natives will be taught from childhood that equality with Europeans is not for them." Black people, he said, "should be educated for their opportunities in life," and asserted that there was no place for them "above the level of certain forms of labor." In the tortured lexicon of apartheid, Africans were considered "temporary sojourners" in white South Africa, wanted only for their labor.

This might sound familiar to students learning the history of Arizona and the Southwest in their Mexican American Studies classes in Tucson high schools. Whites there kept the vast majority of Mexicans at the bottom of a caste system, and Mexicans were paid less even when they did the same jobs as white workers. In the territories taken from Mexico after the 1846–48 invasion and occupation, Mexicans were tolerated because their labor was needed by the white owners of ranches, mines, and railroads. In his book *A Different Mirror: A History of Multicultural America*, Ronald Takaki points out that the owning class of the Southwest appropriated the images and language of slavery. He quotes mine owner Sylvester Mowry: "My own experience has taught me that the lower class of Mexicans . . . are docile, faithful, good servants, capable of strong attachments when firmly and kindly treated. They have been 'peons' for generations. They will always remain so, as it is their natural condition."

In the now-banned *Occupied America,* Tucson students would have read about eugenics proponent and Vanderbilt economics professor Roy L. Garis, who told a congressional committee in 1930 about Mexicans: "Their minds run to nothing higher than animal functions—eat, sleep, and sexual debauchery." Acuña sums up the purpose of schooling in this racist climate: "The mission of the Anglo-American public schools was not to educate, or to create social consciousness, but to condition the newcomer as well as the majority of citizens to accept the corporate society."

In South Africa, the struggle was not merely for better education, but for a better, more equal, more just society. As one journal editorialized during my 1986 stay, "To get rid of gutter education entirely, one would have to get rid of the gutter." At its heart, this is what the Mexican American Studies struggle is about: Will education for young Mexican Americans prepare them for the gutter, to be "peons," or equip them **But if we don't encourage students to ask questions in terms of race, how can we help them make sense of their world—and improve it?** with the critical and academic skills to challenge their historic subordination—to change society?

This brings us back to the racialized roots of the attack on Mexican American Studies in Arizona. In his Dec. 30, 2010, "finding" that Tucson schools were out of compliance with HB 2281, then-Superintendent of Public Instruction Tom Horne (now the Arizona state attorney general) offered a hodgepodge of rumor and racial paranoia. In this legal document, Horne quoted disgruntled former teachers— some named, some anonymous—about how the Mexican American Studies program teaches "racial resentment." Horne quoted at length someone he identified as a retired Tucson teacher, John Ward:

> Impressionable youth in TUSD have literally been reprogrammed to believe that there is a concerted effort on the part of a white power structure to suppress them and relegate them to a second-class existence. This fomented resentment further encourages them to express their dissatisfaction through the iconoclastic behavior we see—the contempt for all authority outside of their ethnic community and their total lack of identification with a political heritage of this country.

This is a theme that John Huppenthal, Horne's successor as superintendent, struck in his campaign ads, pledging to "stop la raza." This is not just a debate about pedagogy, about textbooks, about historical interpretation. It's a debate about the kind of society we want to live in and the values that we want to pass on to young people—and especially the role that race plays in that.

As then-Superintendent Horne wrote in his finding: "Most of these [Mexican American students'] parents and grandparents came to this country, legally, because this is the land of opportunity. They trust the public schools with their children. Those students should be taught that this is the land of opportunity, and that if they work hard they can achieve their goals. They should not be taught that they are oppressed."

The law itself, HB 2281, insists on the "treatment of pupils as individuals" and that the curriculum should not encourage students to see themselves as members of racial or ethnic groups or social classes. The values that the Huppenthals and Hornes of Arizona want students to embrace hark back to those of Horatio Alger: Through individual determination, hard work, and honesty, you will rise in the fundamentally just, colorblind system of capitalism—i.e., "the land of opportunity."

> **Those who promoted HB 2281 don't want students thinking in terms of race, class, ethnicity, or solidarity.**

But if we don't encourage students to ask questions in terms of race, how can we help them make sense of their world—and improve it? Think, for example, about the revelations in the recent Pew Research Center study, *Twenty-to-One*: In 2009, median net white household wealth in the United States was $113,149. For the category Pew defines as "Hispanic," it was $6,325. A ratio of almost 18 to 1. Between 2005 and 2009, Hispanic household wealth declined 66 percent, compared to a 16 percent decline for whites. How do we help students account for these disparities if they aren't allowed to analyze them through a lens of race and of social class? How can young people make sense of the fact that more than twice as many Mexican American children in Arizona live in poverty than white children: 64 percent to 30 percent? Or reflect on what might account for the fact that almost twice as many Mexican Americans as whites in Arizona are incarcerated?

Those who promoted HB 2281 don't want students thinking in terms of race, class, ethnicity, or solidarity. This is intellectually dishonest. Apart from enforcing historical amnesia, it leaves students without the strategic political tools to work for greater equality. Which, I suppose, is a good thing, if your starting point is to "stop la raza."

Teaching Solidarity

How do students consider ways to make things better without solidarity in their conceptual knapsacks? Whether it's the abolition movement, the labor movement, the women's rights movement, the farmworkers movement, the 1968 and 1969 Chicano student walkouts in California, Texas, and Arizona, or the ongoing Immokalee workers struggle in Florida, it has been people organizing for better lives that has made things better, not market forces and the efforts of isolated individuals toiling in a "land of opportunity."

A few years ago, longtime Tucson civil rights activist Salomón R. Baldenegro offered this brief history lesson:

I am of the Chicano generation. We grew up in the 1950s and early 1960s, when American society viewed Americans of Mexican descent as foreigners and there was a concerted campaign by society, particularly the schools, to make us feel inferior and treat us as interlopers in our own land.

We had two choices. We could acquiesce and shuffle through life, hat in hand, picking up society's crumbs. Or we could resist and assert our humanity. We resisted.

This seems to be a pretty good outline of choices for those in Arizona—and all the rest of us—who are struggling over the character of the curriculum. We opt either for a hat-in-hand education or one that equips students to resist.

Bill Bigelow is curriculum editor of Rethinking Schools *magazine. He began teaching high school social studies in Portland, Ore. in 1978. A version of this article was originally published in* Oregon English.

Chapter Sixteen

SAVING MANGO STREET

By Katie Van Winkle

S t. Helens, Oregon, is a rural town about 30 minutes northwest of Portland; it was all I'd ever known. I was used to the flannels and work boots and the fact that most kids' dads worked at the mill. I wasn't allowed to play at a friend's house after I told my mom that my friend's stepdad wouldn't let us in his shed because he was growing funny plants. I shopped at Target for school clothes when we took a rare trip to Portland. Almost everyone I knew was working-class and white.

I first learned about cultural diversity and racial justice in Mr. Sanderson's middle school English class. Sure, we learned about grammar and literary concepts, but Sanderson opened our eyes—or at least my eyes—to the fact that the world was different outside of St. Helens. We read a book called *The House on Mango Street* by Sandra Cisneros and learned about a different culture, but also about a community with striking similarities to our own.

The main character in the novel, Esperanza, a 13-year-old Chicana, grows up in an impoverished neighborhood in Chicago. Mexican American culture and themes of social class and gender are interwoven through the novel's vignettes. I could relate to living in a poor area with a short supply of opportunity. And, like Esperanza, I realized how important it was to remember my roots and to give back to the community from which I came.

RADICALGRAPHICS.ORG

Banned from Middle School

Last year, the St. Helens school board decided to ban *The House on Mango Street* from the middle school curriculum. The district's "reconsideration committee" claimed that the book contained "content too mature for this age group" and expressed "concerns for the social issues presented."

Charles Sanderson contacted me, informing me that the school district had temporarily pulled the book and asking if I could help. First I was angry. Then I was razzed up and ready. But I had doubts. Who was I, some college student, to go up against an entire school district and tell them what they were doing was wrong?

I wrote a letter about how *The House on Mango Street* affected me. The school board could debunk my other arguments, but they could never tell me what I did or did not feel, what I had or had not learned from this book and our discussions in class. *The House on Mango Street* changed me. Cisneros' writing style inspired me to create a series of my own vignettes dealing with my parents' divorce. I learned to heal through the power of writing. Engaging in the classroom discussions about Esperanza and her life introduced new perspectives and ideas. It made me think; it made me realize that there is more to the world than the insular community I was living in. I knew I wouldn't be the only one upset about the threat to *Mango Street*. But how could I assemble a group of protesters when I now lived more than 100 miles away from my hometown? I called an old friend from high school who was known for being strong-willed and possessing a get-it-done attitude: Sam Chapman, also a former student of Sanderson's. I felt better having Sam on my side.

We shouldn't have to defend our right to learn about the world—the real world, not a protected world of make-believe that some adults want to present to students.

After discussing the issue with Sam, I posted a status on Facebook, asking former and current St. Helens students if they remembered reading *The House on Mango Street*, telling them what was happening, asking what impact the book had on them. We got an overwhelming response: "Why would they pull that? It's such a good book!" "How is that fair?" "They don't have the right!"

Fifty-nine comments later, I decided to ask former students to write short testimonials about how they had benefited from having *Mango Street* in their middle school curriculum.

The 10 well-documented testimonials we received covered a range of subject matter and emotion. Arthur Truong, a 2010 graduate, wrote:

[Cisneros] consciously identifies and discusses the presence of Latin American communities, homeless people, and independent women. . . . As a student of ethnic identity, this message was incredibly important. . . . I can understand that you may be worried that by bringing up these social issues in the book, students will treat each other differently. But that's a good thing. By bringing up this kind of social context from a different point of view, students learn about different perspectives in life and how to respect them.

The Mango Street Army

We didn't stop at high school graduates. When I was a junior in high school, I volunteered at the middle school as Sanderson's teaching assistant. I've always been into writing, so he let me create my own writing workshop for a group of 8th graders. Now they were high school seniors. I created a group on Facebook called "The Mango Street Army" and added all the high school seniors I knew. I told them about the situation and asked them to get in contact with classmates.

Sam suggested I call the curriculum director to get clarification as to why *The House on Mango Street* was being banned: Exactly which social issues were they worried about? What was a "reconsideration committee"? Which policy had they used to pull the book?

The curriculum director brusquely referred me to the school board's website to look up the policy. Because of her abrasive response, I sent in my letter and received an emailed reply the next day from a school board member. He thanked me for expressing concern and informed me of a school board meeting the following week and told me how we could speak publicly. Sam and I marked the date.

Speaking Up, Speaking Out

The night before the meeting, I compiled the testimonials into one document. We also had two full-length letters from the Mango Street Army. I made copies to give to the school board members, and prepared what I was going to say.

I was nervous before I spoke at the school board meeting. I worried that I'd look like a fool. But I thought of the papers in my hand, and the stories I was going to share, apart from my own:

> I took away a feeling of identification with myself. I saw the girl struggling with her own identity and trying to find meaning for herself in the neighborhood that she grew up in. . . .

> I personally come from a conservative, Christian home. This novel was indeed appropriate for my peers and me. It opened my eyes to issues that I wish were discussed more often in school. . . .

I stepped up to the microphone and, with shaking hands, pulled my letter up to read. I made eye contact with each board member and tried to keep my voice from shaking. I explained that banning *Mango Street* was not going to preserve the innocence of students and the importance of teaching diversity in our community.

Then Sam read an anonymous student's story from the testimonial sheet:

> There are many life lessons in *The House on Mango Street*, but there is one that helped change me forever although, at the time, I didn't realize I would later become a victim of sexual assault like Esperanza. My junior year I was raped. Back while Mr. Sanderson was teaching this book in my class, some guy stated that it is a woman's fault for being sexually assaulted

and raped. Mr. Sanderson was infuriated at this, and I will never forget his reaction. He was yelling, but the next day he wrote us an apology letter in class and explained why he felt the way he did and he said something along the lines of "If a woman says no, it can never be her fault." . . . Esperanza dreams of leaving Mango Street and her problems behind. She discovered that you can't run from your problems. . . . This book has affected me greatly and I wish I would have absorbed the lessons more at the time. I believe this would be a terrible decision on St. Helens' part if they stopped teaching the lessons of this book.

Sam argued that banning a book that speaks directly about experiences like this one promotes silence. It encourages silence for victims of sexual assault, for those subjected to and hurting from racism, and for those with other real-world problems that need to be discussed.

We both received applause as we said our thank-yous and sat down. The curriculum director gave a short presentation on the board's policy system. A school board member asked her not to discuss anything related to *The House on Mango Street* because it was not on the agenda. Members of the audience called out "Why?"

Making Things Right

Finally, the superintendent spoke, saying that since the issue was already on the table, he would read a formal statement. The statement said that, after review of the reconsideration committee's proposal to pull the book from the middle school curriculum, and after receiving multiple emails and expressions of concern, he had decided not to accept the proposal. He said he would review and amend the rules for the reconsideration committee's membership, function, and power to regulate curriculum based on content complaints.

The crowd applauded, and Sam and I got pats on the back and congratulations.

In these times, schools need to expand students' thoughts concerning major life issues; we need course materials that honestly address race, culture, sexuality, violence, and resistance. We shouldn't have to defend our right to learn about the world—the real world, not a protected world of make-believe that some adults want to present to students. I learned that organized action is sometimes necessary. Sanderson may or may not have intended this, but his class taught me one of the most fundamental lessons of all: When I spot injustice, I need to try to make things right.

Katie Van Winkle is a student at Oregon State University in Corvallis, pursuing a degree in psychology with a minor in writing.

Chapter Seventeen

STANDARDS AND TESTS ATTACK MULTICULTURALISM

By Bill Bigelow

Proponents of "higher standards" and more testing promise that students will learn more and schools will finally be held "accountable." In practice, their reforms are hostile to good teaching and pose a special threat to multiculturalism.

The state where I teach, Oregon, joined the national testing craze well before No Child Left Behind became law. In the late '90s, the Oregon Department of Education gave a glimpse of the test mania to come when it field-tested its first-ever statewide social studies assessments. The tests were a multiple-choice maze that lurched about helter-skelter, seeking answers on World War I, constitutional amendments, global climate, rivers in India, hypothetical population projections, Supreme Court deci-

KATHY SLOANE

sions, and economic terminology. From a close reading of these tests, social studies knowledge is little more than the acquisition of disconnected facts about the world.

The version of standards pressed by "accountability" proponents threatens the development of a multicultural curriculum—one that describes and attempts to explain the world as it really exists; speaks to the diversity of our society and our students; and aims not only to teach important facts, but to develop citizens who can make the world safer and more just.

In a sense, the entire effort to create fixed standards violates the very essence of multiculturalism.

In a sense, the entire effort to create fixed standards violates the very essence of multiculturalism. Multiculturalism is a search, a "conversation among different voices," in the words of Henry Louis Gates, to discover perspectives that have been silenced in traditional scholastic narratives. Multiculturalism attempts to uncover "the histories and experiences of people who have been left out of the curriculum," as anti-racist educator Enid Lee emphasizes. Because multiculturalism is an undertaking that requires new scholarship and constant discussion, it necessarily is ongoing. Yet as researcher Harold Berlak points out, "Standardization and centralization of curriculum testing is an effort to put an end to a cacophony of voices on what constitutes truth, knowledge, and learning and what the young should be taught. It insists upon one set of answers." Curriculum standardization is, as Berlak indicates, a way to silence dissident voices, "a way to manufacture consent and cohesion."

Creating an official, government-approved social studies is bound to be controversial, whether at the national or state level. Thus, according to the Portland *Oregonian,* from the beginning, state education officials "tried to stake a neutral ground," in order to win approval for its version of social reality: "We have tried so hard to go right down the middle between what teachers want, what parents want, and what the [Republican-dominated] Legislature wants," according to Dawn Billings, a Department of Education curriculum coordinator. Not surprisingly, this attempt to be "neutral" and inoffensive means that the standards lack a critical sensibility—an emphasis on conflict and diversity of interpretation—and tend toward a conservative "Father Knows Best" portrait of history and society. For example, one typical 10th-grade benchmark calls for students to "Understand how the Constitution can be a vehicle for change and for resolving issues as well as a device for preserving values and principles of society."

Only? Is this how, say, Frederick Douglass or the Seminole leader Osceola would have seen the Constitution? Shouldn't students also understand how the Constitution can be (and has been) a vehicle for preserving class and race stratification and for maintaining the privileges of dominant social groups? For example, in the 1857 *Dred Scott* case, the Supreme Court held that an enslaved person could not sue for his freedom because he was property, not a human being. Chief Justice Roger Taney declared that no black person in the United States had "any rights which the white man is bound to respect." The abolitionist William Lloyd Garrison called the Constitution an "agreement with Hell" for its support of slavery. And in 1896 the Supreme Court ruled in *Plessy v. Ferguson* that segregation—"separate but equal"—did not violate the 14th Amendment.

Almost 40 percent of the men who wrote the Constitution owned slaves, including George Washington and James Madison. In my U.S. history classes we look at the adoption of the Constitution from the standpoint of poor white farmers, enslaved African Americans, unemployed workers in urban areas, and other groups. Students create their own Constitution in a mock assembly, and then compare their document to the actual Constitution. They discover, for example, that the Constitution does not include the word "slave" or "enslaved person," but instead refers euphemistically to enslaved African Americans, as in Article 4, Section 2: "No person held in service or labor in one state, under the laws thereof, escaping into another, shall in consequence of any law or regulation therein, be discharged from service or labor, but shall be delivered up on claim of the party to whom such service or labor may be due." It's a vicious clause, that sits uncomfortably in the "preserving values and principles" rhetoric of Oregon's standards.

It is probably inevitable that school curricula will reflect the contradictions between a society's myths and realities. But while a critical multicultural approach attempts to examine these contradictions, standardization tends to paper them over. For example, another benchmark—"Explain how laws are developed and applied to provide order, set limits, protect basic rights, and promote the common good"—similarly fails the multicultural test. Whose order, whose basic rights, are protected by laws? Are all social groups included equally in the term "common good"? Between 1862 and 1890, laws in the United States gave 180,000,000 acres (an area the size of Texas and Oklahoma) to privately owned railroad companies, but gave virtually no land to African Americans freed from slavery in the South. Viewing the Constitution and other U.S. laws through a multicultural lens would add texture and depth to the facile one-sidedness of Oregon's "neutral" standards.

> **It is probably inevitable that school curricula will reflect the contradictions between a society's myths and realities. But while a critical multicultural approach attempts to examine these contradictions, standardization tends to paper them over.**

Indeed the "R" word, racism, is not mentioned once in any of the seven Oregon 11th-grade field tests nor in the social studies standards adopted by the state board of education. Even if the only yardstick were strict historical accuracy this would be a bizarre omission: The state was launched as a whites-only territory by the Oregon Donation Act and in racist wars of dispossession waged against indigenous peoples; the first constitution outlawed slavery but also forbade blacks from living in the state, a prohibition that remained on the books until 1926. Perhaps state education officials were concerned that introducing the concept of racism to students could call into question the essentially harmonious world of "change, and continuity over time" that underpins the standards project. Whatever the reason, there is no way that students can make sense of the world today without the idea of racism in their conceptual knapsack. If a key goal of multiculturalism is to account for how the past helped shape the present, and an important part of the present is social inequality, then standards and tests like those adopted in Oregon earn a failing grade.

Despite the publication of state social studies standards and benchmarks, throughout the country, teachers or parents don't really know what students are expected to learn until they see the tests. MetriTech, an out-of-state assessment corporation, developed Oregon's. As Prof. Wade W. Nelson points out in a delightfully frank *Phi Delta Kappan* article, "The Naked Truth About School Reform in Minnesota," "The content of the standards is found only in the tests used to assess them. Access to the tests themselves is carefully controlled, making it difficult to get a handle on what these standards are. It seems ironic to me that basic standards—that which every student is expected to know or be able to do—are revealed only in tests accessible only to test-makers and administrators. This design avoids much of the debate about what these standards ought to be"—a debate that is essential to the ongoing struggle for a multicultural curriculum.

> **It's when you look directly at the tests that their limitations and negative implications for multiculturalism become most clear.**

It's when you look directly at the tests that their limitations and negative implications for multiculturalism become most clear. Test questions inevitably focus on discrete facts, but cannot address the deeper, multifaceted meaning of facts. For example, in the Oregon social studies field tests, one question asked which constitutional amendment gave women the right to vote. Students could know virtually nothing about the long struggle for women's rights and get this question right. On the other hand, they could know lots about the feminist movement and not recall that it was the 19th and not the 16th, 17th, or 18th Amendment (the other test choices) that gave women the right to vote.

Because there is no way to predict precisely which facts will be sought on state tests, teachers will feel pressured to turn courses into a "memory Olympics;" teachers won't be able to spend the time required to probe beneath the headlines of history. For example, in my U.S. history class at Franklin High School in Portland, students perform a role play on the 1848 Seneca Falls, N.Y., women's rights conference, the first formal U.S. gathering to demand greater equality for women. The original assembly was composed largely of middle- to upper-class white women. I wanted my students to appreciate the issues that these women addressed and their courage, but also to consider the limitations imposed by their race, class, and ethnicity. Thus in our simulated 1848 gathering, my students portrayed women who were not at the original conference—enslaved African Americans, Cherokee women who had been forcibly moved to Oklahoma on the Trail of Tears, Mexican women in the recently conquered territory of New Mexico, poor white New England mill workers—as well as the white middle- and upper-class reformers like

Elizabeth Cady Stanton and Lucretia Mott who were in attendance. In this more socially representative fictional assembly, students learned about the resolutions adopted at the original gathering and the conditions that motivated those, but they also saw first hand how more privileged white women ignored other important issues such as treaty rights of Mexican women, sexual abuse of enslaved African Americans, and the workplace exploitation of poor white women, that a more diverse convention might have addressed.

The knowledge that my students acquired from this role play consisted not only of "facts"—although they learned plenty of these. They also exercised their multicultural social imaginations—listening for the voices that are often silenced in the traditional U.S. history narrative, becoming more alert to the importance of issues of race and class. However, this kind of teaching and learning takes time—time that could be ill-afforded in the fact-packing pedagogy required by multiple-choice tests. And after all their study, would my students have recalled whether it was the 16th, 17th, 18th, or 19th Amendment that gave women the right to vote? If not, they would have appeared ignorant about the struggle for women's rights.

In a demonstration of its own shaky grasp of the material on which it tests students, Oregon shows that the reverse is true as well: One can master isolated morsels of fact and remain ignorant about the issues that give those facts meaning. For example, in a test question repeated throughout the seven pilot tests, the state uses the term "Suffragette," an inappropriate and dismissive substitute for "Suffragist." Someone who had actually studied the movement would know this. As Sherna Gluck points out in her book, *From Parlor to Prison,* women in the suffrage movement considered this diminutive term "an insult when applied to them by most of the American press."

Because there is no way to predict precisely which facts will be sought on state tests, teachers will feel pressured to turn courses into a 'memory Olympics'; teachers won't be able to spend the time required to probe beneath the headlines of history.

My global studies students spend the better part of a quarter reading, discussing, role-playing, and writing about the manifold consequences of European colonialism. They read excerpts from Okot p'Bitek's poignant book-length poem, *Song of Lawino* about the lingering psychological effects of colonialism in Uganda; role-play a trial on the colonial roots of the potato famine in Ireland; and examine how Asian economies were distorted to serve the needs of European ruling classes. But when confronted with Oregon's multiple-choice question that asks which continent was most thoroughly colonized in 1914, would my students answer correctly?

As these examples illustrate, in a multicultural curriculum it's not so much facts as it is perspective that is important in nurturing a fuller understanding of society. And sometimes considering new perspectives requires imagination as much as or more than memory of specific facts. For example, my history students read about the people Columbus encountered in 1492, the Taínos—who themselves left no written records—in excerpts from Columbus' journal and articles like José Barreiro's "Taínos: Men of the Good." I ask students to write a story or diary entry from the point of view of a Taíno during the first few days or weeks of their encounter with Spaniards that draws on information in the readings, but goes further. It's necessarily a speculative undertaking, but invites students to turn the "Columbus discovers America" story on its head, encourages them to appreciate the humanity in the people usually marginalized in tales of "exploration." In response, students have written pieces of startling insight. Sure, a multiple-choice test can assess whether students know that Columbus first sailed in 1492, the names of his ships, where he landed, or the name of the people he encountered. But these tests are ill-equipped to assess what students truly *understand* about this encounter.

> **In a multicultural curriculum it's not so much facts as it is perspective that is important in nurturing a fuller understanding of society.**

Necessarily, the "one best answer" approach vastly oversimplifies and misrepresents complex social processes—and entirely erases ethnicity and race as categories of analysis. One question on an Oregon social studies test reads: "In 1919, over 4.1 million Americans belonged to labor unions. By 1928, that number had dropped to 3.4 million. Which of the following best accounts for that drop?" It seems that the correct answer must be A.: "Wages increased dramatically, so workers didn't need unions." All the other answers are clearly wrong, but is this answer "correct"? Since when do workers leave unions when they win higher wages? Weren't mechanization and scientific management factors in undermining traditional craft unions? Did the post-World War I Red Scare, with systematic attacks on radical unions like the Industrial Workers of the World and deportations of foreign-born labor organizers affect union membership?

And how about the test's reductive category of "worker"? Shouldn't students be alert to how race, ethnicity, and gender were and are important factors in determining one's workplace experience, including union membership? For example, in 1919, professional strikebreakers, hired by steel corporations, were told to "stir up as much bad feeling as you possibly can between the Serbians and the Italians." And, as Howard Zinn points out in *A People's History of the United States,* more than 30,000 black workers, excluded from AFL unions, were brought in as strikebreakers. A multicultural awareness is vital if we're to arrive at a satisfactory answer to the above test question. But tests like these reward students for choosing a historical sound bite that is as shallow as it is wrong.

This leads me to an aspect of standardized tests that is especially offensive to teachers: They don't merely assess, they also instruct. The tests represent the authority of the state, implicitly telling students, "Just memorize the facts, kids. That's what social studies is all about—and if teachers do any more than that, they're wasting your time." Multiple-choice tests undermine teachers' efforts to construct a rigorous multicultural curriculum because they delegitimate that curriculum in students' eyes: If it were important it would be on the test.

At its core, multicultural teaching is an ethical, even political, enterprise. Its aim is not just to impart lots of interesting facts, to equip students to be proficient Trivial Pursuit players, but to help make the world a better place. It highlights injustice of all kinds—racial, gender, class, linguistic, ethnic, national, environmental—in order to make explanations and propose solutions. It recognizes our responsibility to fellow human beings and to the earth. It has heart and soul.

Compare that with the sterile fact-collecting orientation of Oregon's standards and assessments. For example, a typical 49-question high school field test includes seven questions on global climate, two on the location of rivers in India and Africa, and one on hypothetical world population projections in the year 2050. But not a single question in the test concerns the lives of people around the world, or environmental conditions— nothing about increasing poverty, the global AIDS epidemic, disappearance of the rainforests, rates of unemployment, global warming, etc., or efforts to address these crises. The test bounds aimlessly from one disjointed fact to another. In the most profound sense it's pointless.

Multiple-choice tests undermine teachers' efforts to construct a rigorous multicultural curriculum because they delegitimate that curriculum in students' eyes: If it were important it would be on the test.

Indeed, the test's random amorality may reveal another of its cultural biases. Oregon's standards and assessments make no distinction between knowledge and information. The state's version of social education would appear to have no raison d'être beyond the acquisition of large quantities of data. But for many cultures, the aim of knowledge is not bulk, but wisdom—insight into meaningful aspects about the nature of life. Writing in the winter 1998–99 issue of *Rethinking Schools,* Peter Kiang makes a similar point about the Massachusetts Teacher Test that calls into question the validity of enterprises such as these. He writes that:

> by constructing a test based on a sequence of isolated, decontextualized questions that have no relationship to each other, the underlying epistemology embedded in the test design has a Western cultural bias, even if individual questions include or represent "multicultural" content. Articulating and assessing a knowledge base requires examining not only what one knows, but also how one knows.

Students "know" in different ways, and these differences are often cultural. Standardized social studies tests nonetheless subject all students to an abstract data-heavy assessment device that does not gauge what or how they have learned. As Kiang points out, test-makers address multicultural criticism by including individual questions about multicultural content—for example, by highlighting snippets of information about famous people of color like Martin Luther King Jr., Cesar Chavez, and Harriet Tubman. But these "heroes and holidays" additions cannot mask the fundamental hostility to multicultural education shown by standards and assessments like those initiated by Oregon.

Spelling out an alternative to culturally biased, superficial "accountability" plans would require another article. In brief, I want the states to abandon the effort to treat teachers as cogs in a delivery system of approved social information. I want departments of education to support me and other teachers as we collaborate to create curriculum that deals forthrightly with social problems, that fights racism and social injustice. I want them to support teachers as we construct rigorous performance standards for students that promote deep thinking about the nature of our society. I want them to acknowledge the legitimacy of a multicultural curriculum of critical questions, complexity, multiple perspectives, and social imagination. I want them to acknowledge that wisdom is more than information—that the world can't be chopped up into multiple-choice questions, and that you can't bubble-in the truth with a No. 2 pencil.

> **Students 'know' in different ways, and these differences are often cultural. Standardized social studies tests nonetheless subject all students to an abstract data-heavy assessment device that does not gauge what or how they have learned.**

Bill Bigelow is curriculum editor of Rethinking Schools *and co-director of the Zinn Education Project. He co-edited* A People's Curriculum for the Earth: Teaching Climate Change and the Environmental Crisis.

SECTION III
LANGUAGE, CULTURE, AND POWER

FAVIANNA RODRIGUEZ

Chapter Eighteen

PUTTING OUT THE LINGUISTIC WELCOME MAT

By Linda Christensen

My friend Karen works as a relatively new principal in a rural Oregon school where the sons and daughters of winery owners rub elbows with the sons and daughters of their field workers. Recently, she recounted a story about a typical day: "When I came into my office after lunch duty, three Latino students sat waiting for me. The students told me the substitute kicked them out for speaking Spanish in class. After verifying the story, I told the substitute her services would no longer be needed at our school."

Karen is a full-time warrior for students. She battles remarkable linguistic prejudice and historical inequities to make her school a safe community for her Latino

MICHAEL DUFFY

students. Before she arrived on campus, for example, school policy excluded Spanish-speaking English language learners from taking Spanish classes. Latino students had to enroll in German classes to meet their world language requirement.

At another urban school, in the Portland area, a group of teachers tallied the grammatical errors their administrator made during a faculty meeting. Their air of superiority and smugness made my teeth ache. This same smugness silences many students in our classrooms when we value how they speak more than what they say.

As educators, we have the power to determine whether students feel included or excluded in our schools and classrooms.

"Nonstandard" language speakers must negotiate this kind of language minefield whenever they enter the halls of power—schools, banks, government agencies, and employment offices. Language inequity still exists, whether it's getting kicked out of class for speaking in your home language or being found unfit for a job, a college, or a scholarship because of your lack of dexterity with Standard English.

As educators, we have the power to determine whether students feel included or excluded in our schools and classrooms. By bringing students' languages from their homes into the classroom, we validate their culture and their history as topics worthy of study.

A Curriculum on Language and Power

Author Toni Morrison (1981) writes about the power of language, and Black English in particular:

> It's the thing black people love so much—the saying of words, holding them on the tongue, experimenting with them, playing with them. It's a love, a passion. Its function is like a preacher's: to make you stand up out of your seat, make you lose yourself and hear yourself. The worst of all possible things that could happen would be to lose that language. There are certain things I cannot say without recourse to my language.

These days, most of our schools and school boards fashion mission statements about "embracing diversity." Multilingual banners welcome students and visitors in Spanish, Russian, and Vietnamese in the hallways of school buildings. But in the classroom, the job of the teacher often appears to be whitewashing students of color or students who are linguistically diverse, especially when punctuation and grammar are double-weighted on the state writing test. If we hope to create positive communities in which students from diverse backgrounds can thrive academically, we need to examine how our approach to students' linguistic diversity either includes or pushes out our most vulnerable learners.

During 30 years as a language arts classroom teacher, I realized that if I wanted my students to open up in their writing, to take risks and engage in intellectually demanding work, I needed to challenge assumptions about the superiority of Standard English and the inferiority of the home language of many of my black students: African American Vernacular English, Black English, or Ebonics. When students feel attacked by the red pen or the tongue for the way they write or speak, they either make themselves small—turning in short papers—or don't turn in papers at all. To build an engaging classroom where students from different backgrounds felt safe enough to dare to be big and bold in their writing, I had to build a curricular platform for them to stand on.

I started this work by intentionally inviting students to tell their stories in their home languages. I brought in August Wilson's plays, Lois Yamanaka's stories, and Jimmy Santiago Baca's poetry to validate the use of dialect and home language. But I learned that this wasn't enough. To challenge the old world order, I needed to explore why Standard English is the standard—how it came to power and how that power makes some people feel welcome and others feel like outsiders.

> **To challenge the old world order, I needed to explore why Standard English is the standard:**

I finally realized that I needed to create a curriculum on language and power that examined the roots of language supremacy and analyzed how schools perpetuate the myths of the inferiority of some languages. I also discovered that students needed stories of hope: stories of people's resistance to the loss of their mother tongues and stories about the growing movement to save indigenous languages from extinction.

Legitimizing the Study of Ebonics/Black English

Depending on how many pieces of the unit I include, this curriculum takes five to 10 weeks. Students watch films and read literature, nonfiction texts, and poetry. They write narratives, poetry, and a culminating essay about language. For their final exam, they create a take-it-to-the-people project that teaches an audience of their choice one aspect of our language study that they think people need to know in order to understand contemporary language issues. The curriculum includes any of the following five segments: Naming as a Practice of Power; Language and Colonization; Dialect and Power; Ebonics; and Language Restoration.

During this unit, we do discuss code-switching, or moving between home language and the language of power—Standard English—during our readings. As a teacher in a predominantly African American school where the majority of students exhibited some features of African American Vernacular English (AAVE, also called Ebonics or "Spoken Soul"), I needed to learn the rules and history of the language so I could help students move between the two language systems. In my experience, teaching black students the grammar structure and history of AAVE evoked pride in their language, but also curiosity. All students—not just African

Americans—benefited from learning that African American language has a highly structured grammar system.

Teaching about Ebonics has been a no-go zone for many teachers since the controversy over a 1996 Oakland School District resolution that recognized Black English as a language of instruction. Stanford linguistics professor John Rickford noted in his book *Spoken Soul:*

> Ebonics was vilified as "disgusting black street slang," "incorrect and substandard," "nothing more than ignorance," "lazy English," "bastardized English," "the language of illiteracy," and this "utmost ridiculous made-up language." (Rickford, 2000, p. 6)

Ebonics also includes distinctive patterns of pronunciation and grammar, the elements of language on which linguists tend to concentrate because they are more systematic and deep-rooted.

As Rickford pointed out, the reactions of linguists were much more positive than those of most of the media and the general public. Although they disagree about its origins, "linguists from virtually all points of view agree on the systematicity of Ebonics, and on the potential value of taking it into account in teaching Ebonics speakers to read and write." (Rickford, 1997)

In an African American literature class I recently taught at Grant High School in Portland, Ore., I introduced the Ebonics part of the language curriculum by giving the 31 students (28 of whom were black) a concept chart and asking them to fill in a definition of Ebonics, write a few examples, and note where it originated. All but one student wrote that Ebonics is slang. Most wrote that Ebonics came out of Oakland or the West Coast or the "ghetto." It was clear that their impressions were negative.

None of the black students in the group used Ebonics/AAVE exclusively. But many of them used aspects of Ebonics in both their speech and their writing. One of my goals was for students to recognize the difference between slang and Ebonics/Black English when they hear it in their school, churches, and homes—and to be able to distinguish it when they are using it. The term "Ebonics" (from ebony and phonics) was coined by Professor Robert Williams in 1973, during a conference on the language development of black children (Rickford, 2000, p. 170). In her essay "Black English/Ebonics: What it be like?" renowned scholar and linguist Geneva Smitherman writes that Ebonics "is rooted in the Black American Oral Tradition and represents a synthesis of African (primarily West African) and European (primarily English) linguistic-cultural traditions" (Smitherman, 1998).

In the class, we read Rickford's essay "Suite for Ebony and Phonics" aloud together paragraph by paragraph, stopping to discuss each part. Is Ebonics just "slang," as so many people have characterized it? No, because slang refers just to the vocabulary of a language or dialect, and even so, just to the small set of new and (usually) short-lived words like chillin ("relaxing") or homey ("close friend") that are used primarily by young people in informal contexts. Ebonics includes nonslang words like ashy (referring to the appearance of dry skin, especially in winter), which have been around for a while, and are used by people of all age groups.

Ebonics also includes distinctive patterns of pronunciation and grammar, the elements of language on which linguists tend to concentrate because they are more systematic and deep-rooted (Rickford, 1997).

We also read "From Africa to the New World and into the Space Age: An Introduction and History of Black English Structure," a chapter from Geneva Smitherman's 1977 book *Talkin and Testifyin: The Language of Black America.* Her discussion of the grammar structure of Ebonics led to a wonderful day of conjugating verbs. For example, we discussed the absence of a third person singular present tense in Ebonics (example: I draw, he draw, we draw, they draw); students then conjugate verbs using this grammar rule. The zero copula rule—the absence of is or are in a sentence—provided another model for students to practice. Smitherman gives as an example the sentence "People crazy! People are stone crazy!" The emphasis on are in the second sentence she points out, intensifies the feeling. I asked students to write zero copula sentences and we shared them in class.

After I started teaching my students about Ebonics, many of them began to understand how assumptions about the supremacy of Standard English had created difficulties in their education.

Empowered by Linguistic Knowledge

After I started teaching my students about Ebonics, many of them began to understand how assumptions about the supremacy of Standard English had created difficulties in their education. One student, Kaanan, wrote:

When I went to school, teachers didn't really teach me how to spell or put sentences together right. They just said sound it out, so I would spell it the way I heard it at home. Everybody around me at home spoke Ebonics, so when I sounded it out, it sounded like home and it got marked wrong. When I wrote something like "My brother he got in trouble last night," I was marked wrong. Instead of showing me how speakers of Ebonics sometimes use both a name and a pronoun but in "Standard English" only one is used, I got marked wrong.

Another student, Sherrell, said:

I grew up thinking Ebonics was wrong. My teachers would say, "If you ever want to get anywhere you have to learn how to talk right." . . . At home, after school, break time, lunch time, we all talked our native language which was Ebonics. Our teachers were wrong for saying our language wasn't right. All I heard was Spanish and Ebonics in my neighborhood. They brainwashed me at school to be ashamed of my language and that almost took away one of the few things that African Americans had of our past life and history.

Throughout the Ebonics unit, I asked students to listen and take notes and see if they could spot the rules of Ebonics at work in the school halls, at home, or at the mall. To celebrate and acknowledge a language that so many of my students spoke without aware-ness, I pointed out Ebonics in class as students spoke. Often, they didn't hear it or recognize it until we held it up like a diamond for them to examine.

> **We signal students from the moment they step into school, whether they belong or whether we see them as trespassers.**

One day my student Ryan handed me an unexpected gift when he asked if I'd ever heard the rapper Big L's song "Ebon-ics." I confessed my ignorance, but I looked it up on the web and downloaded the music and lyrics. The song is clever, but because the performer misunderstands Ebonics as slang, he provided a great audience for my students to rehearse their arguments about Ebonics. In one essay, for example, Jerrell wrote:

> "Ebonics is slang shit," rapper Big L said in his song titled "Ebonics." In this song he tells a lot about the slang that young African Americans use, but this is the problem. He is talking about slang; there is no Ebonics in his lyrics. The misconception people have is that slang and Ebonics are the same thing. The problem is that slang is just a different way of saying things. For example, in his slang you say money, you can also say bread, cheese, cheddar, cash, dough, green, duckets, Washingtons, chips, guap, and many more. However, when you use Ebonics, there is a sentence structure that you have to use. Don't get me wrong, slang and Ebonics go together like mashed potatoes and gravy, but there is a difference between the two. As my classmate said, "Slang is what I talk; Ebonics is how I speak it.

In his end-of-unit reflection, Jayme wrote that he appreciated "the knowledge that was given to us about the language that we speak and how it related to our roots in Africa." Hannah wrote, "Kids who have been taught that the way they speak is wrong their entire lives can now be confident." And I love the sassiness of Ryan's con-clusion: "Ebonics is here to stay and shows no sign of fading away in either the black or white communities. In the words of Ebonics: 'It's BIN here and it's 'bout to stay.'"

Inclusive School Communities

When I took students to local universities to share their knowledge about language during our take-it-to-the-people project, Jacoa told aspiring teachers at Portland

State University, "On my college application, I'm going to write that I'm fluent in three languages: English, Spanish, and Ebonics. Call me if you need more information."

As educators, when we talk about building inclusive communities in which all students can learn, we must also examine how our policies and practices continue to shame and exclude students in ways that may not be readily apparent. We signal students from the moment they step into school, whether they belong or whether we see them as trespassers. Everything in school—from the posters on the wall, to the music played at assemblies, to the books in the library—embraces students or pushes them away. Approaching students' home languages with respect is one of the most important curricular choices teachers can make.

Linda Christensen (lmc@lclark.edu) is director of the Oregon Writing Project at Lewis & Clark College in Portland, Oregon, and a Rethinking Schools *editor. She is author, most recently, of* Reading, Writing, and Rising Up: Teaching About Social Justice and the Power of the Written Word *(2nd edition).*

This article first appeared in the Sept. 2008 issue of *Educational Leadership*. Reprinted with permission. Learn more about ASCD at www.ascd.org.

Writer's Note: In my *Rethinking Schools* article "The Politics of Correction" (Vol. 18, No. 1), I discuss more fully how I address moving students between their home language and the language of power, Standard English.

References

LeClair, T. "'The Language Must Not Sweat': A Conversation with Toni Morrison." *New Republic*. March 21, 1981: 25–29.

Rickford, J. R. (2008). "Suite for Ebony and Phobics," www.stanford.edu/~rickford/papers/SuiteForEbony AndPhonics.html

Smitherman, G. (1977). *Talkin and Testifyin: The Language of Black America*. Boston: Houghton Mifflin.

Smitherman, G. (1998) "Black English/Ebonics: What it be like?" The Real Ebonics Debate. Milwaukee: Rethinking Schools.

Rickford, J. R. & Rickford R J. (2000). *Spoken Soul: The Story of Black English*. New York: John Wiley & Sons.

Chapter Nineteen

MY MOTHER'S SPANISH

By Salvador Gabaldón

My mother, a gifted storyteller, nourished a love of language in all her children. Even before we began school, she would read to us from the Spanish translations of such classic works as Jules Verne's *Twenty Thousand Leagues Under the Sea* and Victor Hugo's *The Hunchback of Notre Dame*.

Mexican music from the radio filled our house in Los Angeles, and my mother taught us to hear the words as well as the melody. Books in Spanish and Spanish-language newspapers filled our home, and she corrected the Spanish we used in writing letters to our family in Chihuahua.

With the wisdom of a young mother, she realized that the foundation of a good education is a love of language. Knowing the importance of English in this country, she made sure we would learn it. Her contribution to that end was to give us a love for her speech, the language she knew best.

ISTOCKPHOTO

Perhaps inevitably, her two sons both became bilingual and both translated their love of language into careers as English teachers. Those of us who teach language minority students in our nation's public schools see the evidence for inter-language literacy again and again: Students who are strong readers in their native language invariably become strong readers in English.

Unfortunately, in the heat of ideological battles, voters sometimes lose their common sense. Who would have thought that Arizonans—a people who have come to respect and admire the culture of our native tribes—would vote for a law, Proposition 203, that is so harmful to our remaining native languages? Or that we would abandon the concept of local control of schools because we fear that the growing use of Spanish in our communities will somehow threaten English?

As Americans, we should know our own language better. Beautifully flexible and seductive in its power, nothing threatens English. It is the language of science, business, the internet, popular culture, and diplomacy. Anyone who feels a desperate urge to protect English is badly underestimating its strength. I have spent my career helping students to discover the splendor of the English language and the richness of its literature. I've yet to meet any group of parents who do not want English for their children.

Parents seeking bilingual education feel exactly the same way. They want English. The only difference is that, like my mother, they want Spanish for their children, too. They are wise enough to see the value of bilingualism.

Yes, Spanish has indeed become our second language, a language with its own power and beauty. It is everywhere: in bookstores, banking machines, phone messages, advertisements, and media of all types. It gives lyrical (and sometimes perplexing) names to our streets and towns, our mountains, valleys, and rivers. It flavors our foods, colors our music, deepens our ties to the land. Those who interpret Spanish as a threat rather than a marvelous resource are the poorer for it.

Those who interpret Spanish as a threat rather than a marvelous resource are the poorer for it.

Sadly, their fear now impoverishes our system of education. Spanish became a convenient scapegoat, blamed for the educational struggles of the children of immigrants. It wasn't the fact that 76 percent of all such children received English-only instruction. It wasn't the disparity of funding between wealthy school districts and poor ones. It wasn't the lack of teacher training on language-acquisition strategies.

No, Spanish was the problem. If we could rid our schools of Spanish, then all children would acquire English "in a period not normally intended to exceed one year."

That was the promise. The reality turned out to be something very different. California launched its experiment with immersion in the late 1990s. In the first few years after their immersion programs began, school officials bragged about test score improvements. They insisted that immersion programs were working, and that children were acquiring English with amazing speed. Then, slowly, the exuberant reports from California began to fade away. Subsequent reports barely made the news. What happened?

In February 2004, California's legislative analysts released a study based on 2.6 million test results, tracking the length of time that it took for students from various language backgrounds to become proficient in English. The students who learned English most quickly were from an Asian American group, Mandarin speakers, averaging 3.4 years. The ones who took longest were from another Asian American group, Hmong speakers, averaging 7.1 years.

> **'English in one year' is a fantasy; literacy in two languages is a treasure.**

The results were exactly what specialists in language acquisition had been saying all along. "English in one year" is a fantasy; literacy in two languages is a treasure.

My mom could have told them that.

Salvador Gabaldón is a Language Acquisition Specialist with the Language Acquisition Department for Tuscon Unified School District in Arizona.

This article first appeared in Latino Perspectives *(www.latinoperspectivesmagazine.com). Reprinted with permission.*

Chapter Twenty

TAKING A CHANCE WITH WORDS
Why are the Asian American kids silent in class?

By Carol A. Tateishi

I received Jeff's essay in a mailing from Joan Cone, an old friend and Bay Area Writing Project teacher-consultant who was teaching at El Cerrito High School in the San Francisco Bay Area at the time. She'd sent it to me mainly to share a powerful piece of writing but also because in my position as director of the Bay Area Writing Project, Joan had worked with me in our project's teacher research program and knew I had long been concerned by what I had noted in Bay Area high school classrooms as a lack of participation by students of Asian descent in the oral language activities of the class.

Being Japanese American, this issue was of both personal and professional in-

JORDIN ISIP

terest. I was aware that high numbers of secondary teachers whose practice I knew well, shared a belief that classroom talk in a variety of modes is a primary means by which students make sense of the world and what they are learning. But in conversations with these same teachers and in my visits to classrooms, the silent Asian American student is a familiar presence.

> **If we believe that the use of language is key to classroom learning, what might it mean if the class includes Asian American students … and significant numbers of them do not participate or participate minimally day in and day out in the oral discourse of the class?**

Although teachers are concerned about this lack of participation in classroom talk, they are also often relatively accepting of these quiet students who don't pose a discipline problem, who turn in homework on time, and in general, get passing grades.

If we believe that the use of language is key to classroom learning, what might it mean if the class includes Asian American students, such as Jeff, and significant numbers of them do not participate or participate minimally day in and day out in the oral discourse of the class? How does their nonparticipation in the active talk of a class affect their learning, or does it? Why don't they participate? What do they understand about the purposes of these orally rich classroom activities? What role might their cultures and home language practices play in their nonparticipation? And, does it matter?

My interest in these questions stems from the fabric of my personal life. Growing up post-World War II in the L.A. Basin, I attended predominantly white schools (my father having bought a house by proxy after the war in an area that discriminated against people of Japanese descent, so there were few of us), but my world outside of school, mainly social life and church life, was mainly among Japanese Americans. I was raised, though, to make my way in the dominant culture, and it started at the dinner table that in my family was a place for talk, orchestrated largely by my dad, sitting at the head of the extra large table he'd built to accommodate six kids. As soon as we all sat down, his questions would start:

"How'd that test go in your math class?"

"Whatever happened to that friend of yours?"

We were a noisy bunch, all vying to keep our dad's attention for that extra minute or two. Although this scene may have been common for white middle-class families in the 1950s, it wasn't for Japanese Americans, attested to by my mother, who sat quietly amidst the jabbering, having been raised as a proper Japanese child to not speak during meals. Not that my dad's upbringing was any different. What was different was his intention. The 1950s was only a decade after the internment of 110,000 people of Japanese ancestry and its shadow loomed large over our everyday lives. My dad believed one reason we were "sold down the river," as he would say, was that we lacked leaders who could make our case and resist government forces. His children would have the words and the confidence to speak up and use language like full-blooded Americans. And for the most part, we did develop the words and the confidence, which served us well in school. But as a teenager trying to fit in among my Japanese American friends, the same rules for speaking served me poorly. As I attempted to negotiate the linguistic borders of school and social life, my conflicting experiences gave me a heightened awareness of culturally patterned differences in the ways people speak and use language.

Now, as an educator, these experiences had taken on an expanded dimension, and I wanted to learn more. Jeff's essay made me think that he would be an interesting student to speak to, and I arranged to spend time in this particular 12th-grade class. Joan and I had talked before about the Asian American students in her classes, and she, too, wanted to learn more about the ways her students used language.

> **As I attempted to negotiate the linguistic borders of school and social life, my conflicting experiences gave me a heightened awareness of culturally patterned differences in the ways people speak and use language.**

Snapshots from the Classroom

During a small-group discussion on my first visit to Joan's class, I sat in Jeff's group, which happened to be made up of students who were all of Asian descent. No one spoke for the longest time while students in the other groups chattered away about the story they'd read for homework, following Joan's directions to share what they didn't understand about the story and to get help from others in their group. Although I grew increasingly uncomfortable with the silence, the students seemed fine with this extended wait time. Finally, Jeff spoke, followed by Dan, and eventually the three girls in the group spoke briefly in voices barely loud enough to hear. And although it was clear they'd done the homework, their comments skirted the assigned questions, no one eager, it seemed, to divulge what they didn't understand in their readings.

I asked Jeff about this later that day. Jeff, a fourth-generation Japanese American whose father was a dentist and who, with his shock of pink hair falling over his forehead, appeared right at home among his peers, said, "I was brought up to believe it was a sign of strength to solve your problems yourself and not to impose them on others. It's really hard for me to bring questions about what I don't understand to class to have others help me find the answer." Jeff's response stopped me in my tracks as I immediately recalled learning the same thing at an early age, that silence is a sign of self-reliance and strength. I was surprised at the abiding strength of this cultural value, extending to this young man whose great-grandfather would have immigrated to this country at the turn of the century. In talking further with Jeff, it emerged that his reluctance to participate was compounded by the negative attitude in Japanese culture toward verbosity in men, something that he'd also learned at home. However, his answer was a point of concern, knowing Joan's belief in collaborative learning and realizing these particular students were not reaping its benefits.

In my next visit, Jeff was leading a whole-class discussion, for the first time according to Joan, of "Seventeen Syllables," a short story by Hisaye Yamamoto that takes place during the 1930s in California's San Joaquin Valley. Central to the story is the relationship between an Issei (first-generation Japanese immigrant) husband and wife where the wife's writing of haiku and the social recognition of her talents make apparent the class differences between them, and challenges the husband's authority within the family. Told from the young daughter's point of view, the story reveals deep-seated emotions by the father, masked through his silence, and the truth behind her mother's move to America due to a shameful romantic liaison. The meaning of silence and the father's inability to express emotions are important themes.

Jeff pulled a desk to the front of the room and started the discussion with a few questions. Soon, other students were answering his questions and raising their own.

Jeff pulled a desk to the front of the room and started the discussion with a few questions. Soon, other students were answering his questions and raising their own, but they appeared puzzled by the key incident in the story where the father destroys the prize given to his wife in a haiku contest:

> [H]e threw the picture on the ground and picked up the axe. Smashing the picture, glass and all (she heard the explosion faintly), he reached over for the kerosene that was used to encourage the bath fire and poured it over the wreckage.

Students wondered why the father hadn't just talked to his wife. Two of the students felt that the father's silence and his abruptness with his wife leading up to this incident were inexplicable and undercut the meaning of the story. Jeff attempted to explain the father's behavior, but it seemed that Jeff was experiencing, himself, the very difficulty he was trying to explain about the father's inability to use language to reveal his thoughts and feelings. Finally, Jeff said, "That's just the way the Japanese are," and he quietly moved the desk back into the row and sat down, frustrated and deflated.

What Students Had to Say

Over time I sat in on Joan's class often and interviewed five students in depth: Jeff and Dan, both Japanese American; Christina and Sandra, who had emigrated from China when they were in elementary school; and Wanda, who had emigrated from Korea when she was in middle school. (I should add that I had started with one-to-one interviews but switched to group interviews when I found that the students seemed to feel that they were failing me by the brevity of their responses.)

For these students, speaking in class was not a simple matter. A recurrent theme throughout our interviews was "You're not supposed to say too much." Jeff was brought up believing that too much talk could "cause disrespect and harsh feelings," while Dan viewed negatively students who were "outspoken." Sandra re-peatedly told me that in her family "We don't talk about feelings," and gender issues compounded the girls' reluctance to talk. Christina summarized their experiences: "In my home, women aren't supposed to speak unless they're spoken to. It's just the way I've been raised. Girls aren't supposed to talk out loud in public and it's just the way I grew up." And, in direct opposition to the way I was deliberately raised, all the girls said they weren't supposed to talk at the dinner ta-ble. In addition, the three girls, who had entered American schools as English learners, continued to worry about their language skills. Wanda commented, "I may not be able to speak as well English as other kids, but I'm scared like, oh, probably they're going to laugh at me . . . so that discourages me from speaking loud in class."

For these students, speaking in class was not a simple matter.

Although all the students tended to be self-conscious about expressing their thinking in class, as our interviews progressed, the students' views of speaking at home began to take on a number of shared qualities:

- Oral language tends to be used functionally.
- Speaking publicly about one's problems is discouraged.
- That restraint in talking is valued.
- You don't talk about feelings or personal experiences.

I was initially surprised that their comments about ways of speaking at home held such commonalities since there were differences among the Asian cultures represented among the students and differences in the features of each of the Asian speech communities. In addition, the students' families spanned close to 100 years of immigration to this country. It could be that the group interview setting may have contributed to this show of commonalities. Even so, the features singled out above shouldn't necessarily be generalized to all students of Asian descent.

What is relevant, though, is to examine these speech behaviors in light of Joan's beliefs about classroom talk that are very likely shared by many progressive class-room teachers, beliefs such as:

- Oral language can be used to negotiate meaning.
- Risk-taking in talk is valued.
- Speaking in class increases engagement.
- Classroom dialogue deepens learning.

When compared with the students' views, the exploratory and engaging nature of this kind of classroom talk was a far cry from the students' ways of speaking at home. In addition, the students had little opportunity to practice or learn about these other ways of speaking in public spaces except in the classroom.

What Students Say Would Help Them

When I asked about what helped or hindered them in speaking in class, the students had definite ideas. They were keenly aware of differences in the sociocultural expectations for speaking in the home and the classroom, and they were unanimous in their preference for small groups. But they felt a strong need to have group leaders, which corresponds to a point made by Professor Lily Wong Fillmore in a conversation I had with her at UC Berkeley where she spoke of a need by Asian American students to be "authored" to speak, a concept that makes sense given the hierarchical nature of many Asian American families. It's not surprising that students might look to an external authority for permission to speak or feel more comfortable with a set of rules or protocols that in themselves "author" turn-taking in speaking. (I realized, too, that this is what my dad had done for my siblings and me as we were growing up.) The students said they felt they could begin to leave behind their hesitations and self-consciousness when they were asked to speak and when the rules for speaking were clear. They felt in these instances they were complying with an external request and the content of what they said was shaped by that request. As Christina stated, "Maybe sometimes I need someone to ask me to say something instead of me moving myself into the group."

> **The students said they felt they could begin to leave behind their hesitations and self-consciousness when they were asked to speak and when the rules for speaking were clear.**

For the students interviewed, to "just, like, join the conversation" (as Christina put it) was the hardest and most unfamiliar way to participate in small-group talk, although they noted that this approach worked for others. They said they needed help in negotiating the open, unstructured nature of the class discussion groups. For example, they were unanimous in their preference for small discussion groups, but they said a group needed to have designated leaders so that, in Sandra's view, "everyone has an equal chance to speak." At one point, Wanda described an "authoring" structure she liked that Joan had used early in the year: "In *The Shipping News,* the whole class got in a big circle. I said 'pass' because I didn't have anything to say, but everybody had a chance to say pass or speak. That was kind of nice."

The concept of "authoring" also shed light on Dan's debate team participation. I had been surprised to learn that he not only was on the team but also had actively recruited new members and was responsible, according to Joan, for the increased number of Asians Americans on the team. In my class visits, though, Dan had not spoken once in the whole-group discussions and had spoken only minimally in small-group discussions. It seemed that the formal structure of debate with its clear rules for speaking gave Dan the authority he needed to speak, liberated him to do so, and, perhaps, gave him the time to plan and craft his words.

A Lot Less Quiet

So far I have focused on the gap between oral language use in the classroom by the Asian American students I interviewed and Joan's expectations for it. I would be remiss, however, to leave a picture of black and white differences. Jeff was the one student who seemed to be straddling the two speech communities, and early on provided an interesting insight about Asian Americans and language use when viewed in a historical context:

> What I think is that Asian Americans (as a significant percentage of the population) are a relatively new minority. A lot of the time they are kept out of the mainstream or keep themselves out of the mainstream—it's kind of ingrained in you like in that "Seventeen Syllables" story where you have to kind of restrain yourself. At the same time as Asian American kids are becoming more American, I think there's less of that restraint and so gradually more Asian American kids and also adults are speaking out more. Maybe 20 years ago or something I'm sure there's quite a big difference compared to now. We're a lot less quiet now.

"A lot less quiet now" is a good way to describe an emerging phase that not only Jeff was experiencing but also one that seems to be just beginning to be played out in Bay Area schools and in San Francisco schools in particular. Based on anecdotal evidence from San Francisco high school teachers, their students are increasingly joining the conversation of the classroom, partly, I think, because they are "becoming more American," but also because of the district's demographics. Close to 40 percent of students are of Asian descent, districtwide, with 31.9 percent Chinese. Numbers make a difference.

They said they needed help in negotiating the open, unstructured nature of the class discussion groups.

Although San Francisco and students like Jeff are showing promising changes, what can teachers do right now that might bring students such as those I interviewed more readily into the talk of the classroom where they can experience and practice the intellectual engagement it can provide?

Recommendations

Although this beginning list of ideas only skims the surface of what is possible, they address the concerns of the students I spoke with—students who said they were raised to wait to speak out of respect for others, who needed to have a definite turn to speak or needed to be called on in order to speak, who needed better understanding of the academic and intellectual purposes of talk in school settings, and who needed scaffolded practice in venturing into talk that might reveal personal feelings and opinions or provoke argument.

- Be aware and knowledgeable of the cultural barriers some students face in attempting to participate in classroom talk.
- Take the same kind of time and effort to teach effective classroom talk as you might for writing response groups or any kind of classroom collaborative work.
- Model strong and weak discussion groups with mock classroom enactments that highlight the why's of the talk.
- Create stable discussion groups as you would for writing groups. Take care in putting students into groups, helping them build trustful communities over time and sensitivity to cultural differences.
- Designate group leaders and develop clear guidelines and protocols with students for how the group works and how talk is conducted and why.
- Debrief the workings of small-group talk regularly to help students develop greater understanding of the dynamics of classroom talk.

Our challenge is to make the rules and purposes governing classroom talk as visible and explicit as possible so that students can acquire new literacy practices and move easily from one speech community to the next in a code-switching mode, not only for the Asian American students but also for their fellow students who need to hear their thoughts and perspectives.

Final Thoughts

While my inquiry has ostensibly been about teaching and learning, the underlying question is, teaching and learning for what? More is at stake than better learning of the curriculum. There are consequences beyond academia. Already a lack of strong verbal skills is impacting Asian Americans and their communities.

Be aware and knowledgeable of the cultural barriers some students face in attempting to participate in classroom talk.

Studies I've looked at point to our underrepresentation in occupations such as journalism, law, and the social sciences that require language skills and personal contact and, instead, a concentration in fields where technical knowledge rather than linguistic and social skills are at a premium. Also, the glass ceiling effect is well known among Asian Americans where candidates tend to do poorly in oral interviews where their lack of verbal fluency translates into a perceived lack of self-confidence and necessary supervisory skills.

And my "for what" question brings me back to my father and his intuitive understanding that language is connected to resistance and social justice, that language is connected to action and consequences.

It mattered in the 1940s and matters again today if Asian Americans have the words and voice to speak up for themselves and their communities. It matters if we have lawyers, writers, activists, educators, business leaders, elected officials, and ordinary citizens who understand the power of language and use it.

Right now, Asian Americans are among the fastest growing segments of the population and are expected to grow to 20 million in this country by 2020. It is increasingly important that Asian American voices, literally, become part of the on-going dialogue that helps shape and inform who we are. A good place to start is the classroom.

Carol A. Tateishi is Director of the Bay Area Writing Project, a University of California at Berkeley program dedicated to improving the teaching of writing in Bay Area schools.

Chapter Twenty-One

BLACK ENGLISH/EBONICS
What it be like?

By Geneva Smitherman

I looked at my hands, they looked new/I looked at my feet, and they did too/I got a new way of walkin/and a new way of talkin.
—Traditional Black Gospel Song

WAYNE STATE UNIVERSITY PRESS

The month after the Oakland School Board passed its resolution, the term "Ebonics" turned 24 years old. Yeah, dass right, the name is more than two decades old. It was coined by a group of black scholars as a new way of talkin bout the language of African slave descendants. Like the message of that old gospel tune "Ebonics" was about transformation, about intellectuals among the Talented Tenth striking a blow for the linguistic liberation of our people. The guru in this group of scholars at that "Language and the Urban Child" conference, convened in St. Louis in January 1973, was the brilliant clinical psychologist Dr. Robert L. Williams, now professor emeritus, Washington University. In the book of conference proceedings Williams published in 1975, he captures the thinking of that historical moment:

> A significant incident occurred at the conference. The black conferees were so critical of the work on the subject done by white researchers, many of whom also happened to be present, that they decided to caucus among

themselves and define black language from a black perspective. It was in this caucus that the term Ebonics was created. [The term refers to] linguistic and paralinguistic features which on a concentric continuum represent the communicative competence of the West African, Caribbean, and United States slave descendant of African origin. It includes the various idioms, patois, argots, ideolects, and social dialects of black people, especially those who have been forced to adapt to colonial circumstances. (1975, Preface, Introduction)

For this group of scholars, the conceptual framework of "Ebonics" represented an avenue for decolonization of the African American mind, a way to begin repairing the psycholinguistically maimed psyche of blacks in America. As Paulo Freire would put it 12 years later, "language variations (female language, ethnic language, dialects) are intimately interconnected with, coincide with, and express identity. They help defend one's sense of identity and they are absolutely necessary in the process of struggling for liberation" (1985, p. 186). Ebonics reaffirms the interrelatedness of language and culture and links Africans in America with Africans around the globe.

> **The conceptual framework of 'Ebonics' represented an avenue for decolonization of the African American mind.**

Ebonics: neither "broken" English, nor "sloppy" speech, nor merely "slang," nor some bizarre lingo spoken only by baggy pants-wearing black kids. Rather, the variety of Ebonics spoken in the U.S. (hereafter USEB) is rooted in the Black American Oral Tradition and represents a synthesis of African (primarily West African) and European (primarily English) linguistic-cultural traditions. The linguistic shape of the words in USEB can readily be identified as Standard English, i.e., the Language of Wider Communication here in the U.S. (hereafter LWC), but these words do not always have the same meaning in USEB as in LWC. Further, there are many words of direct African origin—*e.g., okay, gorilla, cola, jazz*—that are now part of LWC (often without props to us African slave descendants). However, what gives Black Language (un-huh, dat ain no typo, I meant "language") its distinctiveness is the nuanced meanings of these English words, the pronunciations, the ways in which the words are combined to form grammatical statements, and the communicative practices of the USEB-speaking community. In short, USEB may be thought of as the Africanization of American English.

Patterns of Ebonics

In the next section, I discuss the following patterns of USEB: 1) aspectual be; 2) stressed been; 3) multiple negation; 4) adjacency/context in possessives; 5) post-vocalic /r/ deletion; 6) copula absence; 7) camouflaged and other unique lexical forms.

Consider this statement, which comes from some black women just kickin it in the beauty shop (gloss: conversational chit-chat at a hair salon): "The Brotha be lookin good; that's what got the Sista nose open!" In this statement, *Brotha* is USEB for an African American man, *lookin good* refers to his style, his attractive appearance (not necessarily the same thing as physical beauty in USEB), *Sista* is USEB for an African American woman, and her passionate love for the Brotha is conveyed by the phrase *nose open* (in USEB, the kind of passionate love that makes you vulnerable to exploitation). *Sista nose* is standard USEB grammar for denoting possession, indicated by adjacency/context (i.e., rather than the LWC /'s, s'/). The use of be means that the quality of *lookin good* is not limited to the present moment, but reflects the Brotha's past, present, and future essence.

In short, USEB may be thought of as the Africanization of American English.

As in the case of Efik and other Niger-Congo languages, USEB has an aspectual verb system, conveyed by the use of the English verb be to denote iterativity (i.e., a recurring or habitual state of affairs; contrast *He be lookin good* with *He lookin good,* which refers to the present moment only—not the kind of lookin good that opens the nose!). Note further that many black writers and rap artists employ the spellings "Brotha" and "Sista." Now, they ain just tryin to be cute. These orthographic representations are used to convey a phonological pattern derived from the influence of West African languages, many of which do not have an /r/ sound. Also in these language communities, kinship terms may be used when referring to African people, whether biologically related or not.

Of course there is overlap between USEB and colloquial, everyday American English—e.g., use of "ain't," ending sentences with prepositions, double negatives. However, there are critical distinctions that separate linguistically competent USEB speakers from the wanna-bes. For example, the colloquial speaker says *gonna* or *goin* to for the LWC form going to. But the USEB speaker uses the nasalized vowel form, producing a sound close to, but not identical with, LWC gone, thus: "What she go (n) do now?", i.e., in LWC, "What is she going to do now?" Another example is in negation patterns. While those obsessed with the "national mania for correctness" often rail against colloquial speakers' double negatives, USEB is distinctive not only for its negative inversion, but also for its *multiple* negatives, that is, three or more negatives formed from combinations of indefinite pronouns and/or adjectives. Check out this exclamation of complex negative inversion from a devout churchgoer: "Don't nobody don't know God can't tell me nothin!" i.e., in LWC, "A person who doesn't believe in God and isn't saved has no credibility with me."

As mentioned above, USEB words may look like mainstream American English, but the usage and meaning are different. This is the source of a good deal of miscommunication and misunderstanding between USEB and LWC speakers. In response to the question "Is she married?" the USEB speaker may answer "She been married." If the speaker pronounces been without stress, it means the woman in question was once married but is now divorced. If the speaker pronounces *been* with stress, it means she married a long time ago and is still married.

Another example is the use of LWC words that are "camouflaged" (Spears, 1982). For example, in the USEB statement, "She come tellin me I'n [didn't] know what I was talkin bout," the verb come does not denote motion as in LWC. Rather the meaning of come in this context is one of indignation, i.e., in LWC, "She had the audacity to tell me that I didn't know what I was talking about. How dare she!" Yet another kind of cross-communication example comes from semantic inversion. Due to crossover and the popular appeal of Michael Jackson, most people are aware that bad in USEB translates to *good* in LWC; however, lexical items that haven't enjoyed such a high degree of crossover are problematic in these cross-cultural exchanges. For example, consider the following form of address common among many black males: "Yo, Dog!" *Dog* is a linguistic symbol of male bonding, most likely derived from the African American fraternity tradition of referring to pledges as *dogs. Yo, Dog!* was used by a Brotha on lock down (gloss: imprisoned) to address his European American male psychiatrist as an expression of camaraderie. Turns out, though, that this white psychiatrist was not yet down (gloss: hip, understanding of the Black Cultural framework). He misinterpreted the Brotha's greeting and made an issue of the "insult."

The above are only some of the patterns in the grammatical, phonological, and semantic systems of USEB. To explore the full 360 degrees of USEB, we need to move on to styles of speaking. In fact, it is the area of communicative practices—rhetorical strategies and modes of discourse—that cuts across gender, generation, and class in the African American community. USEB speech acts may be classified as follows: l) Call-Response; 2) Tonal Semantics; 3) Narrativizing; 4) Proverb Use/Proverbializing; 5) Signification/Signifyin; 6) The Dozens/Snappin/Joanin. Space limitations will only permit discussion of two of these discourse modes.

Signification, or more commonly, *signifyin,* which can be rendered with or without the phonological and morpho-syntactical patterns of USEB, is a form of ritualized insult in which a speaker puts down, talks about, needles—signifies on—other speakers. In this communicative practice, the speaker deploys exaggeration, irony, and indirection as a way of saying something on two different levels at once. It is often used to send a message of social critique, a bit of social commentary on the actions or statements of someone who is in need of a wake-up call. When signifyin is done with verbal dexterity, it avoids the creation of social distance between speaker and audience because the rich humor makes you laugh to keep from crying. Like Malcolm X, who once began a speech with these words: "Mr. Moderator, Brother Lomax, Brothas and Sistas, friends and enemies." Now, you don't usually begin a speech by addressing your enemies. Thus, Malcolm's signifyin statement let his audience know that he knew inimical forces were in their midst. Or like one of the deacons at this traditional black church, where the preacher would

> **Signification, or more commonly, signifyin, is a form of ritualized insult in which a speaker puts down, talks about, needles —signifies on—other speakers.**

never deal with the problems and issues folk were facing on a daily basis. Rather, he was always preachin bout the pearly gates and how great thangs was gon be at dat home up in the sky. So one day this deacon said to the preacher, "Reb, you know, I got a home in Heaven, but I ain't homesick!"

Signifyin is engaged in by all age groups and by both males and females in the black community. It has the following characteristics: 1) indirection, circumlocution; 2) metaphorical-imagistic (images rooted in the everyday real world); 3) humorous, ironic; 4) rhythmic fluency; 5) teachy, but not preachy; 6) directed at person(s) present in the speech situation (signifiers do not talk behind your back); 7) punning, play on words; 8) introduction of the semantically or logically unexpected.

Types of Signification

There are two types of Signification. One type is leveled at a person's mother (and occasionally at other relatives). Traditionally, this first type was referred to as "The Dozens"/"playin The Dozens." The second type of signifyin is aimed at a person, action, or thing, either just for fun, or for corrective criticism. Today, the two types of Signification are being conflated under a more general form of discourse, referred to as "snappin."

> **Today, the two types of Signification are being conflated under a more general form of discourse, referred to as 'snappin.'**

To fully appreciate the skill and complexity of Signification, we shall analyze in some detail a conversational excerpt involving two Sistas in a group of several at a wedding shower:

Linda: Girl, what up with that head? [Referring to her friend's hairstyle]

Betty: Ask yo momma. [Laughter from all the Sistas on this conversational set.]

Linda: Oh, so you going there, huh? Well, I DID ask my momma. And she said, "Cain't you see that Betty look like her momma spit her out?" [Laughter from all, including Betty.]

Betty and Linda signify on each other. Instead of answering Linda's question directly, Betty decides to inform Linda that the condition of her hairstyle is none of Linda's business by responding with "Ask yo momma." The usual expectation in a conversation is that a speaker's question will be answered honestly and sincerely; thus Betty's unexpected indirection produces laughter from the listeners.

Speech act theory indicates that communication succeeds or fails as a result of the illocutionary, i.e., intended, and perlocutionary, i.e., received, effects of a message. The surface meaning of "yo momma" for those outside the USEB speech community is simply "your mother/mom." However, within the black speech community, the utterance immediately signals that an insult has been hurled. The intended and received meaning of *yo momma* is invective; the game of ritual insult begins with participants creating the most appropriate, humorous, spontaneous, creative, exaggerated/untrue retorts that they can come up with.

The source of the retort "Ask yo momma" probably stems from family patterns in which mothers are consulted ("asked") about all kinds of things, great or small. Fathers may even respond to their children's questions or requests by saying "Ask your mother." In USEB, the speaker does not intend the direct meaning "You should go and ask your mother about this situation." Rather, given the conversational context, the speaker is indirectly saying "Let the game of The Dozens begin." Linda clearly recognizes the entry into this game as indicated by her response, "Oh, so you going there, huh?" Unskilled players, lacking a spontaneous, apposite, humorous retort, would have let the conversation end at this point. However, Linda shows adeptness in playing the game. She regroups momentarily ("Oh, so you going there, huh?") and fires back skillfully. In fact, she "caps" (gloss: wins) this exchange with a more clever retort. Although Betty's use of the intragroup expression, ask *yo momma,* is humorous and sets up a challenge, it is formulaic, simplistic, and stylized. In this instance, it cannot, and does not, beat: "Well, I DID ask my momma and she said, cain't you see that Betty look like her momma spit her out" (Troutman-Robinson and Smitherman, 1997).

To speak Ebonics is to assume the cultural legacy of U.S. slave descendants of African origin.

Although the Rev. Jesse Jackson and Sista Maya Angelou came out in the national news and dissed the Oakland School Board's resolution, they are well versed in USEB. Twenty years ago, in my first major work on USEB, *Talkin and Testifyin,* I quoted both at length and lauded them as linguistic role models, who are adept at capitalizing on the forms of Black Language to convey profound political messages. Like Jesse who is down wit Signification: "Pimp, punk, prostitute, preacher, PhD—all the P's, you still in slavery!" Thus he conveys the message that all members of the African American community, regardless of their social status, are marginalized and disempowered, by virtue of U.S. historically institutionalized racism and skin color bias. (Jesse also uses copula absence here—"you still in slavery"—that has not been found in any of the dialects of British English that came over on the Mayflower, but that is used widely in the languages of West Africa.)

The Dozens

As mentioned above, The Dozens is one of several significant speech acts in USEB. This ritualized game of insult has analogues in West African communicative practices (see Smitherman, 1995, and the several references cited there). Also referred to as "snappin" by many members of the Hip-Hop Nation, The Dozens is like "Yo momma so dumb she thought a quarterback was a refund!"

Sista Maya Angelou is so bad she don't play The Dozens, she play The Thirteens! She uses this USEB discourse mode to critique the actions of blacks and whites.

Here how she do it:

> (The Thirteens Black):
> Your Momma took to shouting
> Your Poppa's gone to war,
> Your sister's in the streets
> Your brother's in the bar,
> The thirteens. Right On. . .
> And you, you make me sorry
> You out here by yourself,
> I'd call you something dirty,
> But there just ain't nothing left,
> cept
> The thirteens. Right On. . .
> (The Thirteens White):
> Your daughter wears a jock strap,
> Your son he wears a bra
> Your brother jonesed your cousin
> in the back seat of the car.
> The thirteens. Right On. . .
> Your money thinks you're something
> But if I'd learned to curse,
> I'd tell you what your name is
> But there just ain't nothing worse
> than
> The thirteens. Right On.
> —Angelou, 1971

African French psychiatrist Frantz Fanon taught that "every dialect, every language, is a way of thinking. To speak means to assume a culture." To speak Ebonics is to assume the cultural legacy of U.S. slave descendants of African origin. To speak Ebonics is to assert the power of this tradition in the quest to resolve the unfinished business of being African in America. While years of massive research (done in the 1960s and early '70s) on the language of this group (mostly by white scholars) did indeed debunk cognitive-linguistic deficiency theory, in its place arose social inadequacy theory.

Although the language was shown to be systematic and rule-governed, since it is not accepted by the white mainstream, difference became deficit all over again, and in the process, Africans in America suffered further dislocation. To speak (of/on/about) Ebonics, to consciously employ this terminology and conceptual framework, as those black scholars did back in 1973, and as the Oakland School Board has done a generation later, is to be bout the business of relocating African Americans to subject position. Large and in charge, as the Hip-Hoppers say, Ebonics, then and now, symbolizes a new way of talkin the walk about language and liberatory education for African Americans.

Dr. Geneva Smitherman is University Distinguished Professor of English at Michigan State University. A linguist and educational activist, she has been at the forefront of the struggle for language rights for over 25 years.

References

Angelou, M. (1971). *Just Give Me a Cool Drink of Water 'fore I Diiie.* New York: Random House.

Fanon, F. (1967). The Negro and language. In *Black Skin, White Masks.* New York: Grove Press.

Freire, P. (1985). *The Politics of Education: Culture, Power, and Liberation* (D. Macedo, trans.). Massachusetts: Bergin & Garvey Publishers Inc.

Smitherman, G. (1995). Introduction. In J. Percelay, S. Dweck, & M. Ivey, *Double Snaps.* New York: William Morrow.

Smitherman, G. (1986). *Talkin and Testifyin: The Language of Black America.* Detroit: Wayne State University Press.

Spears, A. K. (1982). The Black English Semi-Auxiliary *Come. Language,* 58(4), 850–872.

Troutman, D. & Smitherman, G. (1997). Discourse as Social Interaction. In T.A. van Dijk (ed.), *Discourse, Ethnicity, Culture, and Racism* (pp.144–180). London: Sage Publications.

Williams, R.L. (ed.) (1975). *Ebonics: The True Language of Black Folks* St. Louis: Institute of Black Studies.

Chapter Twenty-Two

EBONICS AND CULTURALLY RESPONSIVE INSTRUCTION

By Lisa Delpit

The "Ebonics Debate" has created much more heat than light for most of the country. For teachers trying to determine what implications there might be for classroom practice, enlightenment has been a completely nonexistent commodity. I have been asked often enough recently, "What do you think about Ebonics? Are you for it or against it?" My answer must be neither. I can be neither for Ebonics nor against Ebonics any more than I can be for or against air. It exists. It is the language spoken by many of our African American children. It is the language they heard as their mothers nursed them and changed their diapers and played peek-a-boo with them. It is the language through which they first encountered love, nurturance, and joy.

JEAN-CLAUDE LEJEUNE

On the other hand, most teachers of those African American children who have been least well served by educational systems believe that their students' life chances will be further hampered if they do not learn Standard English. In the stratified society in which we live, they are absolutely correct. Although having access to the politically mandated language form will not, by any means, guarantee economic success (witness the growing numbers of unemployed African Americans holding doctorates), not having access will almost certainly guarantee failure.

So what must teachers do? Should they spend their time relentlessly "correcting" their Ebonics-speaking children's language so that it might conform to what we have learned to refer to as Standard English? Despite good intentions, constant correction seldom has the desired effect. Such correction increases cognitive monitoring of speech, thereby making talking difficult. To illustrate, I have frequently taught a relatively simple new "dialect" to classes of preservice teachers. In this dialect, the phonetic element "iz" is added after the first consonant or consonant cluster in each syllable of a word. (Maybe becomes miz-ay-biz-ee and apple, iz-ap-piz-le.) After a bit of drill and practice, the students are asked to tell a partner in "iz" language why they decided to become teachers. Most only haltingly attempt a few words before lapsing into either silence or into Standard English.

> **So what must teachers do? Should they spend their time relentlessly 'correcting' their Ebonics-speaking children's language so that it might conform to what we have learned to refer to as Standard English?**

During a follow-up discussion, all students invariably speak of the impossibility of attempting to apply rules while trying to formulate and express a thought. Forcing speakers to monitor their language typically produces silence.

Correction may also affect students' attitudes toward their teachers. In a recent research project, middle school, inner-city students were interviewed about their attitudes toward their teachers and school. One young woman complained bitterly, "Mrs. ___ always be interrupting to make you 'talk correct' and stuff. She be butting into your conversations when you not even talking to her! She need to mind her own business." Clearly this student will be unlikely to either follow the teacher's directives or to want to imitate her speech style.

Group Identity

Issues of group identity may also affect students' oral production of a different dialect. Researcher Sharon Nelson-Barber, in a study of phonologic aspects of Pima Indian language, found that, in grades 1 through 3, the children's English most approximated the standard dialect of their teachers. But surprisingly, by 4th grade, when one might assume growing *competence* in standard forms, their language moved significantly toward the local dialect. These 4th graders had the competence to express themselves in a more standard form, but chose, consciously or unconsciously, to use the language of those in their local environments. The researcher believes that, by ages 8 or 9, these children became aware of their group membership and its importance to their well-being, and this realization was reflected in their language.[1] They may also have become increasingly aware of the schools' negative attitude toward their community and found it necessary—through choice of linguistic form—to decide with which camp to identify.

The linguistic form a student brings to school is intimately connected with loved ones, community, and personal identity.

What should teachers do about helping students acquire an additional oral form? First, they should recognize that the linguistic form a student brings to school is intimately connected with loved ones, community, and personal identity. To suggest that this form is "wrong" or, even worse, ignorant, is to suggest that something is wrong with the student and his or her family. To denigrate your language is, then, in African American terms, to "talk about your mama." Anyone who knows anything about African American culture knows the consequences of that speech act!

On the other hand, it is equally important to understand that students who do not have access to the politically popular dialect form in this country are less likely to succeed economically than their peers who do. How can both realities be embraced in classroom instruction?

It is possible and desirable to make the actual study of language diversity a part of the curriculum for all students. For younger children, discussions about the differences in the ways television characters from different cultural groups speak can provide a starting point. A collection of the many children's books written in the dialects of various cultural groups can also provide a wonderful basis for learning about linguistic diversity,[2] as can audiotaped stories narrated by individuals from different cultures, including taping books read by members of the children's home communities. Mrs. Pat, a teacher chronicled by Stanford University researcher Shirley Brice Heath, had her students become language "detectives," interviewing a variety of individuals and listening to the radio and television to discover the differences and similarities in the ways people talked.[3] Children can learn that there are many ways of saying the same thing, and that certain contexts suggest particular kinds of linguistic performances.

Some teachers have groups of students create bilingual dictionaries of their own language form and Standard English. Both the students and the teacher become engaged in identifying terms and deciding upon the best translations. This can be done as generational dictionaries, too, given the proliferation of "youth culture" terms growing out of the Ebonics-influenced tendency for the continual regeneration of vocabulary. Contrastive grammatical structures can be studied similarly, but, of course, as the Oakland policy suggests, teachers must be aware of the grammatical structure of Ebonics before they can launch into this complex study.

Other teachers have had students become involved with standard forms through various kinds of role play. For example, memorizing parts for drama productions will allow students to practice and "get the feel" of speaking Standard English while not under the threat of correction. A master teacher of African American children in Oakland, Carrie Secret, uses this technique and extends it so that students video their practice performances and self-critique them as to the appropriate use of Standard English. (But I must add that Carrie's use of drama and oration goes much beyond acquiring Standard English. She inspires pride and community connections that are truly wondrous to behold.) The use of self-critique of recorded forms may prove even more useful than I initially realized. California State University-Hayward professor Etta Hollins has reported that just by leaving a tape recorder on during an informal class period and playing it back with no comment, students began to code-switch—moving between Standard English and Ebonics—more effectively. It appears that they may have not realized which language form they were using until they heard themselves speak on tape.

> **Although most educators think of Black Language as primarily differing in grammar and syntax, there are other differences in oral language of which teachers should be aware in a multicultural context.**

Young students can create puppet shows or role-play cartoon characters—many "superheroes" speak almost hypercorrect standard English! Playing a role eliminates the possibility of implying that the child's language is inadequate and suggests, instead, that different language forms are appropriate in different contexts. Some other teachers in New York City have had their students produce a news show every day for the rest of the school. The students take on the personae of famous newscasters, keeping in character as they develop and read their news reports. Discussions ensue about whether Tom Brokaw would have said it that way, again taking the focus off the child's speech.

Although most educators think of Black Language as primarily differing in grammar and syntax, there are other differences in oral language of which teachers should be aware in a multicultural context, particularly in discourse style and language use. Harvard University researcher Sarah Michaels and other researchers identified differences in children's narratives at "sharing time."[4] They found that there was a tendency among young white children to tell "topic-centered" narratives—stories focused on one event—and a tendency among black youngsters, especially girls, to tell "episodic" narratives—stories that include shifting scenes and are typically longer. Although these differences are interesting in themselves, what is of greater significance is adults' responses to the differences. C. B. Cazden reports on a subsequent project in which a white adult was taped reading the oral narratives of black and white 1st graders, with all syntax dialectal markers removed.[5] Adults were asked to listen to the stories and comment about the children's likelihood of success in school. The researchers were surprised by the differential responses given by black and white adults.

Varying Reactions

In responding to the retelling of a black child's story, the white adults were uniformly negative, making such comments as "terrible story, incoherent" and not a story at all in the sense of describing something that happened." Asked to judge this child's academic competence, all of the white adults rated her below the children who told "topic-centered" stories. Most of these adults also predicted difficulties for this child's future school career, such as "This child might have trouble reading," that she exhibited "language problems that affect school achievement," and that "family problems" or "emotional problems" might hamper her academic progress.

The black adults had very different reactions. They found this child's story "well formed, easy to understand, and interesting, with lots of detail and description." Even though all five of these adults mentioned the "shifts" and "associations" or "nonlinear" quality of the story, they did not find these features distracting. Three of the black adults selected the story as the best of the five they had heard, and all but one judged the child as exceptionally bright, highly verbal, and successful in school.[6]

This is not a story about racism, but one about cultural familiarity. However, when differences in narrative style produce differences in interpretation of competence, the pedagogical implications are evident. If children who produce stories based in differing discourse styles are expected to have trouble reading, and viewed as having language, family, or emotional problems, as was the case with the informants quoted by Cazden, they are unlikely to be viewed as ready for the same challenging instruction awarded students whose language patterns more closely parallel the teacher's.

This is not a story about racism, but one about cultural familiarity.

Most teachers are particularly concerned about how speaking Ebonics might affect learning to read. There is little evidence that speaking another mutually intelligible language form, per se, negatively affects one's ability to learn to read.[7] For commonsensical proof, one need only reflect on nonstandard English-speaking Africans who, though enslaved, not only taught themselves to read English, but did so under threat of severe punishment or death. But children who speak Ebonics do have a more difficult time becoming proficient readers. Why? In part, appropriate instructional methodologies are frequently not adopted. There is ample evidence that children who do not come to school with knowledge about letters, sounds, and symbols need to experience some explicit instruction in these areas in order to become independent readers. Another explanation is that, where teachers' assessments of competence are influenced by the language children speak, teachers may develop low expectations for certain students and subsequently teach them less.[8] A third explanation rests in teachers' confusing the teaching of reading with the teaching of a new language form.

Reading researcher Patricia Cunningham found that teachers across the United States were more likely to correct reading miscues that were "dialect" related ("Here go a table" for "Here is a table") than those that were "nondialect" related ("Here is a dog" for "There is a dog").[9] Seventy-eight percent of the former types of miscues were corrected, compared with only 27 percent of the latter. She concludes that the teachers were acting out of ignorance, not realizing that "here go" and "here is" represent the same meaning in some black children's language.

In my observations of many classrooms, however, I have come to conclude that even when teachers recognize the similarity of meaning, they are likely to correct Ebonics-related miscues. Consider a typical example:

Text: Yesterday I washed my brother's clothes.
Student's Rendition: Yesterday I wash my bruvver close.

The subsequent exchange between student and teacher sounds something like this:

T: Wait, let's go back. What's that word again? {Points at "washed." }
S: Wash.
T: No. Look at it again. What letters do you see at the end? You see "e-d." Do you remember what we say when we see those letters on the end of the word?
S: "ed"
T: OK, but in this case we say washed. Can you say that?
S: Washed.
T: Good. Now read it again.
S: Yesterday I washed my bruvver. . .
T: Wait a minute, what's that word again? {Points to "brother." }
S: Bruvver.
T: No. Look at these letters in the middle. {Points to "brother." } Remember to read what you see. Do you remember how we say that sound? Put your tongue between your teeth and say "th". . .

The lesson continues in such a fashion, the teacher proceeding to correct the student's Ebonics-influenced pronunciations and grammar while ignoring that fact that the student had to have comprehended the sentence in order to translate it into her own language. Such instruction occurs daily and blocks reading development in a number of ways. First, because children become better readers by having the opportunity to read, the overcorrection exhibited in this lesson means that this child will be less likely to become a fluent reader than other children who are not interrupted so consistently. Second, a complete focus on code and pronunciation blocks children's understanding that reading is essentially a meaning-making process. This child, who understands the text, is led to believe that she is doing something wrong. She is encouraged to think of reading not as something you do to get a message, but something you pronounce. Third, constant corrections by the teacher are likely to cause this student and others like her to resist reading and to resent the teacher.

Language researcher Robert Berdan reports that, after observing the kind of teaching routine described above in a number of settings, he incorporated the teacher behaviors into a reading instruction exercise that he used with students in a college class.[10] He put together sundry rules from a number of American social and regional dialects to create what he called the "language of Atlantis." Students were then called upon to read aloud in this dialect they did not know. When they made errors he interrupted them, using some of the same statements/comments he had heard elementary school teachers routinely make to their students. He concludes:

> The results were rather shocking. By the time these PhD candidates in English or linguistics had read 10-20 words, I could make them sound totally illiterate. . . .The first thing that goes is sentence intonation: they sound like they are reading a list from the telephone book. Comment on their pronunciation a bit more, and they begin to subvocalize, rehearsing pronunciations for themselves before they dare to say them out loud. They begin to guess at pronunciations. . . . They switch letters around for no reason. They stumble; they repeat. In short, when I attack them for their failure to conform to my demands for Atlantis English pronunciations, they sound very much like the worst of the 2nd graders in any of the classrooms I have observed.
>
> They also begin to fidget. They wad up their papers, bite their fingernails, whisper, and some finally refuse to continue. They do all the things that children do while they are busily failing to learn to read.

The moral of this story is not to confuse learning a new language form with reading comprehension. To do so will only confuse the child, leading her away from those intuitive understandings about language that will promote reading development, and toward a school career of resistance and a lifetime of avoiding reading.

The moral of this story is not to confuse learning a new language form with reading comprehension.

Unlike unplanned oral language or public reading, writing lends itself to editing. While conversational talk is spontaneous and must be responsive to an immediate context, writing is a mediated process that may be written and rewritten any number of times before being introduced to public scrutiny. Consequently, writing is more amenable to rule application—one may first write freely to get one's thoughts down, and then edit to hone the message and apply specific spelling, syntactical, or punctuation rules. My college students who had such difficulty talking in the "iz" dialect, found writing it, with the rules displayed before them, a relatively easy task.

To conclude, the teacher's job is to provide access to the national "standard" as well as to understand the language the children speak sufficiently to celebrate its beauty. The verbal adroitness, the cogent and quick wit, the brilliant use of metaphor, the facility in rhythm and rhyme, evident in the language of Jesse Jackson, Whoopi Goldberg, Toni Morrison, Henry Louis Gates, Tupac Shakur, and Maya Angelou, as well as in that of many inner-city black students, may all be drawn upon to facilitate school learning. The teacher must know how to effectively teach reading and writing to students whose culture and language differ from that of the school, and must understand how and why students decide to add another language form to their repertoire. All we can do is provide students with access to additional language forms. Inevitably, each speaker will make his or her own decision about what to say in any context.

But I must end with a caveat that we keep in mind a simple truth: Despite our necessary efforts to provide access to Standard English, such access will not make any of our students more intelligent. It will not teach them math or science or geography—or, for that matter, compassion, courage, or responsibility. Let us not become so overly concerned with the language form that we ignore academic and moral content. Access to the standard language may be necessary, but it is definitely not sufficient to produce intelligent, competent caretakers of the future.

Lisa Delpit is the Felton G. Clark Distinguished Professor of Education at Southern University in Baton Rouge, Louisiana.

©1997 Lisa Delpit *Other People's Children* (New Press: 1995).

Endnotes

1. S. Nelson-Barber, "Phonologic Variations of Pima English," in R. St. Clair and W. Leap, (Eds.), *Language Renewal Among American Indian Tribes: Issues, Problems, and Prospects* (Rosslyn, VA: National Clearinghouse for Bilingual Education, 1982).
2. Some of these books include Lucille Clifton, *All Us Come Cross the Water* (New York: Holt, Rinehart, and Winston, 1973); Paul Green (aided by Abbe Abbott), *I Am Eskimo—Aknik My Name* (Juneau, AK: Alaska Northwest Publishing, 1959); Howard Jacobs and Jim Rice, *Once upon a Bayou* (New Orleans: Phideaux Publications, 1983); Tim Elder, *Santa's Cajun Christmas* Adventure (Baton Rouge, LA: Little Cajun Books, 1981); and a series of biographies produced by Yukon-Koyukkuk School District of Alaska and published by Hancock House Publishers in North Vancouver, British Columbia, Canada.
3. Shirley Brice Heath, *Ways with Words* (Cambridge, Eng.: Cambridge University Press, 1983).
4. S. Michaels and C. B. Cazden, "Teacher-Child Collaboration on Oral Preparation for Literacy," in B. Schieffer (Ed.), *Acquisition of Literacy: Ethnographic Perspectives* (Norwood, NJ: Ablex, 1986).
5. C. B. Cazden, *Classroom Discourse* (Portsmouth, NH: Heinemann, 1988).
6. Ibid.
7. R. Sims, "Dialect and Reading: Toward Redefining the Issues," in J. Langer and M. T. Smith-Burke (Eds.), *Reader Meets Author/Bridging the Gap* (Newark, DE: International Reading Association, 1982).
8. Ibid.
9. Patricia M. Cunningham, "Teachers' Correction Responses to Black-Dialect Miscues Which Are Nonmeaning-Changing," *Reading Research Quarterly* 12 (1976–77).
10. Robert Berdan, "Knowledge into Practice: Delivering Research to Teachers," in M. F. Whiteman (Ed.), *Reactions to Ann Arbor: Vernacular Black English and Education* (Arlington, VA: Center for Applied Linguistics, 1980).

Chapter Twenty-Three

KEEPERS OF THE SECOND THROAT

By Patricia Smith

"Keepers of the Second Throat" was originally delivered as the keynote address at the Urban Sites Network Conference of the National Writing Project, Portland, Ore., April 2010.

Let me introduce you to my mother, Annie Pearl Smith of Aliceville, Ala. In the 1950s, along with thousands of other apprehensive but determined Southerners, their eyes locked on the second incarnation of the North Star, she packed up her whole life and headed for the city, with its tenements, its promise, its rows of factories like open mouths feeding on hope. One day not too long ago, I called my mother, but she was too busy to talk to me. She seemed in a great hurry. When I asked her where she was going, she said, "I'm on my way to my English lesson."

MELANIE CERVANTES

My Mother Learns English

I.
Jittery emigrant at 64, my mother is learning English.
Pulling rubbery cinnamon-tinged hose to a roll beneath
her knees, sporting one swirling Baptist ski slope of a hat,
she rides the rattling elevated to a Windy City spire
and pulls back her gulp as the elevator hurtles heaven.
Then she's stiffly seated at a scarred oak table
across from a white, government-sanctioned savior
who has dedicated eight hours a week to straightening
afflicted black tongues. She guides my mother
patiently through lazy *ings* and *ers,* slowly scraping
her throat clean of the moist and raging infection
of Aliceville, Alabama. There are muttered apologies for
colored sounds. There is much beginning again.
I want to talk right before I die.
Want to stop saying 'ain't' and 'I done been'
like I ain't got no sense. I'm a grown woman.
I done lived too long to be stupid,
acting like I just got off the boat.
My mother
has never been
on a boat.
But 50 years ago, merely a million of her,
clutching strapped cases, *Jet's* Emmett Till issue,
and thick-peppered chicken wings in waxed bags,
stepped off hot rumbling buses at Northern depots
in Detroit, in Philly, in the bricked cornfield of Chicago.
Brushing stubborn scarlet dust from their shoes,
they said *We North now,* slinging it in backdoor syllable,
as if those three words were vessels big enough
to hold country folks' overwrought ideas of light.

II.

Back then, my mother thought it a modern miracle,
this new living in a box stacked upon other boxes,
where every flat surface reeked of Lysol and effort
and chubby roaches, cross-eyed with Raid,
dragged themselves across freshly washed dishes
and dropped dizzy from the ceiling into our Murphy beds,
our washtubs, our open steaming pots of collards.

Of course, there was a factory just two bus rides close,
a job that didn't involve white babies or bluing laundry,
where she worked in tense line with other dreamers:
Repeatedly. Repeatedly. Repeatedly. Repeatedly,
all those oily hot-combed heads drooping, no talking
as scarred brown hands romanced machines, just
the sound of doin' it right, and Juicy Fruit crackling.
A mere mindset away, there had to be a corner tavern
where dead bluesmen begged second chances from the juke,
and where mama, perched man-wary on a stool by the door,
could look like a Christian who was just leaving.
And on Sunday, at Pilgrim Rest Missionary Baptist Church,
she would pull on the pure white gloves of service
and wail to the rafters when the Holy Ghost's hot hand
grew itchy and insistent at the small of her back.
She was His child, finally loosed of that damnable Delta,
building herself anew in this land of sidewalks,
blue jukes, and sizzling fried perch in virgin-white boxes.
See her: All nap burned from her crown, one gold tooth
winking, soft hair riding her lip, blouses starched hard,
Orlon sweaters with smatterings of stitched roses,
A-line skirts the color of unleashed winter.

III.

My mother's voice is like homemade cornbread,
slathered with butter, full of places for heat to hide.
When she is pissed, it punches straight out
and clears the room. When she is scared,
it turns practical, matter-of-fact, like when she called
to say
They found your daddy this morning,
somebody shot him, he dead.
He ain't come to work this morning, I knowed
something was wrong.
When mama talks, the Southern swing of it
is wild with unexpected blooms,
like the fields she never told me about in Alabama.
Her rap is peppered with ain't gots and I done beens
and he be's just like mine is when I'm color among color.
During worship, talk becomes song. Her voice collapses
and loses all acquaintance with key, so of course,
it's my mother's fractured alto wailing above everyone—

uncaged, unapologetic and creaking toward heaven.
Now she wants to sound proper when she gets there.
A woman got some sense and future need to upright herself,
talk English instead of talking wrong.
It's strange, the precise rote of Annie Pearl's new mouth.
She slips sometimes, but is proud when she remembers
to shun dirt-crafted contractions and double negatives.
Sometimes I wonder what happened to the warm expanse
of the red dust woman, who arrived with a little sin
and all the good wrong words. I dream her breathless,
maybe leaning forward in her seat on the Greyhound.
I ain't never seen, she begins, grinning through the grime
at Chicago, city of huge shoulders, thief of tongues.

Chicago Stole My Mother's Yesterdays

Chicago not only stole my mother's tongue, it also stole all her yesterdays. From the moment her battered shoes touched new ground, she wanted Alabama gone, she wanted nothing more than to scrub the Delta from her skin, rid her voice of that ridiculous twang, pretend and then adopt a city sophistication. She thought her *ain't gonnas* and *shoulda dids* and *ain'ts* and *been done hads* signaled ignorance, backwoods, branded her as one of those old-time Negroes. Even years later, after she had married my father, raised a daughter and had to know that her corner was not a promised land but no more than an obscenity of brick, she continued her relentless scrubbing. "I want to talk right before I die," she said, each of her words irreparably Alabama even after she paid an articulate white woman to please fix the mistake of her throat.

And how did my mother's insistence on a blank slate affect me? She slams shut when I ask about the faces in curled-corner Polaroids, when I urge her to tell me what kind of girl she was, when I am curious about her mother, father, grandparents, schooling, baptism, about the steamy hamlet of Aliceville, the stores, schoolhouse, was she fast, was she sullen, did she have the gold tooth then, did she sing? Before her confounding sense of shame, her "Don't know why you wanna know about that nasty ol' down South stuff no way," I was robbed of a history that should have been mine as well as hers.

My husband, on the other hand, has diligently traced his huge raucous family back to the early 1800s. He has remarkably preserved portraits, marriage licenses, death certificates, farm inventory, a rusted scale from his grandfather's store, even a yellowed handkerchief that has been passed gently from hand to hand for more than 100 years. As we pore over the few faded and sun-stained photos my mother has reluctantly parted with, I sound like an impossibility, an orphan with a living parent.

That is my mother, I say, pointing to a teenage stranger with an unmistakable gap-toothed grin. But in every picture she is surrounded by ghosts. I say, "I don't know who that is . . . I don't know who that is," because my mother claims not to remember. In one shot, a ghost turned out to be an aunt I didn't know my mother had.

Right now, if I close my eyes and concentrate, I can't hear my mother's voice. I hear something that sounds like her, but it's a tortured hybrid of the voice she had and the one she wanted so much to have. I've told her story time and time again, and I hear other 50-year-old children tell the same stories of their parents, who spent whole lives trying to reshape their throats, to talk right instead of talking wrong, ashamed of the sound they made in the world.

> **I hear other 50-year-old children tell the same stories of their parents, who spent whole lives trying to reshape their throats, to talk right instead of talking wrong, ashamed of the sound they made in the world.**

How do we lose our own voices? My mother spent her entire life telling me how wrong I was, how my nose was too broad, my hair too crinkled, my skin—Lord, I wish you could be light like cream, like your cousin Demetria. Don't tell anyone your stories, she said, your shameful stories of a mama from Alabama, a daddy from Arkansas, an apartment where roaches dropped from the ceiling into your bed and mice got trapped in the stove, a neighborhood burned down by its own folks right after the riots when that nice Dr. King got killed. Don't tell anyone your stories, stories you should keep to yourself, stories of how your mama and daddy both work in a candy factory, how your auntie lives in those projects, how the apartment we live in's been broken into three times. Don't tell how you live on the West Side, the side everybody tells you to stay away from, and how the school you go to is one of the worst schools in the whole city. And for goodness' sake girl, talk right. If you want to get out of here, ever, you got to talk like white people, and you got to talk about things white people want to hear.

In other words, I was to become a clean, colorless slate, scrubbed of my own history, a slate where people could write my life any way they wanted—any beginning, any middle, any outcome.

How do we lose our own voices, how do we hand our stories over to other people to tell?

The Second Throat

Follow me now to a 6th-grade classroom at Lillie C. Evans Elementary School in Dade County, Liberty City, Miami. For 10 years, I traveled from my home to teach for two weeks. I remember my first day, bounding into the classroom, full of enthusiasm: "I'm here to teach you poetry!" I faced a room of fallen faces: "That's good, but how can you make our lives better?"

I was shocked to learn that these 10- and 11-year-olds had already been told that their voices were not legitimate voices. Look where you live, they'd been told. Look who your mama is, how your daddy in jail. Look how you've lived your whole life in Miami and nobody's ever bothered to take you to see the ocean. Look at all those red marks on your papers, all those bad grades on your report card. Look at that house where you live, how there's no locks on the doors. Look how you've been written off already. In the morning, my kids would come in buzzing about the shots they heard the night before and if anybody knew what had happened, who'd gotten shot. They came in talking gang signs and beatdowns and who went crazy in church with the Holy Ghost and whose brother was locked up now. But when they sat down to write, it was as if they shed their skins and their stories. They'd sit looking blankly at me, their shoulders sagging from sudden shame and the weight of the world: "I can't spell good. I ain't got good handwriting. And Miss Smith, I ain't got nothing to write about."

I spent all my time introducing them to the idea of the second throat. First of all, all your stories are yours. I don't care that you've misspelled this word, that you're using double negatives, and I'll figure out that bad handwriting. What matters is the power that flows through you when you pick up a pen. And you can take any story, even stories that wear on your nerves and sag your shoulders, you can take those stories and you can turn them to triumph. You can pick up a pen and make your whole life make sense. The idea that you can take control of how events affect you—and that includes the mama on drugs, the locked-up brother—the idea that you can process that life through language and come out on the other side a better person, a smarter kid, one who doesn't get beat down by circumstance, but learns how to learn from it.

And they wait. They wait for you. They wait for me. The quiet bespectacled boy with his mind tangled in math is waiting for you. That girl who dressed two sizes too blue is waiting for you. The child who never lifts his eyes is really looking at you, through you, and she is waiting. That tall lanky boy who lives to make everyone laugh is waiting for you. That one white child in a sea of black is waiting for you. That one black child in a sea of white is waiting for you. The one who takes the bus in from the suburbs is waiting for you. Not just the children with the hard, untellable stories, the stories they hold shamed and close to their chests, but any child with a yesterday is looking for a way to sing tomorrow. They wait for you to open another door beyond verb and adjective, punctuation and equation, beyond memorized fact and pop quiz and line and intersection and angle. They wait for you to open a door that leads to their own lives.

> **Any child with a yesterday is looking for a way to sing tomorrow.**

So there is hope. Every single time I walk into a classroom. I tell my story, the story of my parents in the South, the story of growing up in a place that was expected to defeat me. I celebrate every single word a child says, every movement of their pen on paper, and I'm mesmerized when those stories begin to emerge. I stop what I'm doing and I listen. We've got to teach that every utterance, every story is legitimate, that they exist to help you process your own life, to help you move your own life forward, not to complete anyone else's picture of you. Never relinquish control of your own life and the stories that have formed you. Write them down and read them to yourselves if no one else wants to hear. My mother used to say, "Ain't nobody trying to hear that nonsense." In the beginning, it doesn't matter if anyone wants to hear. What matters is what you have to say.

I've told you about my mother, about the tragedy of a voice lost, but now let me tell you about my daddy.

It Began with My Father

Grizzled and slight, flasher of a marquee gold tooth, Otis Douglas Smith was Arkansas grit suddenly sporting city clothes. Also part of the Great Migration of blacks from the South to Northern cities in the early 1950s, he found himself not in the urban mecca he'd imagined, but in a cramped tenement apartment on Chicago's West Side. There he attempted to craft a life alongside the bag boys, day laborers, housekeepers, and cooks who dreamed the city's wide, unreachable dream.

Many of those urban refugees struggled to fit, but my father never really adopted the no-nonsense-now rhythm of the city. He never handed his story over. There was too much of the storyteller in him, too much unleashed Southern song still waiting for the open air. From the earliest days I can recall, my place was on his lap, touching a hand to his stubbled cheek and listening to his growled narrative, mysterious whispers, and wide-open laughter.

Because of him, I grew to think of the world in terms of the stories it could tell. From my father's moonlit tales of steaming Delta magic to the sweet slow songs of Smokey Robinson, I became addicted to unfolding drama, winding narrative threads, the lyricism of simple words. I believed that we all lived in the midst of an ongoing adventure that begged for voice. In my quest for that voice, I found poetry.

Poetry was the undercurrent of every story I heard and read. It was the essence, the bones, and the pulse. I could think of no better way to communicate than with a poem, where pretense is stripped away, leaving only what is beautiful and vital.

Poetry became the way I processed the world. In neon-washed bars, community centers, and bookstores, I breathed out necessary breath, taking the stage and sharing stanzas with strangers, anxious wordsmiths who were also bag boys, day laborers, housekeepers, and cooks. I loved the urgency of their voices and the way they sparked urgency in mine.

Like you and you and you, I'm a storyteller— and so are your children.

So, like you and you and you, I'm a storyteller—and so are your children. I've realized that we only get one life, and I've decided to own mine completely, to celebrate and mourn and lash out and question and believe and argue and explore and love and dismiss and fight on the page, at the front of a classroom, on the stage. No one, no one is authorized to tell that story but you. And if there is shame in that story, you own that shame and you turn it into lesson. If there is darkness in your story, you write toward the light. If there are words you don't want anyone else to hear, you hold those words close. On the other hand, if there is joy threaded throughout that story, you sing it loud enough to rock the rafters. If there is triumph, and there will always be, in some measure, you pull everyone within the sound of your voice, within shouting distance of the page, into that circle of light.

A teacher standing at the front of a classroom is a little bit of religion. It doesn't matter if you are in Portland or Philadelphia or Kentucky or Indianapolis, whether you are overpaid or overlooked, whether your students soar thru their AP classes or stumble through single-syllable words, whether your school is five wings or five stories, it doesn't matter if the buildings are drab and fallen and surrounded by a dying neighborhood or glittering and expansive enough to brag its own ZIP code, it doesn't matter whether your students are colored like snow or sand or soil. For every minute you stand before them, you are the beacon, the whole of possibility, the keeper of the second throat. Like it or not, you are often the first chapter in the story they're writing with their lives. Their parents taught them to speak. Now you must teach them to speak aloud, to keep on speaking, to scream and to sing.

I am Patricia Ann Smith, the daughter of Annie Pearl Smith and Otis Douglas Smith. I am the story they wrote.

Stop. Say your name aloud.

Now find a way to tell your story. And find a way to introduce all those children who wait for you to that second throat.

Patricia Smith's fifth book of poetry, Blood Dazzler *(Coffee House Press, 2008), was a National Book Award finalist. Smith is a four-time individual champion of the national Poetry Slam contest. She appeared in the film* SlamNation *and on the HBO series* Def Poetry Jam. *A selection of her poetry was produced as a one-woman play by Nobel laureate Derek Walcott.*

Chapter Twenty-Four

DEFENDING BILINGUAL EDUCATION

By Kelley Dawson Salas

"Teacher, this is crazy!"

After six days straight of standardized testing in English, her second language, Ana lost it. She laughed out loud and the rest of us laughed with her. As her 4th-grade teacher, I was expected to keep order and continue administering the test (which I did), but I could see where she was coming from. Perhaps it was the rigorous schedule: seven days of testing for three hours each morning. Perhaps it was the tedious format: Listen as each test item is read aloud twice in English and twice in Spanish, then wait for all students to mark an answer, then move on to the next test item. Perhaps it was the random nature of some of the questions.

ALAIN PILON

Whatever it was, Ana knew it didn't make sense. That moment has become a metaphor to me. There are more English language learners than ever in U.S. schools, and yet the policies that affect their schooling make less and less sense.

> **There are more English language learners than ever in U.S. schools, and yet the policies that affect their schooling make less and less sense.**

About 10 percent of all U.S. students—more than 5 million children—are English language learners. This represents a tremendous resource and opportunity. If schools serve English language learners well, at least 10 percent of U.S. students can have highly valued skills: fluency in more than one language and an ability to work with diverse groups of people. If communities give English-speaking students the opportunity to learn side by side with students who speak other languages, an even greater number of students can learn these skills.

But there are obstacles. Although research shows that bilingual education works, top-down policies increasingly push English-only education. To make matters worse, schools serving immigrants are some of the most segregated, understaffed, underresourced schools in the country.

In our Winter 2002/03 editorial, *Rethinking Schools* wrote that "bilingual education is a human and civil right." I think all teachers should defend this right and demand equal educational opportunities for English language learners. It's not just about immigrant students: U.S. society as a whole will benefit greatly when all students have access to bilingual education, and when schools serve English language learners well.

Bilingual Education Works

Research shows that bilingual education is effective with English learners, both in helping them learn English and in supporting academic achievement in the content areas.

A synthesis of research recently published by Cambridge University Press showed that English learners do better in school when they participate in programs that are designed to help them learn English. The review also found that "almost all evaluations of K–12 students show that students who have been educated in bilingual classrooms, particularly in long-term programs that aim for a high level of bilingualism, do as well as or better on standardized tests than students in comparison groups of English-learners in English-only programs."

A synthesis of studies on language-minority students' academic achievement published in 1992 by Virginia Collier found that students do better academically in their second language when they have more instruction in their primary language, combined with balanced support in the second language.

I have seen this in action at the two-way immersion school where I teach 4th grade. Spanish-dominant students who develop good literacy skills in Spanish have a far easier time in 3rd and 4th grade when they begin to read, write, and do academic work in English. Likewise, students who struggle to read and write in Spanish do not transition easily to English reading, and they tend to lag behind in English content-area instruction. High-quality Spanish language instruction starting in kindergarten is essential. Without it, Spanish-dominant students do not get a fair chance to develop good literacy and academic skills in their first or second language.

More Need, Less Bilingual Instruction

Despite the evidence that properly implemented bilingual education works for English language learners, English learners are being pushed into English-only programs or getting less instruction in their primary languages.

Voters in three states (California, 1998; Arizona, 2000; Massachusetts, 2002) have passed referenda mandating "English-only" education and outlawing bilingual instruction. (Colorado defeated a similar referendum in 2002.) Although many parents in these states hoped to get waivers so their children could continue bilingual education, they had more luck in some places than others.

> **Despite the evidence that properly implemented bilingual education works for English language learners, English learners are being pushed into English-only programs or getting less instruction in their primary languages.**

In Arizona, one-third of English language learners were enrolled in bilingual education before voters passed Proposition 203 in 2000. Although Proposition 203 allowed waivers, the state's superintendent of public instruction insisted on a strict interpretation of the law that denied waivers to most parents. Eventually almost all of Arizona's bilingual programs were discontinued; the National Association for Bilingual Education noted in October of 2005 that "bilingual education is simply no longer available" to English language learners in Arizona.

Prior to the passage of Question 2 in Massachusetts in 2002, 23 percent of that state's roughly 50,000 English learners were enrolled in bilingual education. By 2005, only about 5 percent were in bilingual programs. Under the law it is easier for children older than 10 to get waivers, so middle and high school students are more likely to participate in bilingual education than elementary students. Students do not need a waiver to participate in two-way bilingual programs; in 2005 there were 822 students enrolled in two-way bilingual programs.

Resistance Saves Some Programs

In California, the first state to pass an English-only referendum, some schools were able to continue offering bilingual education. The law required all districts to inform parents of their option to continue in bilingual education by signing a waiver; some schools and districts succeeded in getting a very high percentage of waivers and continuing their programs. But by 1999, researchers at the University of California Linguistic Minority Research Institute found that only 12 percent of English learners were in bilingual programs, compared to 29 percent before the law changed.

Even in places where bilingual education is still permitted, top-down pressures threaten to weaken it.

Researchers also found that districts that had a strong commitment to primary language programs were able to hold on to those programs after Proposition 227 passed, while districts that were "not especially supportive of primary language programs prior to 1998" were more likely to do away with primary language instruction altogether.

The 'English-HURRY!' Approach

Even in places where bilingual education is still permitted (by law or by waiver), top-down pressures threaten to weaken it. Since the passage of No Child Left Behind, standardized testing in English has put pressure on schools to teach English earlier and to do it faster.

Bilingual education is still legal in Wisconsin, where I teach. Milwaukee has a districtwide developmental bilingual (also called "late-exit") program. This means that children learn to read and write first in their primary language (in our case, Spanish), and in the early grades they are taught all subjects in Spanish. Once they have gained a strong footing in Spanish, they transition to English and start to receive a larger percentage of literacy and content area instruction in English. Even after making the transition to English, students can continue to get a significant portion of their literacy and content area instruction in Spanish for as many years as they choose to stay in the bilingual program.

But since the passage of NCLB, our district's developmental bilingual program has not fared as well as one might hope. In 2002, Wisconsin did away with all of its Spanish-language standardized tests and began requiring almost all English language learners to take standardized tests in English starting in 3rd grade. (Wisconsin could have purchased and administered tests in Spanish, but chose not to do so because of the cost.)

The English tests have changed classroom instruction for bilingual students in our district. District administrators, many principals, and lots of teachers have bought into the idea that kids must learn English sooner because they must score well on English language tests. "Hurry up and teach kids to read in English! They've got to be ready to take the 3rd-grade reading test in English! They've got to be ready to take the 4th-grade WKCE (Wisconsin Knowledge Concepts Examination) in English!" Suddenly a lot of what we know about second-language acquisition has fallen by the wayside in the scramble to get kids to do well on tests so we can keep schools off the list.

At my school, the year after the law changed, I was part of a team of teachers and administrators that met for months to decide how to respond to the reality that our Spanish-dominant students would be tested in English starting in 3rd grade. We ultimately decided to transition children to English reading in the 2nd and 3rd grades. (We had previously transitioned students to reading in their second language at the end of 3rd grade and beginning of 4th grade.) Other schools in my district have also pushed the transition to English to earlier grades. Still others have reduced primary language instruction in the early grades to make room for direct instruction in English reading (for Spanish-speaking students) as early as 1st grade.

Many administrators and some teachers dismiss concerns with a common refrain: 'This is what we have to do to get them ready for the tests.'

There has been little public discussion about these changes, which contradict the research because they decrease the amount of primary-language instruction and allow less time for students to establish solid literacy skills in their primary language before beginning the transition to second-language literacy. Instead of engaging in discussion about these changes, many administrators and some teachers dismiss concerns with a common refrain: "This is what we have to do to get them ready for the tests."

In a report called "The Initial Impact of Proposition 227 on the Instruction of English Learners," researchers in California described how bilingual instruction changed when English-only testing began:

> English-only testing was observed to have an extraordinary effect on English learner instruction, causing teachers to leapfrog much of the normal literacy instruction and go directly to English word recognition or phonics, bereft of meaning or context. Teachers also worried greatly that if they spent time orienting the children to broader literacy activities like storytelling, story sequencing activities, reading for meaning, or writing and vocabulary development in the primary language, that their students would not be gaining the skills that would be tested on the standardized test in English. They feared that this could result in the school and the students suffering sanctions imposed by the law.
>
> Thus, even in the classrooms that had been designated as bilingual, and where principals often contended that little had changed, teachers revealed that their teaching practices had indeed changed substantially and that their students were receiving much less literacy instruction in their primary language.

Ironically, NCLB does not specify what language students should be taught in, nor does it even require that students be tested in English. It specifies that students must be tested "in a valid and reliable manner," and that they should be given "reasonable accommodations," including "to the extent practicable, assessments in the language and form most likely to yield accurate data on what such students know and can do."

But states have chosen to implement the law in a variety of ways. Most states test students exclusively in English. Some states give English learners extra time to take the test. Another common accommodation is to translate or simplify the English on portions of the test. The state of California allows no accommodations for students who have been in the California schools for one year. Ten California districts have filed suit claiming this violates the NCLB's provision that students be tested in a valid and reliable manner with reasonable accommodations.

Segregation and Unequal Resources

These recent changes in language and testing policies are making a bad situation worse for English language learners, many of whom were already experiencing some of the worst educational conditions in the country.

A study published by the Urban Institute noted that the majority of English language learners are "segregated in schools serving primarily ELL and immigrant children." The study found that these "high-LEP" schools (defined as schools where Limited English Proficient students comprise 23.5 percent or more of the student body) tend to be large and urban, with a student body that is largely minority (77 percent) and largely poor (72 percent). In addition, "high-LEP schools face more difficulties filling teaching vacancies and are more likely to rely on unqualified and substitute teachers," and teachers are "more likely to have provisional, emergency, or temporary certification than are those in other schools."

These recent changes in language and testing policies are making a bad situation worse for English language learners, many of whom were already experiencing some of the worst educational conditions in the country.

Researchers at the University of California, Davis in 2003 found similar disadvantages for the schooling of English language learners, saying they faced "intense segregation into schools and classrooms that place [English learners] at particularly high risk for educational failure."

Advocacy for Immigrants

As conditions and policies worsen for English learners, there is an urgent need for teachers, families, and language-minority communities to speak up in favor of immigrant students and bilingual education.

It is important for English learners to succeed academically and to become bilingual, especially now. Many U.S. cities have majority-minority populations, and more and more people in the United States speak languages other than English. To be able to successfully live in and lead this diverse society, people need to learn how to value and accept others. All children need to learn how to communicate with people whose language and culture are different from their own.

These abilities are highly valued, and many teenagers and adults spend years trying to develop them. Children who are raised from birth speaking a language other than English have a unique opportunity to cultivate these abilities from a young age. Our schools must help them seize that opportunity.

Kelley Dawson Salas, a former elementary teacher in Milwaukee Public Schools, is currently the communications and publications director for the Milwaukee Teachers Education Association.

Chapter Twenty-Five

BILINGUAL EDUCATION WORKS

By Stephen Krashen

Arizona's passage of Proposition 203 aimed at dismantling bilingual education confirms, once again, that a substantial percentage of voters is unaware of the facts about bilingual education. Specifically, much of the public is unaware that bilingual education is very good for English language development.

In my book *Condemned Without a Trial: Bogus Arguments Against Bilingual Education*, I analyze five myths surrounding bilingual education. Below I address two myths that played a particularly important role in the Arizona vote, and look at some of the confusion over media reports on bilingual education, especially in California.

JEAN-CLAUDE LEJEUNE

Myth No. 1: Bilingual Education Keeps Students from Learning English

Saying that educating children in their primary language will help them learn English seems to defy common sense for many people. But providing education in the first language can greatly help second language development. It does this in two ways.

First, when teachers provide students with solid subject matter in the first language, it gives the students knowledge. This knowledge helps make the English children hear and read much more comprehensible.

A child who speaks little English (referred to as "a limited English proficient student") who is knowledgeable about history, thanks to education in the first language, will understand more in a history class taught in English than a limited English proficient child without this knowledge. The child with a background in history will learn more history, and will acquire more English, because the English heard in class will be more comprehensible.

Second, developing literacy in the first language is a shortcut to literacy in the second language. It is easier to learn to read in a language you understand; once you can read in one language, this knowledge transfers rapidly to any other language you learn to read. Once you can read, you can read.

In my interpretation of the research, programs that are set up correctly, that is, that supply background information in the primary language and that provide literacy in the primary language, and, of course, also provide instruction in the second language, typically succeed in teaching the second language.

English in these programs is introduced at the very beginning, in the form of English as a Second Language (ESL) classes. As children acquire more English, and learn some academics through the first language, subject matter is introduced in English gradually, but as soon as it can be made comprehensible.

Controlled studies consistently show that children in such properly organized bilingual classes acquire at least as much English as those in all-English classes and usually acquire more (Willig, 1985; Krashen, 1996). A review of this research was done by Prof. Jay Greene of the University of Texas at Austin, using statistical tools far more precise than those used in previous reviews. Greene concluded that the use of the native language in instructing limited English proficient children has "moderate beneficial effects" and that "efforts to eliminate the use of the native language in instruction . . . harm children by denying them access to beneficial approaches" (Greene, 1997).

Myth No. 2: Bilingual Education Failed in California

A great deal of confusion was caused by newspaper articles that reported that after Proposition 227 passed in California, severely restricting bilingual education, test scores went up. This was widely interpreted as a victory for all-English immersion and a defeat for bilingual education. But this conclusion is incorrect.

First, test scores always go up when a new test is introduced (Linn, Graue, and Sanders, 1990). In California, the SAT9 was introduced at the same time Proposition 227 passed. Linn et al. note that scores increase about 1.5 to 2 points per year after a new test is introduced. Thus, test score inflation accounts for about half of the increase in grades 2 and 3 in the SAT9 reading test since 1998, and all of the increase in grades 4 through 7. It also suggests that SAT9 reading scores in California have actually declined slightly in grades 8 through 11.

Test scores increase for a variety of reasons, and not all of them are related to increased learning. Among the bogus means of increasing test scores are extensive training in test-taking skills and selective testing, i.e., excluding low-scoring children from taking the test. Asimov (2000) suggests that selective testing may have occurred in California. She reported that for some schools in the San Francisco area SAT9 test scores increased in those schools in which the number of students taking the test declined. According to Asimov, "questionable pairings" appeared in 22 Bay Area school districts. Such bogus means are especially likely to be used when strong carrots (financial rewards for teachers if test scores go up) and sticks (threats of school closure if scores go down) are instituted by the state, as they are in California.

Second, there is no evidence linking test score increases to dropping bilingual education. Stanford professor Kenji Hakuta and his associates found, in fact, that test scores rose in districts in California that kept bilingual education, as well as in districts that never had bilingual education (Orr, Butler, Bousquet, and Hakuta, 2000; Hakuta, 2000). Ironically, in the same state that voted to dismantle bilingual education, Arizona, limited English proficient students in bilingual education have outscored those in all-English programs on tests of English reading for the last three years (Crawford, 2000).

A major problem is that nearly all the media focus had been on one district in California—Oceanside. After Proposition 227 passed in 1998, Oceanside dropped bilingual education, enthusiastically embraced English immersion, and test scores went up. But Hakuta and his associates have shown that gains for Oceanside's English learners were similar to gains made in many California schools that retained bilingual education.

There is no evidence linking test score increases to dropping bilingual education.

In addition, the bilingual program that Oceanside dropped was a poor one. In an article in the Sept. 2, 2000, *Washington Post,* Oceanside superintendent Ken Noonan confirmed that Oceanside's "bilingual" program taught only in Spanish until grades 5 or 6. It was therefore not a bilingual program, but a monolingual Spanish program. As noted above, properly organized bilingual programs introduce English the first day, and teach subject matter in English as soon as it can be made comprehensible. An article, Oct. 5, 2000, in the *San Diego Union-Tribune* confirmed suspicions that Oceanside's pre-Proposition 227 efforts were dismal. Before 227, "a lot of students (at Laurel Elementary School) didn't even have books," the article noted (Parnet, 2000).

Controversy in New York

Similar controversy has arisen over recent reports from New York City. The New York Board of Education issued a report on the progress of English language learners that has been interpreted by many as evidence against bilingual education. A casual look appears to show that English-only has the edge: According to the report, for those entering in kindergarten, 84 percent of those in English-only "exited" (acquired enough English to enter the mainstream) within three years, while 73 percent of those in bilingual education did so.

One cannot conclude from these results that bilingual education did worse than English-only. As the authors of the study repeatedly note, there was no control for confounding factors. Most important is the effect of poverty. Students in bilingual education are more likely to be of lower socioeconomic status than students in English-only programs (NCES, 1993). This tendency has been confirmed for New York City by Luis Reyes, a former member of the board of education in New York.

In commenting on a 1994 report from New York City, Reyes noted that "there were a number of middle-class students in the ESL program who came from countries that were more developed . . . kids in the bilingual program came from where they hadn't had full schooling (Hennelly, 1995).

Children who come to the United States with more education in their home country have several important advantages. In addition to having basic food, housing, and health needs adequately met, they live in a more print-rich environment, which has a tremendous impact on school success (Krashen, 1993; McQuillan, 1998). Also, many older children from privileged backgrounds have actually had "de facto" bilingual education, that is, substantial literacy development and subject matter learning in their own language before arriving in the United States. Interestingly, the board of education also found that those who entered with greater competence in their first language exited more quickly than those with less. This is strong evidence for the positive impact of first language development.

It is also interesting to compare the results of the 1994 study and the recent report: For those entering at kindergarten in 1994, 79 percent of all English-only students were exited after three years. In the recent report, it is 84 percent. In 1994, for bilingual education, 42 percent were exited after three years. In the recent report, it is 73 percent. This is an amazing improvement, and is counter to claims that children typically "languish" in bilingual programs for years.

Public Opinion

Surveys consistently reveal strong support for the use of the primary language in school (Krashen, 1996, 1999). The research by Fay Shin of California State University, Stanislaus is particularly informative. Shin did not ask people if they supported bilingual education; instead, she asked about the underlying principles. For instance, she asked whether people thought "developing literacy through the first language facilitates literacy development in English" and whether "learning subject matter through the first language helps make subject matter study in English more comprehensible." Results were encouraging; these principles apparently make good sense. Following are some of the results of Shin's surveys:

Developing literacy through the first language facilitates literacy development in English.

Percent agreement:
Hispanic parents = 53 percent (Shin and Gribbons, 1996);
Korean parents = 88 percent (Shin and Kim, 1996);
Hmong parents = 52 percent (Shin and Lee, 1996);
Administrators = 74 percent (Shin, Anton, and Krashen, 1999);
Teachers = 74 percent (Shin and Krashen, 1996).

Learning subject matter through the first language makes subject matter study in English more comprehensible.

Percent agreement:
Hispanic parents = 34 percent (33 percent were "not sure") (Shin and Gribbons, 1996);
Korean parents = 47 percent (Shin and Kim, 1996);
Hmong parents = 60 percent (Shin and Lee, 1996);
Vietnamese parents = 64 percent (Young and Tran, 1999);
Administrators = 78 percent (Shin, Anton, and Krashen, 1999);
Teachers = 70 percent (Shin and Krashen, 1996).

It is important to note that Shin's subjects were not recent graduates of language education programs, or bilingual teachers.

What these results show is that people agree with the principles underlying bilingual education; the problem seems to be that they are not aware that bilingual education is based on these principles.

Of course, English language development is not the only goal of bilingual education. A second worthy goal is the continuing development of the first language. Research confirms that continuing development of the first language has a positive influence on cognitive development, has practical advantages, and promotes a healthy sense of biculturalism (see, for example, Krashen, Tse, and McQuillan, 1998). But many people still think that the bilingual education "debate" is between rational people who think that children should learn English and irrational fanatics who think children should be prevented from learning English.

If the antibilingual education movement is to be stopped, this misunderstanding needs to be corrected immediately. We need to better get out the message that bilingual educators are deeply concerned about English language development and that properly organized bilingual education programs are very helpful for English language development.

Stephen Krashen is best known for developing the first comprehensive theory of second language acquisition, introducing the concept of sheltered subject matter teaching, and as the co-inventor of the Natural Approach. He has contributed to theory and application in the areas of bilingual education and reading.

References

Asimov, N. (July 22, 2000). Test Scores Up, Test-Takers Down: Link Between Participation, Improvement on School Exam Prompts Concern. *San Francisco Chronicle.*

Crawford, J. (2000). Stanford 9 Scores Show a Consistent Edge for Bilingual Education.

Greene, J. (1997). A Meta-Analysis of the Rossell and Baker Review of Bilingual Education Research. *Bilingual Research Journal* 21(3): 103–122.

Hakuta, K. (2000). Points on SAT-9 Performance and Proposition 227. http://www.stanford.edu/~hakuta/www/research/SAT9/SAT9_2000/ analysis2000.html

Hennelly, R. (1995). NYC Bilingual Study Clarified. *Multicultural Newsletter,* People's Publishing Group International.

Krashen, S. (1993). *The Power of Reading.* Englewood, CO: Libraries Unlimited.

Krashen, S. (1996). *Under Attack: The Case Against Bilingual Education.* Culver City, CA: Language Education Associates.

Krashen, S. (1998). *Condemned Without a Trial: Bogus Arguments Against Bilingual Education.* Portsmouth, NH: Heinemann.

Krashen, S. & Biber, D. (1988). *On Course: California's Success in Bilingual Education.* Los Angeles: California Association for Bilingual Education.

Krashen, S., Tse, L., & McQuillan, J. (Eds.) (1998). *Heritage Language Development.* Culver City, CA: Language Education Associates.

Linn, R., Graue, E., & Sanders, N. (1990). Comparing State and District Test Results to National Norms: The Validity of Claims That 'Everyone Is Above Average.' *Educational Measurement: Issues and Practice* 9: 5–13.

Lisi, P. & Chinn, P. Editorial. *Multicultural Perspectives,* Education Association, Maywood, NJ. 2, 2:1-2.

McQuillan, J. (1998). *The Literacy Crisis: False Claims and Real Solutions.* Portsmouth, NH: Heinemann. New York City Board of Education. (2000). ELL Subcommittee Research Studies Progress Report. New York: Board of Education of the City of New York.

Orr, J., Butler, Y., Bousquet, M., & Hakuta, K. (2000). What Can We Learn About the Impact of Proposition 227 from SAT9 Scores? http://www.stanford.edu/~hakuta/www/archives/syllabi/SAT9/SAT9_ 2000/index.htm

Parnet, S. (October 6, 2000). Test-Score Gains Fill Schools with Pride. *San Diego Union-Tribune.*

Shin, F. & Kim, S. (1998). Korean Parent Perceptions and Attitudes of Bilingual Education. In R. Endo, C. Park, J. Tsuchida, and A. Abbayani (Eds.) *Current Issues in Asian and Pacific American Education.* Covina, CA: Pacific Asian Press.

Shin, F. & Gribbons, B. (1996). Hispanic Parent Perceptions and Attitudes of Bilingual Education. *The Journal of Mexican American Educators,* pp. 16-22.

Shin, F., & Lee, B. 1996. Hmong Parents: What Do they Think About Bilingual Education? *Pacific Educational Research Journal,* 8: 65–71.

Shin, F., Anton, M. & Krashen, S. (1999). K-12 Administrators' Views on Bilingual Education. *NABE News* 22(8): 11-12, 29.

Young, R. & Tran, M. (1999). Vietnamese Parent Attitudes Toward Bilingual Education. *Bilingual Research Journal* 23 (2, 3): 225–233.

Chapter Twenty-Six

RAISING CHILDREN'S CULTURAL VOICES

By Berta Rosa Berriz

How can teachers create a learning environment that honors the diverse family cultures of students within a racist society? Further, how can teachers develop literacy in two languages within a standards-driven curriculum that dictates what each student needs to learn, regardless of cultural and linguistic differences? I work with my colleague Ramona in a large urban school system in Massachusetts. Our journey as teachers is grounded in our search for answers to these questions within our two-way bilingual program classrooms, in which native speakers of Spanish and English are taught in integrated classes in both languages.

JEAN-CLAUDE LEJEUNE

As 3rd-grade teachers, we are committed to quality education for inner-city youth and hold the highest expectations for our students. Our students are African Americans and Latinos whose family cultures differ significantly from mainstream U.S. culture. Thus, they move between two cultural worlds—their home culture and the mainstream culture. Becoming familiar with these two worlds is a developmental process with a double edge: Our students must strengthen their sense of pride in their family culture while at the same time building skills to succeed in mainstream culture. Part of the work of our bicultural classrooms is to live and recreate our own cultures within an integrated learning environment.

> **Our students must strengthen their sense of pride in their family culture while at the same time building skills to succeed in mainstream culture.**

We use a team approach to create a consistent learning environment in which we model cross-cultural respect and cooperation for our students as we learn and teach together from different points of view. Our teaching combines use of the arts and a strong emphasis on writing within a web of relationships essential to our bilingual and bicultural classroom, which includes the teacher, the teacher team, the students, their families, and our community. The arts become tools that celebrate the cultural identity of our students, develop their cultural voices, and strengthen their connection with their family and community. Writing links children's personal experiences to academic learning. This weave of symbols from family cultures and the community becomes the foundation for the development of dual literacy within a standards-driven curriculum.

Two-Way Structure

In our program, the language of instruction is separated by classroom. There are two classrooms with one teacher for each language. I always use English in my classroom and Ramona always uses Spanish in hers. Two groups of students spend an equal amount of time in each language, rotating between Spanish and English classrooms biweekly. Each class group has a mix of students who speak Spanish or English as their native language. Students are becoming bilingual to varying degrees, depending on how long they have been in the two-way program. Teachers speak only one language, while students may use either language as they are acquiring the new language.

The language immersion in our classrooms is supported by team teaching. The team spends time coordinating the development of the curriculum so that it develops sequentially. We do not repeat teaching content. Students follow the development of ideas in one language at a time. For example, a child may start the math investigations unit on patterns in Spanish and finish it in English. In other cases, an entire unit will be presented in one language, and then we move to studying the next unit in the other language. In each classroom, students who are at ease in both languages are resources to their peers in the learning process. Both languages are used as a tool for students to explore and interact with their world.

The integration of students from diverse cultural and linguistic backgrounds is achieved through cooperative learning groups. We do not believe in tracking or ability grouping. Children learn and play together with their peers, many of whom are neighbors in their community. Learning together, they are protected from the harm that segregated student groupings may cause to their spirit and ability to learn. In our child-centered classrooms, the children are language resources for one another. We take care to group students with mixed abilities in each cooperative group. For example, social studies curriculum includes building skills for cooperative learning, cross-cultural understanding, and conflict resolution. Each group will have members who are strong in English, Spanish, reading, writing, drawing, and so on. In our collaborative learning environment, differences are good and necessary for the success of the challenging work of learning two languages.

> **In our child-centered classrooms, the children are language resources for one another.**

There are many principles contributing to the effectiveness of our program, in particular, our use of the arts to develop students' cultural voices, our integrated approach to learning, and our belief that learning happens in a web of relationships, not only among peers but within the wider scope of the community. [For a more complete explanation, see my chapter in the book *Lifting Every Voice: Pedagogy and Politics of Bilingualism*, edited by Zeynep F. Bekont (Cambridge: Harvard Education Publishing Group, 2000), 71–94.]

In this article, I would like to concentrate on how we use writing as the gateway to literacy.

Writing Is a Gateway

Writing, the creation of symbol on a page, is an important step toward literacy. In our classrooms, writing accompanies the arts in the development of biliteracy. Artistic expression and writing are connected in that they are both symbol systems. In the process of making art, a child spends time with images before they take on shape, color, and texture in an art piece. In the same way, writing requires that a child spend time with ideas and bring them out in conversation before they take shape in a manuscript. Both forms of self-expression, arts and writing, have common requisites: a safe place to explore, a personal place to move from, and a community place to share both the process and the message. Many of the writing activities in our 3rd-grade classrooms are based on art projects.

Autobiographical writing, journals, and publishing are three major components of our writing program. Autobiographical writing builds on a personal story and develops academic knowledge of Standard English. Journals provide a safe place to express personal concerns, try out new ideas, and have exchanges in writing with the teacher. Publishing promotes effective communication through writing for general audiences.

Autobiographical writing is key to the positive cultural identity formation of children who have been inhibited by negative immigration experiences or by racism. Student autobiographies are deepened over the course of the year and represent self-discovery, family history, and future dreams. Autobiographies encourage children to reconnect with family stories and name the values in those stories that sustain them. It is significant that the experts on this writing assignment are also the protagonists. Yismilka's words from the introduction to her autobiography exemplify both depth in self-expression and quality writing in her second language:

> I see the world as a dark place. If people depended on helping and saving, we could make a vast difference. The world is a good place to grow in. If we stick together the large difference can take us to an incredible blossom.

We use "sheltering" strategies to enhance the quality of autobiographical writing. One sheltering language development strategy highlights students' prior knowledge in conversations held before writing. For example, sheltering for autobiographical writing may include building descriptive language through talk about family pictures or drawings. In the process of writing their autobiographies, students talk to their classmates about the family pictures. Using oral language, children elaborate with detail as they develop descriptive language for their written life stories. These ideas can be graphically organized for further development around a central theme. Word banks organized on large chart paper categories, such as nouns (names), verbs (actions), adjectives (descriptions), or by topic—such as colors, feelings, textures, or geographical locations—are always on display and are added to by students as their vocabulary expands. Sheltering strategies also include the use of repetitive phrases such as "I know that it is a piñata because. . ." Students are asked to repeat the phrase and fill in as many descriptions of a piñata as they can. Invented spelling, oral dictation, and illustrated response to questions are also part of sheltering strategies for students who are beginning to develop literacy.

Autobiographical writing is key to the positive cultural identity formation of children who have been inhibited by negative immigration experiences or by racism.

Another strong support for good autobiographical writing is simply discussing with students the criteria for evaluating a writing piece. For example, students were preparing artist statements for a schoolwide exhibit that would form part of their autobiographies. In writing, they had to describe the scene that was represented on their family quilt square. The best artist statements would meet the task (stay focused), use a variety of sentence structures, use details, use descriptive language (including smells, colors, adjectives, adverbs), and use good basic mechanics (spacing, margins, indentations, capital letters, spelling, and punctuation). We used a sample quilt square and generated lists of words that would visually describe the art piece by categories such as colors, textures, background, and foreground. The second part of the assignment required students to describe the art-making process. In preparation, they dictated a list of actions involved in making their quilt square. The list generated a repetitive pattern of sentences: "I chose the color . . . because it. . ." Clarifying the assignment, using visual cues, generating lists of words, and using repetitive language patterns are sheltering strategies that enable second-language learners to write effectively. These student-generated lists are resources for the whole class as they compose. The words and ideas have been experienced orally, visually, dramatically, and in writing. This allows for reciprocity between students and teachers. Both players are participants in the learning process and vocabulary development.

> **A variety of genuine writing experiences is woven throughout our day by the frequent use of journals, which accompany many of our classroom activities.**

A variety of genuine writing experiences is woven throughout our day by the frequent use of journals, which accompany many of our classroom activities: morning journals, math journals, science journals, end-of-the-day journals—though different in content, all of these journals provide a safe place for students to try out ideas. I respond to the journals regularly. The personal nature of these exchanges allows me to build friendships with my students and a sense of trust. The interactive morning journal opens the day with a personal dialogue and is written freestyle. Poems or illustrations may be the communicative symbol system on any given morning. There is something peaceful and gentle about morning journal time. While music plays softly, children sit quietly at their desks and make their transition from home to the work of school as they read and respond to my comments. Both reading and writing form part of our written conversations. The following is a poem from a student's morning journal:

Shhhhh.
Listen! to the sound
Higher than the ground
We are black,
We are white,
they are not so tight.
We are Puerto Rican,
We are Dominican,
We are Chinese,
We are Cuban,
We will hold hands and stand.
We are Japanese,
We are Indian,

We are together forever.
Together forever.
    —from "I Am Black," by Myeshia

End-of-the-day journals are strictly academic in nature. A special book with a beautiful cover and quality paper is purchased for this purpose. At the end of the day, one student leads the class in a discussion that generates three main ideas that were learned during the day. Three other students write these in complete sentences on the board. The day closes as students enter their summary of the learning for the day in their end-of-the-day journals. Content-area journals, such as literature-response and math journals, also provide a review and confirmation of the main ideas covered in a lesson or unit.

Real-World Audiences

Our many forms of journaling are important tools for written communication, review, and documentation of academic gains. In telling, writing, and presenting themselves to the world, students realize reciprocity in learning—that is, that students are also teachers.

Bringing student writing to real-world audiences through publishing or the internet also promotes effective communication skills. One such publication project over the internet resulted when 3rd and 5th graders in our school worked together on math stories in their math journals, writing stories about their everyday lives with numbers. News about a bilingual internet exchange project called *De Orilla a Orilla* inspired our students. A group of teachers in New York, California, and Puerto Rico were facilitating exchanges between Spanish and English bilingual students through the internet. Students wanted to participate even though we did not have internet access in the classroom.

Our students' math journals contain stories and describe ways of thinking about math.

Our students' math journals contain stories and describe ways of thinking about math. They write, for example, about how they solved a problem, and include real-life math stories. They enjoyed their math journals and wanted to share them with other students. We decided to participate in *De Orilla a Orilla* by using the internet connection on my computer at home. Students prepared the following announcement for the project on the internet:

Math Journals Take Us Across Grades and Across Cyberspace Warm Greetings from Chilly Boston:

We are students in 3rd- and 5th-grade classes in a two-way bilingual program in Greater Boston. You might be wondering what it means to be a two-way bilingual program (two x bi = multi?). We are African American and Latino kids who are learning about one another's cultures and languages. We study math, science, and social studies in Spanish and English. In math class we have been keeping a math journal and writing math stories with the ideas we are discovering in math class.

Here are some ideas we have been writing about:

The Community We Have Multiplied

In math class we were multiplying, multiplying, multiplying. We read *Anno's Mysterious Multiplying Jar*. We wrote our own versions of the *Multiplying Jar* set in our own communities. Would you like to write with us? Please send us your stories and let us know if you would like to read ours.

I sent the message from my computer at home. A few weeks later, I printed the responses and brought them into class. Although the exchange was difficult to maintain without classroom access to the internet, this collaboration across grade levels strengthened the writing for both groups as they presented their work to an international audience. The literacy circle is complete when children take what they have learned in the classroom and use it in their experiences with the outside world.

Another example of student publishing was preparing student stories in book form for the classroom library. Including quality student writing in the multicultural library inspired children to write their own versions of stories that were popular with the class. One reading group was reading science fiction with animal characters. Their favorite was *Catwings*, by Ursula Le Guin. This story takes place in an urban setting; the wings saved the cats from a terrible fate. Stories sprouted from our students about urban animal families with liberating anatomy. Final edited versions were included in the library for classmates to read.

To summarize, as classroom teachers we emphasize varied ways of developing literacy through writing. Autobiographies, journals, and publishing projects encourage children to express themselves through writing. Second-language learners benefit from sheltering strategies to support the development of their academic language. Children write to be read when their work is validated through publishing.

Berta Rosa Berriz is a National Board Certified bilingual teacher, National Faculty at Lesley University, a dancer, a writer, and storyteller. She is currently the co-lead teacher for the Lower School of the Boston Teachers Union School, an innovative teacher-run pilot school.

Chapter Twenty-Seven

AND THEN I WENT TO SCHOOL

By Joe Suina

I lived with my grandmother when I was 5 through 9 years of age. It was the early 1950s when electricity had not yet entered our Pueblo homes. The village day school and health clinic were first to have it, and to the unsuspecting Cochiti, this was the approach of a new era in their uncomplicated lives.

Transportation was simple. Two good horses and a sturdy wagon met the daily needs of a villager. Only five, maybe six individuals possessed an automobile in the Pueblo of 400. A flatbed truck fixed with side rails and a canvas top made the usual Saturday morning trip to Santa Fe. It was always loaded beyond capacity with people and their wares headed for town for a few staples. The straining old truck with its escort of a dozen barking dogs made a noisy exit, northbound from the village.

A Sense of Closeness

During those years, grandmother and I lived beside the plaza in a one-room house. Inside, we had a traditional fireplace, a makeshift cabinet for our few tin cups and bowls, and a wooden crate carried our two buckets of all-purpose water. At the innermost part of the room were two rolls of bedding—thick quilts, sheepskin, and assorted—which we used as comfortable sitting couches by day and unrolled for sleeping by night. A wooden pole the length of one side of the room was suspended about 10 inches from the vigas and draped with a modest collection of colorful shawls, blankets, and sashes, making this part of the room most interesting. In one corner sat a bulky metal trunk for our ceremonial wear and a few valuables. A dresser that was traded for her well-known pottery held the few articles of clothing we owned and the "goody bag"—an old flour sack Grandma always kept filled with brown candy, store-bought cookies, and Fig Newtons. These were saturated with a sharp odor of mothballs. Nevertheless, they made a fine snack with coffee before we turned in for the night. Tucked securely beneath my blankets, I listened to one of her stories about how it was when she was a little girl. These accounts appeared so old-fashioned compared to the way we lived. Sometimes she softly sang a song from a ceremony. In this way, I went off to sleep each night.

For us children these were the first links to the world beyond the Pueblo.

Earlier in the evening we would make our way to a relative's house if someone had not already come to visit us. There, I'd play with the children while the adults caught up on all the latest news. Ten-cent comic books were finding their way into the Pueblo homes. Exchanging "old" comics for "new" ones was a serious matter that involved adults as well. Adults favored mystery and romance stories. For us children these were the first links to the world beyond the Pueblo. We enjoyed looking at them and role-playing our favorite hero rounding up the villains. Grandmother once made me a cape to leap tall buildings with. It seems everyone preferred being a cowboy rather than an Indian since cowboys were always victorious. Sometimes stories were related to both children and adults at these get-togethers. They were highlighted by refreshments of coffee and sweet bread or fruit pies baked in the outdoor oven. Winter months would most likely include roasted piñon nuts and dried deer meat for all to share. These evening gatherings and the sense of closeness diminished as radios and televisions increased over the following years. It was never to be the same again.

The winter months are among my fondest memories. A warm fire crackled and danced brightly in the fireplace, and the aroma of delicious stew filled our one-room house. The thick adobe walls wrapped around the two of us protectively during the long freezing nights. To me, the house was just right. Grandmother's affection completed the warmth and security I will always remember.

Being the only child at grandmother's, I had lots of attention and plenty of reasons to feel good about myself. As a preschooler, I already had chores of chopping firewood and hauling in fresh water each day. After "heavy work" I would run to her and flex what I was convinced were my gigantic biceps. Grandmother would state that at the rate I was going I would soon attain the status of a man like the adult males in the village. Her shower of praise made me feel like the Mr. Indian Universe of all time. At age 5, I suppose I was as close to that concept of myself as anyone.

In spite of her many years, grandmother was highly active in the village ceremonial setting. She was a member of an important women's society and attended every traditional function, taking me along to many of them. I'd wear one of my colorful shirts she made by hand for just such occasions. Grandmother taught me appropriate behavior at these events. Through modeling she showed me how to pray properly. Barefooted, I greeted the sun each morning with a handful of cornmeal. At night I'd look to the stars in wonderment and let a prayer slip through my lips. On meeting someone, grandmother would say, "Smile and greet. Grunt if you must, but don't pretend they're not there." On food and material things, she would say, "There is enough for everyone to share and it all comes from above, my child." I learned to appreciate cooperation in nature and with my fellow men early in life. I felt very much a part of the world and our way of life. I knew I had a place in it, and I felt good about it.

> **I felt very much a part of the world and our way of life. I knew I had a place in it, and I felt good about it.**

And Then I Went to School

At age 6, like the rest of the Cochiti 6-year-olds that year, I had to begin my schooling. It was a new and bewildering experience—one I will not forget. The strange surrounding, new ideas about time and expectations, and the foreign tongue were at times overwhelming to us beginners. It took some effort to return the second day and many times thereafter.

To begin with, unlike my grandmother, the teacher did not have pretty brown skin and a colorful dress. She wasn't plump and friendly. Her clothes were of one color and drab. Her pale and skinny form made me worry that she was very ill. In the village, being more pale than usual was a sure sign of an oncoming fever or some such disorder. I thought that explained why she didn't have time just for me and the disappointed looks and orders she seemed always to direct my way. I didn't think she was so smart since she couldn't understand my language. "Surely that was why we had to leave our 'Indian' at home." But then I didn't feel so bright either. All I could say in her language was "Yes, teacher," "My name is Joseph Henry," and "When is lunch?" The teacher's odor took some getting used to also. In fact, many times it made me sick right before lunch. Later I learned from the girls this smell was something she wore called perfume.

An Artificial Classroom

The classroom, too, had its odd characteristics. It was terribly huge and smelled of medicine like the village clinic I feared so much. The walls and ceiling were artificial and uncaring. They were too far from me and I felt naked. Those fluorescent light tubes made an eerie drone and blinked suspiciously over me, quite a contrast to the fire and sunlight my eyes were accustomed to. I thought maybe the lighting did not seem right because it was man-made, and it wasn't natural. Our confinement to rows of desks was another unnatural demand made on our active little bodies. We had to sit at these hard things for what seemed like forever before relief (recess) came midway through the morning and afternoon. Running carefree in the village and fields was but a sweet memory of days gone by. We all went home for lunch since we lived a short walk from school. It took coaxing, and sometimes bribing, to get me to return and complete the remainder of the school day.

School was a painful experience during those early years. The English language and the new set of values caused me much anxiety and embarrassment. I couldn't comprehend everything that was happening, but I could understand very well when I messed up or wasn't doing so well. Negative messages were communicated too effectively and I became more and more unsure of myself. How I wished I could understand other things in school just as well.

The conflict was not only in school performance but in many other areas of my life as well. For example, many of us students had a problem with head lice due to the "unsanitary conditions in our homes." Consequently, we received a harsh shampooing which was rough on both the scalp and the ego. Cleanliness was crucial, and a washing of this sort indicated to the class that one came from a home setting that was not healthy. I recall one such treatment and afterward being humiliated before my peers with a statement that I had "She'na" (lice) so tough that I must have been born with them. Needless to say, my Super Indian self-image was no longer intact.

School was a painful experience during those early years.

'Leave Your Indian at Home'

My language, too, was questioned right from the beginning of my school career. "Leave your Indian at home!" was like a school trademark. Speaking it accidentally or otherwise was punishable by a dirty look or a whack with a ruler. This reprimand was for speaking the language of my people that meant so much to me. It was the language of my grandmother, and I spoke it well. With it, I sang beautiful songs and prayed from my heart. At that young and tender age, it was most difficult for me to comprehend why I had to part with my language. And yet at home I was encouraged to attend school so that I might have a better life in the future. I knew I had a good village life already, but this awareness dwindled each day I was in school.

As the weeks turned to months, I learned English more and more. It may appear that comprehension would be easier. It got easier to understand, all right. I understood that everything I had, and was a part of, was not nearly as good as the white man's. School was determined to undo me in everything from my sheepskin bedding to the dances and ceremonies that I had learned to have faith in and cherish. One day I dozed off in class after a sacred all-night ceremony. I was startled awake by a sharp jerk on my ear, and informed coldly, "That ought to teach you to attend 'those things' again." Later, all alone, I cried. I couldn't understand why or what I was caught up in. I was receiving two very different messages; both were intended for my welfare.

> **School was determined to undo me in everything from my sheepskin bedding to the dances and ceremonies that I had learned to have faith in and cherish.**

Values in lifestyle were dictated in various ways. The Dick and Jane reading series in the primary grades presented me pictures of a home with a pitched roof, straight walls, and sidewalks. I could not identify with these from my pueblo world. However, it was clear I didn't have these things, and what I did have did not measure up. At night, long after grandmother went to sleep, I would lie awake staring at our crooked adobe walls casting uneven shadows from the light of the fireplace. The walls were no longer just right for me. My life was no longer just right. I was ashamed of being who I was, and I wanted to change right then and there. Somehow it became very important to have straight walls, clean hair and teeth, and a spotted dog to chase after. I even became critical of, and hateful toward, my bony, fleabag of a dog. I loved the familiar and cozy environment at grandmother's house, but now I imagined it could be a heck of a lot better if only I had a whiteman's house with a bed, a nice couch, and a clock. In schoolbooks, all the child characters ever did was run at leisure after the dog or kite. They were always happy. As for me, all I seemed to do at home was go for buckets of water and cut up sticks for a lousy fire. Didn't the teacher say drinking coffee would stunt my growth? Why couldn't I have nice tall glasses of milk so I could have strong bones and white teeth like those kids in the books? Did my grandmother really care about my well-being?

Torn Away

I had to leave my beloved village of Cochiti for my education beyond 6. I left to attend a Bureau of Indian Affairs (BIA) boarding school 30 miles from home. Shined shoes and pressed shirt and pants were the order of the day. I managed to adjust to this just as I had to most of the things the school shoved at me or took away from me. Adjusting to leaving home and the village was tough enough. It seemed the older I got, the further I got from the ways I was so much a part of. Since my parents did not own an automobile, I saw them only once a month when they came in the community truck. They never failed to come supplied with "eats" for me. I enjoyed the outdoor oven bread, dried meat, and tamales they usually brought. It took a while to get accustomed to the diet of the school. Being in town with strange tribes under one roof was frightening and often very lonely. I longed for my grandmother and my younger brothers and sisters. I longed for my house. I longed to take part in a Buffalo Dance. I longed to be free.

My life was no longer just right. I was ashamed of being who I was, and I wanted to change right then and there.

I came home for the four-day Thanksgiving break. At first, home did not feel right anymore. It was much too small and stuffy. The lack of running water and bathroom facilities was too inconvenient. Everything got dusty so quickly, and hardly anyone spoke English. It occurred to me then that I was beginning to take on the whiteman's ways that belittled my own. However, it didn't take long to "get back with it." Once I reestablished my relationships with family, relatives, and friends, I knew I was where I came from. I knew where I belonged.

Leaving for the boarding school the following Sunday evening was one of the saddest events in my entire life. Although I had enjoyed myself immensely the last few days, I realized then that life would never be the same again. I could not turn back the time just as I could not do away with school and the ways of the whiteman. They were here to stay and would creep more and more into my life. The effort to make sense of both worlds together was painful, and I had no choice but to do so. The schools, television, automobiles, and many other outside ways and values had chipped away at the simple cooperative life I began to grow in. The people of Cochiti were changing. The winter evening gatherings, the exchanging of stories, and even the performing of certain ceremonies were already only a memory that someone commented about now and then. Still, the two worlds were very different and the demands of both were ever present. The whiteman's was flashy, less personal, but very comfortable. The Cochiti were both attracted and pushed toward these new ways that they had little to say about. There was no choice left but to compete with the whiteman on his terms for survival. To do that I knew I had to give up part of my life.

Dr. Joseph H. Suina is a professor emeritus in the College of Education at the University of New Mexico and has numerous publications on culture and education.

SECTION IV
TRANSNATIONAL IDENTITIES, MULTICULTURAL CLASSROOMS

FAVIANNA RODRIGUEZ

Chapter Twenty-Eight

WHAT HAPPENED TO THE GOLDEN DOOR?
How my students taught me about immigration

By Linda Christensen

At Eureka High School, immigration equaled Ellis Island. We watched old black-and-white film strips of Northern Europeans filing through dimly lit buildings. My textbooks were laced with pictures of the Statue of Liberty opening her arms to poor immigrants who had been granted an opportunity to "pull themselves up by their bootstraps" when they passed through America's door:

> Give me your tired, your poor,
> Your huddled masses yearning to breathe free,
> The wretched refuse of your teeming shores.
> Send these, the homeless, tempest-tost, to me,
> I lift my lamp beside the golden door.

JEAN-CLAUDE LEJEUNE

I felt pride at being part of a country that helped the unfortunate, including my own family.

Years later when I visited Angel Island in San Francisco Bay, I learned about another immigration that hadn't been mentioned in my high school or college texts.

Years later when I visited Angel Island in San Francisco Bay, I learned about another immigration that hadn't been mentioned in my high school or college texts. I walked through the deserted barracks where painted walls covered the poems of immigrant Chinese who viewed the "Golden Mountain" through a barbed wire fence. I felt angry that yet another portion of U.S. history had been hidden from me. Between 1910 and 1940, the "tired, poor, wretched refuse" from Asian shores were imprisoned on Angel Island before being accepted as "resident aliens" or rejected at the "golden door." As historian Ronald Takaki notes, "Their quarters were crowded and unsanitary, resembling a slum. 'When we arrived,' said one of them, 'they locked us up like criminals in compartments like the cages in the zoo.'"[1] Turning their anger and frustration into words, the Chinese carved poems on the building's wooden walls. Their poems stood in stark contradiction to the Statue of Liberty's promise:

America has power, but not justice.
In prison, we were victimized as if we
    were guilty.
Given no opportunity to explain, it was
    really brutal.
I bow my head in reflection but there is
    nothing I can do.[2]

All Europeans were eligible for citizenship once they passed through Ellis Island, a right denied to Asians until the mid-1940s.

In 1995 when California voters passed Proposition 187, I decided to teach about immigration, not just the traditional version, but the more dangerous and unspoken immigration that denies access to large numbers of potential immigrants based on color or politics.

Beyond these political reasons, I had personal and educational reasons to teach this unit. It was the last quarter of the year in Literature in U.S. History, a combined junior level untracked history and English class that met 90 minutes a day for the entire year. The days had warmed up and the students smelled summer. If I said the word "essay," "interior monologue," or "role play," I could hear a collective moan rise from the circle and settle like stinky fog around my head.

For three quarters, my planning book had been filled with lessons attempting to teach students how to become critical readers of history and literature. They'd written essays, critiques, short stories, personal narratives, poems, and interior monologues analyzing their own lives as well as the history and contemporary issues that continue to deprive Native Americans of land and economic opportunities. They'd also reflected critically on the enslavement of Africans, starting with life in Africa before slavery as well as forced immigration and resistance. We examined the literature and history of the Harlem Renaissance, the Civil Rights Movement, and contemporary issues. They read and critiqued presidential speeches, historical and contemporary novels and poems written by people from a variety of backgrounds. They were ready to do their own investigation and teaching—putting into practice their analytical skills.

Fourth quarter I wanted them to conduct "real" research—not the scurry-to-the-library-and-find-the-closest-encyclopedia-and-copy-it-word-for-word kind of research, but research that made them ask questions about immigration policies, quotas, and personal stories that couldn't be lifted from a single text. I wanted them to learn to use the library, search for books, look up alternative sources, find the Ethnic NewsWatch, search the Oregon Historical Society's clipping files, photo files, and rare documents room. I wanted them to interview people, read novels and poetry that told the immigrant's story in a more personal way. Through this kind of thorough research, I hoped they would develop an ear for what is unsaid in political speeches and newspaper articles, that they would learn to ask questions when their neighbors or people on the bus began an anti-immigrant rap.

I wanted them to interview people, read novels and poetry that told the immigrant's story in a more personal way.

Setting the Stage

I started fourth quarter by outlining my goals and expectations. I do this each term, so students know what kinds of pieces must be in their portfolio, for example, a literary essay comparing two novels, an essay exploring a historical issue, a poem that includes details from history, etc. As part of the opening of the quarter ceremonies, I passed out an outline of their upcoming project. I wanted a lengthy deadline so students would have the opportunity to work the entire quarter on the project.

Before students started their research, I modeled how I wanted the lessons taught by presenting Chinese and Japanese immigration. While students who come through the Jefferson network of elementary, middle, and high schools get at least surface background knowledge of Native Americans and African Americans, they appear to know less about Asian or Latino literature or history. In fact, students are often surprised that the Japanese and Chinese faced any prejudice.[3]

During the lessons on Japanese Americans, students examined Executive Order 9066 signed by President Roosevelt, which gave the military the right to force Japanese Americans from their homes and businesses into camps surrounded by barbed wire and guard towers. Because these "resident aliens" and U.S. citizens were allowed to take only what they could carry to the "camps," they were forced to sell most of their possessions in a short period of time. Students read "Echoes of Pearl Harbor," a chapter from *Nisei Daughter* by Monica Sone, where she describes her family burning their Japanese poetry, kimonos, breaking their Japanese records, destroying anything that could make them look like they cherished their Japanese heritage. Students wrote moving poetry and interior monologues imagining they were forced to leave their homes, businesses, and treasured possessions. "Becoming American," was written by Khalilah Joseph:[4]

> I looked into the eyes of my Japanese doll
> and knew I could not surrender her
> to the fury of the fire.
> My mother threw out the poetry
> she loved;
> my brother gave the fire his sword.
> We worked hours
> to vanish any traces of the Asian world
> from our home.
> Who could ask us
> to destroy
> gifts from a world that molded
> and shaped us?
> If I ate hamburgers
> and apple pies,
> if I wore jeans,
> then would I be American?"

I came across *Beyond Words: Images from America's Concentration Camps,* a fascinating book of personal testimony and artwork produced in the camps: black-and-white drawings, watercolors, oil paintings, and pieces of interviews that gave me a window into the lives of the imprisoned Japanese. While I showed slides of the artwork, students I prompted ahead of time read "Legends from Camp" by Lawson Inada, "The Question of Loyalty," by Mitsuye Yamada, and segments of the internees' interviews that matched pictures on screen. With images and words of the prisoners in their minds, students wrote their own poems. Thu Throung's poem is called "Japanese Prisoners":

> Guards watch us.
> They wrap us around
> in barbed wire fences
> like an orange's meat
> that never grows outside its skin.
> If the orange's skin breaks,

the juice drains out.
Just like the Japanese behind the
    wire fence.

We watched and critiqued the somewhat flawed film *Come See the Paradise,*[5] and talked about the laws that forbade Japanese nationals from becoming citizens or owning land. Students read loyalty oaths imprisoned Japanese American citizens were forced to sign. After learning about the "No No Boys," men who refused to sign the oath, and their subsequent imprisonment in federal penitentiaries, students argued about whether or not they would have signed the loyalty oath if they'd been interned.[6]

Students wrote moving poetry and interior monologues imagining they were forced to leave their homes, businesses, and treasured possessions.

Students also looked at the number of immigrant Chinese allowed in the country compared to European immigrants. For example, in 1943 when Congress repealed the Chinese Exclusion Act because of China's alliance with the United States against the Japanese, 105 Chinese were allowed to enter Angel Island while 66,000 English immigrants passed through Ellis Island.[7]

The Research Begins

Students started on their own projects during the same time period I presented the Chinese and Japanese immigration. They had two 30-minute sessions the first week to discuss what they knew, itemize what they needed to find, and list the resources they had (people to interview, books at home, potential videos to use, outside resources like Vietnamese, Russian, or Latino teachers or districtwide coordinators.) During the following weeks, while I continued my presentations, they were given varied amounts of time to conduct research: 45 minutes to prepare for the library, a full day at the library, additional 90-minute periods as we got closer to deadline, etc. At the end of each period of "research/preparation" time, students turned their information in to me so I could see if they made headway, ran into a block, needed a push or help. During this research period, I moved between groups, listening in, asking questions, making lists of questions they raised, but didn't answer, questioning literary choices when a piece was by a writer from the immigration group but didn't deal with any of the issues we were studying.

During this time, it was not unusual to see some of my students gathered around a television in the hallway outside my door or in the library as they watched and critiqued videos, looking for potential sections to show to the class. Travis, Roman, and Sophia, who were individual researchers, could be seen translating notes or cassette tapes for their stories. Sometimes they met to talk over stories or ideas for their presentation.

The Mexican group had the most members—too many, really. They watched videos together and then split the rest of the work: Danica and Komar collected and read books to find a story; Shannon researched Cesar Chavez and wrote a profile to hand out to the class; Heather gathered information for a debate on Proposition 187; Stephanie and Stacey coordinated the group, collecting information from each subgroup, fitting research into a coherent lesson plan, and creating a writing lesson that would pull information together for the class; Rosa, the only group member fluent in Spanish, talked with recent immigrants in ESL classes and the Latino coordinator to find speakers, videos, and stories to feed to her group.

Before I end up sounding like a movie script starring Michelle Pfeiffer, let me quickly insert into this idyllic classroom a word or two of other things you might see: kids whining and competing for my attention, RIGHT NOW; students gossiping about a fight, a guess-who's-going-out-with. . ., an upcoming game, or a movie they saw last night; a sly student attempting to take advantage of the chaos to catch up on math or Spanish; the slippery students who said they were going to the library or to see an ESL coordinator, but who actually sneaked into the teachers' cafeteria for coffee or outside for a smoke. There were also two students who attended regularly and might have learned something through other people's work, but who produced no work themselves, and a few others who rode the backs of their group's work, contributing a little in spurts, but not making the sustained efforts of most students. The ESL coordinators and librarians and I developed an easy communication system regarding passes. I called students and parents at home to talk about their lack of work. While the calls pushed the back-riding students who made some effort, I failed to bring the "slackers" into the research fold.

Besides the usual chaos a teacher might expect when turning over the curriculum to students, I simultaneously hit another problem. I'd set up immigrant groups that I knew would have some interesting and contradictory stories because I was familiar with their history and literature. While students did accept some of the groups I'd proposed: Mexican, Haitian, Cambodian, Irish, and Vietnamese, others argued vehemently that they be allowed to choose the immigrant group they would study. Our previous lessons on resistance and solidarity had certainly taken root within each of the class members, and I was the object of their solidarity. A few wanted to research their own family's immigration stories: Greek, Jewish, Macedonian, and Russian. Several African American students wanted to study immigrants from Africa or from the African Diaspora. Most were happy to study Haiti, one of my original groups; one student chose to study Eritrea, since Portland has a larger population of Eritreans than Haitians. I agreed; in fact, he made an excellent choice. We ended our first rounds with the following research groups: Cambodians, Eritreans,[8] Greeks, Haitians, Irish, Jewish, Macedonians, Mexicans, Russians, and Vietnamese. This first dialogue marked the end of my control over the history and literature presented in class. And I was nervous

This first dialogue marked the end of my control over the history and literature presented in class.

because I knew almost nothing about Greek and Macedonian immigration and not much more about the Russians.

Ultimately, the contrast between groups made for great discussion. In my class of 31 students, three had emigrated from Vietnam, one from Russia, one from Cambodia; several students were second-generation Americans from Greece, Ireland, Nicaragua, and Mexico; half of the class' ancestors had been enslaved Africans, and one girl's grandmother was the only surviving member of her family after the Holocaust. But I can imagine a more homogenous classroom where this might not be the case. In my high school English class more than 20 years ago, 29 students were white and one was black. Around Portland today, I can cite similar profiles. These ratios would have made me demand more diversity in the research if all students wanted to study their own heritage. I do think it is important to negotiate the curriculum with students, and I'm sure some students would be more interested in researching their own past than researching the past of others, but sometimes, in order to surface issues of race and class inequality, it is necessary to move beyond our personal histories.

Research Problems

Prior to the beginning of the unit, I spent time in the public library and the Oregon Historical Society (OHS) library, finding sources, articles, books, practicing computer research programs, before bringing my students across town. OHS officials were friendly and helpful, but told me that I couldn't bring the entire class to their library: I'd have to bring one or two at a time after school or on Saturdays. And they closed at 5 p.m.

I wanted students to learn the 'whole truth,' not just a watered-down version that left out facts that might complicate the issues.

In addition to limited library time, I discovered that the easily accessible research materials did not have a critical page in their spines; they just restated the textbook version. I wanted students to learn the "whole truth," not just a watered-down version that left out facts that might complicate the issues. I figured that part of research is getting lots of material and then deciding what is important to present so that others hear a fuller truth. But when I discovered that much of what students were reading only told one side of the immigration story—the same side I learned in high school—I made an effort to put other facts in students' hands as well. We searched computer files of Ethnic NewsWatch and alternative news and magazine sources. Although many students dutifully read the computer-generated articles, most of these pieces were too academic or required extensive background knowledge to understand. If we had relied solely on these sources of information—either textbook or alternative—many students would have come away with material that they might have been able to cite and copy into a readable paper, but they wouldn't have understood much about the underlying political situations their immigrant group faced.

After the library research, I linked students with people or information that might provide facts and stories not available in the library. The Haitian group, for example, read articles but hadn't comprehended what was going on: Who was Papa Doc? How was the United States involved? What was happening with Aristide? I distributed copies of the Network of Educators on the Americas' (NECA) booklet *Teaching About Haiti,* which gave them historical and political analysis they needed in order to make sense of the newspaper and magazine articles. The novel *Krik? Krak!* by Edwidge Danticat developed their personal connection; she gave faces and voices to the people on the boats, to those who lived in fear. The names in the newspaper became real: Aristide, Tontons Macoutes, boat people, refugees. (The group's enthusiasm for the novel caught on. I'd purchased five copies, and there were arguments over who got to read *Krik? Krak!* after group members finished.)

Students became wonderfully devious researchers, using their own connections to gain information. They learned to find back doors when the front doors closed and windows when all of the doors were locked. But sometimes these backdoor, through-the-window–type researches posed another problem: What if personal history omitted vital historical facts and perspectives? While I could help students who studied immigrant groups that I knew something about, I had little time to read and research the Macedonians, Greeks, and Russians.

Students became wonderfully devious researchers, using their own connections to gain information.

Travis was thoroughly confused when his research revealed a snarled web of history involving Greece, Bulgaria, and a historic trade route through the mountains. His research took him back to 146 B.C., when Rome conquered the Kingdom of Macedonia, and forward to today. He wanted to know why his grandfather immigrated. Instead of untangling the web of Macedonian history, he spent time with his grandfather, talking, asking questions, going through photo albums, relying on his personal relationships to decode the past. He arranged for a day at the Macedonian lodge, where he interviewed men his grandfather's age about their immigration experiences. Because of my own limited knowledge of events in Macedonia, I let him. This was history via personal story—how much or how little of the history was included, I wasn't sure.

Likewise, when Meghan and I met one Saturday at the Oregon Historical Society, we discovered the letters James Mullany, an Irish immigrant, wrote to his sister in Ireland in the mid-1800s. In one letter, he pleaded with his sister not to mention that he was Catholic: "their [sic] is a strong prejudice against them here on account of the people here thinking it was the Priests that caused the Indian war three or four years ago."[9] Interesting. But in another letter he wrote of the Snake Indians who attacked a train of 45 whites, "only 15 survived but some of them died of starvation. . . . [A] company of soldiers . . . found them living of [sic] the bodyes [sic] of them that were killed by the [I]ndians." Could we count these letters as historic evidence? Whose voices weren't included? What stories might the Snake Indians have told?

Students using voices of immigrants or novels to tell the history created a dilemma for me: What happens when personal narratives exclude the stories of large groups of other people or neglect important historical facts? When and how do I intervene? If students tell only their own stories or draw on personal testimonies, is that "inaccurate" history? As an English teacher who weaves literature and history together, who values personal stories as eyewitness accounts of events and who encourages students to "tell their stories," I began to question my own assumptions.

The Vietnamese group, occupying Tri's corner between the windows and closet, underscored my "history versus personal story" dilemma. Their student-told account emphasized a pro-American stance around the Vietnam War but said nothing, for example, of U.S. support for French colonialism, its creation of "South Vietnam," or its devastating bombardment of the Vietnamese countryside. How could I challenge the story these students grew up hearing from parents and elders in their community?

With Meghan's research, we'd studied historical accounts of Native Americans in the Northwest, so we knew that Mullany's letters lacked facts about land takeovers and Indian massacres. But I didn't have time to teach the unit on Vietnam that Bill Bigelow and I developed when we taught the class together, so I also worried that the rest of the class would come away without an understanding of the key role the United States played in the Vietnam War; and without that understanding, how would they be able to critique other U.S. interventions?

> **I learned a lesson: Personal story does not always equal history. This lingers as a vexing teaching dilemma.**

I talked with Cang, Tri, and Thu and gave them resources: a timeline that reviewed deepening U.S. involvement in Vietnam and numerous readings from a critical standpoint. I also introduced them to the film *Hearts and Minds,* which features testimony from numerous critics of the war, as well as prominent U.S. antiwar activists like Daniel Ellsberg. Without a sustained dialogue, this insertion seemed weak and invasive, more so than my talks with Travis and Meghan, because their research was at a greater distance from their lives. But I learned a lesson: Personal story does not always equal history. This lingers as a vexing teaching dilemma.

The Presentation

Once presentation deadlines hit, students argued over dates and order—who got to go first, last, etc. Our biggest struggle came around the issue of time. Students lobbied for longer time slots. The Mexican group was especially ardent. They'd found great movies as well as short stories, informational videos, and a guest speaker from PCUN, the local farm workers union, about working conditions and the boycott of Garden Burgers, a veggie burger sold in stores and restaurants across the country. They figured they needed at least a week, possibly two. We had five weeks left: four for presentations and a last sacred week to finish portfolios and evaluations. Rosa said, "Look how many days you used when you taught us about the Japanese and Chinese. Two weeks on each! Aren't the Latinos as important as the Asians?" They bargained with single person groups, like the Russians and Greeks, for part of their time.

A week or so prior to presentations, groups submitted detailed lesson plans. I met formally with each group to make sure all requirements were covered, but also questioned choices. During previous weeks, I'd read every proposed story and novel selection, watched each video, went over writing assignments: I didn't want any surprises on their teaching day.

> **The power of my students' teaching was not in just the individual presentations, but also in the juxtaposition of these histories and stories.**

The power of my students' teaching was not in just the individual presentations, where students provided historical information in a variety of mostly interesting and unique lesson plans, but also in the juxtaposition of these histories and stories. Students created a jazz improvisation, overlaying voices of pain and struggle and triumph with heroic attempts to escape war, poverty, or traditions that pinched women too narrowly into scripted roles. Their historical research and variety of voices taught about a more varied history of immigration than I'd ever attempted to do in the past.

But the presentations were also like improvisation in that they were not as tightly connected and controlled as a rehearsed piece I would have conducted. There were off notes and unfinished strands that seemed promising but didn't deliver an analysis that could have strengthened student understanding of immigration. Few students found research on quotas, few had time left in their presentation to engage in a discussion that linked or compared their group to another. The Haitian group, for example, tied our past studies of Columbus and the Taínos to present Haiti, but didn't develop the history of Duvalier or Aristide or the involvement of the United States.

Although presentations varied in length and depth, most gave us at least a look at a culture many students weren't familiar with, and at best, a strong sense that not only did racial and political background determine who gets into this country, but also how they live once they arrive.

The Cambodian group arranged for Sokpha's mother to come to class, as well as a viewing of the film *The Killing Fields*. Sokpha's mother told of her life in Cambodia, of hiding in the deep tunnels her father built to keep them safe from U.S. bombs, of her fear of snakes at the bottom of the tunnel that scared her almost as much as the bombs. She talked about the Khmer Rouge, the Vietnamese, and the United States. On her father's deathbed, he said, "Go to America. Leave Cambodia." She did. Shoeless, nine months pregnant with Sokpha, and carrying a 3-year-old on her back, she walked for three days and three nights from Cambodia into Thailand, dodging land mines that killed some of her fellow travelers. She also spoke of difficulties here—how her lack of language skills have kept her from finding a good job, her reliance on Sokpha, the breakdown of their culture, the Americanization of her children.

The Haitians presented background history tying the modern struggle in Haiti with previous history lessons; their strengths were chilling descriptions of the refugees, their choice of story, their research into Haitian culture, and their writing assignment. Read aloud by a male and a female student, the two-voice story, "Children of the Sea," portrayed a political young man who dared to speak out against the Haitian government, writing to his lover as he rides a sinking boat in search of refuge in the United States. His lover writes of the increased military violence of the Tontons Macoutes, who make parents have sex with their children, rape and torture suspected supporters of Aristide.

Cang, from the Vietnamese group, recounted Vietnam's history through a timeline. Thu's stories of escape and life in the refugee camps created nightmare scenes for her fellow students of drownings, rapes, and the difficulties of families who got separated. Tri pointed out the geographical settlements of immigrant Vietnamese and their induction into the United States. He talked about the struggle of the Vietnamese shrimp fishermen in the Gulf, the attempts of the KKK to drive the fishermen out of the region,[11] and the creation of Little Saigon in California, a space where the Vietnamese have forged a community inside the United States, not unlike many immigrants who came before them.

The student writing assignments generated excellent poems and personal narratives. After Sophia spoke about her mother's experiences, she said her inheritance from her mother was the strength to pursue her goals even when she faces opposition. Her assignment for the class: "Write about something you treasure from your family. It might be an heirloom, like a ring, but it can also be a story, a memory, a tradition, a personal trait. Write it as a poem, a personal narrative, or a story." Komar Harvey wrote an essay about his family's love of music:

> **The student writing assignments generated excellent poems and personal narratives.**

> You can hear music on the porch before you enter our house. Tunes climb through those old vinyl windows and mailbox and drift into everybody's ears in the neighborhood. If you came during the holiday season you could hear the Christmas bells chiming through the static of that old crackling phonograph needle. You hear the rumbling voice of Charles Brown as if he were digging a hole up in the living room, 'Bells will be ringing.' . . . Nobody graces our door during those Christmas months without a little Charles ringing his bells in their ears.

After talking about the efforts of his grandfather's struggles to get to the United States, Travis asked students to write a personal narrative about an obstacle they overcame in their life. Cang wrote about his difficulty learning English in the face of classmates' ridicule. His narrative had a profound effect on students. I have not changed or corrected his language because it is part of the story:

[After he left Vietnam, he was in the Philippines.] In 1989 we came to America. That's when I started to go to school. I went to all of the classes I had, but I felt the blonde and white-skinned people not respected me. They make joke over the way I talk. . . . I'll never give up, I say to myself. . . . One day I'm going to be just like them on talking and writing, but I never get to that part of my life until now. Even if I can understand the word, but still I can't pronounce it, if I do pronounce it, it won't end up right. Truly, I speak Vietnamese at home all the time, that's why I get used to the Vietnamese words more than English, but I'll never give up what I have learned. I will succeed with my second language.

The Mexican group took several days for their presentation. They taught about the theft of Mexican land by the United States, immigration border patrols, the effect of toxic sprays on migrant workers, the migrants' living conditions in Oregon. During this time, we also debated Proposition 187: Should the United States deny services to undocumented immigrants? Then the presenters asked the class to write a persuasive essay taking a point of view on the question.

On our last day, students overwhelmingly voted that immigration was the unit they both learned the most from and cared the most about.

One day we watched the movie *Mi Familia,* about a "Mexican" family whose original homeland was in California. As we watched, we ate tamales and sweet tacos that Rosa and her mother-in-law lugged up three flights of stairs. Then we wrote food poems that tied us to our culture. Sarah LePage's "Matzah Balls" is a tribute to her grandmother:

Grandma's hands,
wise, soft, and old,
mold the Matzah meal
between the curves of each palm.
She transforms our heritage
into perfect little spheres.
Like a magician
she shapes our culture
as our people do.
This is her triumph.
She lays the bowl aside
revealing her tired hands,
each wrinkle a time
she sacrificed something for our family.

Evaluation

On our last day, students overwhelmingly voted that immigration was the unit they both learned the most from and cared the most about. Komar, the first to speak, said, "I never realized that Cambodians were different from Vietnamese. Sokpha's family went through a lot to get here, so did Tri's, Thu's, and Cang's." Stacey, a member of the Haitian group added, "I learned that the United States isn't just black and white. I learned that my people are not the only ones who have suffered in this country." Khalilah noted that she hadn't realized what research really meant until she struggled to find information about the Haitians. While others added similar points about various groups or presentations they learned from, Travis summed up the conversation by saying, "I didn't know anything about Proposition 187 or the discrimination immigrants have faced because that wasn't part of my family's history. I didn't know that there was discrimination about who got in and who was kept out of the United States, and now I do."

I felt that students learned from each other about immigrants' uneven and unfair treatment. The Statue of Liberty's flame and rhetoric had met with a history, told by students, that dimmed her light. But they had also learned lessons that would alter their interactions with the "Chinese"—actually Korean—storekeeper at the intersection of Martin Luther King Jr. and Fremont. At Jefferson, one of the most offensive scenes I have witnessed in the hallways or classrooms is the silencing of immigrant Asian, Russian, and Mexican students as they speak their own languages or struggle to speak English. Throughout the year, Cang, Thu, and Tri's personal testimony during discussions or read-arounds about the pain of that silencing as well as their stories about fighting with their parents or setting off firecrackers in their school in Vietnam created much more awareness in our classroom than any lecture could have. I credit our study of history, for example, the Mexican-American War, as part of that change, but through this student-led unit on immigration, I watched students crack through stereotypes they had nurtured about others. Students who sat by their lockers on C-floor were no longer lumped together under the title "Chinese"; they became Vietnamese, Cambodian, Laotian. Students no longer mimicked the sound of their speech as a put-down. Latino students who spoke Spanish near the door on the west side of the building were no longer seen as outsiders who moved into the neighborhood with loud cars and lots of children, but as political exiles in a land that had once belonged to their ancestors. The Russian students who moved together like a small boat through the halls of Jefferson were no longer odd, but seekers of religious freedom.

Throughout fourth quarter, I tossed and turned at night questioning my judgment about asking students to teach such an important part of history—and the consequence that much history would not be taught. But after hearing their enthusiasm and their changed perceptions about their classmates, the world, and research, I put my critique temporarily on hold. Turning over the classroom circle to my students allowed them to become the "experts" and me to become their student. While I lost control and power over the curriculum and was forced to question some key assumptions of my teaching, I gained an incredible amount of knowledge—and so did they.

Linda Christensen (lmc@lclark.edu) is director of the Oregon Writing Project at Lewis & Clark College in Portland, Oregon, and a Rethinking Schools *editor. She is author, most recently, of* Reading, Writing, and Rising Up: Teaching About Social Justice and the Power of the Written Word *(2nd edition).*

Bibliography

Asian Women United of California (1989). *Making Waves: An Anthology of Writings by and About Asian American Women.* Boston: Beacon Press.

Chin, F., Chan, J. P., Inada, L. F., & Wong, S. (1991). *Aiiieeeee! An Anthology of Chinese American and Japanese American Literature.* New York: Penguin Books.

Danticat, E. (1991). *Krik? Krak!* New York: Vintage Books.

Gesensway, D. & Roseman, M. (1987). *Beyond Words: Images from America's Concentration Camps.* Ithaca, NY: Cornell University Press.

Harvey, K., Joseph, K., & LePage, S. (1996). *We Treasure Music. Rites of Passage.* Portland, OR: Jefferson High School.

Houston, J. W. & Houston, J. D. (1973). *Farewell to Manzanar.* Boston: San Francisco Book Company/ Houghton Mifflin.

Inada, L. F. (1993). *Legends from Camp.* Minneapolis, MN: Coffee House Press.

Kim, E. H. (1982). *Asian American Literature.* Philadelphia: Temple University Press.

Lai, H. M., Lim, G., & Yung, J. (1986). *Island: Poetry and History of Chinese Immigrants on Angel Island 1910–1940.* San Francisco: San Francisco Study Center.

Lowe, F. (1988). *Carved in Silence.* San Francisco: National Asian American Telecommunications Association.

Okada, J. (1957). *No-No Boy.* Boston: Charles E. Tuttle Co.

Sone, M. (1953). *Nisei Daughter.* Seattle: University of Washington Press.

Sunshine, C. A. & Menkhart, D. (1994). *Teaching About Haiti* (3rd ed.). Washington, DC: Network of Educators on the Americas.

Takaki, R. (1989). *Strangers from a Different Shore: A History of Asian Americans.* New York: Viking Penguin.

Yamada, M. (1976). *Camp Notes.* San Lorenzo, CA: Shameless Hussy Press.

Endnotes

1. Takaki, R. (1989). *Strangers from a Different Shore: A History of Asian Americans.* New York: Viking Penguin. (p. 237)
2. Lai, H. M., Lim, G., & Yung, J. (1986). *Island: Poetry and History of Chinese Immigrants on Angel Island 1910–1940.* San Francisco: San Francisco Study Center. (p. 58)
3. I have to thank my former student Mira Shimabukuro, who pointed out my own lack of attention to these groups, and Lawson Inada, professor at Southern Oregon State College, who served as my mentor in these studies.
4. Many of the student poems used in this article are printed in our literary magazine, *Rites of Passage.*
5. For example, like many films about an oppressed people, *Come See the Paradise,* features a white man in the lead role.
6. Wakatsuki Houston, J. & Houston, J. D. (1973). *Farewell to Manzanar.* Boston: San Francisco Book Company/Houghton Mifflin. (p. 58)
7. Lowe, F. (1988). *Carved in Silence.* San Francisco: National Asian American Telecommunications Association.
8. The student studying Eritreans left school, so I will not report on his project.
9. Letters from James Mullany to his sister Mary Mullany, August 5, 1860. Oregon Historical Society Mss 2417, p. 10.
10. Mullany, November 5, 1860, p. 14.
11. See the film *Alamo Bay,* which despite its "white hero main character" flaw, does tell some of the story

Chapter Twenty-Nine

BRINGING GLOBALIZATION HOME

By Jody Sokolower

"Globalization is complicated," I admitted to my 12th-grade economics class, all immigrants, all English language learners (ELLS). "But migration is a key aspect of globalization, and every single one of you is an expert on migration. So we're going to start our study of globalization with migration."

I believed that starting with my students' own immigration experiences would push them to a deeper emotional level. In my experience, deep emotions lead to deep learning. But I was worried, too. The class included students from Mexico and El Salvador who came to this country out of economic desperation. Other students, including individuals from Yemen, Japan, and Pakistan, came from more

GAIL GELTNER, TIMES OF WAR AND PEACE

privileged backgrounds. I hoped I could lead in a way that the diversity would enrich our learning, not feed tensions based on class or culture.

It's difficult to find good social science text sources for ELLs. Writers and publishers tend to "accommodate" ELL students by eliminating the complexity and contradictions in the content. But limited English doesn't mean limited capacity for critical thinking. I usually look for strong materials and then expand, rewrite, or excerpt as needed. I knew I wanted to use *Rethinking Globalization: Teaching for Justice in an Unjust World* as the basis for my curriculum, but it needed adaptation for ELLs.

The first challenge was providing a definition of globalization that would tie the course together. My experience in a mainstream class the year before was that many students "got" pieces of globalization—like sweatshops and the World Trade Organization (WTO)—but never saw the system as a whole. They got the trees, but not the forest. I hoped that explaining the definition up front, posting it on the wall, and referring back to it periodically would help students keep both trees and forest in view. Unfortunately, there's no simple, quick definition of globalization. After comparing definitions in a range of books and websites, I ended up writing my own:

Unfortunately, there's no simple, quick definition of globalization.

Globalization—More than ever before in history, there is one world economy. This pressure toward one world economy is called globalization. Globalization is the struggle for control of the earth's resources—natural resources, human resources, and capital resources. There are eight elements of globalization:
1. Migration.
2. Big companies are international companies.
3. Resources are international.
4. Free trade agreements.
5. World Bank and International Monetary Fund (IMF).
6. Sweatshops.
7. Environmental problems.
8. Increased communication among peoples—the basis for resistance.

Before I introduced the definition, we did a gallery walk: I created collages with three to five images representing each of the elements of globalization and posted them around the room. I asked students to circulate and look at each collage. Then I asked the following questions: What are five important details you see in this collage? What do you think this collage is about? What questions do you have about this collage? What questions does this collage raise about the world? We had a lively discussion of each collage and it helped me begin to explain the elements of globalization.

Then, as I promised that first day, we began with migration. We watched *Uprooted: Refugees of the Global Economy,* which introduces globalization in the context of three migration stories: Maricel from the Philippines, Luckner from Haiti, and Jessy and Jaime from Bolivia. As we watched the video, I asked students to take notes: Why did these people have to leave their countries? What were their thoughts and feelings about migrating? What problems did they have as immigrants? Is anything about their experiences similar to yours? Each time I stopped the video for discussion, common threads emerged: "Even though Maricel studied hard in school, there were no jobs for her—that's just like in Pakistan." "Jessy and Jaime missed their children so much—my father didn't see us for 12 years." "My uncle's factory in El Salvador moved to Nicaragua—like Luckner's moved to China." "Everyone in the movie has problems with immigration papers. In my family some of us have papers to be here and some of us don't—I feel scared all the time." I used this opportunity to open a discussion about the many reasons why some immigrants don't have legal documents. "In this class," I concluded, "everyone is welcome, and we don't want to put anyone in danger. Please be careful what you ask and what you share. And can we agree that what we discuss in class stays in class?" Everyone agreed.

Why did these people have to leave their countries? What were their thoughts and feelings about migrating? What problems did they have as immigrants? Is anything about their experiences similar to yours?

Then we started to collect our own information. I sent students home with global migration oral interview worksheets. Their assignment was to interview a parent or older relative who had migrated to the United States. The interview questions were keyed to the elements of globalization. For example: What are the most important economic and natural resources in your country? Which resources are publicly owned? Privately owned? How has the economy changed in the past 20 years? Why did you migrate to the United States? I encouraged students to interview family members in their first language and then translate the answers into English.

My expectations for this activity were modest. I figured we'd gather some information about natural resources and industry that we could use later in the semester, and collect data on why people migrate. I included questions about which resources are publicly and privately owned to lay groundwork for our study of the World Bank and IMF later in the semester, but I expected many question marks on the surveys.

Two days later, when students returned with the completed surveys, we posted the information on butcher paper and compiled it by region. As they waited for their chance to write their responses on one of the charts, the students spontaneously clustered in groups, watching the findings go up and tracking patterns. One pattern that emerged was how often families were separated by migration. Another was the career sacrifices parents make: Beza's father had been a principal in Ethiopia but works as a teacher's aide here; Maria's father was an engineer in Pakistan, but here he does clerical work.

I was amazed at the depth of information we received and the time that parents and other relatives spent in sharing a wealth of experience and knowledge. We got great information on resources, public and private ownership, changes in the economy—everything. As an engineer in Pakistan, Maria's father had a professional's understanding of energy resources. José's cousin knew firsthand about the North American Free Trade Agreement (NAFTA) and how he and his family were forced off their land in Mexico when the price of corn fell year after year. Every family had personal stories and specific pieces of information that contributed to the global picture we were creating.

> **The enthusiasm my students and their families demonstrated for this project made me realize what a mistake it is to ignore families as resources.**

High school educators don't talk much about the importance of the connection between home learning and school learning. The enthusiasm my students and their families demonstrated for this project made me realize what a mistake it is to ignore families as resources. This is particularly true for immigrant students, who sometimes feel they must leave their family and culture behind to "make it" in the United States.

One part of the survey that elicited rich results was the question "How has immigration to the United States affected your family?" Hamza's father said, "[The positive effects are that] my family is getting a good education, jobs, and dreams come true. [The negative effects are that] my family has to work full time during their studies. We have less time to spend in the house. We have less time to sit together and talk." During our class discussion Delia said, "I never knew what it was like for my father when he first came from Mexico until I just asked him now. I had no idea how hard it was."

I asked the students to use the information from their survey as background for writing the story of their own migration or the story of one of the people they interviewed. And I requested that all the stories be written in first person. I read them a couple sample immigration stories and gave them a word count (400 words). When the stories were complete, we read them aloud in small groups.

Building Community

Asking students to share the complexity and pain of their families' migrations was a risk, but it did push class discussions to a deeper level as students shared their feelings and the feelings of their families. This deeper level of connection with the material built class community. As one student said in her end-of-year evaluation, "When I am sharing my ideas with the group, I feel very friendly because people are talking very nicely to each other—with respect, no racism." It also enabled the students to engage with academic material that was very difficult for their level of English language development. The most marked result from my perspective was their willingness, spring of senior year, to think critically about the world economy.

One of the many strengths of *Rethinking Globalization* is the emphasis on rooting globalization in the history of colonialism. During our very first discussions of globalization, José asked, "Why are some countries so much richer than others?" Astri asked, "Why do some countries have so many resources and others so few?" I wanted to make sure that every student understood that power and wealth in the current situation is based on what happened during centuries of colonialism and imperialism.

The center of our study of colonialism was the "Six Building Blocks of Colonialism": stealing resources, cash crops, factories instead of crafts, drawing borders, holding up the hierarchy, and west is best (adapted from *Rethinking Globalization,* p. 35). After we discussed the building blocks, students created booklets with drawings that illustrated each building block. From looking at the drawings, I could tell at a glance whether they understood the concepts.

Then we headed for the library. The assignment was to pick a country that was colonized and create a poster explaining how each of the six building blocks applied to that country's history. The students worked in teams of two or three. Many of them chose their own countries and they brought their prior knowledge of colonialism to the patterns we discussed in class. The class discussion was broadened by history learned in schools in Pakistan, Mexico, Indonesia, Taiwan, China, Brazil, Yemen, and Japan. Faryal wrote the following:

> It connects with my life because Pakistan and India were one country when the British came to take over. The British people made it very hard for my people and made conflict between them. Pakistan and India got separated. Some Indian people stayed in Pakistan with the Muslim people, and most of the Pakistani people are in India and can't come to live with their own people. I learned a lot from this topic because now I actually know how and why everything happened.

Asking students to share the complexity and pain of their families' migrations was a risk, but it did push class discussions to a deeper level as students shared their feelings and the feelings of their families.

Tackling 'Free Trade'

One of the most complicated aspects of globalization is the role of the World Bank and the IMF. I was searching for a concrete and personal way to introduce structural adjustment policies and the IMF when my cousin reminded me that credit card debt balloons in very similar ways to IMF debt. What's more important for young adults to understand than the pitfalls of those seductive pieces of plastic?

I downloaded a couple of credit card offers aimed at college students. We went through them line by line, defining terms and reading the small print together. Raymond, calculator in hand, showed us on the board what happens if you charge $1,000, miss a payment, and then pay the minimum amount each month for a year.

This worked well as an introduction to *Life and Debt in Jamaica,* an excellent video on the role of the IMF, World Bank, and WTO policies on postcolonial Jamaica. The impact of IMF policies on the dairy industry, farming, banana plantations, and manufacturing are all illustrated in depth. Michael Manley, former president of Jamaica, explains why he felt he had to accept the IMF loan and conditions; IMF and World Bank leaders explain why they believe their policies are good for Jamaica; and Jamaican farmers, workers, and economists describe the impact on their lives and on the country. The voiceovers and accents are difficult for English language learners, so we went slowly and stopped frequently for interpretation and discussion. As we watched the video, students created dialogue journals. On the left side of the page, they recorded quotations and described significant images from the video. On the right side, they wrote personal reflections and reactions. Alvin applied his new understanding of free trade policies to migration from his homeland, Hong Kong:

> In some countries, there are a lot of people with no jobs because their businesses were destroyed by free trade. Because of the problem of getting jobs, people immigrate to other countries and settle down there. In Hong Kong in 1997, the year it was returned to China, people were scared there would be a financial storm because free trade is changing China. That's why people started immigrating to Canada or somewhere else.

One student's reflections took the form of a poem:

> Debt is like a deep and dark circle,
> It has a way in, not a way out.
> Debt is like a deep and dark circle,
> It puts conditions on you.
> Debt is like a deep and dark circle,
> It makes you non-independent.
> Debt is like a deep and dark circle,
> It always goes up, but lets you go down.
> Debt is like a deep and dark circle,
> But you can come out by being together.

At the end of the semester, I gave the class a choice of culminating activities. Somewhat to my surprise, the students decided to create a text for English language learners on globalization. We brainstormed a list of the most important things we learned over the semester, and the students narrowed the list down to eight chapters:

Somewhat to my surprise, the students decided to create a text for English language learners on globalization.

1. What Is Economics?
2. Migration: We Are Part of Globalization
3. Colonialism: The Roots of Globalization
4. What Is Globalization?
5. The IMF and Poor Countries in Debt
6. Sweatshops, Free Trade, and Fair Trade
7. Globalization Means the Whole World Can Fight for Justice
8. Economics Is the Fight for Resources: The War in Iraq

I developed a framework for the chapters and an assignment sheet, and the students divided themselves into eight groups. Each group was responsible for developing a list of the information that should be included in their chapter and for assigning sections. In addition to the core information, each chapter included personal reflections, an illustration, focus questions, vocabulary, and activities. By now we were well into May of their senior year, but everyone wrote at least two drafts of their section and a reflection as well as collaborating with their teammates on the other pieces. The students submitted their final drafts on flash drive or via email; I compiled and edited the final text. When we were finished, we had a 53-page spiral-bound book, *Globalization: Economics in the 21st Century, Immigrant Students Teach Students.*

> **One of the most complicated aspects of globalization is the role of the World Bank and the IMF.**

My favorite part of the book is the reflections at the end of each chapter because there I can see the critical thinking process. For example, here Shoaib reflects on Chapter 4, "What Is Globalization?"

> The big countries are getting stronger and more powerful, and small countries are getting weaker. The big countries are taking air, land, and a lot of resources from other countries. After learning all about globalization and the dilemmas of global trade, my point of view is that the world is getting worse and worse. With no tariffs on products, it seems like big countries have most of the power in the world. It is destroying the world economy. If I were the president of the United States, I would change all the world and make everyone equal. I would make the whole world one country and live in peace.

Next Steps

Of course the next step is to use the student-generated textbook with the next generation of students. Ideally there would be a progression, with each new class using the previous year's text as a springboard for their own. Stay tuned. . . .

On the end-of-year evaluation, I asked students what skills they thought they had improved. More than half of the responses were specifically related to critical thinking about the world. For example, "I've become more aware and sensitive about the changes of people's lives because of economic problems." "We understand what is the real meaning of migration. It was important to me because I also migrated to another country." But the most exciting response was the suggestion from several students that we should have returned to look at the economies of their home countries in the light of their new understanding of globalization. Their eagerness to apply what we learned to reanalyzing the situation of their home countries is the best evidence of what we accomplished.

One aspect of the curriculum that didn't work as well as I had hoped was the unit on resistance. After so much appalling information on the injustices of globalization, I hoped my students would feel excited by the opportunities that increased global connection provides for international solidarity. We read articles, researched organizations on the internet, and watched several videos, but this section lacked the fire and intensity of other parts of the semester. Next time I will integrate resistance into each unit; when it's tacked on at the end, it just doesn't work. I will also prioritize bringing in speakers (or maybe we'll take a field trip to Bolivia!). One of my colleagues had an additional suggestion: Students need explicit support in going from classes with progressive, critical perspectives to "the rest of the world." In other words, I need to help them navigate the distance between the view of globalization we studied and the one they may encounter in their next economics class.

> **Their eagerness to apply what we learned to reanalyzing the situation of their home countries is the best evidence of what we accomplished.**

When I decided to use the students' own migration as the starting point for studying globalization, I was operating partly on instinct. I hoped it would engage students at the beginning, but I saw migration as an isolated "element," one detached piece of the globalization story. I didn't really grasp myself how central it was to the global web. It took the students and their parents to show me the way. Here is how Rizwana, Mariam, and Yaneli described the connection in their introduction to their chapter, "Migration Is Part of Globalization":

Migration is part of the world economy today. It is a big piece of globalization. The changes in the world economy are good for some countries and bad for other countries. If there are no jobs in your own country or if there is a war, many people have to migrate to other places in the world. That is part of globalization. Because we are a class of students who were all immigrants to the United States, our family stories are a good way to begin to understand globalization.

We closed the year by writing poems to express our hopes for the future. Here is Delia's:

The world shall be one nation
Where there is no discrimination for skin color

Where the word humanity has presence
As the water sparkling through the mountains
The world shall be unity
As the ants lining together form a group
Working for each other and helping each other
The world shall be never defeated
It shall be so strong that even
Wars or natural disasters won't
Make it fall down
There shall be a world where
The words war, hatred, and ambition
Don't exist
Because the world shall be love, peace
Freedom and friendship.

Jody Sokolower is currently managing editor of Rethinking Schools. *Previously she taught social studies and English to middle and high school students in the California Bay Area.*

Resources

BOOKS:

Bigelow, B., & Peterson, B. (Eds.) (2002). *Rethinking Globalization: Teaching for Justice in an Unjust World.* Milwaukee: Rethinking Schools.

Cho, E., Paszy Puente, F., Louie, M., & Khokha, S. (2004). *Bridge: Building a Race and Immigration Dialogue in the Global Economy.* Berkeley, CA: Inkworks Press.

VIDEOS:

Uprooted: Refugees of the Global Economy. National Network for Immigrant Rights and the Interfaith Coalition for Immigrant Rights, 2002. Bilingual with English/Spanish subtitles.

Life and Debt. Stephanie Black, director. New Yorker Films, 2001.

Zoned for Slavery: The Child Behind the Label. National Labor Committee, 1995.

Chapter Thirty

ARRANGED MARRIAGES, REARRANGED IDEAS

By Stan Karp

Jihana was one of my favorite students. By the time she was a senior, we had been together for three years, first in a sophomore English class and then through two years of journalism electives where students produced school publications and learned desktop publishing. Jihana's bright-eyed intelligence and can-do enthusiasm made her a teacher's dream. Her daily greeting in our busy journalism office was "Hi, Mr. Karp, what needs to be done?" I used to joke that she'd get straight A's until the end of her senior year when I'd have to fail her so she couldn't graduate and leave. It was corny, but she always laughed. Jihana was one of a growing number of Bengali students in my Paterson, N.J., high school. Along with increasing numbers of Latin American, Caribbean, Middle Eastern, Central European, and other immigrants, these new communities had transformed the school in the 20 years I'd been there as a teacher. What had once been a predominantly white, then later a primarily black and Latino student population was now

DONNA DECESARE

thoroughly international. The teaching staff, however, remained mostly white, with a limited number of teachers of color.

Increasingly, some of my best students each year were young Bengali women. Some, like Jihana, covered their heads with scarves in keeping with Muslim tradition. A few wore the full veil. Others wore no special dress. Many seemed reserved and studious. Others gradually adopted the more assertive, outgoing styles of the city-wise teens around them.

An Arranged Marriage

By the time Jihana was a senior it was natural for me to ask, during one of the many extra periods she spent in the journalism office, what her postgraduation plans were. She said she wanted to go to college, perhaps to study medicine, and was considering several schools. But, she added, a lot depended on whether she had to get married.

I knew enough about Jihana, and about the Bengali community, to know that she wasn't referring to a premature wedding prompted by an unplanned pregnancy, but to the possibility of an arranged marriage. Jihana made it pretty clear that she wasn't ready to get married. She was anxious to go to college and to move out of a household where she felt she had too many cleaning chores and childcare duties and not enough personal freedom. She said the outcome partly depended on what happened with her sister, who was several years older and also a candidate for marriage, and on whether her family decided to send them both back to Bangladesh in the summer for possible matches. I listened sympathetically and made schoolteacher noises about how smart I thought she was and how I hoped she'd get the opportunity to attend college. Unsure of just what my role, as a white, male, high school teacher, could possibly be in this situation, I halfheartedly offered to speak to her family about her college potential if she thought it would help. Jihana smiled politely and said she'd keep me posted. I went home thinking about Jihana's situation. I was upset, even angered, by the thought that this young woman's promising prospects and educational future could be sidetracked by a cultural practice that seemed to me hopelessly unreasonable and unfair. No matter how I tried to come to terms with it, the custom of arranged marriages was completely alien to my own sensibilities and to my expectations for my students. I kept thinking of how my own high school-aged daughter, raised at home—and at least nominally at school—to think in terms of gender equality and independence, would laugh in my face if I ever sat her down and tried to tell her my plans for her marital future.

> **Unsure of just what my role, as a white, male, high school teacher, could possibly be in this situation, I halfheartedly offered to speak to her family about her college potential.**

I also thought, and not for the first time, about what my responsibilities were as a public school teacher, and how I should manage this mix of my own strongly held personal opinions, concern for my students' well-being, and respect for the cultural differences that were increasingly evident in my school community.

As both a political activist and a classroom teacher, I'd wrestled with these issues often. On the one hand, I'd come to believe that effective classroom teaching, especially in schools with a history of failure and pervasive student alienation, was inherently "political," in the sense that it had to take the social context of schooling and of students' lives as a primary point of departure. I tried to encourage students to "talk back" to the world we studied, and, wherever possible, to take action in response to ideas and issues. These premises informed any number of choices I made daily about curriculum, classroom organization, and how to channel in particular directions the "oppositional energy" I found in most teenagers. It also meant I frequently tried to take real situations in my students' lives, both in and out of school, as starting points for research, writing, and class discussion. At the same time, I know it is neither appropriate nor fair for teachers to restrict the curriculum to only those views and ideas that they personally agree with. Since teachers have power over students, it's especially necessary to be sensitive to issues of intimidation, the rights of dissent, personal privacy, and freedom of choice. In some ways, the closer issues hit to home, as in Jihana's situation, the more careful teachers must be, particularly where racial, cultural, and class differences are involved. At first glance, Jihana's problem seemed personal and private, not readily the stuff of classroom discussion. It had social roots and cultural dimensions like other student concerns that had become the subject of class assignments or research. But it seemed to call for an individual, personal response on my part, rather than a pedagogical one, and I had real trouble imagining what that response should be.

> I also thought about how I should manage this mix of my own strongly held personal opinions, concern for my students' well-being, and respect for the cultural differences that were increasingly evident in my school community.

Reluctant to Intervene

As a rule, I have generally been reluctant to intervene at home when it comes to handling personal and family issues with my teenage students. Though I've always supported parents' participation in their children's education, for me this usually has meant support for parent participation in governance and policymaking processes, or finding ways to include parent and family experience in my curriculum.

But when personal (as opposed to strictly academic) problems arise with secondary-age students, I've always hesitated to "call home" too quickly. Most of the 15- to 18-year-olds I deal with are emerging adults who've been semi-independent to varying degrees for years: holding down jobs, assuming family responsibilities, traveling the world, dealing with the courts and immigration authorities, and even coping with parenthood themselves. Others come from difficult family situations that are not always supportive or, not infrequently, may even be the source of the problems they choose to share with me. In the normal course of a year, it's not unusual for me to deal with teenagers who are wrestling with everything from homelessness, pregnancy, and sexual identity to depression, domestic violence, and drug abuse.

When my students bring such issues to me, I've always felt that my first allegiance was to them, to listen sympathetically and to offer whatever advice or access to services I could manage, and not, primarily, to act as a surrogate for, or even mediator with, parental authority. Yes, there have been occasions when my judgment, or the legal responsibilities that are periodically spelled out in nervous memos from central office, compel me to pick up the phone or make a home visit. But in general I take my signal about whether home intervention on my part makes sense from my students, and most of the time it doesn't. There have also been times when I've passed on information about where to get birth control or other kinds of counseling services (for example, for gay teens) that I knew might not be fully endorsed at home.

In Jihana's case I tried to imagine what I could possibly say to her family about the situation: "Hi, I'm Jihana's teacher, and as a politically progressive, pro-feminist, privileged white male, I think your plans for Jihana are a medieval abomination."

I don't think so.

The problem was figuring out the dividing line between responding to the needs of my students and interfering inappropriately with 'other people's children.'

But the more I thought about it, the more I realized that the problem wasn't finding more diplomatic ways to voice my opinions; the problem was figuring out the dividing line between responding to the needs of my students and interfering inappropriately with "other people's children." I also thought about another student I had some 10 years earlier, Rafia, who faced this same situation. Rafia was the youngest of four daughters in a Bengali family. Smart, sophisticated beyond her years, and ambitious, Rafia was anxious to go to college despite her family's objections. As I encouraged her and helped her fill out applications during her junior and senior years, it was Rafia who first made me aware that many Bengali families did not think girls should go to college, and that she and her sisters were facing, with varying degrees of dread, the prospect of arranged marriages. I was horrified at the idea, and said so. In fact, as I recall, my main reaction consisted of expressing my outrage that women were oppressed this way in her culture. I told her I didn't think anyone had the right to tell her who to marry, and that it was much more important for her future to go to college than to please her parents. I even suggested that it was more important to choose college than to avoid a break with her family, and that, even if they got upset, they would probably get over it. I somewhat flippantly told her she could stay at my house for a while if she decided to run away.

Learning a Lesson

When Jihana's story jogged my memory, it was with more than a little embarrassment that I recalled how my reaction to Rafia had been foolish, and not a little arrogant. At the time I had acted as if the most important response to Rafia's dilemma was to show her that not everyone was as "backward" as her parents, and that there were swell, "enlightened" folks like myself who believed in her right to shape her own future and education. In effect I was showing off the "superior" values and "advanced" thinking of "progressive Western culture," especially of radicals like myself, and contrasting it to the "underdeveloped practices" of her own community, which I encouraged her to reject. I had also reacted as if what I thought and how I felt about the issues raised by her predicament were of paramount importance, and should be the point of departure for my response. Looking back, it seemed that the problem wasn't that I was wrong to oppose the custom of arranged marriages or to make my opinions known, but that I did it in a way that was essentially self-serving, and as a practical matter, not very helpful. I had basically denounced what I, as an outsider, saw as "deficient" in her culture and encouraged her to turn her back on it.

While my sympathies may have been well meant, my advice was culturally insensitive and wildly impractical. And it probably just reinforced Rafia's sense of alienation and being trapped.

Fortunately, Rafia was sharp enough to appreciate my personal support and ignore my advice. Instead of running away or openly breaking with her family, she steadfastly argued for her chance to attend college while continuing to excel in school. Eventually, she got her father's permission to go to college (though she was forced to study engineering instead of the humanities she preferred). The experience had stayed with me over the years, and now that a similar situation had arisen, I was anxious to do better by Jihana. A couple of weeks passed after our first conversation, and it became clear that nothing decisive would happen with Jihana's situation until the summer came. Still looking for a way to lend support, one day I suggested to Jihana that she consider writing a story about arranged marriages for our student magazine. I mentioned briefly my experience with Rafia and asked how the growing community of female Bengali students in the high school felt about this and related issues. Instead of dwelling on my own opinions, I tried to emphasize that she wasn't the only one facing these issues, and that she could perform a service for both Bengali students and the rest of the school by focusing on a set of concerns that had gotten little attention. Jihana seemed interested but hesitant. She was a good writer but generally took less ambitious assignments, like covering school news or activities. She expressed some concern that her family would

> **Looking back, it seemed that the problem wasn't that I was wrong to oppose the custom of arranged marriages or to make my opinions known, but that I did it in a way that was essentially self-serving.**

be offended if they found out, and that, in the tight-knit Bengali community, it might be hard to keep it a secret even if she published a piece anonymously. I asked her to think it over and told her she could get credit for writing the article even if she decided in the end not to publish it. I also told her, as I told all my students, that we could consider the implications or consequences of going public later, but she should write what she really thought and not censor herself in advance.

> **I was hoping to use the tremendous potential that writing has, not only to help students express their ideas and feelings but also to help them develop the skills, and sometimes the distance, needed to analyze complicated topics and clarify issues.**

I was hoping to use the tremendous potential that writing has, not only to help students express their ideas and feelings but also to help them develop the skills, and sometimes the distance, needed to analyze complicated topics and clarify issues. Although I hoped Jihana would eventually publish, it seemed valuable to have her organize and express her thoughts for her own purposes as well. After a few days, and after double-checking that she wouldn't have to publish the piece if she wasn't comfortable, she agreed. She asked for help making an outline, so we arranged a story conference.

A Broader Context

When we started discussing how to organize the article, Jihana said she wanted to deal first with stereotypes and misconceptions that Westerners had about Muslims. She said she wanted to put the issue of arranged marriages in a broader context of Muslim culture, which had a variety of customs and practices that she felt were misunderstood. Muslim women were not "slaves," she said, and not everyone did things the same way. When it came to marriage, there was a range of practices, and in many cases, Muslim women did have choices and varying degrees of input into the decision.

This led to a discussion of women and marriage customs in general, and how women have faced oppression and male supremacy in all cultures. We also talked about the generational conflict between young Bengalis (and other younger immigrants) raised in the United States, and their parents, rooted in more traditional "old country" customs, and how this exacerbated the struggle over marriage practices. Jihana told me stories about families that had been torn apart by these differences, as well as others where parents and children had found common ground and happy endings. As we talked, several things started to become clear. By locating the issue of arranged marriages inside the broader issue of women's rights, which cuts across all cultures and countries, it became easier for Jihana to address the topic without "stigmatizing" her own community. If Bengali women had to wrestle with arranged marriages and male dominance, the supposedly more "liberated" sexual culture of the United States presented women with its own set of problems: higher levels of sexual assault, single teenage parenthood, divorce, and domestic violence. Generational conflict between old ways and new also cut across cultures and made the issue seem more universal, again allowing it to be addressed in a context that didn't demonize one particular group.

Finally, it was clear that speaking on behalf of Bengali women, instead of just against the practice of arranged marriages, tended to make Jihana feel more empowered than isolated. She was still determined to question the imposition of marital arrangements against the woman's will, but would do so in the context of defending Muslim culture against stereotypes and as part of a critique of women's oppression as a whole. Added to the protection she felt from not having to publish her work if she chose not to, assuming this positive stance on behalf of herself and her peers seemed to give her the safe space she needed from which to address these difficult issues. By the end of our conversation, she seemed ready to go. Within a week or two, Jihana was back with her article. "Do Muslim women have any rights?" she began.

> **By locating the issue of arranged marriages inside the broader issue of women's rights, which cuts across all cultures and countries, it became easier for Jihana to address the topic without 'stigmatizing' her own community.**

> Do they make their own decisions? Are they allowed to think? Are they prisoners in their own homes? There are many stereotypes held by Westerners about the position and role of Muslim women. . . . These notions are based upon the lack of knowledge Westerners have of Islam.

> Women, regardless of their culture or society, have suffered tremendously over inequality and have had to fight for a firm place in their society. During the Roman civilization, a woman was considered to be a slave. The Greeks bought and sold their women as merchandise rather than accept them as human beings. Early Christianity regarded their women as "temptresses," responsible for the fall of Adam.

> In pre-Islamic times, as well as in certain places today, a female child is thought of as a cause for unhappiness and grief. Baby girls were sometimes buried alive after birth. But gaps in wealth, education, and justice between men and women can be found everywhere and just can't be explained by religion.

Jihana went on to discuss "some issues about the rights of a Muslim woman [that] stem from the issue of marriage." She wrote about the varying degrees of choice women may have in different families, the generational conflict, the problems associated with patterns of marriage in the United States. ("Some Muslim families say that while the Westerners seem to be 'more free,' their society is not working too well.") She cited examples to show that "as in all marriages, whether arranged or not, some work and some do not."

Though many of the Bengali students Jihana spoke to declined to be quoted by name, she did find one senior who "extremely disagrees with arranged marriages" and who thought "all Muslim women should be given an opportunity and the privilege to choose the person that they want to spend the rest of their lives with."

> **At bottom, Jihana's 'balancing act' was an affirmative statement about her place and her rights in her community.**

After exploring the issues from several sides, Jihana came to a balancing act that suggested her own personal struggle:

Arranged marriages and other Muslim customs of life, like the covering of the body and not dating, may seem to be burdensome to women of most Western cultures, but for Muslim women it's their way of life. We were brought up to follow and believe that these practices were the right ways of life. It is up to us as individuals to see that we follow what is expected of us. . . . The Muslim religion, in my opinion, can include double standards. . . . In many cases males are allowed to do certain things that females can't. . . . For example, when a male does get married without his parents' permission, it is OK, but if a female does the same thing it is not OK. This is so because in the Holy Koran it states that a woman has to follow certain things. For example, it is a woman's duty and obligation to bring up her children according to the ways of Islam. She has to look after the family and has absolute control over domestic affairs. She must wear a covering cloak when meeting adult men outside her family. She is her husband's helpmate. Islam recognizes the leadership of a man over a woman, but that does not mean domination.

In conclusion, women should have the freedom and right to do something they're interested in doing or accomplishing. They should go forward with their education if they want to continue it, with the help and support to do so. Women can cook and clean, but they could also do more.

At bottom, Jihana's "balancing act" was an affirmative statement about her place and her rights in her community. And though writing the article didn't resolve her dilemma, it did, I think, support her in her efforts to speak up for herself, and offered a way for her to develop some useful perspectives on her situation. It also helped focus attention on issues that she and her Bengali peers were wrestling with inside the school community.

New Pride

Though Jihana had originally balked at the idea of publication, by the time she was done she used the computer skills she'd learned in class to create a two-page layout for our magazine with her article, her byline, and her picture under the title, "Muslim Women: Where Do We Belong?" She seemed proud of it, and so was I, especially as I reflected on what I'd learned myself.

Switching the focus from my own reactions to my student's point of view, and developing a deeper appreciation of the need to deal with issues of cultural difference with more humility and care, had led me to a more effective and more appropriate response. I was still just as opposed as ever to arranged marriages, and still saw contradictions in Jihana's balancing act about the codes of Islam. But because I hadn't begun with an attack on the cultural norms of her community, I had managed to find a way that, to some degree at least, both supported and empowered her. As it turned out, Jihana's willingness to raise such issues was not limited to our magazine. One morning in the spring, I found her working feverishly in the journalism office on a list of "Bengali Concerns" for the next Student Government Association meeting. The list had a tone familiar from earlier days of student activism, but it had specifics I'd never seen before. It read:

1. How come there aren't more Bengali SGA members?
2. There is a lack of Bengali students involved in school activities. We need more participation and more representation of the Bengali people.
3. We need Bengali-speaking guidance counselors and teachers.
4. We need Bengali mentors.
5. How come the history teachers never teach about Bangladesh and its culture when they teach world history?
6. Why isn't there Bengali student representation when the school presents a panel of students to represent the school?
7. How come all the newsletters that go home from the school are either in Spanish or in English? How come you can't send letters home that are in Bengali? That way the parents will know what is going on in their children's school. The lack of communication with the Bengali parents is a reason why many don't attend the Home-School Council meetings.

New Steps for Jihana

Around the same time that these concerns were being presented to the student government, preparations were under way for an assembly presentation of Bengali dance and traditional dress. Like many other schools, my high school was still in the relatively superficial stages of addressing multicultural issues, and tended toward food festivals and holiday celebrations. But the assembly program tapped the energy of many Bengali students, and Jihana had gotten involved. One afternoon, soon after our magazine had appeared, she came to the journalism office and asked if I could fax a copy of her article to a reporter from a local newspaper. She said she'd been interviewed in connection with the upcoming assembly program, but had left some things out. "I was trying to explain myself to the reporter and couldn't get the words out right," she said. "I told him I had written an article explaining what I thought, and it was all in there. I promised to send it to him." The article she had been hesitant to write and reluctant to publish had become a personal position statement.

As we headed into the last weeks of the school year, I occasionally asked Jihana if there were any new developments. There weren't any on the marriage front, but she did get accepted to several colleges and began to make plans to attend a state university. When we parted at year's end, I made her promise to let me know how things turned out. About a month later, I returned from a trip to find a slightly ambiguous message. Jihana had called to say hello and to invite me to a wedding. Taken aback, and fearing that this might be her way of letting me know that marriage had won out over college, I called her at home. She was in good spirits and busy getting ready to move into the dorms on her new campus. The invitation was to her sister's wedding, Jihana explained, and if I could come I'd get a chance to see some more of how Bengali marriage customs worked. Unfortunately, I wasn't able to attend, but Jihana promised to show me the proceedings on videotape.

Like many other schools, my high school was still in the relatively superficial stages of addressing multicultural issues, and tended toward food festivals and holiday celebrations.

In September Jihana started college classes. A few weeks later, I got a note describing her new life. "College is OK," she wrote, "not that great as everyone said it would be. Maybe it is just me. I never realized how difficult my classes would be and so large in lectures!! I am taking an Arabic class so that I can be trilingual!"

"I have to go home every weekend, but I don't mind," she wrote. "I have a new status in my family; everyone respects me more, and I also don't have to do any more housework. Isn't that great??!!" I had to agree that it was.

The names of students in this article have been changed.

Stan Karp taught English and Journalism to high school students in Paterson, N.J. for 30 years. He is currently director of the Secondary Reform Project for New Jersey's Education Law Center, and an editor of Rethinking Schools.

Chapter Thirty-One

WELCOMING KALENNA

An early childhood teacher strives to make all her students feel at home

By Laura Linda Negri-Pool

When I was a child, our home was filled with the sounds of Spanish, mariachi music, and boisterous conversations. At home, my Nana cooked enchiladas, menudo, and tamales. During family celebrations we broke piñatas, danced, and hung papel picados. I was surrounded by six siblings, multiple cousins, tíos, and tías. My home was filled with light, color, art, texture, and love.

My school, in contrast, was drab, white, and unappealing.

I recall only one time when my Mexican American identity was validated during elementary school. When I was in 3rd grade, my mother organized a Cinco de Mayo event at our school. My father, siblings, and I cut out the papel picados,

HEIDI STAMBUCK/UNIVERSITY OF ARKANSAS

made the piñatas, formed the papier-mâché sculptures, and created paper flowers. Seeing my culture represented at school made me feel at home there for the first time.

I want my students to have more than one memory like that. I've taught preschool for 27 years, and I feel passionate about embracing families from nondominant cultures into the early childhood communities I work in.

As the result of a personal process of identity and cultural reclamation, I came to understand how my personal experiences influence this passion.

My experiences inspired me to find ways to make other marginalized children and families see themselves and their lives reflected in our classroom community.

Welcoming Kalenna

One fall day a few years ago, I held an open house to welcome the new children and families enrolled in our preschool program. When Kalenna entered our classroom, I immediately felt an affinity with her. Kalenna's dark, thick hair and chocolate brown skin set her apart from most of the other 14 children in the class. Our community college lab school served predominantly European American children whose parents were taking classes. Her mother, Diane, spoke with an accent that made me wonder if English was not her first language.

"Do you speak a language in addition to English?" I asked Diane.

She smiled and answered, "Marshallese." Our journey had begun.

I sensed Diane's feeling of relief and surprise when I asked about her language history. I knew from my own experiences what it was like to not be seen, to be treated with a question mark. I wondered how many times others had asked her, as they had me, "what she was" rather than respectfully and authentically inquiring about her. My question was an open and honest acknowledgment of her differences.

Over the next few months, I tried to infuse our classroom environment with the sounds, textures, and objects that surrounded Kalenna in her home.

Over the next few months, I tried to infuse our classroom environment with the sounds, textures, and objects that surrounded Kalenna in her home.

First I had to learn about the Marshall Islands. I had no idea where or what the Marshall Islands were, let alone anything about the Marshallese language and culture. I started with a map, where I learned that the Marshall Islands are a collection of 1,225 islands and islets in Micronesia. From the internet, I learned about the ongoing struggle of the Marshallese people to maintain their language and culture given their history of domination by Germany, Japan, and the United States. Following World War II, the United States conducted nuclear tests on the islands—including Bikini Atoll. These tests exposed many inhabitants to high radiation levels.

After gaining some knowledge of her origins, I was able to begin to speak more confidently with Kalenna's family. I began regular conversations with Diane, each of us sharing information about our family and culture.

I discovered a website with Marshallese music and language. I printed a list of simple words and phrases and brought it to the classroom. I showed Diane what I had found and asked her to translate a song into Marshallese. Each morning the children, student teachers, and I sang a greeting song utilizing the home languages of the children and adults present in our classroom, including Spanish, Chinese, and Afrikaans. Diane taught us how to sing our good morning song in Marshallese.

I asked Diane if she could help me locate items from the Marshall Islands that the students might use in the classroom. She brought in a hat, a basket, clothing, a hairpiece, and a necklace. We incorporated them into our dramatic play area. The children frequently wore the hairpiece and hat. The large basket with shells held an assortment of classroom materials throughout the year. The children loved wearing the seashell necklaces. They knew that the items belonged to Kalenna and treated them with care and respect.

After gaining some knowledge of her origins, I was able to begin to speak more confidently with Kalenna's family.

I invited Diane to record the book *No, David!* by David Shannon, on audiotape in Marshallese. The book was a favorite in our classroom due in part to the artwork, the simple text, and message of unconditional love. In the story, a little boy repeatedly gets in trouble for typical misbehaviors, including making a mess, overfilling the bathtub, and playing with a baseball in the house. The story concludes with the mother expressing her enduring love for him despite his antics. The children already could "read" each page in English. I partnered Diane with a mom who spoke Spanish. Together they recorded the book in their home languages. The mothers joined us at circle time to read the book aloud and to allow us to hear their voices on tape. From then on, Kalenna listened frequently to her mother's voice reading *Jaab, David*.

Bridging Cultures

One of my best memories of Kalenna is of the day she brought some of "her music" to class. I had invited her mother to share music that they listened to at home, in part because I was having difficulty locating Marshallese music.

Kalenna and I went to the CD player and began to listen. At first we listened to it as background music while the students played. Later Kalenna went to the large rug area. I began to move to the music and told her how much I liked it. Then she began to dance. As she danced, a magnificent smile appeared on her face. She clearly had a specific routine that she'd learned for that particular song. I began to mimic her movements. When the song ended, I rewound the tape and started it again. She began to teach me the moves. We laughed and moved, reveling in our intimate shared enjoyment. The other children watched, pausing in their own play to see our scene unfold. Later, some came and joined us. Kalenna's delight was evident as our dance continued. I had finally touched her where she lived.

A few years ago a former teacher of mine told me that he always pictured my face while reading of a young Mexican woman in the novel *The Pearl*. I was shocked. I never knew that he saw me as Mexican, that he associated me with the language, the culture, and the stories. I was touched, yet felt a loss. The loss was about not having my identity validated some 25 years earlier.

How I yearned to have a teacher who could see me, hear me, and dance with me.

Laura Linda Negri-Pool has worked in the field of early childhood education for more than 30 years. She is currently the Education Coordinator for Nike Child Development Programs in Beaverton, Ore.

Chapter Thirty-Two

EDWINA LEFT BEHIND

By Sören Wuerth

T he woman from the state education department had come to show us "the
data." She stood in an auditorium, in front of Ketchikan school district's some
300 teachers and staff and began a choppy Powerpoint presentation describing the standards on how students should soon be judged.

The official, dressed in a black blouse and black sport jacket, called herself a
"recovering" math and middle school teacher.

During her presentation, which I'd seen before, we were quizzed on the meaning of acronyms and asked multiple-choice questions about No Child Left Behind.
Judging from comments and muffled heckling behind me, I was not the only teacher who considered the education department's presentation demeaning.

As I listened, I reflected on Edwina, a student in the 12th-grade language arts
class I taught last year in the remote Cu'pik Eskimo village of Chevak. Chevak

SÖREN WUERTH

School is the dominant feature in the rural, western Alaska village. Just over 300 students shuffle from small, modular homes to the K–12 school, leaning into the wind most of the year to get there, crossing swells of snow drifts in the winter.

> **Edwina was tough. She had a round face, always wore the same sweatshirt and oval glasses, and maneuvered through two communities rife with drugs and alcohol like a running back moving past hapless opponents.**

Edwina was tough. She had a round face, always wore the same sweatshirt and oval glasses, and maneuvered through two communities rife with drugs and alcohol like a running back moving past hapless opponents.

Edwina's family lived in the coastal village of Hooper Bay, but she attended Chevak's school 20 miles inland, hoping her education would be superior to that of the neighboring village. On weekends, she'd leave her grandmother's place and drive a snowmobile 40 miles across frozen tundra, in weather that dipped to 60 below, to visit her home village. Edwina beat up boys who picked on her brothers, swore, and chewed tobacco. She turned to her schoolwork with the same rugged self-assurance.

A senior, Edwina needed to pass the state's High School Graduation Qualifying Exam to receive a diploma. Early in the year, I downloaded practice tests the state education department offered on its site. The sample test was three years old and students were so familiar with it they had many of the answers memorized.

Edwina didn't complain. She took the test seriously, as she did most of her school assignments. She remained after class to finish projects, always smiling, easily falling into laughter. She was a good writer. One of her stories, detailing the time she got lost riding through a blizzard behind her father on his snowmobile, eventually appeared in a journal of high school writing. A disciplined student, Edwina maintained a straight-A average throughout her school career. When a storm gripped the village and other students decided not to go to school, Edwina would invariably trudge through wind-packed snow to ensure an immaculate attendance record.

As the woman from the state droned on about formulaic assessment, I thought of how, as far as the state was concerned, Edwina's entire education—all that she'd learned and all that she had endured to obtain it—would come down to one test.

Kids in the village struggle to memorize vocabulary and concepts with which they have no connection. A counselor in my village told me the story of an elementary student who began crying during a test. When the counselor asked her what was wrong, the girl pointed to the word "curb" and said she didn't know what it meant. In her community, on a dusty knoll above thousands of acres of barren tundra, residents travel on dirt paths with four-wheelers and snowmobiles.

It seems every teacher who has worked in Alaska's rural school system has a story of the cultural ignorance of standardized tests. A question that stumped a student in my wife's 2nd-grade class asked for the best choice on how to get to a hospital: boat, ambulance, or airplane. Since the nearest hospital is 300 miles away, the student circled the logical, yet "incorrect," answer: airplane.

In Alaska, only about 40 percent of Native students graduate from high school, compared to almost 70 percent for all other ethnicities combined. There were 13 dropouts in Chevak the year I taught there. Generally, white students pass high-stakes tests at double the rate of their Native counterparts. In the region encompassing Chevak, an area the size of Iowa and dotted with more than 50 villages, only about a quarter of the students pass reading tests.

Edwina had lived her entire life in the remote villages of Hooper Bay and Chevak. It's a desolate region where the wind blows almost constantly across a vast delta of winding rivers, sloughs, and subarctic tundra. Edwina had to work hard to support her family. Her anna (grandma) and atta (grandpa) as well as other family members relied on her to help prepare food, cook, wash laundry, run to the village store, and perform hundreds of other tasks.

She tried to stay awake in class and, when I joked with her once about her sleepiness, she erupted in uncharacteristic anger: "I've been up all night working, babysitting, helping my anna and atta!"

Yet, the state graduation-qualifying exam would not ask about her snowmobiling experience, subsistence hunting on the frozen ocean, collecting driftwood, or preparing a traditional sauna called a "steam."

Worried about previous years' lackluster test results, Edwina took a supplementary class, from another teacher, designed specifically to "teach to the test." In my classroom, I deviated from language arts units geared toward critical thinking, inquiry-based learning, and cultural literacy, and devoted several weeks of classroom instruction to review test strategies, test content, and preparation. We analyzed sample tests, practiced using the process of elimination to discard distracting choices, and even discussed cultural biases in test questions.

It seems every teacher who has worked in Alaska's rural school system has a story of the cultural ignorance of standardized tests.

But in a village where kids are raised with a linguistically distinct form of English—called village English—and where young people struggle daily with the effects of economic hardship, domestic violence, and cultural disintegration, tests that ask students to compare personal digital assistants are irrelevant. Alaska Natives in rural villages have far greater concerns. With Alaska's Native communities suffering from the highest rates of fetal alcohol syndrome, teen suicide, and child abuse in the nation, staying healthy—and even alive—is the paramount motive.

I tried to take these real concerns into consideration in my classroom by making learning relevant to conditions my students faced in their communities while maintaining high expectations in an academically rigorous curriculum. We read books by Native American authors such as Sherman Alexie, reconstructed traditional narratives into plays, and analyzed comparisons between "home" language and Standard English.

I conducted a grant-writing unit so students could realize an authentic outcome for composition. Edwina wrote an introduction to a grant that was ultimately awarded to her senior class.

Little did I know, however, how severely high-stakes tests would undercut my efforts to motivate my Alaska Native students for reading and writing.

Near the end of the year, the counselor came into my classroom. She stood solemnly by the door, as someone would who is about to deliver the news of a death in the family. She held the test results and waited until students were sitting down.

> **Little did I know, however, how severely high-stakes tests would undercut my efforts to motivate my Alaska Native students for reading and writing.**

When the seniors looked at their test scores, some seemed unfazed by the results. Edwina, however, said she felt sick.

Because she didn't pass the test, Edwina didn't get a diploma when she graduated later that spring. None of her female classmates did.

Edwina wrote a letter about her shattered hopes and her view of schools—how she'd "been working hard in school all this time" since kindergarten, how she wanted to earn the diploma her older sister never received, how she's afraid she'll end up living with her mother the rest of her life. When she read her letter aloud, other students in class fell silent.

I suggested she send her letter to the editor of the Bethel paper, but drawing attention to oneself and one's problems is not customary among the Cu'pik Eskimo.

In Ketchikan, the department of education representative closed her presentation, saying, "Everyone's goal is to increase student achievement."

Edwina accomplished that goal. The state and the school district failed her.

Sören Wuerth is an educator, writer and activist currently teaching high school language arts in Anchorage.

Chapter Thirty-Three

WHO CAN STAY HERE?

Confronting issues of documentation and citizenship in children's literature

By Grace Cornell Gonzales

everal years ago, the bilingual elementary school where I taught in East Oakland was subject to an attempted U.S. Immigration and Customs Enforcement (ICE) raid. Rumors began to fly early in the school day among students and teachers—ICE agents had been seen parked several blocks away from the school. The campus went into a panic, terrified that the agents would apprehend parents on their way to pick their children up from school. Office staff and parent volunteers called each family at home, instructing them to send only documented friends or relatives to get their children at the end of the day. The administration

RICHARD DOWNS

contacted the press. Soon, Mayor Ron Dellums and members of the Oakland police force were gathered outside, denouncing the fear tactics being used by ICE.

While politicians made statements outside, it was my job inside to calm down a class of 1st graders who were all too aware of what an ICE raid meant. They knew their parents could be taken away or that they themselves could be forced to suddenly leave the familiarity of their homes and schools. As my students were playing outside during recess, a news helicopter began to circle above the playground. Half of my class came running back inside, panicked, hysterical, in tears, saying that *la migra* was coming in helicopters to get them. It was almost impossible to assuage that fear—to tell them that they were safe here and no one would take them away. Especially because I didn't really know if that was true.

The ICE agents never actually entered our school that day. Perhaps this was because intimidation had been their only goal, or perhaps the barrage of media attention put them off. However, I later learned that several other schools in East Oakland and South Berkeley were subject to similar intimidation tactics that day—ICE agents parked nearby, watching and waiting for parents and students to leave the campus. At one East Oakland elementary school, a mother was apprehended by ICE agents in the school hallway before the start of classes. She was led away in front of her 6-year-old daughter and gathered parents and staff.

Though many of these books dealt with border crossings, very few addressed issues of documentation and unequal access to citizenship.

Though such a dramatic brush with immigration enforcement didn't reoccur during the two years that I worked at that school, each year many teachers, myself included, were asked by parents to write letters on their behalf for immigration hearings. And each year I knew of at least one student whose mother or father was deported.

So when I set about compiling a list of children's picture books that deal with immigration issues, the memories of that attempted ICE raid and the deportation hearings were fresh in my mind. I found books that dealt with many themes: intergenerational ties and gaps, peer pressure and friendship, and, of course, language barriers and language learning.

What caught my attention was one theme that was missing. Though many of these books dealt with border crossings, very few addressed issues of documentation and unequal access to citizenship in any meaningful way. Indeed, most skirted around the topic, leaving unexplained holes in their narratives of immigration. Others explicitly sent the message that citizenship in this country is equally attainable by all—a fact that many of my students clearly know to be false from their own life experiences.

It is understandable that children's book authors are reticent to address such controversial and political issues in their books, especially in the current climate. Taking a strong stance on undocumented immigration and unequal access to citizenship could limit their audience. Many might consider the issues involved—deportation, the separation of families, economic and racial discrimination—too frightening or "adult" for the children who will read their books. Yet when I think about my students' fear on the day that ICE came near our school, I can't escape the realization that many of our children deal with these issues on a daily basis. These powerful experiences and fears make their way into students' school lives, whether we want them to or not.

When we create immigration units or read picture books about immigration to our children, I do not believe we have the luxury to avoid these topics. Indeed, I believe that if we do we risk marginalizing the students who cannot choose to ignore these issues in their daily lives. Of course, children should never be prompted to share sensitive personal information or disclose their immigration status, but these topics can be discussed safely through a literary lens. If we want to provide literature that helps children understand their world better and realize that they are not alone in the ways they feel and the problems they face, it is important to critically analyze children's books about immigration. What kinds of messages do they send to students about documentation and access to citizenship?

With all of this in mind, I identified three broad categories of books according to the extent to which they explore or obscure these themes. Here are a few examples to illustrate each category. I hope that this provides a framework for critical analysis of children's literature about immigration and is helpful to teachers planning curriculum or adding to their classroom libraries.

Creating the Image that Citizenship Is Equally Available to All

The first category comprises books that choose to ignore issues of undocumented immigration and unequal access to citizenship, portraying a world in which U.S. citizenship is equally (and often easily) available to all people. The most extreme example of this that I encountered is *A Very Important Day,* by Maggie Rugg Herold, in which families from the Philippines, Mexico, India, Russia, Greece, Vietnam, the Dominican Republic, China, Egypt, Ghana, Scotland, and El Salvador all joyously celebrate as they make the trip downtown to the courthouse to receive their papers and to be granted citizenship. They happily swear loyalty to the United States of America and recite the Pledge of Allegiance, waving tiny American flags as they exit the courthouse.

This book strongly implies that each family has had an equal opportunity to apply for citizenship, whether from Scotland or Ghana. They have all followed the same equitable legal process that is described in the epilogue. For a child unfamiliar with the economic, linguistic, and political issues that make U.S. citizenship far more attainable for some than others, this book creates a false sense of security—look, our system is working well! For a student who is undocumented or whose parents are undocumented, this book raises many unanswered questions— why can't we just go down to the courthouse, recite the Pledge of Allegiance, and become citizens if everyone else can? Unless a teacher is willing to engage with these issues and discuss the author's underlying assumptions with the students, this book could do more harm than good in a classroom setting.

The second book in this category, *How Many Days to America? A Thanksgiving Story,* by Eve Bunting, does portray immigration and border crossings as difficult, but the barriers suddenly and inexplicably disappear in the end when the need arises to create a happy ending. This book tells the wrenching story of a family that is forced to leave an unnamed Latin American country, fleeing from political oppression. They board a fishing boat to travel to the United States. Their journey is arduous—the motor breaks, the soldiers in their country shoot at them from the shore, their food and water run out, people become ill, and what little they have left is taken by thieves. When they finally arrive at the shore of the United States, they are greeted by soldiers who give them food and water but do not let them land. "They will not take us," the father comments sadly, but he refuses to explain why.

Yet suddenly, the next day, the boat makes landfall on U.S. shore again. This time there are no soldiers, but instead a large crowd of people who welcome the family and usher them into a shed with tables covered with delicious food. They explain that it is Thanksgiving and tell the new arrivals about the significance of that day in the United States. The book ends with a description of how "Father gave thanks that we were free, and safe—and here." The little sister asks if they can stay. "Yes, small one," the father replies. "We can stay."

This book clearly sets up a false expectation: No matter the struggle that it takes to get to the United States, once here, you are safe and you are allowed to stay. Yet this is so clearly not the case for many undocumented immigrants, and many children recognize that, despite their family's arduous journeys to this country, they still face the dangers of deportation, exploitation, and discrimination on U.S. soil. Just as this book stays silent on the reasons why the soldiers initially refuse to allow the family to land, it all too swiftly conjures up a happy ending when many questions still remain in the mind of a critical reader. Like *A Very Important Day,* it ignores the possibility that citizenship might not be attainable for all people who set foot on U.S. shores.

Someone Else's Problem

If the first category is comprised of books that ignore issues of documentation and equitable access to citizenship completely, the second category includes books that hint at these themes but do not explore them. They imply that the aforementioned dangers exist, yet avoid putting the main characters at any real risk. The message that they send is that deportation and the separation of families does occur, but that such things usually happen to someone else.

The first of these books, *My Diary from Here to There/Mi diario de aquí hasta allá,* by Amada Irma Pérez, is the diary of a girl who immigrates to the United States from Mexico. Although her father is a U.S. citizen, the family must wait a long time near the border while her father secures their green cards. The narrator expresses sadness at how she cannot see her father and fear that he will not be able to get green cards for the rest of the family. Yet they wait patiently, the green cards finally arrive, and the family is able to cross the border legally and be reunited. Interestingly, on the bus into the United States, the police arrest a woman without papers. This incident is mentioned but not discussed, leaving children on their own to question why some immigrants have documents and others do not.

Another book, the charming *Super Cilantro Girl/La superniña de cilantro*, by Juan Felipe Herrera, tells the story of Esmeralda, a child whose mother is stopped at the U.S.-Mexico border despite the fact that she is a U.S. citizen. Worried about her mother, Esmeralda dreams that she turns green like a bunch of cilantro, grows into a giant, and flies to the border to set her mother free. Here Herrera paints a vivid picture:

> She gawks at the great gray walls of wire and steel between the United States and Mexico. She stares at the great gray building that keeps people in who want to move on.

In the dream, Esmeralda rescues her mother. When the soldiers begin chasing her, she makes green vines and bushes of cilantro grow up and erase that border, declaring that the world should be *sin fronteras*—borderless. However, when Esmeralda wakes up in the morning, she discovers that everything was a dream and that her mother is already safely back home.

This book hints at the terror that children experience at the prospect of their families being split apart, but it does not actually put the characters in real danger. Esmeralda's mother is a citizen and does not truly run the risk of being separated from her family. In the foreword, Herrera expresses concern about families that are kept apart by borders and shares his wish that some superhero could abolish such borders and bring those families back together. However, his choice to make Esmeralda's mother a citizen in no danger of actually being barred from returning home still sends the message that family separation, deportation, and detention centers are all part of a dream from which you can wake up. If they are real dangers, they exist only in the lives of others.

Tackling the Subject

The final category includes the handful of books I found that do deal with issues of documentation and unequal access to citizenship head on. In *Hannah Is My Name,* by Belle Yang, a family immigrates to San Francisco from Taiwan. Though they apply for green cards, they wait more than a year to hear back from the government. During this time, the narrator's parents must work illegally to make ends meet. Hannah's mother is fired from her job in a clothing factory when the boss realizes that she doesn't have papers, and her father is constantly on the watch for immigration agents as he works at a hotel. One of Hannah's friends, Janie, a child from Hong Kong, is deported because Janie's father is discovered working at a Chinese restaurant before his family receives their green cards. And one day, while Hannah is visiting her father's work, she and her father are forced to flee from an immigration raid. From then on, her father must work at night. In the end, the story concludes happily—the family finally receives the green cards and is allowed to stay. In the process, however, the author exposes several key issues, including the seemingly arbitrary nature of the immigration process (e.g., papers can be delayed for extended periods of time without explanation) and the fact that many families must work illegally to survive while applying for documents.

América Is Her Name/La llaman América, by Luis J. Rodríguez, deals with many other harsh issues facing immigrant communities: neighborhood violence, unemployment, language barriers, and, importantly, racism, an issue that is not directly addressed in any of the books reviewed above. América's mother is called a "wetback" when she goes to the market. In school, América's ESL teacher, Ms. Gable, scornfully refers to her as an "illegal." América's confusion is heartbreaking:

> How could that be—how can anyone be illegal! She is Mixteco, an ancient tribe that was here before the Spanish, before the blue-eyed, even before this government that now calls her "illegal." How can a girl called América not belong in America?

This is a powerful question to pose to students, one that could generate much discussion. Fortunately, América finds release from the pressures of her life through writing poetry, discovering her voice and her place in this new passion. Her family and her teacher, who are initially skeptical, finally support her, telling her that she will be a real poet some day. "A real poet," the book concludes. "That sounds good to the Mixteca girl, who some people say doesn't belong here. A poet, América knows, belongs everywhere."

Teaching Critical Thought

The books critiqued above are only a few of the many that are available. However, although there are many children's books that deal with the experiences of Asian and Latin American (specifically Mexican) immigrants, there is a paucity of literature that tells the stories of immigrants from other places in the world, such as Africa or the Middle East. I urge teachers to seek out books that do represent these populations when building their classroom libraries, especially books that choose to tackle the difficult issues surrounding immigration status and citizenship. This is especially important if we want immigrant students to recognize that they are not the only ones who face struggles in the United States—that many different groups share similar experiences and that this may in turn be due to the existence of larger systemic injustices.

I have reflected on the books above from the perspective of a teacher whose class includes immigrant students, many of whom are undocumented or have undocumented family members. However, I believe that it is just as important for teachers who do not have immigrant students to look critically at the books about immigration available in their classrooms. In all probability, children who do not confront these issues in their daily lives are the least likely to question the portrayals of immigration in the books they read.

> **None of these books stands alone—read them aloud and make them the subject of group discussions.**

Finally, and most importantly, I want to emphasize that none of these books stands alone, regardless of whether they choose to confront or evade the topics of documentation and inequitable access to citizenship. Read these books aloud and make them the subject of group discussions before adding titles to the classroom library for independent reading. This is to assure that the sensitive issues involved can be treated with care, given the attention they deserve, and dealt with in a safe environment mediated by a caring adult. If our goal is to develop students who think critically about their own lives and about the world around them, teachers should be integrally involved in guiding children as they discover, explore, and analyze all of these books. I have tried to provide a framework to help us, as educators, look closely at the messages sent by the books about immigration that we choose for our classrooms. Thinking critically about the books ourselves is the first step in facilitating thoughtful dialogue among our students.

Grace Cornell Gonzales is a bilingual elementary school teacher in San Francisco, and an editorial associate of Rethinking Schools.

References

Bunting, Eve. *How Many Days to America? A Thanksgiving Story.* New York: Clarion, 1988.

Herold, Maggie Rugg. *A Very Important Day.* New York: Morrow Junior Books, 1995.

Herrera, Juan Felipe. *Super Cilantro Girl/ La superniña de cilantro.* San Francisco: Children's Book Press, 2003.

Pérez, Amada Irma. *My Diary from Here to There/Mi diario de aquí hasta allá.* San Francisco: Children's Book Press, 2002.

Rodríguez, Luis J. *América Is Her Name.* Willimantic, Conn.: Curbstone Press, 1997.

Rodríguez, Luis J. *La llaman América.* Willimantic, Conn.: Curbstone Press, 1998.

Yang, Belle. *Hannah Is My Name.* Cambridge, Mass.: Candlewick Press, 2004.

Chapter Thirty-Four

AQUÍ Y ALLÁ
Exploring our lives through poetry— here and there

By Elizabeth Schlessman

Allá en las montañas,
para entrar no necesitas
papeles, estás libre.

There in the mountains,
to enter you don't need papers,
you are free.

SCOTT BAKAL

driana's steady gaze accompanies her sharing of her poem during our Aquí/ Allá (here/there) poetry unit. Her words are met with silence and sighs, nods and bright eyes. She gets it, I think. In this verse of her poem, Adriana suddenly pushes beyond a contrast of the smells of pine and the cars of the city streets. She voices her critique of the world through her poem, contrasting two important places in her life—the city and the mountains.

The opportunity and space to find our voices—to see, name, analyze, question, and understand the world—is an invitation I work to create again and again in our 5th-grade dual language classroom about 30 minutes south of Portland, Ore. Labels and statistics define our school as 80 percent Latino, 70 percent English language learners, and more than 90 percent free and reduced lunch. My students spend 50 percent of their academic day in Spanish and the other half in English. Cultures, however, are not so easily equalized. The dominant culture—one in which much of my own identity was formed—can too easily shutter and silence the multifaceted, complex cultures of students' lives. My daily challenge is to pull up the details and experiences of their lives so that they become the curriculum and conversation content of our classroom.

Our Aquí/Allá poetry unit did just that. It surfaced the layers and parts of lives often overpowered by a common classroom curriculum. It created spaces where students could analyze and name the details of their lives.

In the past few years, the bilingual poetry and stories of Salvadoran writer Jorge Argueta have been an invaluable resource in my classroom. I've used poems from *Talking with Mother Earth* for homework and class analysis during a study of eco-systems, the story *Xochitl and the Flowers* to lead into persuasive writing, and *Bean Soup* to teach personification, similes, and beautiful poetic language. As I scanned books for a poem that would raise the level of vivid imagery in my students' narrative writing, I returned to this trusted source. Argueta's poem "Wonders of the City/Las maravillas de la ciudad," from his book *A Movie in My Pillow/Una película en mi almohada,* has the potential to pull the everyday details of students' lives into a place of power. It is a tightly packed representation of the tension of bridging cultures and places, something most of my students negotiate on a daily basis.

"Wonders of the City" has a simple and accessible structure, particularly for language learners, a category that fits all of my students at one time or another during our 50/50 day. (See page 271.) The introductory stanza hints at the irony of the poem: "Here in the city there are/wonders everywhere." The second stanza surprises the reader with a puzzling observation: "Here mangoes/come in cans." As the reader wonders why someone would eat a mango from a can, the third stanza calmly counters, "In El Salvador/ they grew on trees." The repetitive contrast pattern and concrete details are simple windows to the profound dissonance of longing for one place while living in another.

Breaking Down a Model, Building Up a Draft

After reading the poem out loud a few times and discussing the meaning, we read the poem again, this time as writers. I prefaced this reading with our usual writers' questions: "What do you observe or notice about the writing?"

"The author is contrasting two places."

"There is repetition, a pattern—here, there."

One Spanish language learner, Ben, surprised me by noticing the parallel language structure: "When the author talks about 'here,' he writes in present tense. When he talks about 'there,' he uses past tense."

When the responses to the open-ended question began to dwindle, I probed for more. "What does Jorge Argueta do to show the contrast? What details does he choose to compare?" "He contrasts food." Students had a harder time naming the author's content choices. I pointed out the use of everyday details, like the comparison of the packaged wonders of the city with mangoes and chickens in a more natural environment.

We ended our discussion of the poem's meaning with the questions "What do you notice about the author's attitude toward the two places?" "What feelings does Jorge Argueta convey in the poem?" "Does he seem to like one place more than the other?" Students noticed the irony: "He likes El Salvador more." We talked about how the culture that is labeled by the world as "more advanced" and full of technological wonders is often missing the richness and connections to the natural world that are an integral part of indigenous cultures.

After discussing the poem's irony, I asked students to think about contrasts in their own lives, suggesting possibilities that would open the assignment to all: home/Grandma's house, the United States/another country, school/nature, Oregon/another state. Miguel's eyes lit up when he received an affirmative answer to his question "Can I contrast life in school and video games?"

Once students had chosen their topics, they began using a two-column Aquí/Allá list to generate ideas for their poems. We looked back at the poem to notice how the author contrasted mangoes in both countries, how he compared mango to mango, and not mango to melon. I shared my own list of ideas comparing school with nature. While

I help students question the aquí and value the allá.

I, too, wanted to write a poem contrasting two countries, I knew that many of my students had lived their whole lives in our community.

There is nothing "mini" about a brainstorming session in my classroom. I find that the more ideas we share during the prewrite stage of the writing process, the more excited, confident, and successful my students are as they begin their writing. We shared lists once students had a few ideas down. "Here in the United States we celebrate Halloween; there in Mexico they celebrate Day of the Dead," read Juliana. While validating the observation (especially since we were listing ideas on Oct. 29), I realized that our challenge to show, not tell, had followed us across genres.

"How might you show the reader how people are celebrating Halloween or Day of the Dead so that the reader can see the difference? What do you see on Halloween? What do people do to celebrate El día de los muertos?" I asked. Students eagerly shared their experiences of families gathering to honor ancestors and loved ones. Ana Maria suggested, "Maybe you could say, 'Here we knock on doors in our costumes/There families gather at the cemetery.'"

As students shared some of their ideas, I tried to push them to critique and value. I tried to explicitly value the allá: "I wish more people here celebrated Day of the Dead. What a powerful way to remember loved ones."

Students continued to share ideas: "The money is different," said Carlos. "You play different games." "The stores are different," Mayra observed. "Here I need to speak two languages to be understood, and there only Spanish." "In Florida it is hot, and in Oregon it is rainy."

I responded with questions that would generate word pictures: "What does the money look like? How could you show the reader the difference in appearance or value?" "How are the toys different? Where and what do children play?" "How do people dress or what do they do that might show us the difference in weather?" "What do you see and hear in the market?" As students headed off to write their drafts, I reminded them to write with vivid images instead of generalities.

> **The more ideas we share during the prewrite stage of the writing process, the more excited, confident, and successful my students are as they begin their writing.**

Some days during writing workshop you can hear pencils scratch and thoughts flow directly from the brain to the page. Not on our first Aquí/Allá drafting day. The clamor of questions and conversations continued as pencils carved thoughts in the white spaces between blue lines. "Alejandra! What do you call the toys the kids play with in Mexico?" asked David. "Which toys?" "The ones that you spin, the ones. . ." "Oh, yeah, " I heard Roberto murmur from across the room.

Noticing, Naming, and Applying

At the end of the initial drafting session, we gathered in a circle on the floor. Students read a few of their favorite lines or their entire poem to the class. This in-progress read-around motivates students by providing an immediate audience, allows them to borrow and adapt ideas from others, and helps me develop revision mini-lessons. We all work together to notice and name what students are already doing so that others can try the technique in their own writing.

The bulk of my teaching about writing happens once students have a working draft that can be revised. Although all the students had easily applied the "here/there" structure to their poems, most students were struggling to show details instead of telling them. Their energy until this point had been focused on identifying the contrasts instead of crafting an image.

The next day began with a series of revision invitations that I listed on the board as I introduced them. "When Erica writes, 'Aquí dicen trick-or-treat,' she inserts dialogue in her poem. You might try the same technique in your own writing today."

Next, I used a student poem as a revision possibility. "Dalia uses personification in her poem when she says, 'Over there in Mexico there is brilliant yellow lightning/that cuts the sky like a cake.' Go back and find a place where you might add personification."

Later, as I conferenced with individuals, I noticed David's "Aquí dicen hello, goodbye/Allá dicen hola, adios." He also wrote that children play with "wooden tops that dance."

Eva revised her lines about paletas:

Aquí venden
paletas dulces y sabrosas
"ay que ricas, que deliciosas"
Allá en México
hay paletas picosas
con chile
color fuego ardiente
"ay, ay, ay, me pica me pica
quiero agua"

Here they sell
sweet and tasty paletas
"oh, how yummy, how delicious"
There in Mexico
there are spicy paletas
with chile
burning fire color
"oh, oh, oh, it's hot, it's hot
give me water"

Fernando moved from "They are different" to:

Aquí los zapatos son famosos
por la marca y cómo se mira
Allá no les importa mucho
de cómo se mira
nomás les importan
si duran y están baratos

Here shoes are famous
for the brand and look
There it doesn't matter a lot
what they look like
it only matters
if they last and are cheap

Luis used a subtle form of personification:

Aquí hay trabajos de sudando
y de dolor de pie a cabeza

Here there are jobs of sweating
and ache from foot to head

Toward the end of our work on the poems, students met in small response groups. They shared their poems with one another, writing down favorite lines and images, describing cultural contrasts, trying to name what they noticed. In one group we paused to think about how much more sense it makes to play with a top or a ball than it does to buy a $200 video game system. In another we marveled over the personal relationships and interactions involved in buying tomatoes and onions in the market.

Students read their favorite lines from others' poems during a whole group share. As I passed from one group to the next, Alex exclaimed, "Wow, you should read Juliana's poem. It is really good":

> Aquí cuando llueve
> sólo caen gotitas pequeñas
> que bailan en el piso
>
> Allá los truenos caen
> y casi te desmayas del miedo
> los relámpagos caen
> pueden romper a la mitad un árbol
>
> *Here when it rains*
> *only tiny drops fall*
> *that dance on the floor*
>
> *There the thunder falls*
> *and you almost faint from fear*
> *lightning falls*
> *it can break a tree in half*

Taking It Beyond Our Walls

Alex wasn't the only one who thought our poetry was "really good." When I shared our poems with Catherine Celestino, a 2nd-grade teacher whose class my students knew as "reading buddies," she responded with an invitation: "Could your 5th graders teach the poem to my 2nd graders?"

The plan to teach our reading buddies to write Aquí/Allá poems blasted fresh energy and relevance into our work. "When I plan a lesson for you, I always think about the goal of expressing our lives and views through the writing of a poem, as well as the skills I want to teach you in your writing. What are our goals as we teach our reading buddies?" I asked.

Students broke into groups of three or four to create a list of the important skills they had learned while writing their poems. We shared ideas with the whole group

The Bilingual Stories and Poetry of Jorge Argueta in the Classroom

Talking with Mother Earth/Hablando con madre tierra

I first discovered the writing of Jorge Argueta as I was searching the school library for Spanish language poetry that could deepen students' understanding of ecosystems. In the book *Talking with Mother Earth/Hablando con madre tierra* I found a bilingual poem that spoke to the ways in which our lives are connected to both living and nonliving things in the natural world that surrounds us. The poem "Stones" centers on the metaphor of stones as our sacred ancestors. I ask students to read the poem with a family member or someone at home, talk about the meaning, and then write a reflection. In class, we analyze the poem's literary devices, theme, and meaning, and later compare those elements in the poems "Ancestors of Tomorrow" and "Giant Sequoias" from the book *Iguanas in the Snow/Iguanas en la nieve* by Francisco X. Alarcón.

Xochitl and the Flowers/Xochitl, la niña de las flores

When I teach persuasive writing, I look for stories that depict a local conflict that gets resolved through community action. The picture book *Xochitl and the Flowers/Xochitl, la niña de las flores* is based on a true story about an immigrant family living in San Francisco. The family longs to connect their new world to the full life they left behind in El Salvador, and decides to begin a flower-selling business on an empty lot next to their apartment. I stop reading the story when the family's landlord forces the family to close the flower shop. Students brainstorm what justification both sides have as support for their opinion/stance on the issue, and then have a class debate. We return to read the end of the story and learn that the neighbors join forces and convince the landlord to allow the family to reopen their nursery.

Bean Soup/Sopa de frijoles

Bean soup is a seemingly common, everyday staple. In this poetic picture book, Argueta honors each and every ingredient and step of preparing bean soup with vivid use of nature-based personification and similes. The poem compares ingredients to sunrise, sunset, soil, and moon, revering them as well as the source of sustenance—the earth. My students and I read and reread, and then reread the poem again, deepening our appreciation of its language and meaning. We chart and analyze examples of similes and personification. Finally, students practice the techniques, writing and revising their own celebrations of everyday foods in their lives. We share poems in a read-around and bind a collective poetry book for the classroom library.

and then, together, determined which were most important. We decided that the prewriting and revision goal would be to use a list with commas, sensory details, and similes. The students defined the most important editing goals as taking out unnecessary words and deciding where to use line breaks.

"Who doesn't have a partner? Raise your hand." As we entered Mrs. Celestino's 2nd-grade classroom, students formed pairs and settled into work.

"What does your grandma's house look like? What kinds of things do you find there?" I heard Adriana ask her partner.

I saw students develop new strategies to scaffold learning: "We've decided that I will write one line for my partner and he will write the next." "I'm writing down whatever she tells me on this paper, and then my partner is copying the words onto hers." Jessica, Michelle, and Alex were dividing the Aquí/Allá columns horizontally and adding categories: food, names, toys, activities.

"Aquí we speak Spanish, allá we speak another language," I heard 2nd grader Alma explain to Mayra. Most students who had compared the United States and Mexico focused on the English in the *here* and the Spanish in the *there*.

"Can you teach us some words in your other language?" I asked in Spanish as I lowered myself to the rug to join the conversation. Alma smiled with the confidence of an expert as she told me the words for tortilla and water. Mayra and I repeated the new words, practicing and trying to learn the sounds. I moved across the room, and Mayra helped Alma move from oral idea to a new line in her poem: "Here we say tortilla and agua, in Mexico we say 'sheck' and 'nda'," she wrote.

When we returned to the room after our first teaching session, I heard about successes and frustrations. "My partner picked Mexico and she can't remember what Mexico is like." We talked about the importance of picking a place you know and remember well, and brainstormed some possible local choices. "My partner just sits there." "We've already written a whole page!"

Stepping Back and Learning Forward

I feel fortunate each time we shake to the surface parts of students' home lives, traditions, languages, and cultures, as well as their views of the world around them. I can't completely know and understand the allá of every student's life, but I can join Jorge Argueta in his critique of the "wonders" of aquí. I can create space for students to name the details and cultures of their lives in the classroom curriculum. I can help students question the aquí and value the allá. Next year I will ask even more questions, probe for more details, and leave more spaces for talking and sharing and critiquing the contrasts of our lives.

Students often follow me as we head out to the playground, eager to share a thought or experience that they weren't comfortable enough to share in class. We head out to mid-morning recess after drawing and labeling detailed diagrams of crickets during a study of ecosystems. Andrea hesitates for a moment as some of

Wonders of the City	**Las maravillas de la ciudad**
Here in the city there are	Aquí en esta ciudad
wonders everywhere	todo es maravilloso
Here mangoes	Aquí los mangos
come in cans	vienen enlatados
In El Salvador	En El Salvador
they grew on trees	crecían en árboles
Here chickens come	Aquí las gallinas vienen
in plastic bags	en bolsas de plástico
Over there	Allá se dormían
they slept beside me	junto a mí
—Jorge Argueta	—Jorge Argueta

---

her classmates sprint off, eager to join the game of tag or secure the best swing.

"We eat crickets at home. You know, they are really good with a little bit of lemon and salt," she tells me, staring off in the distance as she stands at my side. "Really?" I ask, turning to face her. "What do they taste like? How do you catch them?" Andrea continues to talk, and, as we line up to head back to the classroom, we share her cricket connection with the class.

How can I continue to open spaces so that rich moments of linguistic and cultural revelation are not chance conversations on the peripheries of the playground and hallway, but a central core of the classroom curriculum? How can I help students bridge the conflicting cultures of their lives?

Elizabeth Schlessman Barbian is a bilingual educator. She taught 4th and 5th grade in a Spanish dual language immersion classroom in Woodburn, Ore., for five years.

Notes

"Wonders of the City," by Jorge Argueta, is reprinted from *A Movie in My Pillow/Una película en mi almohada* with permission of the publisher, Children's Book Press, San Francisco. (www. childrensbookpress. org). © 2001 by Jorge Argueta.

All conversations and student work in this article were originally in Spanish. Student work was translated by the author.

The words "sheck" and "nda" come from the Oaxaca Amuzgo language, spoken in the village of San Pedro Amuzgos in Oaxaca, Mexico. The spelling of the words is taken directly from 2nd-grade student work.

Resources

Alarcón, Francisco X. *Iguanas in the Snow/ Iguanas en la nieve.* San Francisco: Children's Book Press, 2001.
Argueta, Jorge. *Bean Soup/Sopa de frijoles.* Toronto: Groundwood Books, 2009.
Argueta, Jorge. *Talking with Mother Earth/Hablando con madre tierra.* Toronto: Groundwood Books, 2006.
Argueta, Jorge. *Xochitl and the Flowers/ Xochitl, la niña de las flores.* San Francisco: Children's Book Press, 2003.

Chapter Thirty-Five

PUTTING A HUMAN FACE ON THE IMMIGRATION DEBATE

By Steven Picht-Trujillo and Paola Suchsland

While politicians debate immigration policy, many of our high schools in Southern California and across the country are places where immigration issues are not just academic, abstract discussions but rather the real-life drama that many of our students face on a daily basis. For those of us working with immigrant populations, we have in our students living examples that we can use to bring the immigration issue to the forefront and teach all of our students, both immigrants and descendants of immigrants, so that they can have a better understanding of the issue as it relates to their fellow students and their community. This past school year at our high school we joined forces to teach a unit on immigration to our students, using our students' own immigration experiences to form a curriculum that we will be able to use in future classes.

MICHAEL DUFFY

We teach at Valencia High School, in Placentia, Calif., on the northern edge of Orange County. Traditionally considered a conservative "white" enclave of Southern California, Placentia is undergoing major demographic changes. Valencia High School, the oldest of Placentia's three high schools, was established 70 years ago and now serves a student population of more than 2,500. English language learners constitute 22 percent of the student body, and just over half the school's students are Latino. However, Valencia is diverse, with 31 percent of the students officially categorized as "white" (non-Hispanic, including a variety of immigrant Europeans such as Germans, Romanians, and Albanians, as well as Lebanese, Indians, Pakistanis, and others); 12 percent Asian (Korean, Vietnamese, Chinese, and Filipino students predominate); and 3 percent black (African American as well as African and Caribbean immigrants). Our school's population reflects the huge demographic shift that has occurred throughout Orange County over the past 20 years; the result is that our county is now decidedly less "white" than the stereotypical image depicted in television programs such as *The OC* and *Laguna Beach*.

To be admitted to a university in the California State University system, a student must have two years of study in a language other than English; and to enter the University of California system, a student must have at least three years of study. Therefore, we have a large percentage of students studying Spanish, followed by French and Japanese.

As teachers in the same department, we always look for ways to have our students interact, as this cross-class engagement has language and cultural benefits for both groups.

Steve teaches first- and third-year Spanish to students from various ethnic backgrounds, while Paola, a native of Mexico, teaches second- and third-year classes in Spanish for native speakers. The vast majority of her students are first- or second-generation immigrants from Mexico, some of whom arrived only recently. As teachers in the same department, we always look for ways to have our students interact, as this cross-class engagement has language and cultural benefits for both groups.

The 2006 U.S. House of Representatives bill that declared all undocumented immigrants to be felons and imposing draconian penalties on those knowingly assisting such immigrants triggered an intense debate in the school. Since a number of our school's students participated in the 2006 May Day marches in Orange County and Los Angeles in support of immigrants' rights, we decided that this year we wanted to engage students in several joint lessons to increase their understanding of these issues. We especially wanted to make them more aware of the circumstances facing many of our students whose families have recently emigrated from Latin America.

To align our lessons with the California Standards for Foreign Language Instruction, Steve chose to begin our "Immigration Unit," as we called it, during the chapter in his class' Spanish 3 textbooks titled "La riqueza cultural" ("Cultural Richness"), which teaches vocabulary and grammar within the context of the immigrant experience and our students' cultural heritage. Students learn how to express topics dealing with the challenges associated with arrival in a new country, talking about future plans and goals, discussing their accomplishments and successes, and expressing intention and purpose. This chapter comes late in our second semester and coincided perfectly with the one-year anniversary of the May 1st marches. Likewise, "La Experiencia Migrante" ("The Migrant Experience"), a unit in Paola's textbook, includes poems and short stories depicting the lives and struggles of immigrants' families coming to the United States. Some of Paola's students live with the constant worry of either being deported or having their parents deported.

Against this backdrop, we began to put together lessons and activities to have our students become more aware of the realities of immigrants and their contributions to American society, and to promote greater appreciation of the commonalities we share in our pursuit of the American dream. All activities, projects, readings, and films that we used during this unit aligned with both the language and culture standards. Since this was our first year to teach this unit, we often created as we went along, but the end result laid the groundwork for what we feel will be an outstanding unit next year.

> **We began to put together lessons and activities to have our students become more aware of the realities of immigrants and their contributions to American society.**

To begin this unit, we brought our classes together to have our students read excerpts from Francisco Jiménez's book *Cajas de cartón,* an account of the author's experiences as an immigrant child in California during the 1940s. We chose this text in order to draw parallels between undocumented immigrants of that period with those of today. The first time our classes met together we read sections aloud in Spanish in small groups, with Paola's students helping Steve's with their pronunciation and comprehension. It was also a chance for our students to get to know each other and to feel comfortable with one another.

Another activity that our two classes shared was the bilingual skits prepared by the students. We combined our classes to form groups of four to five students, with at least two native speakers in each group. Students wrote and prepared short skits that they later presented to the combined classes. Each group randomly drew from a list of situations and prepared their skits in Spanish (or English if it fit the situation). We came up with the topics based on real-life events that were being reported in the news.

The topics included: 1) a family in Mexico discusses the pros and cons of immigrating to the United States; 2) politicians on both sides of the spectrum debate immigrant issues; 3) an encounter between Minutemen and immigrants at the U.S.-Mexico border; 4) a family in California receives a deportation order and decides whether the U.S.-born children will stay or leave; 5) a raid at a California business that employs undocumented workers.

All of these situations were either derived from news articles that we had read or were gleaned from our own experiences living in Orange County, home to an estimated 185,000 undocumented immigrants.

Each group of students randomly chose one of the five topics that were written on slips of paper. Immediately some groups responded positively to their selected topics while others expressed disappointment and wanted to change to a different topic. We had each group keep their selected topic and challenged everyone to make the effort of putting themselves in the shoes of others and to act accordingly, even if it meant taking a role completely opposite from their own closely held beliefs. As they started to work in their groups, many of the students from both classes seemed uneasy and tried to make light of their topics, jokingly taking extreme positions with each other in order to gauge the attitudes of the other students in their groups. However, as their work progressed it became obvious to us that they were putting their efforts into developing their roles and working to create cogent arguments either for or against immigrants' rights. An additional challenge for many of Steve's students was to prepare a role in Spanish that would convey the emotional intensity that came so easily for Paola's students. After working together for nearly a full class period, the students seemed ready to begin presenting, so we planned to start the skits in the next day's class, reserving the entire hour for the presentations and discussion.

> **We challenged everyone to make the effort of putting themselves in the shoes of others and to act accordingly, even if it meant taking a role completely opposite from their own closely held beliefs.**

As we anticipated, many of these topics struck a nerve with Paola's immigrant students, and some of the presentations became very emotional. We noticed how some of Paola's students were especially animated as they took on the role of the perpetrator instead of the victim in their situations (e.g., the immigration officer or the manager who refuses to pay fair salaries to undocumented workers). Still, we also saw mixed feelings of frustration and kindness from my students, who had difficulty arguing anti-immigrant positions in front of their peers. One of Steve's students had taken an adversarial role in her skit as a politician arguing against immigrants and stopped several times in order to address the class directly, saying, "I don't really feel this way, I'm just playing a role." During the presentation of the skits there seemed to be a feeling of mutual respect and understanding, and we had no discipline or behavior problems.

During this unit Steve wanted to engage his students in a project that would not only put their language skills to use but that would give them cause to reflect on their own immigrant heritage, regardless of whether they or their own parents were immigrants or their family had been in the United States for centuries. To reach this aim he decided on posters in which they would include graphic representations of their heritage (photos, maps, flags, drawings, cultural artifacts, etc.) along with an original written piece. The written portion could be in the form of a personal letter, a diary entry, a newspaper article, or a short essay written in the first person as if the student were their immigrant ancestor, a parent, or themselves. The only stipulation was that they incorporate vocabulary from our textbook and show command of the grammatical structures that they employed in their writing.

In Steve's case, his maternal ancestors were not actually immigrants to the United States; rather, the United States came to them after the Mexican-American War and subjugated them under the oft-violated terms of the Treaty of Guadalupe Hidalgo. Therefore, while we used the term *inmigrante* during this unit, he explained to his students that we were using the word as an all-encompassing term to include anyone who wasn't indigenous to the United States, regardless of the circumstances under which their ancestors arrived here. Steve had no Native American or African American students in his class during this unit, but that would bring a whole other voice to the discussion that he hopes we can develop in next year's class.

For Steve's students whose ancestors may have come to the United States 100 or more years ago, the project required that they use their creative powers to make educated assumptions about the circumstances surrounding their chosen ancestor's reasons for coming to the United States, based on what they might have learned in their U.S. or world history classes, or perhaps from parents or family members. Often, these students had to make up the ancestor, but doing so helped them understand why that ancestor would have made the sacrifices of leaving his or her native land to come to a new country. Most of Paola's students are from recently immigrated families so their documents often related to a parent or grandparent.

We also saw mixed feelings of frustration and kindness from my students, who had difficulty arguing anti-immigrant positions in front of their peers.

After creating their posters, students presented them to the class, after which they were put up on the walls in both of our classrooms. One of our aims was for Paola's students to see Steve's in a different light and to understand that most of them too were descended from people who came to this country in search of the same opportunities. Although we didn't formally assess their responses this time around, we were happy to see her students actively engaged in poring over the posters, and we will definitely include more discussion to gauge their responses in our next unit. Some of the written documents on the posters were written as letters from the immigrant ancestor (or parent, as many of them were) to a loved one left behind. Many of these were touching accounts of the challenges the person faced in a new land, and sometimes expressed regret for having left parents or loved ones behind. Other documents were written as diary entries, expressing the pain of discrimination and marginalization in what was supposed to be a land of liberty for all. The posters' vibrancy and creativity made Steve's classroom into a virtual art gallery for the last month of school and students were eager to see each other's posters and read their accounts.

All of Paola's students wrote a personal narrative in Spanish about their family's circumstances of coming to the United States, including reasons for leaving their homeland, challenges they faced after arrival, and hopes for the future. When she assigned the personal narratives she had her students use fictional names so that only she would know who wrote which narrative. She also had them change the names of the characters involved in their stories to avoid any accidental divulging of the authorship of any given piece. These narratives were especially poignant, as they talked about the hardships involved in crossing through the desert or being smuggled by ruthless coyotes or living with the fear of being deported or having their families torn apart.

When Paola assigned the personal narratives to her students, some were hesitant but excited to be able to tell others their story. On the other hand, about a third of her class, mostly recent immigrant students, had a difficult time writing about events that were still fresh wounds in their hearts. We realized then that many of the personal stories had no happy endings. Paola had to encourage her students, especially the ones having trouble writing or who did not want to tell their story, to use writing as a tool that would allow them to heal their inner scars. The students were given the option to undertake an alternative assignment more generically related to immigration if they did not want to pen their personal experiences, and indeed there was one student who in the beginning refused to put his experience on paper. But after seeing his fellow classmates focused on writing their accounts he told Paola, "Ms. Ledezma, my family has suffered a lot and I have to tell their story so others will know how they suffered."

> **We realized that we needed to create a unit to empower both of our classes to become agents of change.**

As Paola had hoped, students were able to complete and share their personal narratives in class because of the encouragement to write. To groups of five or six students, she randomly handed out essays to read aloud and then discuss, but the authors' identities were not divulged.

These narratives are valuable documents and will be useful for our unit next year when we have our students read them in the target language and realize that these amazing stories are from their classmates' lives. These, more than anything, put a human face on the immigration issue and in the future we hope will help students understand that regardless of whether a person immigrates to this country with documents or without, the motivation is the same: to secure the best opportunities for us and our families.

During our frequent lunch conversations, we often discussed the immigration situation, especially as it relates to undocumented immigrants. Steve sometimes had to deal with his own students' negative and derisive comments about Mexican immigrants, while Paola was comfortable discussing immigration issues openly with her students, with whom she could easily relate. It was during those conversations that we realized that we needed to create a unit to empower both of our classes to become agents of change. For Paola's students, by putting themselves in the shoes of others, they gained a better understanding of those who fight against undocumented immigrants and they learned to discuss and defend their own positions in the immigration debate in both English and Spanish. For Steve's students, they came away with a deeper understanding of the issues and how they relate to their fellow classmates. As one student commented, "I never really thought about these things before, but now I realize that when they talk about immigrants in the news, they're talking about my friends and classmates."

The Brazilian education theorist and activist Paulo Freire once said that "washing one's hands of the conflict between the powerful and the powerless means to side with the powerful, not to be neutral." With this unit we tried to get our students to understand the position of the powerless in the immigration debate. On the one hand, Steve's students are siding with the powerful since they remained relatively uninformed on the immigration debate even though many of them are from families who have immigrated to the United States legally and enjoy a certain level of economic success. Since many of them live without the constant fear of losing everything and being deported, many had never given this issue a second thought until we discussed it in class.

> **With this unit we tried to get our students to understand the position of the powerless in the immigration debate.**

By not using their voice and being heard, Paola's students were likewise siding with the powerful. This unit was an opportunity for them to raise their voices and to begin their first steps toward empowerment. Most of them immigrated to this country without documents or were born in the United States to undocumented parents. Prior to this unit, the national debate surrounding immigration was becoming more intense, so Paola brought in articles from the Spanish-language press about various proposals for immigration reform, and her students were eager to talk about the issue. Her classroom became what she liked to call a "sanctuary city," as she sought to create a loving and welcoming environment where her students would feel safe talking about their experiences. For her as a Mexican immigrant and having been undocumented herself for more than five years, she could relate to their fears and frustrations.

One of our fears in doing this unit was the anticipation of combining our classes. We had previously brought students together in an earlier unit to create plays depicting Aztec legends, so they were already somewhat familiar with each other, but not in the context of dealing with a controversial topic such as this. For this unit, Paola confided to Steve that she worried about how students would respond, especially because more than half her students are English language learners and had said how hard it was for them to speak English with Steve's students. His students too had reservations. They felt like the native Spanish speakers made fun of them for their poor Spanish skills. Also, we were apprehensive about our students' parents: How would they react? Would they complain about the unit and our politicizing of the subject matter, insisting that we just stick to the curriculum? We prepared for the worst by always having the unit's objectives and the standards ready to justify our work.

Moreover, we had to challenge ourselves to present multiple sides of the arguments and not appear to force our personal agenda on students. Paola, once undocumented herself, was concerned that her personal situation might prevent students from expressing opposing points of view. She had shared her personal story with her students and had told them about her support for the legalization of millions of immigrants in the United States. Through our personal and professional experiences working with immigrant students, as well as the personal relationships we have with undocumented friends and relatives outside of the classroom, we are both passionate about the immigration issue and we feared that a class discussion about such a heated topic could result in chaos and/or disciplinary problems. Thankfully, our fears never materialized and the experience turned out to be overwhelmingly positive. Contrary to our fears, discussions never got out of hand, nor did we have to deal with irate parents. The curriculum provided students ample opportunity to put themselves in someone else's shoes.

Putting a human face on immigration issues has been one of our most challenging tasks, and at the same time has been one of the most rewarding experiences that we have had in our relatively short teaching careers.

Putting a human face on immigration issues has been one of our most challenging tasks, and at the same time has been one of the most rewarding experiences that we have had in our relatively short teaching careers. As teachers who strive to be agents of change, there came a moment when we realized that we could not just dispassionately talk about the issue, but rather we needed to act upon it by bringing it into our classrooms. By doing so we hope we have planted the seeds so that our students can begin to effect change in their communities and work to change attitudes of those around them. As language teachers we don't always have opportunities to raise students' social awareness or to address global social justice issues, so for us this unit was the opportunity we were waiting for. We hope that it is just the beginning.

Steven Picht-Trujillo and Paola Suchsland are Spanish teachers at Valencia High School in Placentia, Calif.

Resources

READINGS

During this unit we had our students read a book excerpt dealing with immigration issues from the 1940s along with a contemporary article about the experience of a Mexican family in San Diego. These readings were the initial activity for this unit and were used in order to give students a feel for how these issues have not changed substantially in the United States since the early 20th century.

Cajas de cartón: relatos de la vida peregrina de un niño campesino, by Francisco Jiménez, Chapter 1: "Bajo la alambrada." This book is the author's account of his family's illegal entry into the United States from Mexico during the 1940s. (Available in English: *The Circuit,* by Francisco Jiménez, Chapter 1: "Under the Wire.")

"Column One: A family's painful split decision." *Los Angeles Times* article from April 27, 2007, by Anna Gorman, tells the story of parents who were deported to Tijuana, leaving their three U.S.-born children in San Diego so that the children might have greater opportunities in life.

FILMS

During this unit we watched three films relating to immigrants from Latin America, in which our students were able to meet a handful of immigrants and learn their stories.

El Norte, by Gregory Nava. (In Spanish, English, and Mayan languages with English subtitles) This film tells the story of a Guatemalan brother and sister who flee their country's civil war during the 1980s and shows the harrowing events crossing the U.S.-Mexican border as they immigrate to Los Angeles. Edited version for classroom use available from Teacher's Discovery, www.teachersdiscovery.com.

"Immigration." This is an episode of Morgan Spurlock's FX Network series *30 Days* that deals with an undocumented immigrant family in Los Angeles and the anti-immigrant Minuteman who lives with them for 30 days. The program sparked a number of lively in-class debates and discussions. (In both English and Spanish with English subtitles) Available from iTunes.

Farmingville. This is a PBS P.O.V. documentary by Carlos Sandoval and Catherine Tambini dealing with the impact of undocumented immigrants on a suburban New York community and the community's sometimes violent reaction to their presence. Available from www.amazon.com. This documentary is primarily in English with some Spanish (English subtitles).

SECTION V
CONFRONTING RACE IN THE CLASSROOM

FAVIANNA RODRIGUEZ

Chapter Thirty-Six

BROWN KIDS CAN'T BE IN OUR CLUB

By Rita Tenorio

A few years before I became the principal at La Escuela Fratney in Milwaukee, I sat down one day with seven of the children in my 1st-grade class. It was early in the year and we were getting to know each other. We talked about how we were alike, how we were different. "Our skin is different," one of the children said. I asked everyone to put their hands together on the table, so we could see all the different colors.

One of my African American students, LaRhonda,* simply would not. Scowling, she slid her hands beneath the tabletop, unwilling to have her color compared to the others.

It was a reaction I had seen before. I teach at La Escuela Fratney, an ethnically diverse school in a racially mixed working-class Milwaukee neighborhood. My students typically include black kids, white kids, and Latinos. They have many things in common. Recess is their favorite time of day. Friendships are a priority. They want to "belong" to a group and they are very conscious of where they fit in a social sense.

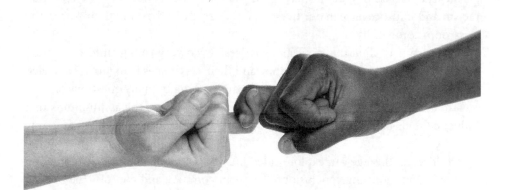

And they all "know" that it is better to be light-skinned than dark-skinned.

Even though my students have only six or seven years of life experience by the time they reach my classroom, the centuries-old legacies of bias and racism in our country have already made an impact on their lives. I have seen fair-skinned children deliberately change places in a circle if African American children sit down next to them. An English speaker won't play with a Latino child because, he says, "He talks funny." On the playground, a group of white girls won't let their darker-skinned peers join in their games, explaining matter-of-factly: "Brown kids can't be in our club."

> **Even though my students have only six or seven years of life experience by the time they reach my classroom, the centuries-old legacies of bias and racism in our country have already made an impact on their lives.**

As teachers, we have to acknowledge that we live in a racist society and that children typically mirror the attitudes of that society. Between the ages of 2 and 5, children not only become aware of racial differences, but also begin to make judgments based on that awareness. They do this even though they may not be able to understand, in an intellectual way, the complexities of race and bias as issues.

Teachers have a responsibility to recognize the influence of racism on themselves and their students. And we can help children learn the skills and strategies they will need to counteract it in their lives. At Fratney, our 1st-grade teaching teams have put those ideas at the center of our practice.

Are They Too Young for This?

Many people would say that children at this age are too young to deal with these serious issues. I too had real questions at first about what was actually possible with young children. Can you have "real" conversations with 6-year-olds about power, privilege, and racism in our society? Can you make them aware of the effects that racism and injustice have in our lives? Can they really understand their role in the classroom community?

The answer to all of these questions is "yes." Even very young children can explore and understand the attitudes they and their classmates bring to school each day. They have real issues and opinions to share, and many, many questions of their own to ask. In this way they can begin to challenge some of the assumptions that influence their behavior toward classmates who don't look or talk the same way they do.

Children at this age can explore rules and learn about collecting data, making inferences, and forming conclusions. They can compare and contrast the experiences of people and think about what it means. They can, that is, if they are given the opportunity.

At Fratney, which serves 400 students from kindergarten through 5th grade, we discuss issues of social justice with all of our students. During the past several years, those of us teaching 1st grade have developed a series of activities and projects that help us to discuss issues of race and social justice in a meaningful, age-appropriate way.

We strive to build classroom community by learning about each other's lives and families. We ask our students to collect and share information about their families and ancestry. For example, we might talk about how they got their names, how their families came to live in Milwaukee, which holidays they celebrate and how. And at every step we help the children to explore the nature of racial and cultural differences and to overcome simplistic notions of "who's better" or who is "like us" and who isn't.

These activities include:

Me Pockets

This is always a class favorite. Each child takes home a letter-sized clear plastic sleeve, the kind used to display baseball cards. We ask students to fill the pockets with photos, pictures, drawings, or anything else that will help us know more about them and the things that are important in their lives. They return the pockets within a week and put them into a three-ring binder that becomes the favorite classroom book to read and reread.

The individual pockets reflect the cultural and socioeconomic diversity of the families. Some students put lots of photos or computer images in their pockets. Others cut pictures out of magazines or make drawings. Our experience is that every family is anxious to share in some way, and family members take time to help their children develop the project.

If someone doesn't bring their Me Pocket sheet back, the teachers step in to help them find pictures or make the drawings they need to add their page to the binder.

I'm always amazed at how quickly the children learn the details about each other's lives from this project: who has a pet, who takes dance classes, who likes to eat macaroni and cheese. The children know there are differences among them, but they also love to share the things that are alike.

Children at this age can explore rules and learn about collecting data, making inferences, and forming conclusions.

"Look, Rachel has two brothers, just like me."

"I didn't know that Jamal's family likes to camp. We do too!"

Each of the teachers also completes a Me Pocket sheet. The students love looking at the picture of me as a 1st grader, seeing my husband and children, and learning that chocolate cake is my favorite food.

Partner Questions

Each day we take time to teach the social skills of communicating ideas with others and listening to another person's perspective. We use this time to "practice" those skills with role-playing activities and problem-solving situations they or we bring to the group. For example, we might ask such questions as: What is the meanest thing anyone has ever said to you? Why do you think some people like to use put-downs? The children take a few minutes to talk about this with a partner. Some are willing to share with the whole group afterward. We might then role-play the situation as a group and look for ways to respond, such as speaking back to insults.

'Someone Special'

By the end of October, during the time of Halloween, Día de los Muertos, and All Souls' Day, we learn about how people remember their ancestors and others who have died or who are far away. We set up a table and students are encouraged to bring in pictures or artifacts to display. They bring a remarkable variety of things: jewelry, a trophy won by a departed relative, a postcard that person sent them, or perhaps the program from a funeral. And they bring many, many stories. Again, the teachers also participate and share stories of those who have gone before us. We get great responses from our students and from their families.

Let's Talk About Skin

Another important conversation I have with my students focuses on the varieties of skin color we have in our group. Usually when we begin this discussion, some children are uncomfortable about saying "what they are" or describing the color of their skin. In particular, children with very dark skin—like LaRhonda, who would not even put her hands on the table—are often reluctant to join in. Meanwhile, the white kids often boast about being "pink." Though we've never talked about this in class before, there is definitely a strong implication that it is better to be lighter.

Each day we take time to teach the social skills of communicating ideas with others and listening to another person's perspective.

Many children are amazed that this topic is put out on the table for discussion. The looks in their eyes, their frequent reluctance to begin the discussion, tell me that this is a very personal topic.

As part of the lesson, we ask the students if they have ever heard anyone say something bad or mean about another person's skin color. The hands shoot up.

"My mom says that you can't trust black people."

"My sister won't talk to the Puerto Rican kids on the bus."

"Mara said that I couldn't play, that I was too black to be her friend."

They continue to raise their hands and this conversation goes on for a while. We talk about ways we've heard others use people's skin color to make fun of them or put them down. We talk about what to do in those situations.

As we continue to discuss issues of race, we teachers often introduce our personal experiences. I tell them about the first time I realized that black and white people were treated differently. I share my experience being one of the few Latinas in my school. And we try to ask questions that really intrigue the students, that invite them to try to look at things with a different perspective, to learn something new about the human experience and be open-minded to that idea: Do people choose their colors? Where do you get your skin color? Is it better to be one color than another? Lots of our conversations revolve around a story or a piece of literature.

With a little work, we can expand this discussion of skin color in ways that incorporate math lessons, map lessons, and other curricular areas. We've done surveys to see how many of our ancestors came from warm places or cold places. We ask children to interview their relatives to find out where the family came from. We create a bulletin board display that we use to compare and learn about the huge variety of places our students' relatives are from. We graph the data of whose family came from warm places, who from cold, who from both, or don't know.

As part of the lesson, we ask the students if they have ever heard anyone say something bad or mean about another person's skin color.

Skin Color and Science

Our class discussions of skin color set the stage for lots of "scientific" observations.

For example, I bring in a large variety of paint chips from a local hardware store. The students love examining and sorting the many shades of beige and brown. It takes a while for them to find the one that is most like their own skin color.

In the story *The Colors of Us,* by Karen Katz, Lena learns from her mother that "brown" is a whole range of colors. Like the characters in the story, we take red, yellow, black, and white paint and mix them in various combinations until we've each found the color of our own skin. Then we display our "research" as part of our science fair project.

In another exercise, inspired by Sheila Hamanaka's *All the Colors of the Earth,* students are asked to find words to describe the color of their skin, and to find something at home that matches their skin color. Then we display the pieces of wood and fabric, the little bags of cinnamon and coffee, the dolls and ceramic pieces that "match" us.

As we continue these explorations, dealing concretely with a topic that so many have never heard discussed in such a manner, students begin to see past society's labels. It is always amazing to children that friends who call themselves "black," for example, can actually have very light skin. Or that children who perceive themselves as "Puerto Rican" can be darker than some of the African American children.

Writing About Our Colors

As children begin to understand the idea of internalizing another's point of view, they can apply that understanding by examining different ideas and alternatives to their own experiences. As they learn to express themselves through reading and writing, they can learn to challenge stereotypes and speak back to unfair behavior and comments.

Once students have had a chance to reflect on skin color, they write about it. Annie wrote: "I like my skin color. It is like peachy cream." James wrote: "My color is the same as my dad's. I think the new baby will have this color too." And Keila wrote: "When I was born, my color was brown skin and white skin mixed together."

When LaRhonda wrote about mixing the colors to match her skin, she said: "We put black, white, red, and yellow [together]. I like the color of my skin." How far she had come since the day she would not show us her hands.

Tackling Issues

These activities have an impact. Parents have spoken to us about the positive impression that these activities have made on the children. Many children have taken their first steps toward awareness of race. They are not afraid to discuss it. They now have more ways in which to think about and describe themselves.

Yet these activities are no guarantee that children have internalized anti-racist ideas. So much depends on the other forces in their lives. We are still working on making these activities better: doing them sooner in the year, integrating them into other subjects, deepening the conversations, finding other stories or activities to support them. Each year's group is different, and we need to incorporate their experiences and understandings. I learn something new every time. They challenge my consciousness too.

We rely on our schools to be the place for a multicultural, multiracial experience for our children. We want to believe that learning together will help our students to become more understanding and respectful of differences. Yet so often we do not address these issues head-on. It is unlikely that sensitivity and tolerance will develop, that children will bridge the gaps they bring to school from their earliest days, without specific instruction.

Personally, I want to see more than tolerance developed. I want children to see themselves as the future citizens of this city. I want them to gain the knowledge to be successful in this society. Beyond that, though, I want them to understand that they have the power to transform society.

When students see connections between home and school, when lessons challenge them to look at the issue of race from multiple perspectives, we take the first steps in this process.

Rita Tenorio has taught at the elementary level for over 30 years. She recently retired from her position as principal at La Escuela Fratney in Milwaukee.

Chapter Thirty-Seven

WHAT COLOR IS BEAUTIFUL?

By Alejandro Segura-Mora

Most of my kindergarten students have already been picked up by their parents. Two children still sit on the mat in the cafeteria lobby, waiting. Occasionally, one of them stands to look through the door's opaque windows to see if they can make out a parent coming. Ernesto,* the darkest child in my class, unexpectedly shares in Spanish, "Maestro, my mom is giving me pills to turn me white."

"Is that right?" I respond, also in Spanish. "And why do you want to be white?"

"Because I don't like my color," he says.

"I think your color is very beautiful and you are beautiful as well," I say. I try to conceal how his comment saddens and alarms me, because I want to encourage his sharing.

"I don't like to be dark," he explains.

His mother, who is slightly darker than he, walks in the door. Ernesto rushes to take her hand and leaves for home.

SNAP VILLAGE

Childhood Memories

Ernesto's comment takes me back to an incident in my childhood. My mom is holding me by the hand, my baby brother in her other arm, my other three brothers and my sister following along. We are going to church and I am happy. I skip all the way, certain that I have found a solution to end my brothers' insults.

"You're a monkey," they tell me whenever they are mad at me. I am the only one in my family with curly hair. In addition to "monkey," my brothers baptize me with other derogatory names—such as Simio (Ape), Chineca (a twisted and distorted personification of being curly, and even more negative by the feminization with an "a" at the end), and Urco, the captain of all apes in the television program *The Planet of the Apes*.

As we enter the church, my mom walks us to the front of the altar to pray before the white saints, the crucified white Jesus, and his mother. Before that day, I hadn't bought into the God story. After all, why would God give a child curly hair? But that day there is hope. I close my eyes and pray with a conviction that would have brought rain to a desert.

"God, if you really exist, please make my hair straight," I pray. "I hate it curly and you know it's hard. So at the count of three, please take these curls and make them straight. One, two, three."

With great suspense I open my eyes. I reach for my hair. Anticipating the feel of straight hair, I stroke my head, only to feel my curls. Tears sting my eyes. As I head for one of the benches, I whisper, "I knew God didn't exist."

For Ernesto, the pill was his God; for me, God was my pill. I wonder how Ernesto will deal with the failure of his pill.

A Teachable Moment

I can't help but wonder how other teachers might have dealt with Ernesto's comments. Would they have ignored him? Would they have dismissed him with a "Stop talking like that!" Would they have felt sorry for him because they agree with him?

As teachers, we are cultural workers, whether we are aware of it or not. If teachers don't question the culture and values being promoted in the classroom, they socialize their students to accept the uneven power relations of our society along lines of race, class, gender, and ability. Yet teachers can—and should—challenge the values of white privilege and instead promote values of self-love.

As teachers, we are cultural workers, whether we are aware of it or not.

Young students, because of their honesty and willingness to talk about issues, provide many opportunities for teachers to take seemingly minor incidents and turn them into powerful teaching moments. I am grateful for Ernesto's sincerity and trust in sharing with me. Without knowing it, Ernesto opened the door to a lively dialogue in our classroom about white privilege.

To resurface the dialogue on beauty and skin color, I chose a children's book that deals with resistance to white privilege (a genre defined, in part, by its scarcity). The book is *Niña Bonita,* written by Ana María Machado and illustrated by Rosana Fara (1996, available in English from Kane/Miller Book Publishers). The book tells the story of an albino bunny who loves the beauty of a girl's dark skin and wants to find out how he can get black fur. I knew the title of the book would give away the author's bias, so I covered the title. I wanted to find out, before reading the book, how children perceived the cover illustration of the dark-skinned girl.

> **Young students, because of their honesty and willingness to talk about issues, provide many opportunities for teachers to take seemingly minor incidents and turn them into powerful teaching moments.**

"If you think this little girl is pretty, raise your hand," I said. Fourteen hands went up.

"If you think she is ugly, raise your hand," I then asked. Fifteen voted for ugly, among them Ernesto.

I was not surprised that half my students thought the little girl was ugly. Actually, I was expecting a higher number, given the tidal wave of white dolls that make their way into our classroom on Fridays, our Sharing Day, and previous comments by children in which they indicated that dark is ugly.

After asking my students why they thought the girl on the book cover was ugly, one student responded, "Because she has black color and her hair is really curly." Ernesto added, "Because she is black-skinned."

"But you are dark like her," Stephanie quickly rebutted to Ernesto, while several students nodded in agreement. "How come you don't like her?"

"Because I don't like black girls," Ernesto quickly responded. Several students affirmed Ernesto's statement with "yes" and "that's right."

"All children are pretty," Stephanie replied in defense.

Carlos then added, "If you behave good, then your skin color can change."

"Are you saying that if you are good, you can turn darker?" I asked, trying to make sure the other students had understood what he meant.

"White!" responded Carlos.

"No, you can't change your color," several students responded. "That can't be done!"

"How do you know that your color can change?" I asked, hoping Carlos would expand on his answer.

"My mom told me," he said.

"And would you like to change your skin color?" I asked.

"No," he said. He smiled shyly as he replied and I wondered if he may have wished he was not dark-skinned but didn't want to say so.

Carlos' mother's statements about changing skin color reminded me of instances in my family and community when a new baby is born. "Oh, look at him, how pretty and blond-looking he is," they say if the baby has European features and coloring. And if the babies came out dark, like Ernesto? Then the comments are "¡Ay! Pobrecito, salió tan prietito"—which translated means "Poor baby, he came out so dark."

I hear similar comments from co-workers in our school's staff lounge. A typical statement: "Did you see Raul in my class? He has the most beautiful green eyes."

It is no surprise that so many students must fight an uphill battle against the values of white privilege; still other students choose not to battle at all.

Challenging the Students

In an attempt to have students explain why they think the black girl in *Niña Bonita* is ugly, I ask them, "If you think she is ugly for having dark skin, why do you think her dark skin makes her ugly?"

"I don't like the color black," volunteers Yvette, "because it looks dark and you can't see in the dark."

"Because when I turn off the light," explains Marco, "everything is dark and I am afraid."

> It is no surprise that so many students must fight an uphill battle against white supremacist values; still other students choose not to battle at all.

Although most of my kindergarten students could not articulate the social worthlessness of being dark-skinned in this society, I was amazed by their willingness to struggle with an issue that so many adults, teachers included, ignore, avoid, and pretend does not exist. At the same time, it was clear that many of my students had already internalized the values of white privilege.

At the end of our discussion, I took another vote to see how students were reacting to *Niña Bonita;* I also wanted to ask individual students why they had voted the way they had. This second time, 18 students said the black girl was pretty and only 11 said she was ugly. Ernesto still voted for "ugly."

"Why do you think she is ugly?" I asked, but this time the students didn't volunteer responses. Perhaps they were sensing that I did not value negative answers as much as I did comments by students who fell in love with *Niña Bonita*. In their defense of dark skin, some students offered explanations such as "Her color is dark and pretty," "All girls are pretty," and "I like the color black."

Our discussion of *Niña Bonita* may have led four students to modify their values of beauty and ugliness in relation to skin color. Maybe these four students just wanted to please their teacher. What is certain, however, is that the book and our discussion caused some students to look at the issue in a new way.

Equally important, *Niña Bonita* became a powerful tool to initiate discussion on an issue that will affect my students, and myself, for a lifetime. Throughout the school year, the class continued our dialogue on the notions of beauty and ugliness. (One other book that I have found useful to spark discussion is *The Ugly Duckling*.

This fairy tale, which is one of the most popular among early elementary teachers and children, is often used uncritically. It tells the story of a little duckling who is "ugly" because his plumage is dark. Happiness comes only when the duckling turns into a beautiful, spotless white swan. I chose to use this book in particular because the plot is a representation of the author's value of beauty as being essentially white. I want my students to understand that they can disagree with and challenge authors of books, and not receive their messages as God-given.)

When I have such discussions with my students, I often feel like instantly including my opinion. But I try to allow my students to debate the issue first. After they have spoken, I ask them about their views and push them to clarify their statements. One reason I like working with children is that teaching is always a type of experiment, because the students constantly surprise me with their candid responses. These responses then modify how I will continue the discussion.

I struggle, however, with knowing that as a teacher I am in a position of power in relation to my young students. It is easy to make students stop using the dominant ideology and adopt the ideology of another teacher, in this case my ideology. In this society, in which we have been accustomed to deal with issues in either-or terms, children (like many adults) tend to adopt one ideology in place of another, but not necessarily in a way in which they actually think through the issues involved. I struggle with how to get my students to begin to look critically at the many unequal power relations in our society, relations that, even at the age of 5, have already shaped even whether they love or hate their skin color and consequently themselves.

At the end of our reading and discussion of the book, I shared my feelings with my students.

"I agree with the author calling this girl 'Niña Bonita' because she is absolutely beautiful," I say. "Her skin color is beautiful."

> **I struggle, however, with knowing that as a teacher I am in a position of power in relation to my young students.**

While I caressed my face and kissed my cinnamon-colored hands several times happily and passionately, so that they could see my love for my skin color, I told them, "My skin color is beautiful, too."

I pointed to one of my light-complexioned students and said, "Gerardo also has beautiful skin color and so does Ernesto. But Gerardo cannot be out in the sun for a long time because his skin will begin to burn. I can stay out in the sun longer because my darker skin color gives me more protection against sunburn. But Ernesto can stay out in the sun longer than both of us because his beautiful dark skin gives him even more protection."

Despite our several class discussions on beauty, ugliness, and skin color Ernesto did not appear to change his mind. But, hopefully, his mind will not forget our discussions.

Ernesto probably still takes his magic pills, which, his mother later explained, are Flintstones vitamin C. But I hope that every time he pops one into his mouth, he remembers how his classmates challenged the view that to be beautiful one has to be white. I want Ernesto to always remember, as will I, Lorena's comment: "Dark-skinned children are beautiful and I have dark skin, too."

Names have been changed.

Alejandro Segura-Mora is a facilitator and founder of Mind Growers, a consulting organization dedicated to helping schools close the racial achievement gap and lead all students to excellence.

Reflection Activity

If this is an individual reflection, reflect on, and respond to, the following question.

If you are having a group discussion, write and share your individual response to the following question:

If your skin could speak, what would it say?

Chapter Thirty-Eight

RACE: SOME TEACHABLE—AND UNCOMFORTABLE—MOMENTS

By Heidi Tolentino

"**Y**ou can never know what it's like to be black," Carlen said sharply. The class went silent.

It was the fourth week of school and my juniors had just begun Sue Monk Kidd's *The Secret Life of Bees*. The novel is set in South Carolina in the mid-1960s. Something intrigued me about the perspective and the interracial relationships during such social upheaval. I chose this book because I love the characters, but also because it opens the door to discussions of racial justice—both historically and today.

ZACH BARTEL

Growing up the only Asian American student in my community, I promised myself that I would never walk away from issues of race in a classroom setting. Thus, for my 11th-grade American literature class, I choose multicultural literature that explores how race plays out in characters' lives, which I hope will in turn trigger discussions about how race plays out in our lives. One of my aims is to help students—especially my predominantly white students—recognize that life in our society confronts us with choices about whether and how we will act to counter racism. Too often, "racism" is reduced to how people treat one another on an interpersonal level. But I wanted them to think in broader terms about this country's history of legislated racism and the lingering patterns of inequality produced by that history. Some of this curriculum I can map out in advance in lesson plans, but part of this work is improvisational, and I know I need to be alert to the unpredictable, and sometimes uncomfortable, ways that students respond to this teaching.

> **One of my aims is to help students—especially my predominantly white students—recognize that life in our society confronts us with choices about whether and how we will act to counter racism.**

As part of Portland's annual "curriculum camp," I worked with a group of high school teachers to create a unit around *The Secret Life of Bees* as a stepping stone for teaching about the human effects of institutionalized racism. I began the unit in my 11th-grade language arts classes at Portland's Cleveland High School, an urban school, but one that is more than 75 percent European American. My students and I were early in the unit and just beginning our exploration of the impact of segregation in the lives of characters in the novel.

I opened our reading of *The Secret Life of Bees* by examining the dichotomy between the lives of whites and blacks in the South during the 1960s. I used Spike Lee's documentary *Four Little Girls* to help students gain insight into the chasm between the two communities. The film focuses on the bombing of the 16th St. Church in Birmingham, Ala., by white supremacists. This African American church was the center of civil rights activity there at the time of the bombing; the congregation was focused on helping black citizens gain the right to vote. Four young girls were murdered and Spike Lee focuses both on the repercussions of their deaths and how members of the community honored their lives through continuing civil rights activism. I chose this film to begin our unit because it is a powerful look at the blatant and violent racism that existed in 1965 and the struggle of African Americans and their white allies to fight for equal rights through their push to register African American voters. This was our starting point.

Shortly after watching the film, I initiated a discussion on a scene from *The Secret Life of Bees* in which Rosaline, one of the book's African American characters, is arrested while on her way to register to vote. We reflected on what we'd learned about work for voting rights, and I brought out copies of the Louisiana voting rights test given to African Americans who tried to register. [A PDF of this test is available at http://www.rethinkingschools.org/static/img/archive/17_02/Vote_test.pdf.]

We examined the tricks used in the test to keep African Americans from voting. I set the scene for them: "Imagine the fear that must have come with walking through that door, seeing the men with rifles standing a few feet behind you, and being handed a test, given 10 minutes to finish, and realizing that there was no way for you to pass." The students were appalled and kept pointing out new questions for us to examine and to try to decode them, and finally concluded that there was no way to decode trick questions. They couldn't take their eyes off the document.

As students put the tests away, I noticed Evan watching the clock from his desk, and I walked over and joked, "Stop counting down the minutes until you can run from the classroom." He shushed me and told me he was timing Jessie to see if she could finish the test in 10 minutes. She wrote frantically as she sat hunched over the paper. Without glancing up she said, "I want to know what it was like."

Suddenly, from across the room I heard, "You can never know what it's like. You will never understand." I turned quickly to see the fury on the face of one of my African American students as she glared at Jessie. Jessie looked up from the test, her pencil poised over the paper, and stared across the room.

I knew I had to make a choice quickly and either cut off discussion or open the door all the way. I decided to let it swing wide open. I said: "Talking about issues of race is so difficult. It's painful. Most adults don't want to touch it and will silence others when they do. But I've found that at our school students will discuss it, and I want to give you room to do so. You need to know that when you say something in this class, you have to be ready to explain yourself and have an open discussion about it as a class."

I motioned to the student who had confronted Jessie and said, "Carlen, tell us what you meant." I sat down at a student desk and the room went completely silent. The students sat rigidly at their desks, and the tension in the room was palpable.

Suddenly, from across the room I heard, 'You can never know what it's like. You will never understand.'

Carlen took a deep breath, leaned forward, and said pointedly to Jessie who was seated directly across from her, "You can never know what it's like to be black." Her face became more serious with each word, her tone angry. "I also don't understand why white people always say, 'I want to know what you're feeling and know what it feels like.' You don't want to know what it feels like to walk down the street and have white women clutch their purses. You don't want to know what it's like to be different every single day. You can't want to know because it's horrible."

Jessie pushed her blond hair back from her face and came right back at her and said, "But should I just remain ignorant then? Don't you think it's important for me to try and understand so that things can change? Race is a huge issue in 2006 and things haven't changed and I think we have to learn to change things." Her voice shook just the slightest bit, but she looked determined. No one made a sound.

"But there is nothing you can do to understand it. You are white and you will always be white and you won't ever know what it's like to be me." Carlen never shouted, but the intensity of her words filled the room.

"But don't I have to try? Shouldn't I try?" Jessie's voice sounded desperate.

"But, why? What will it change?" Carlen sat back in her seat and I felt 34 pairs of eyes turn my way.

The girls looked at each other for a moment, and I stepped toward them. I told them how much I appreciated their honesty and that I wanted them to feel that they could always stop our discussions to be honest about what they were feeling and thinking. I explained that we were not going to end this conversation for good—we would come back to it over and over so they should reflect on today and think about what they'd heard, felt, and thought. In retrospect, I wish I had stopped the class and had them journal about what occurred so that they could gain some perspective in the moment. But, if I had, the following discussion may never have happened.

The N-Word

I breathed a sigh of relief as we returned to the book and Rosaline, who was on her way to register to vote. Before we began to read, I explained that in the next section and in sections to come, the N-word would be used, and I wanted them to understand my policy around that word. I explained that because of its painful history, I ask students not to say the word when we read aloud. Instead, I have them say N. I also explained that we would naturally never use that word in the classroom at any time or toward anyone. Just as a student continued our read-aloud, I noticed a hand out of the corner of my eye. In my gut, I knew that something was coming. I'd known the student for two years and I knew his penchant for creating chaos, but I asked anyway. "Joe, do you have a question about the book?"

"No, but I have a question about the N-word. Why can black people use it and white people can't?"

Voices exploded from every corner of the room. "Are you a complete idiot for bringing that up now?" "Why are you trying to start something?" "What is wrong with you?"

I silenced the class and, with an inner grimace, thanked Joe for asking such a difficult question. What I really wanted to say was "We don't have time for that question now. Just don't use the N-word." But I knew that this was a pivotal point in my year and if I wanted to push kids, I had to push myself. I asked the students to close their books.

Internally I was shaking. *What was I going to say? How did I let it get this far? Why wasn't I prepared for this?* I had five seconds to come up with something.

I explained to students that words that are historically used against a community in hate are often taken back by that community and turned around and used as words of power. I told them about my 6th-grade experience when I told my parents that we played "smear the queer" at school that day and how my parents almost jumped out of their chairs trying to cover my mouth. They explained why that word was never to be used again in our house, because it was derogatory and disrespectful. I never forgot that, so when a friend of mine used "queer" years later when talking about her own community, I was taken aback. I asked her about its use and she explained how the gay and lesbian community had taken it back and used it as a word of power. I told kids that the N-word had an even more horrific past and so much pain connected to it and we had to be careful when dealing with it.

Joe was not appeased. He peered out at me from behind his glasses, "But why can't white people use it?"

I explained that even within the African American community, there was a split about whether or not to use the N-word and that the debate was heated and might always be that way. I noticed some students raising their hands, waving them around, and I had to make another split-second decision. I knew that they wanted to put their two cents in about the topic, and I was usually open to hearing what everyone had to say, but this was different. We had already had an intense blowup and two of my African American students looked uncomfortable and were not making eye contact with anyone.

> **In solidarity with my African American students, I had shut down a discussion that most of the class wanted to have, and I wasn't sure that I had made the right choice.**

I knew what it felt like to be one of the only students of color in a classroom and to have to wait for other students to make comments that were stereotypical and painful. I knew the feeling in the pit of my stomach as I waited for the comment and knew everyone was looking at me and waiting for my reaction. So I continued: "But if you are not a member of that community and have never had that word used against you in hate, you don't get to be part of the debate." The hands slowly lowered. "The African American community can discuss its use and debate its power, but we won't use that word here and I hope you won't use it anywhere."

The class was silent for a few moments. No one spoke or moved and they seemed to ponder what I was saying. In solidarity with my African American students, I had shut down a discussion that most of the class wanted to have, and I wasn't sure that I had made the right choice; I followed my instincts and they were the only thing that I had in that moment. There were only a few minutes left in class, and I reminded them that this would not be our last discussion and that they should continue to bring up these important questions. I reiterated their reading homework and the bell rang.

Second Thoughts

Before Carlen left the room, Jessie walked over to her and said, "I'm sorry, Carlen. I hope you know that I wasn't trying to make you angry. I just really wanted to know what it felt like." Carlen simply nodded.

I asked Carlen to stay after class so that I could talk to her because she looked upset. After the students filed out, Carlen and I sat down and she began to cry. "I hate this. I hate having to deal with this. Why does it happen over and over?" I hugged her and we sat there for a moment. "Why do I always have to defend people of color? Why do I always have to explain?" I wanted to comfort Carlen, but my internal struggles were so heavy from such an intense class and the fear that I had done and said everything wrong, that I was at a loss for the right words.

I told Carlen, "I'm so proud of you for how openly you spoke and how willing you were to go to that place."

"But it didn't help. It never helps."

"I think it helped more than you will ever know. You got people thinking. But you didn't get to say everything, and I think you need to write about it. I want you to go home and write down everything that comes to mind about today. Reflect on it and get as angry as you need to. We'll meet tomorrow and talk about it again."

Carlen nodded and seemed to relax a bit. I sent her to the library to write and I went to my desk and put my head down. I was overwhelmed both emotionally and physically. I took a moment to email Carlen's mom because I wanted her to know what to expect when Carlen came home. I needed someone to talk to, and I needed some help in processing the day.

> **When I encourage students to think about race in an almost all-white classroom, do I do it on the backs of my students of color? Do I force them to carry a load that is too heavy just to help white students begin to deal with their own issues of race?**

I found our school campus monitor, Joann. She had been my ally for the past three years. Like me, she had grown up mixed-race (African American and European American) and was also the only person of color in her community. We had spent hours talking about issues of race and how to work with students around those issues. Outside of school, she worked with African American writers in the community and African American at-risk youth and had amazing insight into how to confront difficult topics.

So I asked her, "When I encourage students to think about race in an almost all-white classroom, do I do it on the backs of my students of color? Do I force them to carry a load that is too heavy just to help white students begin to deal with their own issues of race? It was too heavy for me, so am I just doing the same thing to them?"

She reminded me that many, perhaps most, teachers feel so much discomfort confronting issues of race that they try to avoid it in their classes. I was talking about race in a way that not everyone was willing to take on and it was always going to be uncomfortable—for students and for me. But hadn't we said that we worked with kids because of what we both experienced in our youth? Students of color were forced to carry the load of racism every day because racism is entangled in every aspect of their lives. As educators we have to find ways to be their allies and be sensitive to how our work in the classroom affects them.

Carlen's Story

The next day, Carlen returned with a letter that she wrote to the class. I asked her if I could read it aloud and she agreed. The following is an edited version of what she wrote:

> Yesterday in class was very intense for everyone because of the subject matter and no matter how many times you can say you were comfortable sitting there, it is a fact that no one was. I don't regret anything I said yesterday because I meant every word. When Jessie said that she wanted to take the test to get a feel for what it was like, my first reaction was to give her the benefit of the doubt and to think of it as just a statement. That was only half of my brain saying to keep my mouth shut . . . the impulse part of me always speaks up and I commented back as everyone knows. But I shouldn't have forgotten that Ms. T. makes everything a discussion. Although I am not the only person of color in the classroom, I always have something to say . . . and yesterday I did. Honestly, I was about to cry because I am tired of having to talk about racism and tired of having to feel this way once again because I always get offended. It hurts to have to think about the people out there that don't think you deserve to be in a classroom with them or to even be alive. It makes me feel like as a black person I am stripped of my rights, confidence, value, and self-image every time I have to open a book or see a movie about slavery or racism. After class and the discussion was over, Ms. T. and I talked. I was really upset and I hate to admit it, but I cried. It didn't upset me that Jessie made that statement or that it became a big deal. I was upset because I will never be able to explain to anyone who isn't a person of color what it is really like. I can't just walk in a store and not be watched or followed. I can't make people feel safe around me when they assume that I want to steal something of theirs. I don't get automatic respect from white people; I have to try even harder because someone always has a stereotype. I make jokes all the time, but it's only because I wish it made me feel better about who I am and the race I am. I'm not saying I am ashamed and I have never wanted to be white. I just wish I didn't have to be so different or so judged. But everything having to do with the subject just makes me want to leave the room, but I can't let my people down by not getting through it. . . . Hopefully yesterday taught everyone something. But I also realize it only makes me stronger every day. I hope you all don't hate

I talked to them about the idea of sympathy versus empathy—that it is not possible for us to feel what people in other times or circumstances felt, but that it's crucial that we attempt to understand how the conditions in people's lives affect them.

me and I hope you understand where I am coming from and who I am as a person. But, to end it with four encouraging words. . .

> Peace and love, everyone,
> Carlen

Students were silent after I finished reading. They applauded Carlen and thanked her for her writing. I talked to them about the idea of sympathy versus empathy—that it is not possible for us to feel what people in other times or circumstances felt, but that it's crucial that we attempt to understand how the conditions in people's lives affect them. And from this empathy we can consider ways that we can work to make the world a more just place for everyone.

Looking back, I wish that I had stopped myself before handing students my conclusions, and instead asked them to write a reflection about what had happened the day before. It could have been something that they wrote to me or something that they wrote to Carlen or to Jessie, which I would read and give to them later. I missed an opportunity to use their writing as a means for them to reflect on crucial issues. I want students to gain insight because they come to realizations, not because I tell them. This writing might not have elicited realizations, but it would have given them an opportunity to express what they felt and wondered, which could have led to a valuable discussion.

Jessie

After class I stopped Jessie as she was leaving and commended her for what she had said the day before. I told her that I knew how strong Carlen's anger must have felt, yet she did not back down. I was so impressed by her courage. She told me that she wished she hadn't started the conflict and that she hadn't meant anything by it, but she really wanted to explain what had motivated her. She gave me a thoughtful look before she left but didn't say any more.

My own role in prompting the blowup in class continued to gnaw at me. Hadn't I put Jessie in that situation? Hadn't I asked her, and the entire class, to "imagine the fear" of people who took the voting test? Hadn't Jessie simply done what I'd asked of all my students? Wasn't this attempt at historical imagination a crucial component of social justice teaching?

My own role in prompting the blowup in class continued to gnaw at me.

Perhaps. And yet Jessie's attempt to imagine the impact of racism in people's lives felt presumptuous to Carlen—like Jessie was proposing to understand something that her white privilege would never permit her truly to grasp.

But what about Jessie? How did the exchange affect her? Jessie and I didn't talk at length about the incident until the last day of school when I shared a draft of this article with her. Jessie explained that she felt "cornered" that day and had felt unable to express what she truly meant or felt. I think that she was politely telling me that I hadn't helped open a space for her to speak. I'd allowed the conversation to happen, but hadn't made it safe enough for her to express her intent or her confusion. She told me that she wished that she had been brave enough to speak her piece and help the class understand that she wasn't trying to "be black," but rather hoped to understand the severity of the situation so that she could better understand the extent to which institutionalized racism affects an individual's daily life.

Jessie and Carlen's responses were both legitimate; how does my teaching honor each of these? This is an issue I'm still pondering.

Lessons Learned

I learned many things from this experience both about my teaching and about myself. I realized that I hadn't appreciated how uncomfortable it can be to teach about race, even though I considered myself an anti-racist teacher. It's one thing to map out lesson plans on a novel about the Civil Rights Movement, but students' reactions cannot be "scripted" in the same way that a lesson plan can be. Anti-racist teaching requires a willingness to go where students' responses take us. I have to be willing to go deeper than just interactions between characters in a book.

I realized that I have to keep myself from being bound by my own calendar and recognize when students are engaged. I have to remember that learning comes in the cracks when we are open and willing to deal with the uncomfortable conversations, the unpredictable questions, and the spontaneous outbursts. I can choose books, films, and other resources that create opportunities to discuss racism, but that is not enough without being open to allowing the tough conversations to happen. I have to be willing to make mistakes and not have all of the answers and let my students learn without me always leading them there. I have to be willing to deal with the unexpected if I want to truly be an anti-racist teacher.

Heidi Tolentino teaches English at Cleveland High School, an urban school in the Portland Public School District.

Chapter Thirty-Nine

EXPLORING RACE RELATIONS

By Lisa Espinosa

"I don't want my daughter going to the high school with all the blacks." That's what one of my students' mothers said when I first began teaching. While her comment took me aback, it wasn't the first time I had heard such racist comments from people in the Latino community.

Although I had not heard my own students, most of whom are Mexican Americans, make blatant racist comments, I had heard adults mention "loud black people" or express fear of black people moving into the community. My own parents were caring people, but they had biases and prejudices against blacks—mostly

EDEL RODRIGUEZ

stemming from lack of education and experience. I wondered how this racial divide affected my students.

I had chosen to teach in a predominantly Mexican community in Chicago because, as a Mexican American woman, I felt a connection to the students there. I hoped to use our shared culture as a means of validating my 7th graders' experiences. And I wanted to help my students become more politically aware by exposing them to issues and ideas I didn't encounter until college.

Comments such as the one my student's mother made reminded me that part of teaching my students about who they are in the world and how to overcome oppression means helping them see the commonalities between their struggles and those of other people of color.

But starting a dialogue about it with them wasn't easy. I did not want to disrespect my students' families, and I did not want my students to perceive me as doing so. I had struggled with this issue before and believed that by bringing in my personal experiences I could help my students feel more comfortable. But I must admit that sharing my own family's biases was not something I enjoyed. I couldn't help feeling as if talking about this made me somehow disloyal to my family—and maybe even my culture.

I am very proud of my Mexican American heritage, and I want to help foster that pride in my students. At the same time, I feel people of color need to unite to fight against the oppression and systemic racism in our society. In the current political climate—with attacks on public schools, immigrants, the poor, and new tax breaks for the wealthy—it is easy for people of color to narrow their vision and "fight for scraps" instead of joining together to fight against common oppression. In fact, those in power in our society count on the divisions among the powerless to maintain their positions.

In order to introduce my students to these concepts, I began integrating content into my curriculum that I believed would help them see connections between the struggles of blacks and Latinos in this country. I hoped that this would help them develop a sense of alliance between themselves and African Americans.

This is the story of some of the efforts I have made—sometimes only partially successful ones—to teach about issues of racism and to begin a conversation with my students about their own racial biases. These are not snapshots of amazing transformations among my students, but glimpses of efforts I've made to challenge my students—and myself—to examine a topic that often goes unacknowledged.

A Process of Discovery

Examining racial biases has been a learning experience for my students, but it has been just as much a process of discovery for me. Growing up in a working-class Mexican immigrant household, I didn't listen to National Public Radio and read the *New York Times*. I didn't know about progressive causes because there was nobody to inform me about them. Unlike my parents, I was able to go to college. But, during college, I was also busy raising my children, so my main concern was making sure I stayed in school and graduated. Because of my background, I continually feel as if I'm trying to play catch up—even when it comes to knowing about my own cultural history. So, when I teach my students about the Chicano Movement, in many ways, I'm learning right along with them.

But whoever is doing the teaching, one thing is certain: Racism still affects the lives of African Americans and Latinos (as well as other people of color). According to *Minding the Gap,* a 2003 report funded by the Human Relations Foundation of Chicago, the Jane Addams Policy Initiative, and the Center for Urban Research and Learning at Loyola University, Latinos and African Americans in the Chicago area continue to face disparities in areas such as housing, economic opportunity, access to public transportation, and health care. In 2001, for example, African Americans in Chicago were five times more likely to be denied conventional mortgages than whites, while Latinos were two-and-a-half times more likely than whites to be denied. Although income levels grew for all racial groups in Illinois between 1990 and 2000, Latino and African American men still earn less than half of their Asian and white counterparts. And Latinos (29 percent) and African Americans (24 percent) in Illinois have the highest rates of nonelderly persons without health insurance.

> Part of teaching my students about who they are in the world and how to overcome oppression means helping them see the commonalities between their struggles and those of other people of color.

These numbers demonstrate that systemic injustices continue to affect both blacks and Latinos. But for a person growing up in a racially isolated neighborhood, it's sometimes hard to get that perspective. I grew up in a very segregated community in Chicago in the 1980s, and I don't remember ever having black classmates in the public elementary school I attended. Today many students in Chicago public schools face similar circumstances: In 2003, 50 years after the *Brown v. Board of Education* decision, 343 of Chicago's 602 schools are racially isolated, with 90 percent or more of their students sharing the same racial background, according to statistics from the Chicago Board of Education. When I asked my students how many of them had black friends, few raised their hands. Some had had African American teachers at school, but most have had little, if any, personal interaction with black people.

I tried to do three things in my class throughout the year: provide background knowledge about the history of racism and discrimination in this country and how that has led to the inequalities that exist today; look at current issues that affect people of color; and examine how the media create and perpetuate negative images of people of color. Here I will focus on curriculum that I developed around certain resources that I gathered, most of which focus on the African American experience. Because I was doing this as part of my language arts class, where I need to cover many other topics, I can't always explore these topics as deeply as I would like.

One of the resources I used to discuss current issues affecting poor urban youth in our city is the book *Our America: Life and Death on the South Side of Chicago,*

> **When I asked my students how many of them had black friends, few raised their hands.**

by LeAlan Jones and Lloyd Newman. This book, which grew out of two radio documentaries, examines life in a public housing development from the perspectives of two African American teenagers, 13-year-old LeAlan Jones and 14-year-old Lloyd Newman. (Along with the book we listened to the original radio documentary.)

To provide some historical background about the Civil Rights Movement, I used the book *Freedom's Children: Young Civil Rights Activists Tell Their Own Stories,* by Ellen Levine. Finally, to examine how the media create and perpetuate stereotypes of African Americans, we watched the documentary *Ethnic Notions* and read relevant articles in magazines and newspapers.

'Our America'

The book *Our America* was at the center of our unit. This book helped me raise some current issues that affect poor urban youth, such as inadequate housing, lack of community resources, and the prevalence of violence in their community. I required all my students to keep a dialogue journal. Through reading the journal entries I was able to get a sense of how they were connecting with LeAlan and Lloyd, the protagonists of the book. LeAlan and Lloyd write a lot about the lack of resources in their community and the biases that people who were not from their community have against them. These were things I knew my students could relate to. Many of them compared LeAlan and Lloyd's environment with their own.

Several students wrote about the death of a 5-year-old boy in the book. Although I never forced my students to share their writing, as the unit progressed they became more comfortable sharing. Lilia,* who had recently been in a car accident that seriously injured her mother and killed her 3-year-old nephew, wrote, "It was sad because I've seen a person dead already and it reminded me of the accident that I was in." She read this aloud in class, and although it made me sad that she had experienced such a tragedy, I felt it could be healing for her to begin sharing some of her feelings about it.

Many students wanted to discuss how economic and social circumstances can lead children to resort to disruptive and even violent behavior. Angelica wrote, "This made me think that some kids were treated wrong and maybe in school they act all tough but what they really want is love and friendship." Although these reflections did not deal directly with race, the fact that my students were empathizing with LeAlan and Lloyd was an important beginning.

'Ethnic Notions'

To begin a conversation about the origins of stereotyping and misrepresentation of African Americans, we watched the documentary *Ethnic Notions*. Although the language of the video is difficult, with sufficient teacher guidance it can be a valuable teaching tool. It depicts different images that have been used throughout this country's history to represent African Americans. For example, blacks were either depicted as docile—"the happy slave"—as a defense of slavery, or as savages after the Civil War to justify the need to go back to the "good old times in the Southern plantation."

Because the video *Ethnic Notions* is so complex, it is helpful to show it over the course of several days. I used words from the film as our weekly vocabulary, and wrote comprehension questions to help guide my students along the way. I also reviewed with them the different historical periods that the video references: antebellum (pre-Civil War), Civil War, Reconstruction, and Redemption.

Many students wanted to discuss how economic and social circumstances can lead children to resort to disruptive and even violent behavior.

To understand some of the concepts in *Ethnic Notions*, students need to have some familiarity with the idea of media representation. Since we had started the year looking at media depictions of men and women, my students were already familiar with these concepts. Before watching the video, I explained to my students that the video was going to explore different portrayals of African Americans throughout different historical periods in this country. Although using this video was a time-consuming process, I believe that it is worth the time and energy, and it's a film we often refer back to throughout the year.

To connect the negative media images of African Americans in *Ethnic Notions* to current portrayals of Latinos in the media, I brought in copies of the "Ask Dame Edna" column in the February 2003 issue of *Vanity Fair* that had caused a stir among Latinos across the country. In the column, which is a spoof of advice columns, Dame Edna "jokingly" responds to a dilemma from a fictionalized reader who says she wants to learn French, but everyone keeps telling her to learn Spanish instead. Dame Edna responds, in part: "Who speaks [Spanish] that you are really desperate to talk to? The help? Your leaf blower?"

Like many other readers, my students did not think her comments were funny or appropriate. Some of them wrote letters to the editors of the magazine. Alberto wrote, "I think *Vanity Fair* was wrong in putting Selma Hayek on the cover of the magazine and at the same time printing Dame Edna's comment. They tried to get Hispanics to buy their magazine but at the same time, they insult Hispanics with such a racist comment. I believe Vanity Fair owes Hispanics an apology." Javier wrote, "When I read it, it made me feel bad . . . and if you just say it was a joke, well it was a joke that hurt feelings." And Mara wrote, "I love my culture and when I grow up I will find a way to make Hispanics look great in front of everybody's face."

Historical Context

After we explored past and current media representations, I thought it would help to provide some background on the Civil Rights Movement. The book *Freedom's Children: Young Civil Rights Activists Tell Their Own Stories* helped me to provide historical background that my students could relate to. It includes first-person accounts from activists who were teenagers during the Civil Rights Movement and photographs of the teenagers and major events.

Because we were pressed for time, I decided to read the first chapter together in class and then divide the six remaining chapters among the six reading groups in my class. I had each group summarize the major facts of one event and choose one teenager from the corresponding chapter to read and write about.

Mara wrote, 'I love my culture and when I grow up I will find a way to make Hispanics look great in front of everybody's face.'

Looking back, I realize that my students needed more guidance with each chapter. Next time I teach this, I'll provide a set of questions for each chapter. When the groups finished that assignment, I asked them to design posters that included facts about the events and words from the young activists. Then I had them teach their classmates about what they'd learned. Although my students wanted to create skits for each of their chapters, finishing this project took much longer than I anticipated, so we postponed that idea. These activities helped my students get a better sense of the impact of the Civil Rights Movement and the role teenagers can play in creating social change. It also set the stage for our later discussion of the Chicano Movement and allowed us to later compare and contrast the two movements.

In a class discussion, I asked my students whether they thought building alliances with other people of color, specifically African Americans, was important. Miriam said, "I think it would be good to start alliances because they probably don't know many Mexicans and we could teach them not to believe all the stereotypes about us and we could learn too." Judging by the students' journals, I think my efforts were paying off. Eddie wrote, "We would have more power working together." Jacinto wrote, "I think it is important because the more united you are the more you get done." And Iris added, "I think they should form an alliance because the bigger we are, the better things we will probably get from the government."

As a result of this last conversation, we are planning to start a correspondence with a 7th-grade class of predominantly African American students. My students are very excited about this.

I don't want to give the impression that some of my students haven't been resistant to the idea that building solidarity with African Americans is important. For example, there have been times when students have expressed a belief that Latinos need to help themselves and that African Americans "already get too much help." But these are exactly the kinds of ideas I'm trying to address in my classroom. In a sense, these kinds of comments give me a chance to further educate my students.

In her book *De Colores Means All of Us,* Elizabeth Martínez writes, "Building alliances calls for us to break down the walls of mutual prejudice that exist. To do so we need to hammer out strong tools. One is simply education: learning about each other's history, current experience and culture, beginning very young." By exploring media depictions of African Americans and Latinos and the history of the Civil Rights Movement, I feel we're headed in the right direction.

Lisa Espinosa is a teacher, healer and writer. She has taught on the south side of Chicago for over 10 years.

Chapter Forty

RECONSTRUCTING RACE

By Nathaniel W. Smith

"Really just think it's so terrible that people judge other people for their race. I don't see how they can be so stupid! I don't care if you're black, yellow, or green. I only see people as people."

When one of my students made this comment, his classmates applauded. Yet he was the same student who, not a day later, noticed that one of our classroom windows had a broken handle. He laughed, saying the school was "so damn ghetto." And he openly talked about rap music as "complete crap. It's not even music—even I can get on a microphone and just talk!"

COURTESY OF GREG FRENCH COLLECTION WITH ASSISTANCE FROM GREG FRIED

I wondered how I would even begin to get at the contradictions in this student's mind.

Yes, we should "all get along," as another student once earnestly implored. But before we can, we must first understand the degree to which we don't get along. This seemed especially difficult considering the population I was working with. I taught in Central Bucks School District in Bucks County, Pa., which is approximately 98 percent white, and 95 percent middle-class or higher. There was not much in the way of racial and socioeconomic diversity among my 10th- and 12th-grade students, who were tracked into honors, standard, and basic classes.

As a white teacher in a predominantly white school I wanted to help students see their own whiteness and the ways it has shaped their lives.

Comments like the ones above were not those of a few idiosyncratic individuals, they were refrains, repeated again and again, often in the exact same wording. I wanted to develop a curriculum that made race enormous, difficult, and personal, when many students defined it as stupid, simple, and external.

As a white teacher in a predominantly white school I wanted to help students see their own whiteness and the ways it has shaped their lives. I wanted to confront my students' perceptions that "I don't think it has anything to do with me—I don't even have a race. I'm just normal." I thought I would begin by helping them understand race as a specifically social construct.

The Breakthrough

"Mr. Smith, why are you teaching us history in our English class?" Students wondered why, in a course on American literature, I would devote multiple days to discussions of race. I explained to the students the interrelation of literature and the societies in which the authors lived, often pointing out that one couldn't understand modern music without understanding modern times.

As my course contained a unit on slave narratives and another on the Harlem Renaissance, I justified race discussion as requisite to understanding the context of the literature. So by the time our semester together had come and gone, I had taught several lessons that addressed the concepts of race, the historical development of race, and the challenges to race presented by the constant creation of multiracial people.

I had found readings and role plays, personal accounts, and documentary films. We acted out and discussed Twain's controversial *Pudd'nhead Wilson,* created graphic novels representing the autobiographies of Frederick Douglass and Harriet Jacobs, and even watched samples of the PBS film *Race: The Power of an Illusion.* Like many teachers with a passion, I bent the rules of the district curriculum requirements in favor of lessons I thought more pressing. But with all these lessons I ran into the same problem.

Constructing race, the daily practice of ascribing roles and identities to physical features, is a matter of active perception. If race affects the way you are treated by others in the world, it necessarily depends upon what race they suppose you to be. My curricular premise is that individuals can discover and address their own racism more effectively when they understand that all race categories are political lines drawn in the sands of cultural and genetic diffusion and evolution.

Constructing race, the daily practice of ascribing roles and identities to physical features, is a matter of active perception.

I can say it clearly enough, but lectures never bring the result I'm really after. If race is perceptual, it must be challenged on the level of perception. My lessons based on reading and discussion failed to produce activities that revealed to students how they construct race through their own vision and sense of identity.

Then in February 2002, I was doing some background research on Frederick Douglass, and I stumbled across Gregory Fried's article "True Pictures." (It's available on the web at http://www.mirrorofrace.org/common.php.) The pictures he had found were the perfect starting point.

Before we began, I told the students we were going to start working with slave narratives soon, and I thought this would be a good exercise for laying the groundwork. As I handed each student one of two photographs, I explained that these were taken around the time of emancipation (1863, to be precise), and that Frederick Douglass had hoped to use them to educate people against slavery.

Then I gave them three minutes to write a description of the photo. "Describe it, explain what's happening and who the characters are. Then explain how you think it might have been used in an antislavery campaign. If this were an antislavery campaign ad, what might be the slogan?" I avoided mentioning the race of the people in the photographs. The students spent the next few minutes reacting to these pictures. Though I cut off the original captions, I included the names for ease of discussion after.

Afterward, I asked them to share what they wrote. Students guessed that the picture of Isaac and Rosa arm in arm is symbolic of an interracial harmony campaign, a Benetton-style depiction of black and white together in youthful innocence. "The white girl and the black boy together arm in arm is a sort of vision for the future—there's hope for us to all live together," wrote one student.

Someone else suggested that Isaac and Rosa show that "the little white girl is safe playing with the little black boy."

For the second picture, students had a range of explanations, though often again the idea of safety emerges: "It shows that a black man can know more than a white person—he can teach them to read. And it sort of says, these white kids are safe with this black man."

Alternatively, some students argued, "the white kids are teaching the black man to read, kind of saying that he can learn just as well as white people and should be given a chance."

In addition to using this activity with my own classes of predominantly white students, I've also used it with classes of adults. Every time groups of people have debated these photos, they have described the pictures as photos of black and white people together.

Once students aired their reactions, I revealed to them that every person pictured was an emancipated slave. They had all been socially known as black, made to live as slaves. They were unable to own property, unable to vote, unable to pursue their rights through legal institutions. So, I asked my students: Were they in fact black, or were they white?

> **Though I never asked anyone the race of the people pictured, all respondents (without exception) included it in their descriptions.**

Though the debate was a stuttering one at this point, students began to engage in some disagreement. Before moving on, I tried to point out one constant in this exercise: When we're not thinking about race, we guess race and attach significance to it. Though I never asked anyone the race of the people pictured, all respondents (without exception) included it in their descriptions. Their interpretations of the meaning of the photos were all completely dependent on the assumed racial identities of the subjects. This point makes it much harder for students later to claim they don't see race at all.

'Is Mr. Smith a White Guy?'

I then changed the topic, volunteering to be a contemporary example. "OK, so the next question is: Is Mr. Smith a white man? Yes or no?" I asked. "Raise your hand if you think Mr. Smith is a white guy."

Across all the groups I've worked with, only one person has ever suggested that they thought I might have been mixed—because I have curly hair. "So, without asking, and without knowing my parents or how I might identify, everyone here has quietly agreed that I'm white. So how do you know?"

GREG FRENCH COLLECTION / GREG FRIED

On the board I made a list of the things that made me white to them. Kids had a lot of fun with this (though it was tough to avoid reacting to the descriptions, as some were quite unflattering); it's a rare opportunity to pick apart their teacher's appearance. "You have a thin nose! White skin! Thin lips! Blonde hair! Blue eyes! You talk white! You walk like a white man! You wear khakis and a button-up shirt! European ancestors!" The list of evidence was long, and the students threw out comments faster than I could write them on the board.

Once the list was up, I turned it around. "So, of all these things, which ones are indispensable?

Which ones make me absolutely white?" I challenged each one. "If I had fuller lips, would I still be white? Are there white people with brown or black hair? Are there white people with brown eyes? White people who speak 'Ebonics'—are they still white? If a black man wears a button-up shirt, is it harder to tell that he's black?" We went down the list until the students were unable to defend my whiteness. Still, they vehemently argued: "You just know."

Again I asked, "But what about Isaac and Rosa? Why didn't we 'just know' with them?"

Following this exercise, the ensuing debate has always been deep and often heated, tightly focused on what qualifies people for their race. No one tried to claim they didn't "see" the race of the teacher or the people pictured—they had already revealed assumptions about race in their answers. All the students assumed and interpreted race, regardless of whether they considered themselves prejudiced, regardless of whether they were looking at an emancipated slave in an old photograph or a white teacher standing in front of the classroom.

> **All the students assumed and interpreted race, regardless of whether they considered themselves prejudiced, regardless of whether they were looking at an emancipated slave in an old photograph or a white teacher standing in front of the classroom.**

With the rug pulled out from under the categories, we then moved on to discussing how, with all this uncertainty, we ever decide that a person is of a specific race. Using the traits students listed for categorizing my race, I suggested that all the qualities fit under one of three headings: color, culture, or ancestry. I then asked them, which of these provides the key? Is one category more important than the others? Students break down along unpredictable lines and bring forth some very interesting answers. One of the most strongly defended criteria is color.

A few questions quickly defeated the color argument. Students said I was white because of my white skin, so I held up a piece of blank paper. "So if I'm not exactly white in color, how white do I have to be to fit?" If students reversed it and claimed that "black people are people with black skin," I asked them to define the exact range of tones. What about darkly tanned white people? Thanks to tanning salons, there's often someone who identifies as being white in the room with skin darker than that of Malcolm X, who they all agreed was black. And what of the emancipated slaves in the pictures? Most came to accept that people with darker skin may be white, and people with very light skin may be black. Inevitably, the kids argued about Michael Jackson, and the conversation took on a life of its own.

I offered similar challenges to those who would ground race in culture. My students often mocked white students who "wish they were black." I had students explain to me how a person "acts black." What are the behaviors? "They try to talk Ebonics. They're always blasting DMX in the parking lot! They wear low baggy pants with their boxers hanging out. I know someone like that who's always trying to convince people she is black!"

If a person has adopted black culture, would we say that person is acting black? Wouldn't he or she just become black? What if this black-acting person had a black great-grandparent they didn't even know about? Who would argue that a "black-acting" person with African ancestry is not in fact black?

In the face of these ambiguities, students often drew the line at the most "scientific" seeming category—genetics. "You can look like whatever, but you either have African ancestors or you don't" is a typical student remark.

I asked about adoptees. Imagine I was adopted and didn't know my ancestry. Imagine that tomorrow I meet my real parents and one of them is black. Is it possible for a person to be black and not even know it? If this happened, would I be right to come to school tomorrow and say I am black? If not, does that mean black is something other than having African ancestry? If yes, then how could everyone have assumed I was white? I find students often split right down the middle as to whether I would be legitimately black or white in that scenario.

Another response to the ancestry argument revolved around historic black figures. I asked students if Malcolm X and Frederick Douglass were black men, and they said yes. Then I revealed to them that both men had European ancestry. If ancestry is the key to race, why doesn't that ancestry make them white? Why is it that in the game of race, even the slightest African ancestry trumps European ancestry? And in my case, students say they know I'm white because I have European ancestry—but how does one "see" ancestry?

In fact, one sees only physical traits—not the familial lines or genes from which they might be derived. Here students came full circle to the point of admitting that ancestry does not clearly correlate with race—skin tone and culture matter a lot too. So the argument is circular: A person is black because we decide they are black enough, and there is no single defining quality one must possess.

My purpose wasn't to clarify race, but to blow it apart. To do that I had to bring out the complex challenges that exist on all sides of the race definition. The point was to raise questions and make a mess rather than let students off with neat and easy answers. No more raising your hand just to say, "Racism is bad."

In fact, one sees only physical traits—not the familial lines or genes from which they might be derived.

But at this point I needed to be aware of a real danger. Students, particularly those white students who feel excluded in race discussions, may try to run with the principle that "race isn't real."

As one student said, "This just proves that all this race stuff is a bunch of people worked up about nothing." Obviously, this was not my intended result. So we got into a conversation about the word "real."

I said to the students, "Many people will say that God is not real. As with race, there is no 'scientific' evidence. Let's imagine for a moment those people are right, that there isn't a God. Even if that's true, think of the role the idea of God has played in world history. Think of all the huge religious organizations in almost every country, and the influence those religions have had in the world. Think of how many people refer to God every morning in the Pledge of Allegiance, how God is written on every coin and bill in the United States. Even if God is just something people made up—does that mean it hasn't affected us?" Even the most irreligious of students agreed that the idea of God affected them; in fact I've found the atheist-identified students to be quite upset about how often they are reminded of

My purpose wasn't to clarify race, but to blow it apart.

their status as outsiders. There is a parallel to those who would rather not see race, those who wish it would go away—wishing doesn't make it so. No matter whether race is grounded in science or ideology, it has a long and powerful history, one that has determined the shape of our society in ways no individual can escape.

Bringing It Home, Literally

Once students had some time to soak in these ideas, I ended with an exercise that literally brought the lesson home. Before doing so, I gave some words of introduction, as this piece could serve to alienate some students if not handled delicately. I explained to students that often we think only of certain populations as not knowing their heritage. It is a widely acknowledged tragedy of slavery that so many family lines were severed and cannot be retraced. This is likewise the case with many populations who may have fled oppressive circumstances in their countries of origin. When one thinks of people not knowing their heritage, one might think of adoptees first. But the truth of the matter is, few if any of us truly know our heritage in the way we imagine it. Think of all the people who describe themselves as "Irish and German" or some other two- or three-part combination. Can this really capture the genetic history of any individual?

For this exercise, I produced a simple blank diagram of the family tree, reaching back five generations. I then ask students to fill in the names of every relative they can. If one looks at the spreading numbers of ancestors—32 great-great-great-grandparents, 16 great-great-grandparents, eight great-grandparents, four grandparents, and two parents—there are 62 progenitors to name. I have yet to meet a student who could name them all. If one could, it still wouldn't identify the race of those individuals, even if there were pictures of them all.

I tried to minimize the discomfort for students who may have hesitations about revealing this kind of information by emphasizing that we are all on the same ground when it comes to our ancestry. None of us knows "where we come from," even if we know our parents and grandparents. I didn't ask students to share their trees, or even to feel compelled to fill them in there and then. The point was simply to visualize the vast numbers of people that came before us, and the inadequacy of the simplified descriptions most of us inherit.

I grew up being told I was Scots-Irish and a little bit of Native American, but when I started to examine this tree and ask my family members, I discovered many countries of origin that had not been told to me (Hessian, German, and British), several branches of the tree for which there was no information, and absolutely no confirmation of the "bit of Native American" that I had always been told of.

As a group we then discussed the significance of the holes in all our knowledge. If being African American means having African ancestry, how many of us know whether we are African American? How do any of us know we are any specific race at all? Some students will begin insisting on their whiteness, but most quickly realize they have no evidence to stand on. As one student said, "I don't know—maybe I am black—or African American, or whatever, for all I know."

The point was simply to visualize the vast numbers of people that came before us, and the inadequacy of the simplified descriptions most of us inherit.

Another of my students, the same one who said he didn't see race, came back to me a week after the lesson. "Mr. Smith, I went home and asked my grandmother how we know we're white. I asked her if she knew if we had any black ancestors. She got really angry and started yelling that 'of course we don't have any n––s in the family!' I didn't expect her to care so much about it. I quit asking about it after a while, but she never did say she had any evidence. When I showed her that [ancestry chart], she couldn't fill it out either. She tore it up." I worried I might have caused a family rift, or that I might be explaining myself to the principal soon, but at the same time I couldn't help but be happy that my student had taken it upon himself to seek answers—and he was sharp enough to recognize that no answer satisfies.

Of course, there are dangers. In my experience, no single lesson is received and applied the same way across all students, or even any two students. Some students will shut down in the face of this mess-making—others will select from the many potential implications the one they most want to hear, "race isn't real." It's a danger, though I would argue all educational practice is fraught with danger.

I believe it is promising to bring high school students to this level of thinking about race. If it is not an immutable, biological fact, then race must be a changing social fact. And if it has changed in the past, it can be changed now. Whatever dissatisfies us about the issue does not have to be accepted, looked at with resignation, and considered an inevitable part of our lives. Though it hardly guarantees that all students adopt a conscious, activist, anti-racist stance, it arms them against simple and reductive thinking about race, which is always dangerous regardless of the intent.

Nathaniel W. Smith is a lecturer at the University of Pennsylvania's Graduate School of Education, where he teaches courses in diversity, intercultural communication, and urban

Chapter Forty-One

PRESIDENTS AND SLAVES
Helping students find the truth

By Bob Peterson

During a lesson about George Washington and the American Revolution, I explained to my 5th graders that Washington owned 317 slaves. One student added that Thomas Jefferson also was a slave owner. And then, in part to be funny and in part expressing anger—over vote fraud involving African Americans in the then-recent 2000 election and the U.S. Supreme Court's subsequent delivery of the presidency to George W. Bush—one of my students shouted, "Bush is a slave owner, too!" "No, Bush doesn't own slaves," I calmly explained. "Slavery was finally ended in this country in 1865."

Short exchanges such as this often pass quickly and we move onto another topic. But this time one student asked: "Well, which presidents were slave owners?"

She had me stumped. "That's a good question," I said. "I don't know." Thus began a combined social studies, math, and language arts project in which I learned along with my students, and which culminated in a fascinating exchange between my students and the publishers of their U.S. history textbook.

After I admitted that I had no clue exactly which presidents owned slaves, I threw the challenge back to the students. "How can we find out?" I asked.

> **After I admitted that I had no clue exactly which presidents owned slaves, I threw the challenge back to the students.**

"Look in a history book," said one. "Check the internet," added another. I realized that I had entered one of those "teachable moments" when students show genuine interest in exploring a particular topic. Yet I had few materials about presidents and slaves, and no immediate idea of how to engage 25 students on the subject.

I also recognized that this was a great opportunity to create my own curriculum, which might help students look critically at texts while encouraging their active participation in doing meaningful research. Such an approach stands in sharp contrast to the "memorize the presidents" instruction that I suffered through growing up, and which too many students probably still endure. I seized the opportunity.

First, I had a student write down the question—"Which presidents were slave owners?"—in our class notebook, "Questions We Have." I then suggested that a few students form an "action research group," which in my classroom means an ad hoc group of interested students researching a topic and then doing something with what they learn. I asked for volunteers willing to work during recess. Several boys raised their hands, surprising me because I would have guessed that some of them would have much preferred going outside to staying indoors researching.

Action Research by Students

At recess time, Raul and Edwin were immediately in my face. "When are we going to start the action research on the slave presidents?" they demanded. I told them to look in the back of our school dictionaries for a list of U.S. presidents while I got out some large construction paper. The dictionaries, like our social studies text, had little pictures of each president with some basic information. "Why doesn't it show Clinton?" Edwin commented. "He's been president forever." I think, yeah, Clinton's been president four-fifths of this 10-year-old's life. But I kept that thought to myself and instead replied, "The book is old." "Why don't they just tell whether they have slaves here in this list of presidents?" asked Edwin. "They tell other things about presidents." "Good question," I said. "Why do you think they don't tell?"

"I don't know, probably because they don't know themselves." "Maybe so," I responded. "Here's what I'd like you to do. Since slavery was abolished when Lincoln was president, and since he was the 16th president, draw 16 lines equal distance from each other and list all the presidents from Washington to Lincoln, and then a yes-and-no column so we can check off whether they owned slaves."

I was soon to find out that filling in those columns was easier said than done.

When my students and I began investigating which presidents owned slaves, our attempts focused on traditional history textbooks and student-friendly websites from the White House and the Smithsonian Institution. These efforts turned up virtually nothing. We then pursued two different sources of information: history books written for adults and more in-depth websites.

I brought in two books that were somewhat helpful: James Loewen's *Lies My Teacher Told Me* (Simon and Schuster, 1995) and Kenneth O'Reilly's *Nixon's Piano: Presidents and Racial Politics from Washington to Clinton* (Free Press, 1995). By using the indexes and reading the text out loud, we uncovered facts about some of the presidents. We also used the web search engines Google and AltaVista and searched on the words "presidents" and "slavery." We soon learned we had to be more specific and include the president's name and "slavery"—for example, "President George Washington" and "slavery." Some results were student-friendly, such as the mention of Washington's slaves (and some of their escapes) at www.mount-vernon.org/slavery. There was also a bill of sale for a slave signed by Dolly Madison, the wife of president James Madison (for a link to the document see http://www.rethinkingschools.org/static/img/archive/17_02/Vote_test.pdf). Many websites had a large amount of text and were beyond the reading level of many of my students. So I cut and pasted long articles into word processing documents so we could search for the word "slave" to see if there was any specific mention of slave ownership.

> **When my students and I began investigating which presidents owned slaves, our attempts focused on traditional history textbooks and student-friendly websites. These efforts turned up virtually nothing.**

In their research, students often asked, "How do we know this is true? Our history books aren't telling the truth, why should we think this does?" I explained the difference between primary and secondary sources and how a primary source—like a bill of sale or original list of slaves—was pretty solid evidence. To help ensure accuracy, the students decided that if we used secondary sources, we needed to find at least two different citations.

Bits and Pieces of Information

In the next several days the students, with my help, looked at various sources. We checked our school's children's books about presidents, our social studies textbook, a 1975 *World Book Encyclopedia,* and a CD-ROM encyclopedia. We found nothing about presidents as slave owners. I had a hunch about which presidents owned slaves, based on what I knew in general about the presidents, but I wanted "proof" before we put a check in the "yes" box. And though my students wanted to add a third column—explaining how many slaves each slave-owning president had—that proved impossible. Even when we did find information about which presidents owned slaves, the numbers changed depending on how many slaves had been bought, sold, born, or died.

> **In our research, most of the information dealt with presidential attitudes and policies toward slavery. It was difficult to find specific information on which presidents owned slaves.**

In our research, most of the information dealt with presidential attitudes and policies toward slavery. It was difficult to find specific information on which presidents owned slaves. To help the investigation, I checked out a few books for them from our local university library. Overall, our best resource was the internet. The best sites required adult help to find and evaluate, and I became so engrossed in the project that I spent a considerable amount of time at home surfing the web. The "student-friendly" websites with information about presidents—such as the White House's gallery of presidents (www.whitehouse.gov/history/presidents)—don't mention that Washington and Jefferson enslaved African Americans. Other popular sites with the same glaring lack of information are the Smithsonian Institution (http://smithsonianeducation.org/educators/lesson_plans/idealabs/mr_president.html) and the National Museum of American History (http://www.americanhistory.si.edu/presidency). As we did the research, I regularly asked, "Why do you think this doesn't mention that the president owned slaves?" Students' responses varied, including "They're stupid"; "They don't want us kids to know the truth"; "They think we're too young to know"; and "They don't know themselves." (Given more time, we might have explored this matter further, looking at who produces textbooks and why they might not include information about presidents' attitudes about racism and slavery.) During our research, my students and I found bits and pieces of information about presidents and slavery. But we never found that one magic resource, be it book or website, that had the information readily available. Ultimately, though, we discovered that two presidents who served after Lincoln—Andrew Johnson and Ulysses S. Grant—had been slave owners. While the students taped an extension on their chart, I explained that I was not totally surprised about Johnson because he had been a Southerner. But it was a shock that Grant had owned slaves. "He was the commander of the Union army in the Civil War," I explained. "When I first learned about the Civil War in elementary school, Grant and Lincoln were portrayed as saviors of the Union and freers of slaves." When I told the entire class how Grant's slave-owning past had surprised me, Tanya, an African American student, raised her hand and said, "That's nothing. Lincoln was a slave owner, too." I asked for her source of information and she said she had heard that

Lincoln didn't like blacks. I thanked her for raising the point, and told the class that while it was commonly accepted by historians that Lincoln was not a slave owner, his attitudes toward blacks and slavery were a source of much debate. I noted that just because a president didn't own slaves didn't mean that he supported freedom for slaves or equal treatment of people of different races.

I went into a bit of detail on Lincoln, in part to counter the all-too-common simplification that Lincoln unequivocally opposed slavery and supported freedom for blacks. I explained that although it's commonly believed that Lincoln freed enslaved Americans when he signed the Emancipation Proclamation, the document actually frees slaves only in states and regions under rebellion—it did not free slaves in any of the slaveholding states and regions that remained in the Union. In other words, Lincoln "freed" slaves everywhere he had no authority and withheld freedom everywhere he did. Earlier, in Lincoln's first inaugural address in March of 1861, he promised slaveholders that he would support a constitutional amendment forever protecting slavery in the states where it then existed—if only those states would remain in the Union.

Slave-Owning Presidents

By the time we finished our research, the students had found that 10 of the first 18 presidents were slave owners: George Washington, Thomas Jefferson, James Madison, James Monroe, Andrew Jackson, John Tyler, James K. Polk, Zachary Taylor, Andrew Johnson, and Ulysses S. Grant. Those who didn't: John Adams, John Quincy Adams, Martin Van Buren, William Henry Harrison, Millard Fillmore, Franklin Pierce, James Buchanan, and, despite Tanya's assertion, Abraham Lincoln. The student researchers were excited to present their findings to their classmates, and decided to do so as part of a math class. I made blank charts for each student in the class, and they filled in information provided by the action research team: the names of presidents, the dates of their years in office, the total number of years in office, and whether they had owned slaves. Our chart started with George Washington, who assumed office in 1789, and ended in 1877 when the last president who had owned slaves, Ulysses Grant, left office.

> **By the time we finished our research, the students had found that 10 of the first 18 presidents were slave owners.**

We then used the data to discuss this topic of presidents and slave-owning within the structure of ongoing math topics in my class: "What do the data tell us?" and "How can we construct new knowledge with the data?" Students, for example, added up the total number of years in which the United States had a slave-owning president in office, and compared that total to the number of years in which there were non-slave-owning presidents in office. We figured out that in 69 percent of the years between 1789 and 1877, the United States had a president who had been a slave owner. One student observed that only slave-owning presidents served more than one term. "Why didn't they let presidents who didn't own slaves serve two terms?" another student pondered.

Using the data, the students made bar graphs and circle graphs to display the information. When they wrote written reflections on the math lesson, they connected math to content. One boy wrote: "I learned to convert fractions to percent so I know that 10/18 is the same as 55.5 percent. That's how many of the first 18 presidents owned slaves." Another girl observed, "I learned how to make pie charts and that so many more presidents owned slaves than the presidents who didn't own slaves." During a subsequent social studies lesson, the three students who had done most of the research explained their frustrations in getting information. "They hardly ever want to mention it [slaves owned by presidents]," explained one student. "We had to search and search." Specific objectives for this mini-unit, such as reviewing the use of percent, emerged as the lessons themselves unfolded. But its main purpose was to help students to critically examine the actions of early leaders of the United States and to become skeptical of textbooks and government websites as sources that present the entire picture. I figure that if kids start questioning the "official story" early on, they will be more open to alternative viewpoints later. While discovering which presidents were slave owners is not an in-depth analysis, it pokes an important hole in the godlike mystique that surrounds the "Founding Fathers." If students learn how to be critical of the icons of American past, hopefully it will give them permission and tools to be critical of the elites of America today. Besides uncovering some hard-to-find and uncomfortable historical truths, I also wanted to encourage my students to think about why these facts were so hard to find, and to develop a healthy skepticism of official sources of information. I showed them two quotations about Thomas Jefferson. One was from a recently published 5th-grade history textbook, *United States: Adventures in Time and Place* (Macmillan/McGraw Hill, 1998), which read: "Jefferson owned several slaves in his lifetime and lived in a slave-owning colony. Yet he often spoke out against slavery. 'Nothing is more certainly written in the book of fate than that these people are to be free'" (p. 314). The other quotation was from James Loewen's *Lies My Teacher Told Me*. Loewen writes:

> Textbooks stress that Jefferson was a humane master, privately tormented by slavery and opposed to its expansion, not the type to destroy families by selling slaves. In truth, by 1820 Jefferson had become an ardent advocate of the expansion of slavery to the western territories. And he never let his ambivalence about slavery affect his private life. Jefferson was an average master who had his slaves whipped and sold into the Deep South as examples to

While discovering which presidents were slave owners is not an in-depth analysis, it pokes an important hole in the godlike mystique that surrounds the 'Founding Fathers.'

induce other slaves to obey. By 1822, Jefferson owned 267 slaves. During his long life, of hundreds of different slaves he owned, he freed only three and five more at his death—all blood relatives of his. (p. 140)

We talked about the different perspective each quote had toward Jefferson and toward what students should learn. My students' attention immediately turned to the set of spanking new history textbooks that had been delivered to our classroom that year as part of the districtwide social studies adoption. Some students assumed that our new textbook *United States* (Harcourt Brace, 2000) was equally as bad as the one I quoted from. One student suggested we just throw the books away. But I quickly pointed out they were expensive, and that we could learn from them even if they had problems and omissions.

I then explained what an omission was, and suggested that we become "textbook detectives" and investigate what our new social studies text said about Jefferson and slavery. I reviewed how to use an index and divided all page references for Jefferson among small groups of students. The groups read the pages, noted any references to Jefferson owning slaves, and then reported back to the class. Not one group found a single reference. Not surprisingly, the students were angry when they realized how the text omitted such important information. "They should tell the truth!" one student fumed.

> **I then explained what an omission was, and suggested that we become 'textbook detectives' and investigate what our new social studies text said about Jefferson and slavery.**

No Mention of Racism

I wanted students to see that the textbook's omissions were not an anomaly, but part of a pattern of ignoring racism in America—in the past and in the present. In the next lesson, I started by writing the word "racism" on the board. I asked the kids to look up "racism" in the index of their social studies book. Nothing. "Racial discrimination." Nothing.

"Our school should get a different book," one student suggested. "Good idea," I said, "but it's not so easy." I told my students that I had served on a committee that had looked at the major textbooks published for 5th graders and that none of them had dealt with racism or slavery and presidents.

Students had a variety of responses:

"Let's throw them out."

"Let's use the internet."

"Write a letter to the people who did the books." I focused in on the letter-writing suggestion and reminded them that before we did so, we had to be certain that our criticisms were correct. The students then agreed that in small groups they would use the textbook's index and read what was said about all the first 18 presidents, just as we had done previously with Jefferson. None of the groups found any mention of a president owning a slave.

Letters as Critique and Action

In subsequent days, some students wrote letters to the textbook publisher. Michelle, a white girl, was particularly detailed. She wrote: "I am 11 years old and I like to read and write. When I am reading I notice every little word and in your social studies book I realize that the word "racism" is not in your book. You're acting like it is a bad word for those kids who read it." She went on to criticize the book for not mentioning that any presidents had slaves: "I see that you do not mention that some of the presidents had slaves. But some of them did. Like George Washington had 317 slaves. So did Thomas Jefferson. He had 267 slaves." She continued: "If you want to teach children the truth, then you should write the truth." (Michelle's letter and some of the student-made charts were also printed in our school newspaper.)

We do students a disservice when we sanitize history and sweep uncomfortable truths under the rug.

We mailed off the letters, and moved on to new lessons. Weeks passed with no response and eventually the students stopped asking if the publishers had written back. Then one day a fancy-looking envelope appeared in my mailbox addressed to Michelle Williams. She excitedly opened the letter and read it to the class.

Harcourt School Publishers Vice President Donald Lankiewicz had responded to Michelle at length. He wrote that "while the word 'racism' does not appear, the subject of unfair treatment of people because of their race is addressed on page 467." He also argued: "There are many facts about the presidents that are not included in the text simply because we do not have room for them all."

Michelle wrote back to Lankiewicz, thanking him but expressing disappointment.

"In a history book you shouldn't have to wait till page 467 to learn about unfair treatment," she wrote. As to his claim that there wasn't room for all the facts about the presidents, Michelle responded: "Adding more pages is good for the kids because they should know the right things from the wrong. It is not like you are limited to certain amount of pages. . . . All I ask you is that you write the word 'racism' in the book and add some more pages in the book so you can put most of the truth about the presidents."

Michelle never received a reply.

Improving the Lesson

Michelle and the other students left 5th grade soon after the letter exchange. In the flurry of end-of-year activities, I didn't take as much time to process the project as

I might have. Nor did I adequately explore with students the fact that most non-slave-owning presidents exhibited pro-slavery attitudes and promoted pro-slavery policies.

But the larger issue, which critical teachers struggle to address, is why textbook publishers and schools in general do such a poor job of helping students make sense of the difficult issues of race. We do students a disservice when we sanitize history and sweep uncomfortable truths under the rug. We leave them less prepared to deal with the difficult issues they will face in their personal, political, and social lives. Granted, these are extremely complicated issues that don't have a single correct response. But it's important to begin with a respect for the truth and for the capacity of people of all ages to expand their understanding of the past and the present, and to open their hearts and minds to an ever-broadening concept of social justice.

I believe my students learned a lot from their research on presidents and slaves—and clearly know more than most Americans about which of the first 18 presidents owned slaves. I'm also hopeful they learned the importance of looking critically at all sources of information. I know one student, Tanya, did. On the last day of school she came up to me and amid the congratulatory goodbyes and said, "I still think Lincoln owned slaves."

"You are a smart girl but you are wrong about that one," I responded. "We'll see," she said, "You didn't know Grant had slaves when the school year started! Why should I always believe what my teacher says?"

Bob Peterson (bob.e.peterson@gmail.com) is an editor of Rethinking Schools *and former president of the Milwaukee Teachers' Education Association. He taught 5th grade in Milwaukee Public Schools for 30 years.*

Some of the students' names in this article have been changed.

Author's Note: About two years after I completed the research on slave-owning presidents with my students, a wonderful website called UnderstandingPrejudice.org was put up by folks at Wesleyan University. This site includes extensive information on presidents who owned slaves (see www.understandingprejudice.org/slavery). I learned from this website that three presidents not on my list also owned slaves: Martin Van Buren, William Henry Harrison, and James Buchanan. I was grateful for the additional information on this website, which opens up all sorts of new teaching possibilities.

Chapter Forty-Two

FROM SNARLING DOGS TO BLOODY SUNDAY

By Kate Lyman

"I'm not teaching about civil rights this year," my colleague asserted.
"Not teaching about civil rights?" I responded. My teaching buddy and partner had teamed with me in tackling "controversial issues" at the 2nd/3rd-grade level—AIDS, the "discovery" of America, and homophobia, to name a few. I couldn't believe that she was not going to join me in planning the civil rights unit.

My partner explained that a parent of a child who was continuing in her 2nd/3rd-grade combination class had objected to the unit on civil rights the previous year. "There was too much violence," she had said. Her daughter had been frightened.

Knowing that I would miss our joint planning sessions and sharing of materials

BETTMANN/CORBIS

and ideas, I nevertheless decided to go ahead with the unit.

My own experience growing up in an exclusively white and economically priv-ileged suburb of Milwaukee had isolated me from the issues of the Civil Rights Movement. When, as a high school student in the 1960s, I finally became informed in a U.S. history class about the events in the South and the segregation and dis-crimination in my own city, I was appalled. I started on the long road to try to better understand issues of racism and to do what I could to act on the inequities in our society.

Unlike the suburb I grew up in, my school attendance area is culturally, politi-cally, and socially diverse. More than 50 percent of the students come from families of color, most of them low-income. There are also low-income and working-class white families, and a smattering of middle-class families from a new development.

> **I had previously received a generally positive response to the civil rights unit. Parents had shared resources, such as a battered but prized painting of Rosa Parks.**

I had previously received a generally positive re-sponse to the civil rights unit. Parents had shared re-sources, such as a battered but prized painting of Rosa Parks. One grandmother came in to teach us freedom songs and talk about her efforts in the 1960s to organize an NAACP chapter in Oklahoma. My former principal and a few teachers had disapproved of teaching such deep and heavy issues to young children. However, I could recall only one negative comment from a parent: "Why are you still teaching black history when it's past February?" In fact, even though I generally started the unit on or around the observance of Martin Luther King's birthday, related activ-ities integrated into all subject areas extended past January and February and, de-pending on student interest and the depth of the projects, into the first few weeks of March.

I planned the civil rights unit within the context of a discussion of human rights and children's rights, in honor of the upcoming 50th anniversary of the United Nations Universal Declaration of Human Rights, signed on Dec. 11, 1949. It was during that discussion that my students had agreed that among basic rights for children is the right "to not be judged by the color of our skin." This idea was a logical lead-in to the Civil Rights Movement.

We began by reading biographies about Martin Luther King Jr. and gave him his due as a strong and gifted leader. But I also wanted to go beyond the platitudes often taught in elementary classes. I discarded worksheets in my files that summed up the Civil Rights Movement in simplistic language such as "Dr. King decided to help the black people and white people get along better."

One especially useful book was *I Have a Dream*, by Margaret Davidson, and for 14 days we read a chapter a day from the book. While written in clear and fairly simple language, the book goes way beyond others in its genre in the complexity of its coverage of the Civil Rights Movement.

We used a variety of books, videos, poetry, and music to follow the history of racial discrimination and segregation. We studied not only King but many other people who worked together to overturn unfair laws and practices, especially the children: Ruby Bridges, the Little Rock Nine, the children in the Birmingham children's march, the students in the sit-ins, and Sheyann Webb, the 8-year-old voting rights activist in Selma.

Sections from the PBS documentary series *Eyes on the Prize* were invaluable in helping my students witness history. They were entranced by the 1957 footage of the nine Little Rock high school students who faced angry mobs as they desegregated Central High. They cheered when one of the students, Minnijean Brown, got so infuriated with the daily intimidation that she finally poured a bowl of chili on her harasser's head. They watched with awe as the children in Birmingham, Ala., in 1963 joined the protests against segregated facilities and then stood their ground even as they were being slammed against the wall by the power of the hoses held by Bull Connor's firefighters.

My students were especially captivated by the story of the Birmingham children's crusade. The class participated in a role play about how these high school students helped desegregate public facilities in the city.

Jerome, an African American student with a gift for the dramatic, made a remarkable Martin Luther King. Imitating King's style for oratory, Jerome addressed his classmates who were playing the children gathered in the church after their first encounter with police brutality. Repeating the lines I gave him from the book *I Have a Dream*, he challenged the crowd: "Don't get bitter. Don't get tired. Are we tired?" The students role-playing the Birmingham children responded before I had a chance to give them their lines. "NO!" they shouted, standing up and shaking their fists.

> **We studied not only King but many other people who worked together to overturn unfair laws and practices, especially the children: Ruby Bridges, the Little Rock Nine, the children in the Birmingham children's march, the students in the sit-ins, and Sheyann Webb, the 8- year-old voting rights activist in Selma.**

A Parent's Concern

I was halfway through the unit, feeling good about how the kids were conceptualizing the conviction of the civil rights activists—as well as how their enthusiasm was extending into reading, writing, and math activities—when Joanne, one of the eight African Americans in the class, handed me a letter from her mom. The letter expressed opposition to the civil rights unit, pointing out that Joanne had never witnessed hatred and brutality toward blacks. Joanne, she said, had "no experience with police and guns, snarling dogs, hatred, people who spit and/or throw soup at others." Joanne felt afraid at bedtime because of the "true stories" she remembered from the books and movies.

I had anticipated that such issues might come up, and had tried to take steps to deal with the children's reaction to the violence of racism. For example, before we began the Emmett Till section in *Eyes on the Prize,* we had discussed how scary some of these historical events were. Third-grade students, who had been exposed to some of the content the year before, shared some feelings of fear, but also affirmed that they wanted to learn more about what they had been introduced to in 2nd grade. I assured the class that acts that the Ku Klux Klan and others had committed with impunity could not go unpunished today.

Third-grade students, who had been exposed to some of the content the year before, shared some feelings of fear, but also affirmed that they wanted to learn more.

I also knew I couldn't pretend that racial hatred is a thing of the past, however. I knew that many of my students were aware of the racist acts of violence reported in the national news. I also knew that many encounter racist name-calling or other biased acts in school and in their neighborhoods.

I hadn't seen signs that Joanne had been upset; in fact, her contributions to class discussions revealed a fascination with the topic. However, I was glad that Joanne's mom had communicated to me a problem that I might have missed.

As Joanne's mom had suggested, and in fact, as I would have done anyway, I took Joanne aside to talk with her. She said that the story of Emmett Till had bothered her, but that the rest had been OK. Cheerful and positive, as usual, Joanne dismissed my concern, and said she wanted to learn more.

I asked her to let me know if something was troubling her. I decided to watch her closely for signs of distress or withdrawal and to ask her frequently if she was doing all right. I also said she had the option to leave if the content disturbed her. But then I received another communication from her parents that she was to be excused from all books, movies, and poems that showed hatred toward blacks. I thought back to my teaching partner's reason for not teaching about the Civil Rights Movement.

I thought of a few other parents and one other teacher (all middle-class African Americans, like Joanne's mom) who had told me that they didn't want slavery or racism taught about in schools because that was all behind them and they didn't want it dredged up. It was too painful. It was over. It made them out to be victims. Joanne's mom said that she wanted her daughter to know only the positive parts of the movement—the love and the happiness—not the snarling dogs and hatred toward blacks.

I was in a quandary. Was it possible to teach in any depth about the Civil Rights Movement without including the violence and the racism? On the other hand, as a white teacher, was it presumptuous of me to decide to teach something that offended an African American parent? I knew that I couldn't put myself in her or Joanne's shoes. I can't know what it is like to be a racial minority is this country. And as a parent of three children, I know that parents have insight into their children that a teacher might lack.

I respect the right of parents to communicate their concerns and, if possible, I try to address them by altering what I do in the classroom. However, I knew that my obligation went beyond Joanne and her parents. I needed to think about what was best for all my students.

Assessing the Reactions of the Students

I watched my students carefully. It soon became apparent that my African American and biracial students (nine out of 25) were gaining strength and self-confidence during the unit. They were participating more frequently in class, sharing information that they had learned from the many books available in the class and relating what they were learning about the Civil Rights Movement to their own lives.

I knew I had to think of Joanne. But I also had to think of Keisha, Jasmine, Monique, and Jerome.

Take Keisha, who had often drifted off to sleep through our other units and when called on would ramble. During the unit, she suddenly found her voice. In preparation for our enactment of the Birmingham children's march, for example, I talked to the class about what it meant to be "in character" in a drama. I told them to think about how they would feel if they were the people marching for their rights.

"I know," broke in Keisha, "you would be serious. You wouldn't be acting silly or nothing, because this is about getting your freedom. And you are marching for your mother or your father or your sister or your brother or for your children or your grandchildren, not just for yourself."

The next morning, Keisha brought in a friend from another class. "I have something to share," Keisha said. "Yesterday, at the community center, LaToya and me made up a speech, like Martin Luther King."

Her friend pulled out a rumpled sheet of paper and they proceeded to present their speech to the class:

> **Jasmine surprised me one morning with a life-sized portrait of Ruby Bridges that she had made in the after-school program by taping together smaller pieces of paper.**

> Martin Luther King Jr. and Me. Martin had a dream that black people would be treated equally. But I have a dream that we would hold hands and study together, read together, and play together. I have a dream that we would go to the mall together, come to school together, and learn together as one. One day Rosa Parks refused to give up her seat on the bus to a white person. Things have gotten better now. Thank you.

Keisha later chose to do her human rights biography project on Harriet Tubman. She read all the books she could find on the topic and wrote her longest, most coherent piece in her journal on Tubman. And once, when the class was having a particularly difficult time settling down, Keisha yelled out, "Hey, would you all be acting like this if Martin Luther King was here?"

Jasmine, a biracial girl with a long history of discipline problems at the school, took to heart the story of 6-year-old Ruby Bridges. Jasmine surprised me one morning with a life-sized portrait of Ruby Bridges that she had made in the after-school program by taping together smaller pieces of paper. She wrote about Ruby Bridges in her journal and in a letter to Wisconsin Gov. Tommy Thompson on another topic, she asked, "Have you heard of Ruby Bridges?"

One day, Jasmine approached me in confidence, "Kate, you might not know this, because it's a secret, but I'll tell you something I've been doing."

"I'd like to know, Jasmine," I responded, expecting a confession of some wrongdoing.

"Well, Kate, sometimes, when I'm sitting at my table, I just pretend I'm Ruby Bridges. I pretend that the other kids sitting at my table are those people yelling at me because I'm black and they don't want me in their school. And, just like Ruby, I ignore them and just go on doing my work. I do it real good, just like Ruby. I was doing it just before at math time."

And then there were Monique and Jerome. Previously two of my biggest troublemakers, during this unit they became the two I could count on to be on task for reading, writing, and other activities. Monique, who had previously disrupted numerous group discussions or cooperative projects, suddenly became the model student: "Shhhhh, everybody!" she'd admonish. "I want to hear this!"

Jerome found a connection from home. "My mom told me that we all need to learn about this because it could happen again," he said. He told the class about when the people next door to his apartment house had put up a sign to prevent kids from cutting through their yard on their way to school. The sign had said "Private. Stay out of our yard. No niggers."

Many of the other students talked about how they, too, would have been discriminated against if they had lived in the South during Jim Crow. (I also had four Hmong students, one Cambodian American, two Filipino Americans, two born in Mexico, and one with a Mexican-Indian grandparent.) "I would have had to use the 'colored only' drinking fountain because I'm part Filipino," Anita would remind the class. At the drawing table I heard one girl say, "You know, we would all have been discriminated against, because I'm part Mexican, you are Hmong, and you are both black."

Chris and many of the other white kids in our school come with attitudes that are the products of the racism that divides our neighborhood.

I also watched the reactions of the European American students. There were fewer white kids than children of color in the class and, although we had learned about many brave white activists, the whites were definitely not shown in a positive light in most of the material. I watched to see if the European Americans were engaged in our discussions and if they showed any signs of discomfort. Chris was tentative at first, hanging back, sometimes fooling around with another white boy. But then he started to participate more and more in the discussions and role plays. As we were watching a video, *My Past Is My Own,* in which a white teenage gang assaults the black students at a lunch counter sit-in, Chris moved close to where I was sitting.

"I don't like this part," he confided in me. "If those kids were friends of mine, I'd tell them, 'Hey, leave them alone. What you're doing isn't right.'"

The next day, Chris decided to write a letter to Rosa Parks relating his admiration for her courage.

Chris and many of the other white kids in our school come with attitudes that are the products of the racism that divides our neighborhood. I came to the conclusion that they, as much as, or even more than, the children of color, needed to hear the story of the racial hatred and the saving power of a nonviolent movement. There may come a time when they find the courage to say, "What you're doing isn't right."

Despite the positive changes I witnessed in many of my students, the opposition of Joanne's parents kept nagging at me. We kept in touch through notes and conversations. I heard, on the one hand, that they supported what I was doing; yet Joanne was still to be kept out of all activities related to the unit. I talked over the situation with colleagues and friends, including the principal, who encouraged me to go on with the unit. (In the 1st grade, a parent had complained to the principal that the teacher had not gone into enough depth in presenting the history of civil rights.)

I also spoke with an African American man, the grandfather of a student, who had presented to my class several years ago. He had proudly brought in a huge photograph of the Edmund Pettus Bridge and had told how he joined the voting rights march on "Bloody Sunday," March 7, 1965, and crossed that bridge only to be attacked by local and Alabama state police officers armed with weapons and tear gas. I invited him back to speak to the class and also asked his opinion on my dilemma, sketching out the objections to the civil rights unit. His voice, heretofore somewhat soft and distant, became strident.

One day, when Joanne was out of the room, I told the class that Joanne's parents objected to her learning about the Civil Rights Movement.

"Hey, that's what we were all marching for!" he said. "We were marching for the right for our kids and all kids to learn about the history of black folks. And it's not like it's over and done with. They might try to keep their kid from knowing about it now, but sooner or later they'll find out and then it will be a shock. Better to learn now what we were all fighting for!"

I decided to also ask the opinion of my students. I was finding it hard to put off questions of why Joanne was dismissed to work in the library each time we worked on the unit. Even though I assigned different work for Joanne, some members of the class were protesting that she was playing on the computers while they were working on their writing and reading. One day, when Joanne was out of the room, I told the class that Joanne's parents objected to her learning about the Civil Rights Movement.

I also asked the class if they thought it was an important topic. The consensus was that it was "very, very important." The reasons came out faster than I could record them: "So if that stuff happened again, we could calm down and be strong." "It might happen again and then we'd have to go and march." "The KKK is still alive and they don't like blacks and Filipinos." "It makes us smarter to learn about this, and then if we have kids and they wanted to learn about it, we could teach them." "When we go to another grade, we will know not to call people names like Darkie." "If you learn about it, you get to go to higher grades and get to go to college." "Dr. King, he was trying to tell us that we could have a better life." "We want no more segregation, no more fights, no more KKK burning down houses." "So it don't happen no more."

We went on with our work. At this point in the unit, the focus was on presenting a student-written screenplay of *Selma, Lord, Selma* (which in turn was based on the Disney television special). Not wanting Joanne to miss what was becoming an even more central part of our curriculum, I suggested to Joanne's parents that they watch the tape of the television special. Since it was shown on *Wonderful World of Disney*, I figured I couldn't go wrong there. I also gave them copies to read of the screenplay that the class had written. I again was told that Joanne could not participate.

The rest of the students, however, immersed themselves in the drama. Jasmine transformed herself into the role of Sheyann Webb, the brave 8-year-old participant in the Selma voting rights movement. She held her head high and sang "Ain't Gonna Let Nobody Turn Me 'Round" with a voice pure in tone, perfect in pitch, and strong in conviction. Monique turned all her energies into not only acting the part of Rachel West, Sheyann's friend, but also keeping the rest of the class on task and in role. Jerome continued as Martin Luther King, changing the words of his speech every practice but never failing to perform the part of the orator and leader of the people. It was clear that the play was cementing the history of the Civil Rights Movement in the minds and hearts of every student.

Several days before the final performance, Joanne's parents approached me in the hall. They wanted her to participate, although they were concerned it might be too late.

Several days before the final performance, Joanne's parents approached me in the hall. They wanted her to participate, although they were concerned it might be too late. They never explained what had led them to change their minds. I knew that Joanne was feeling left out, especially since the class had also been working on their play in their music and movement classes.

Despite my earnest efforts to excuse Joanne to the library whenever we read or discussed material related to civil rights, Joanne, a very bright and curious girl, had not only managed to pick up a lot of information, but had also learned the songs in the play. Joanne took on her role as a voting rights activist in *Selma, Lord, Selma* as smoothly as if she had been practicing it for three weeks with the rest of the class. She not only marched to the courthouse, singing "Kumbaya" and demanding the right to vote, but she also participated in a slow-motion pantomime of the "Bloody

Sunday" confrontation, as marchers attempting to cross the Edmund Pettus Bridge were met with the troopers' sticks, cattle prods, and tear gas.

After Joanne and the others recover from the violent attack and rise to the occasion of singing "Ain't Gonna Let Nobody Turn Me 'Round" this time with added significance to the words, Jasmine (Sheyann) narrates: "We were singing and telling the world that we hadn't been whipped, that we had won. We had really won. After all, we had won."

The Lessons of Selma

The Selma story instructs us that out of unspeakable violence and defeat can come resolution and victory. Out of Bloody Sunday came renewed participation and power in the Civil Rights Movement, resulting in the Voting Rights Act of 1965 and the success of the second Selma to Montgomery March.

Can the Civil Rights Movement be taught without teaching about segregation, racial hatred, and violence? I don't think so. It is against the backdrop of the firehoses and the snarling dogs that the Birmingham children found their strength to sing, even as they were hauled off to jail. When Martin Luther King was denied the right to sit in the front of a shoe store or to play with his white friends, the seeds of his leadership were planted. It does not make sense to teach the Civil Rights Movement without teaching about the separate bathrooms and KKK. Furthermore, to do so wouldn't be history. It would be a lie.

Can the Civil Rights Movement be taught without teaching about segregation, racial hatred, and violence? I don't think so.

Despite the controversy my unit engendered, I did not regret my decision to proceed. Even though the behavior and academic focus of students like Keisha, Jasmine, Jerome, and Monique did not remain at that peak, they still remembered those weeks as the best part of the school year. And as we moved into learning about the struggles of other groups of people for equal rights, or as we talked about issues of justice and tolerance in the classroom, we always had the Civil Rights Movement to look back to for inspiration.

As Keisha said in her end-of-the-year evaluation: "I liked giving my speech in class about Martin Luther King and Rosa Parks, too. They fought for freedom and the right to vote. They are so cool to do that and march and give us freedom. [If they hadn't done that,] me and you would not be together today and be learning."

Kate Lyman has been teaching kindergarten through 3rd grade in the Madison, Wisconsin School District for 37 years.

The names of the children were changed to protect their identities.

Chapter Forty-Three

'IF THERE IS NO STRUGGLE...'
Teaching a people's history of the abolition movement

By Bill Bigelow

"**W**ho here would have been against slavery if you suddenly found yourself living in those times?" I've asked a version of this question to many U.S. history classes over the years. Every student raises a hand. "So what exactly would you have *done* to end slavery?"

Puzzled looks are generally the response to this question. What *should* we do, what *can* we do, when we are confronted by the enormity of an injustice like slavery? It's not an easy question for my students, and it wasn't an easy question for the people who opposed slavery in those times. The answers were struggled over in the abolition movement, one of the most significant social movements in U.S. history, but underappreciated in today's history curriculum.

A few summers ago, my wife, Linda, and I vacationed in upstate New York. We went to visit John Brown's grave site at North Elba, near Lake Placid. Brown was executed Dec. 2, 1859, by the state of Virginia shortly after leading a raid on the Harpers Ferry arsenal, hoping to trigger an antislavery rebellion.

FREDERICK DOUGLASS

LUCRETIA COFFIN-MOTT

LIBRARY OF CONGRESS

LIBRARY OF CONGRESS

In a nearby town, we went to a talk, part of a lecture series on abolitionism, by scholar Eric Foner. Foner's thesis was that the abolition movement was the foundation of virtually all social justice movements in the United States. It led to the first antiwar movement, against the U.S. invasion and occupation of Mexico (1846–48), which abolitionists saw as a land grab to expand slavery. (Henry David Thoreau coined the term "civil disobedience" in defending his willingness to go to jail for his refusal to pay taxes to support the war.) The abolition movement seeded the movement for women's rights in the United States: The leaders of the first gathering of women to demand rights as women, at Seneca Falls, N.Y., in 1848, were abolitionists like Lucretia Mott and Elizabeth Cady Stanton. For all its imperfections, the abolition movement was this country's first multiracial movement. And it was the first anti-racist movement in U.S. history, demanding an end not only to slavery but also to racial segregation and discrimination in the North. As Foner writes in *The Story of American Freedom,* "The origin of an American people unbounded by race lies not with the founders, who by and large made their peace with slavery, but with the abolitionists. . . . [A]bolitionists invented the concept of equality before the law regardless of race, one all but unknown in American jurisprudence before the Civil War."

> **The abolition movement was the foundation of virtually all social justice movements in the United States.**

U.S. history textbooks and curricula tend to marginalize the abolition movement. For example, Oregon's state social studies standards mention "abolitionists" only once in the 8th-grade benchmarks, and not at all in the high school standards. One of my favorite quotes is from Amy Goodman, host of the radio/TV program *Democracy Now!* Goodman says that journalism needs to go where the silences are. The same can be said of the school curriculum. And one of the greatest silences is about the fact that social movements have transformed the United States—that everything good and decent about our society is the product of people working together to make things better.

But like so much other media, textbooks prefer to regard social progress as the product of great individuals. Ask a typical group of students, "Who freed the slaves?" and they'll say Abraham Lincoln. Yet Lincoln was never an abolitionist. In fact, the Great Emancipator was not even an abolitionist when he signed the Emancipation Proclamation—a document that carefully listed the regions, county by county, where enslaved people were to remain enslaved, "as if this proclamation were not issued." Earlier, in March 1861, during his first inaugural address, Lincoln had not been president for five minutes before he quoted one of his own pro-slavery speeches: "I have no purpose, directly or indirectly, to interfere with the institution of slavery in the states where it exists. I believe I have no lawful right to do so, and I have no inclination to do so. . . ." He then promised to enforce the Fugitive Slave Act and to support a constitutional amendment "to the effect that the federal government shall never interfere with the domestic institutions of the states, including that of persons held to service." Lincoln left a complicated legacy—and no doubt, through the course of the Civil War he came to espouse positions held by white and black abolitionists—but he began his presidency by promising slave owners that they could keep people enslaved forever.

Foner's talk about the significance of the abolition movement inspired me to rethink how I had been approaching the antislavery struggle in my classes. First, I realized that I needed to spend more time teaching it. I wanted to find teaching strategies that would underscore the difficult choices that confronted the abolition movement. Instead of having students simply read about the abolition movement or listen to me talk, I wanted to engage them as movement participants, so that the strategic dilemmas of ending slavery would unfold in class. In other words, I wanted a *people's* pedagogy to match the bottom-up people's history I hoped to impart to my students.

'You Are a Member of the American Anti-Slavery Society'

I created a role play in which every student in class portrayed a member of the American Anti-Slavery Society (AASS). As the AASS, the class would encounter some of the difficult strategic choices that confronted the actual organization throughout its history. I'd be present as teacher to observe and take notes, but I would play no role in their deliberations. My hope was that students would taste a bit of the uncertainty but also the exhilaration that actual antislavery organizers experienced as they sought to abolish the greatest injustice of their time.

A little context: When I first taught this to my 10th-grade U.S. history classes, I was at Franklin High School in southeast Portland. My classes at Franklin were largely white and working-class, with relatively small numbers of African Amer-

SOJOURNER TRUTH

LIBRARY OF CONGRESS

ANTI-SLAVERY MEETINGS!

A Quarterly Meeting of the Worcester County South Division Anti-Slavery Society, to be attended by

STEPHEN S. & A. K. FOSTER,

CHARLES LENOX REMOND,

AND

SAMUEL MAY, Jr.

Will be held as follows: In the

METHODIST CHURCH, at Millville,

Saturday Evening, July 1st,

AT 7½ O'CLOCK.

AT BLACKSTONE TOWN HALL

SUNDAY, July 2d A. M. and P. M.

Commencing at 10 o'clock.

And again in the METHODIST CHURCH at MILLVILLE, Sunday Evening at 5 o'clock. The public are invited to attend.

LIBRARY OF CONGRESS

ican, Asian American, and Latino students. According to state standards, slavery and the antislavery movement were supposed to be taught in the 8th grade, not high school—a mandate I consistently ignored. The idea that students should finish their study of U.S. slavery in the 8th grade seemed absurd. With no exit tests or curriculum cops around, it was an easy order to disobey. Prior to this role play, my students engaged in a simulation on the dynamics of the African slave trade; watched a slide lecture on the slave trade and U.S. slavery; examined laws pertaining to slavery; and read, wrote about, and discussed Chapter 7 from Howard Zinn's *A People's History of the United States,* "Slavery Without Submission," up to the point where Zinn discusses the abolition movement.

Autobiography of an Abolitionist

I began this lesson by telling the class that we were going to do a role play on the movement to end slavery in the United States, and that each of them would become a member of the American Anti-Slavery Society, the most significant abolition organization in the country. I distributed a role sheet and we read it aloud. The role begins:

> "You are a member of the American Anti-Slavery Society, an organization founded in 1833 to end slavery in the United States. Your members include both blacks and whites. To you, slavery is the central evil in American life. Of all the injustices, this one—that allows human beings to own other human beings and to treat them purely as property—is far and away the worst."

The role sheet goes on to describe aspects of slavery and some of the first actions against slavery, and concludes by reminding the students-as-abolitionists that "it's one thing to oppose slavery and quite another thing to know what to do about it. There is sharp debate among abolitionists—people who want to end slavery. How can we end this enormous evil? That is the question we face." [Teaching materials for this role play can be found at http://www.rethinkingschools.org/static/archive/25_02/bigelow_roleplay.pdf]

It is one thing to oppose slavery and quite another thing to know what to do about it.

To encourage students to connect more personally to their role as abolitionists, I asked them to write their autobiography, to imagine the experiences that led them to dedicate their lives to the fight against slavery. I emphasized to them what a remarkable thing it was for someone to become an abolitionist—slavery was the dominant institution in the United States. It had existed here for more than 200 years, was protected by the Constitution and U.S. Supreme Court rulings, and was the single most profitable "industry" in the country. By the birth of the abolition movement, most U.S. presidents had owned slaves. I asked:

"What motivates you to work against your government and for equality? How did you come to think that you could make a difference in the world?"

I told students that they were free to choose their gender, age, race, social class, and region of the country. To help them find a route into their autobiographies, I offered a number of general scenarios that summarized the histories of actual abolitionists—both black and white—but I also told students that these needn't limit them. For example:

- Your father was a slave owner. You witnessed firsthand the conditions of enslaved African Americans.
- You escaped from slavery. You know from your own experience the horrors of being enslaved. Every day of your life you can't stand the fact that people just like you are still being whipped, still being sold apart from their families, still being abused—just because of the color of their skin.

I hoped that the autobiography writing assignment would help students imagine lives of commitment, to consider experiences that might lead one to dedicate one's life to something beyond simply making a living, enjoying one's family, and having a good time. But I'm aware that an assignment like this also invites stereotype—that despite previous lessons, students wouldn't have enough background to plausibly describe someone's transformation into an abolitionist. That didn't bother me. Reading students' writing alerted me to areas I needed to teach in greater depth, and the objective was less exact historical accuracy than it was for students to spend time "inside" an individual committed to racial justice and to radically changing the society. I wanted them to try on the personas of individuals who had created lives of activism and defiance.

This assignment produced some of the best writing of the year. I'm tempted to include lots of examples, but I'll stick to two different approaches. This first is from Nicole McDonald, a kind, quiet, and bookish student who fired to life when we talked about women's issues in class. Nicole's character is a young white woman raised in the North:

I was brought up in a staunch Christian home by my father and elder brothers, my mother having passed away giving birth to my brother a year younger than me. Living without a woman, none of us were quite sure how a girl was supposed to act. I'm sure I had the queerest upbringing in all of New England. I didn't start wearing skirts until I was 10 because my father did not want to spend the money on an entire wardrobe just for myself when my brothers' hand-me-downs were as good as anything. I worked with the boys in the barn and in the fields. I had to, they needed my help. I was always big for my age, and never had a problem with physical labor. But none of this tells how I entered the antislavery movement. All I can say is that I know what it feels like. No, I have never been whipped. I have never been forced to pick cotton in the fields, torn from my family and all that I know. But as I entered society, I realized, really, I do not have much freedom either. I cannot get a job besides being a teacher, and even then only if I do not date or am not married. My shackles are invisible. I am given the illusion of freedom, but not the reality. In reality, I am as much a slave as anybody. My situation is immovable except into marriage. And then I will be like a servant.

Mariya Koroteyev, a big-hearted, religious, Russian immigrant, took her autobiographical story in a different direction. She imagined herself enslaved as "Maggie":

I leaned against the tree with closed eyes. I took a moment to catch my breath. "You!" I heard the watcher yell. "Get moving. Don't waste precious time." So once more I took my heavy basket and began to pick. Row by row, basket by basket, under the burning sun, I picked cotton and so did the other slaves. When the day came to an end and the sun, understanding our pain, hid behind the mountain, I heard the whistle ordering us to go back to our cabins, for the day's work was over.

Mariya's character, Maggie, learns that a friend has been killed for stealing food. Distraught, she decides to run away and is joined by two other friends:

As we crossed the border of Canada, I was filled with joy. "Larrie!" I shouted. "We are free!" "Free, free," my words echoed through the cave where we stopped to make our new home. Then it was quiet. We each thought of the horrible place we had escaped, and Matt was first to reply: "We are," he said. "But I think about the millions of others." And so did I. I thought of the four girls in my cabin, and the hundreds of slaves who were beaten in the fields, and my eyes filled with tears. "I wish I could help," I whispered. "I wish I could."

A successful abolition role play builds on students steeped in their collective anti-racist imagination. I hoped the lesson would teach students that the abolition movement, by and large, saw racism as the enemy, and not only slavery.

Ultimately, Maggie begins attending antislavery meetings, joins the abolition movement, and volunteers her house as a stop on the Underground Railroad.

Other abolitionists who students created included a dockworker who encounters slave auctions where he sees "how carelessly families are torn apart"; an enslaved woman who cannot bring herself to raise her daughter to be a slave, and remembers her own mother's stories of Africa retold through the years; a white worker disgusted by parasitic slave owners—"Where I come from, no matter who you are, you take care of and clean up after yourself"; and a young white woman from a tight-knit, devoutly Christian family, frustrated by her parents' inability to "take their devotion one step further" to become abolitionists:

"I have no patience for anyone who is too self-absorbed to care about the suffering of others simply because of their skin color."

Our class formed a circle and we read aloud and appreciated these one by one, creating an aural tapestry of abolitionist resistance. It was worth spending a substantial amount of class time listening to these stories, both because a read-around in which students express such humanity is a great community builder, but also because a successful abolition role play would depend on students steeped in their collective anti-racist imagination.

Strategic Dilemmas of the Abolition Movement

The day following the conclusion of our read-around, I distributed a handout with five strategic dilemmas that faced the AASS at different points from its founding in 1833 until 1858:

- Should the AASS support "colonization" schemes to send people freed from slavery to Africa?
- Should the AASS spend time and money opposing racial discrimination in the North as well as attempting to end slavery in the South?
- Should the AASS support efforts to gain greater equality for women?
- Should the AASS support armed attempts to resist enforcement of the Fugitive Slave Act?
- Should the AASS support John Brown either with guns or money?

These were actual historical dilemmas, although I took some liberty in suggesting that they were each debated in an assembly of AASS members. Here's an example from the handout:

Situation: It's 1848. Many of the people in the abolition movement are white women. As they worked against slavery, many women began to feel that they, too, were heavily discriminated against. Even in some antislavery gatherings, women are not allowed to speak or to be leaders. In almost every state, married women cannot own property. Women's husbands even own the wages that women earn. In almost every state, the father can legally make a will appointing a guardian for his children in the event of his death. Should the husband die, a mother can have her children taken away from her. In most states, it is legal for a man to beat his wife. New York courts have ruled that, in order to keep his wife from nagging, a man can beat her with a horsewhip every few weeks! Women are not allowed to vote in any state.

A number of prominent women—many of them, perhaps most, active in the abolition movement—have organized a women's rights convention for Seneca Falls, N.Y., in July of this year. Some of the organizers would like the American

Anti-Slavery Society to endorse this gathering. This will be the first time that women in the United States have organized a meeting to discuss the condition of women.

- **Question:** Should the American Anti-Slavery Society publicly endorse this gathering?
- **Arguments:** Those in favor argue that the abolition movement should stand against all oppression, including the oppression of women. They argue that women abolitionists would be more effective if they were allowed to speak publicly. Some supporters also believe that the women's rights movement would bring in many people who have not been active in abolitionist work, and that this could ultimately strengthen the movement against slavery. And besides, they argue, we're trying to build a society based on equality and freedom from all oppression.

Others argue that this is nonsense, that this threatens to divide antislavery forces. They argue that without question, the greatest evil of our time is the enslavement of black human beings by white human beings, and that as bad off as some white women have it, this discrimination cannot be compared to slavery. Opponents argue that associating the American Anti-Slavery Society with women's rights will confuse and divide our supporters—and will weaken the antislavery movement.

We went over one of the questions as an example. I told students: "These were real issues that antislavery activists faced. I want you to think about each of these questions as if you're a member of the American Anti-Slavery Society." I told them they'd be discussing and making decisions about these questions in a large AASS meeting, but first I wanted them to discuss the dilemmas in small groups. I divided them into groups and urged them to stay in the "roles" that they'd created through their autobiographies, and asked them to try to reach agreement about the best course of action for their organization. These are tough questions, and my hunch was that their whole-class discussion would be richer and more democratic if students had thought about the issues beforehand in small groups.

As the students talked about the thorny questions that the abolition movement faced, some continued to represent the individual they'd created in their autobiography, and some abandoned their character in favor of trying to figure out what they personally thought was the best course of action. Either was fine with me; the autobiographies had served their purpose by getting students into an abolitionist mindset.

I gave the small groups a class period (about 50 minutes) to talk through the issues and to write down preliminary thoughts on what they felt was the best course of action for each strategic choice. As I circulated through the classroom, I noticed that there was no unanimity in students' opinions on these questions. I told them that it was fine if they couldn't agree because we'd be talking about these issues as a whole class the following day, but that I wanted them to make their best attempt to reach consensus.

Students Run Their Own Abolitionist Meeting

LIBRARY OF CONGRESS

The next day, we arranged our desks in a circle. This was the first "whole-group" role play that my U.S. history students had encountered. I explained: "The real abolitionists didn't have a teacher there to guide their discussion. They were on their own. That's how it's going to be in here, too. I'll sit at my desk and take notes on your discussion, but how you run your discussion and the decisions you make about each question will be up to you. The only requirements are that you do your best to take this seriously, and that you *discuss* the questions and don't simply bring them to a vote." I shared that, in watching students do whole-group role plays over the years, the best route is to raise hands and have each speaker call on the next speaker. "Be sure to decide on a process to carry on your conversation before you begin, or people will just start calling things out, and it can get chaotic."

One of my two classes doing this activity decided to choose a trusted student to chair the proceedings; the other class followed my suggestion and called on each other. Neither was problem free, but by and large both worked fine. In whole-group role plays, there is almost always a rough period that tries my patience, but the students' struggle to do this *together* without an adult leader is itself a key piece of the lesson.

Before we began, I emphasized that, even though we may now think the end of slavery was inevitable, there was no way abolitionists could have known with certainty that it would end. In fact, territories open to slavery had spread, and slavery became more legally entrenched between the founding of the AASS in 1833 and 1858 (the year the AASS debated my students' final question). I urged them to approach each question thoughtfully and seriously. In real life, these decisions had life-and-death consequences.

Each class began a bit haltingly. But the first question, about whether the AASS would support sending people who had been freed from slavery to Africa, was the easiest, both for students and for the real AASS. As the African American abolitionist Maria W. Stewart said, before she would go to a strange land, "the bayonet shall pierce me through." (Stewart was the first U.S.-born woman to speak in public and leave written texts of speeches.)

I was delighted by the seriousness and passion that students brought to these discussions. Frankly, these went on much longer than I'd planned, but I'd promised students that as long as they were engaged in discussing the issues, I wouldn't interrupt or hurry them. I sat at my desk and took careful notes on their arguments.

Here is a sampling of one class's discussion about whether they should consider armed resistance to oppose enforcement of the 1850 Fugitive Slave Act:

Austin: There are so many other ways to make our point other than with violence.

Luke: Austin said that there are so many nonviolent things to do. Name one.

Tim: Think of when you walk by a house and there is a little yapping dog tied on a leash. You walk by day after day. You don't pay any attention to the dog. You know that it can't hurt you. That's who we are. The abolitionists are that yapping dog, and we're not making any difference at all. We have to unleash the dog and it has to bite the slave owners on the butt.

Tiffany: Well, if we're that dog, and that dog does bite, then we're going to get put to sleep. The whole government and army is going to come down on us and we'll be destroyed.

Eron: People keep saying that we need to find other ways besides violence. Fine. What other ways? The bounty hunters are rounding up blacks. What if the bounty hunters started rounding up white people in the North? Would we still urge nonviolence then? Would we just sit back and say let's stay nonviolent and continue to publish our pamphlets and speak in churches as they are destroying our lives?

Alex: I like the yapping dog analogy. We need to go after them. We can't just look at the legalities. They'll just change the law anytime they feel like it.

Tiffany: People are saying that the law is unimportant. It's not unimportant. If it were unimportant, then why are we trying to pass a law outlawing slavery? It's not like the choice is to be violent or to do nothing. We could develop a strategy to help freed blacks. We could establish communities of armed blacks for self-defense. We don't have to attack people but we can help people defend themselves.

Eron: If we are going to abide by this fugitive slave law, we can't win. We have to fight this law.

Ilantha: I thought Tiffany's solution was good. We organize communities of people who can stay together to defend themselves.

Nick: I like that too. We train people in self-defense. To defy the bounty hunters.

Eron: We have to force the judges and courts to see our point. The only way we have to do that is to revolt.

Jaimie: Yeah. Violence will get their attention. But once they're attacked, the government will try to do away with us.

Tim: People are saying that violence is doomed to fail. What about the American Revolution? What about the Boston Tea Party? We could be the hicks and farmers of the American Revolution. The ones who threw out the British. Just because we're outgunned doesn't mean that we're doomed to lose.

Eron: I don't think that Tiffany's idea of self-defense solves anything. We're throwing them to the dogs. "Let them defend themselves. We don't want to get involved." But we have numbers. We have to get out people to defend them.

The students voted 15 to 11, with several abstentions, to reaffirm their commitment not to attack bounty hunters first, but decided to help communities of freed African Americans arm themselves for self-defense. My students' discussion mirrored the frustration and disagreement within the abolition movement about what to do in the face of the increasingly aggressive measures by pro-slavery forces. Eron was becoming the John Brown of the class, even if he wrongly assumed that the "we" of the abolition movement was all white. Others refused to waver from a strict adherence to nonviolence.

Students took most of two class periods to discuss the issues. In each class, I began the second day by reading to them my verbatim notes from the previous day. I was impressed by students' intensity and thoughtfulness, and wanted them to appreciate each other as intellectuals. They were rapt as they listened to me read the back-and-forth of their arguments. This reading helped students re-enter their roles, and reminded them where they left off. We also talked about their decision-making process and analyzed when they made progress and when they tended to spin their wheels.

In our class discussion following the role play, I asked students to predict how they thought the abolition movement had resolved these questions. Not surprisingly, their curiosity to know what "really happened" was much greater because they had tried to figure out the same questions themselves. I wanted them to recognize the growing militancy of the abolition movement. I also hoped the lesson would teach students that the abolition movement, by and large, did see racism as the enemy, and not only slavery. In his first speech as an abolitionist, Frederick Douglass argued that "Prejudice against color is stronger North than South; it hangs around my neck like a heavy weight. It presses me out from my fellow men. . . . I have met it every step the three years I have been out of slavery."

There were important facts that I wanted students to know and historical figures I wanted to introduce. But my main teaching aim was to show students that the movement for racial justice wasn't simply a matter of one thing happening after another—it wasn't the smooth unfolding of History leading to Freedom. I wanted students to see that history is a series of choice-points and there is nothing inevitable about the direction of society, that where things move depends on how we analyze the world and how we act on that analysis. People like them—not only famous leaders—make history.

Bill Bigelow is curriculum editor of Rethinking Schools *and co-director of the Zinn Education Project. He co-edited* A People's Curriculum for the Earth: Teaching Climate Change and the Environmental Crisis.

Chapter Forty-Four

THE HISTORY ALL AROUND US
Roosevelt High School and the 1968 Eastside Blowouts

By Brian C. Gibbs

A text can be anything: a poem, a map, an old letter. To spur great learning, it needs to be provocative, powerful, open to multiple interpretations, and, above all, it needs to teach something profound. I use one of the greatest texts imaginable—Theodore Roosevelt High School in East Los Angeles.

Roosevelt High was constructed in 1923 in Boyle Heights. Like the neighborhood itself, Roosevelt has grown. Originally built to house up to 800 students, it is now home to more than 5,000 students. The original building sat on less than three acres of land but now engulfs more than 10. When I arrived in 1994, 21 years old and full of nervous excitement, I was amazed at the sheer size of it and intrigued by its many hidden corners. I remember wondering about the school's ghost stories. Were they true or just urban myths? I always thought that there was a good assignment in there somewhere, but it took years to come to me.

As part of the school's 75th anniversary celebration in 1998, glass cases were erected with paraphernalia from each of Roosevelt's decades—prom photos, 1920s-style football helmets, old faculty photos. One year my students and I were talking about the political message of monuments and I thought about those cases.

"A monument can be anything from a statue, to a painting, to a park or project named for someone," I told the students. "You know the display cases up front, near the main office?"

Dead silence.

"You know, the glass cases with the old stuff? Have you looked at them?"

"Well, I've looked at them, but not

CHICANO STUDENTS WALKOUT and . . . MARCH to HAZARD PARK and . . . CONFRONT STENGEL & CADWELL with DEMANDS

looked at them, you know what I mean, Mister?" Martin asked with a sly smile. I did know what he meant.

"Field trip!" I announced. "On your feet and follow me!"

I took my students to the glass cases, pointing out the photographs and memorabilia, reminding them that all of these were *monuments* and asked them to think about not only what was there but also what wasn't, who chose to display these things, and why. During the impromptu tour a student found her mother in a photograph: "I didn't know she was on the drill team. She never told me!" Another student found a photograph of Coach Burgueno, popular math teacher and winning basketball coach, as a student.

On the way back to the classroom I hung a quick right to show them a small memorial garden for Mike Morrell, a powerful and popular teacher who had died of AIDS 16 years before. Students arrived back in the room, hot and a little cranky. "There were no tours listed on the syllabus," one student complained. The bell rang, students left, and so ended my spontaneous lesson plan. I hoped the students had gained something from the tour but I wasn't convinced.

During lunch one day that week, I saw a student of mine pointing out Morrell's memorial to a friend, and at different times caught some of my students looking quizzically at the glass cases outside the hall. It also came up in class, with students referencing items in the glass cases: "Oh yeah, that wouldn't help at all, just like that ridiculous leather football helmet in the case."

I realized that the impromptu tour helped students see their campus and their school differently. They were actually looking at the campus. It was no longer just a run-down school that was *chafa* (East LA-speak for cheap), a place where they were forced to be.

Building Curriculum on a Building

I habitually wander during my free period. It helps me reflect on the day and plan for the next. I kept trying to figure out how I could expand what had already begun to happen with my students, turn the school into a full-fledged text. I knew that students from area high schools had staged a walkout in the late 1960s over the racism obvious in the deteriorated buildings, wretched pedagogy, lack of college planning, and narrow curriculum that students were force-fed, but I didn't know much about it. I began my research by reading books, watching the film series *Chicano! History of the Mexican American Civil Rights Movement,* and searching the archives of the *Los Angeles Times* and the school newspaper. I also spoke to older faculty who had been staff or students back in the late 1960s. Slowly a lesson began to develop that could bring my unit on rights and struggle home to my students in East Los Angeles.

I wanted to turn the school into a full-fledged text.

GEORGE RODRIGUEZ

The unit I planned was an examination of the struggle for human and civil rights for women, African Americans, and Mexican Americans in the United States from the 1920s until the present day. I decided to begin with the 1968 Eastside Blowouts. The essential question I chose was: "How do we create change?"

I began the unit by asking students: "What would you be willing to do to create change? If you felt that women, African Americans, Latinos, or another group had no rights and you believed they should have those rights, what would you be willing to do to change that?"

"So, this is back in time?" a student asked.

"It could be back in time or the present, but what would you be willing to do?"

"You mean like kill somebody?"

"Well, would you be willing to die? Dr. King said, 'A man who will not die for something is not fit to live.' Would you agree with that? There are people in history who have given up everything in the hope that one day they and their people would have rights or equality. So what I'm asking is, what would you be willing to do for some massive change that you want?"

"I'm not willing to do anything," a student said. "Isn't that like the government's job or something?"

"Well, the sad truth of it is that no rights have ever been given. Aldous Huxley said, 'Liberties are not given, they are taken.' In other words, all the rights we have today, others before us organized, fought, and struggled for them.

"Think of a right that is really important to you—the right to vote, maybe, the right to go to school, the right not to be drafted into the Army for a war you think is wrong. Then think what you would be willing to do to get that right for yourself or for other folks." To feed their thoughts, I briefly described a few things activists have done and why. The list included hunger strikes, sit-ins, taking the risk of being beaten up or arrested, getting expelled from school.

I asked students to write about this question for a few minutes. When everyone had something on paper, I asked them to turn to the person next to them and talk about what they wrote and why. Then students shared briefly with the full class. It turned into a heated discussion. Some of the highlights:

"I would spend some money but not all of my money."

"I would risk getting hit if it were something really important like the right to vote or to stop violence to women or something like that . . . but it would have to be important and I'd have to be mad."

"I'd be willing to risk getting expelled if other people were doing it with me. I don't think I could do it alone."

"I'd do everything but get expelled; I'd rather risk my life than get kicked out of school. My mom would make sure that I didn't get into heaven if I got kicked out."

For homework, I had students interview two adults in their home about what they would be willing to do.

Field Trip to a Staircase

The next day I told students, "Exciting news, we're going on a field trip." Student faces filled with momentary exuberance but then quickly fell.

One student voiced dismay. "Is it one of those *chafa* school tours again?"

"It's a field trip of the mind," I said, attempting my best Rod Serling. "Follow me, stay close, if you fall behind, you get left behind." I took students out of the bungalow, across the asphalt, past the fountain, across the grass, up the steps, and into the main building. We continued down the hall until we came to a long, wide stairwell that leads to the front of the building and into the quad in the middle of the school.

"Sit down on the steps near the handrails; it's important for the story," I told the students.

"We have to sit on the ground?" a student asked.

"It won't kill you, I promise," I replied.

After a few moans, students took their seats and I told them the story with passion and flourish, pacing up and down the stairwell:

In 1968, the Mexican American students of East Los Angeles realized that the schools in East LA—Garfield High, Wilson, Lincoln, and Roosevelt—were underserving their students. Going into the college track and on to college wasn't encouraged, corporal punishment, swats, were used far too often, there were very few Mexican American teachers, students were punished for speaking Spanish, and their culture was under attack. A small group of students became angry and wanted to fight back. They wanted to protest, to show their anger. They formed a small group with representatives from all four campuses to organize a way to respond. All the students had been members of a youth program the previous summer and had met

EDUARDO "EDDIE" LOPEZ

Lincoln High School history teacher Sal Castro. Castro convinced the students that they had to go through steps, do their homework first, think carefully, and then act.

The students put together a survey and took it to as many students as they could in the East LA high schools. They brought the results to the school board, hoping that they would listen and enact change. When they didn't, the students decided to risk everything and walk out. The word about the walkout spread; it was set to begin the next morning. At 9 a.m. on March 3, 1968, students walked out of Lincoln and Wilson high schools. No one took them seriously at first, expecting that they would go quietly back to school, but they didn't. The next day students again walked out of Lincoln and Wilson high schools, but that day, Garfield and Roosevelt joined them.

On the third day, students walked out again, only this time, Roosevelt students chose to stage a sit-in and they sat exactly where you are. They were sitting-in when the LA County Sheriff's Department and members of the LA Police Department burst in on them wearing helmets and riot gear. The police rushed the students and beat them with their batons.

My students had sat in absolute silence up until this part of the story, when they issued a few gasps. "No way!" several students whispered. And "Are you serious?"

I continued:

The police didn't ask the students to move. They considered them dangerous radicals and started swinging their nightsticks at them almost immediately. A few students attempted to hang on to the railings, but most broke immediately and ran up the steps and in the opposite direction. The police chased them up the stairs, down the hall, and through the back door.

"Let's go!" I ushered students up, and we walked back down the hallway and out the back door.

"They just kept beating them?" a student asked. "The cops just kept attacking them, kept beating them?"

I continued the story:

Yes, once the violence started, it didn't end until the students were pushed against the fence, there was nowhere else for them to run. The beatings continued as the students attempted to resist. Eventually, some students were arrested.

My students stood in shocked silence, mouths open and angry.

For homework I asked students to record what they remembered from the story, to explain what the students were willing to risk to cause change, and to make an argument as to whether their decision was correct. I asked everyone to write at least two pages.

The next day I began class by asking: "Was their action justified? Was it worth getting beaten up and arrested for? Is it what you would have done?"

"Yes!" some students immediately shouted. Others weren't sure: "If it was something more important, I mean, it was important, but to get beat like that."

I then divided students into partner pairs to discuss their responses. After a few minutes, I asked: "So, what do we think? Did the students make the right choice?"

Comments ranged from "They absolutely did the right thing" to "What did it really accomplish?"

Most students were convinced that action should have been taken, but they weren't convinced as a class what that action should be. Next, I showed the actual footage of what happened, as depicted in Part 4 of *Chicano!*: "Fighting for Political Power." Immediately prior to showing the film clip, I asked students to record and reflect on at least five major events depicted in the film and to record at least eight quotes from participants in the action.

The question 'What would you be willing to do?' became the touchstone for the unit and for the rest of the year.

The film footage is strong. It provoked reactions when students saw their school and when they witnessed the violence that took place. They were moved, more than I expected. For homework I asked students to reflect on the quotations they had chosen: "Write at least three sentences for each, explaining whether the film offers evidence that supports or challenges your thoughts about whether the students' actions in 1968 were correct. The quotes and your responses will be the basis for a seminar discussion tomorrow."

Did They Do the Right Thing?

When students arrived the next day, we again headed to the stairwell. Once there, I divided students into groups of four. Students sat around the stairwell, sharing quotes and their thoughts about them. The discussions began in whispered tones, but soon voices rose and students were pointing to areas of the stairwell where students sat-in in 1968 and where the police burst in.

"Can we move around a little? We'll stay focused, we just want to look around some more," a student asked.

"Haven't you been in this stairwell a million times?" I asked.

"Yeah, but I just realized that I never really looked at it before."

After a few minutes, I asked each team to choose the most powerful quote or moment from the film to share and explain why they chose it. Each team shared in turns. Their responses were in hushed tones at first, reverential to the stairwell, which had seemed to grow into hallowed ground:

"It wasn't a quote so much or a specific thing, but the whole thing, that students were willing to risk everything for their education."

"The scene I keep thinking about is the one where the students are outside . . . up against the fence. I mean they had nowhere to run . . . and they were running away. I can't believe the police would do that to them. That's just fu . . . I mean messed up."

The stairwell has become a monument to be recognized and honored.

"We liked what Moctesuma Esparza said when he told the media, 'We the students have a message and we're asking you to convey it.' When the reporter tried to argue with him, he just walked away. It was like he was saying, 'That's our demand and we'll be here until it's fulfilled.'"

By the end of the class period, there was no resolution; instead, there was disagreement everywhere. About half thought the students did the right thing in 1968, about a fourth thought that the students did the right thing but were insane, and the final fourth were convinced that there must have been a better way. Their concluding homework assignment was to return to their original writing about what they would be willing to do to fight for something that was important to them.

When the complaints arose—"Didn't we do this already?"—I explained, "It's to see whether you've changed your mind, to catch you growing."

The question "What would you be willing to do?" became the touchstone for the unit and for the rest of the year. Whether we were studying suffragist Alice Paul's hunger strike, Dr. King in the Birmingham Jail, *Johnny Got His Gun* author Dalton Trumbo's decision not to testify before the House Un-American Activities Committee, or the Berrigan brothers' decision to burn draft cards in Catonsville, Md., their choices always were compared with the choices of the high school students and the strength they showed in East Los Angeles. Difficult, distant, and powerful ideas became clearer and closer to home.

My students never again looked at the stairwell in quite the same way. When I'm lucky, I'll catch one of them explaining what happened to a friend or sibling. Whether they agreed with the protesters' choices or not, their school's stairwell has become a monument to be recognized and honored.

Brian C. Gibbs formerly taught history and American government at Roosevelt High School in Los Angeles. He is currently a doctoral student in curriculum and instruction at the University of Wisconsin-Madison.

Chapter Forty-Five

FOR MY PEOPLE

Using Margaret Walker's poem to help students 'talk-back' to stereotypes and to affirm their self-worth

By Linda Christensen

"I don't understand how you could walk into that building day after day for 22 years," the older woman at the copier told me. "I have to go in there once a week, and I fear for my life every time I walk up those stairs. All of those black boys with their hoodlum clothes—sweatshirt hoods pulled up over their heads, baggy pants—I'm afraid they're going to knock me down the steps and steal my purse."

I looked at her and remembered Damon and Sekou, young black men I taught at "that building": Jefferson High School, Portland, Ore. I remembered their brilliance, imagine their faces—one was at law school, one was at NASA. I thought of Kanaan's huge heart, of Frank's humor. I thought of Aaron Wheeler-Kay's poem written after we visited an art museum exhibit of Carrie Mae Weems' work:

SUSAN LINA RUGGLES

I Went Looking For Jefferson
and I found. . .
all the nations of the world
wrapped in baggy jeans
sweatshirts
braids.
Closed minds slowly opening
like doors under water.
Jefferson is our whetstone
the blade is our mind.

There was no blade to open the mind of the woman at the copy machine. I'd met her before in countless other closed minds through the years: people—teachers, parents, reporters, students from other schools—who sized up those who attended or worked at Jefferson based on stereotypical images, usually without ever venturing inside our classrooms.

Students and Stereotypes

Students, particularly students who don't fit the social norm because of their race, language, sexual orientation, weight, or ability to purchase the latest fashions, bear the brunt of such stereotypes. They sometimes share their anger and frustration at inappropriate times and in inappropriate ways. But the classroom can be a safe place for students to not only talk back, but also to affirm their right to a place in the world.

The classroom can be a safe place for students to not only talk back, but also to affirm their right to a place in the world.

During the years I worked at Jefferson, I found it necessary to help students "talk back" to disrespectful and untrue stereotypes of our school. In one particularly helpful assignment, they write a poem as their way of "talking back."

I began by reading Margaret Walker's powerful poem "For My People." Walker's poem teaches about the hardship that African Americans endured, but also celebrates the triumphs of her people. She ends the poem with an exhortation: "Let a new earth rise. Let another world be born. . . . Let a race of men now rise and take control!"

We looked at how Walker constructs her poem with the repeating phrase "For my people." She uses the phrase as an introduction to her theme for that stanza and follows it with a list. For example:

For my people everywhere singing their slave songs
repeatedly: their dirges and their ditties and their blues
and jubilees, praying their prayers nightly to an
unknown god, bending their knees humbly to an unseen power

Walker's poem teaches the strength of using repetition and lists in poetry. I also pointed out the rhythm of the line—"their dirges and their ditties and their blues and jubilees," and the repetition of sounds—singing slave songs, dirges and ditties, and praying prayers.

Then I asked students to create a list of their "people." I told them to think of all of the communities they belonged to. I list mine on the board as a way to stimulate them to think beyond their immediate categories. My list consisted of Jefferson, poor whites, working class, Norwegians, Germans, teachers, feminists, social activists, women, mothers, overweight people, environmentalists.

I often used Jefferson as a model because it's the one community we all shared. We catalogued reasons to celebrate our school: the diverse student body, the many languages heard in the halls, the Jefferson dancers and the gospel singers, Michele Stemler's Spanish classes, the powerful student-created murals on the walls. Then I asked them to pick one of their communities and list what they could praise about it. I also asked them to think about any common misconceptions people have about any of their "people" and suggested that they might "talk back" to those judgments in the poem I asked them to write.

My student Cang Dao wrote in his poem "Race":

People don't know how I feel
"You can't talk like us."
The words hurt me more than
It hurts them to say.
I'm getting an attitude.
Too many jokes,
I can't accept it.
What's wrong about me
That may not be accepted by them?
Is it the way I look or
The way I talk?
How many languages can you speak?
I speak four.
Is there something from
Me that you want?
My beautiful brown eyes or
My lovely skin?
Don't get jealous.

When Cang wrote this poem, we discussed how kids made fun of his newcomer English, but we also discussed how he can speak more languages than most of the student body. He embedded pieces of that talk in his poem.

Lori Ann Durbin, then a senior in my Writing for Publication class, was a transplanted cowgirl who ended up at Jefferson High School. Her poem "Country

Folk" celebrates that heritage:

> For my folk, two-steppin', shit-
>   kickin' pioneers.
> Blue collar, redneck, bowlegged
>   horsemen. . .
> This is my song to you.
> Moonshiners, horse ranchers, hill
>   billy roots,
> wild women, bare feet, it's nothin'
>   or it's boots,
> twangy sweet fiddle, songs about
>   our lives,
> maybe sappy to everyone else, but
>   that's how we survive.
> Fishin', singin', ridin' bareback in
>   the field,
> tight cowboy butts and Wranglers.
> I love the way they feel.
> Tailgate parties, couples in the
>   barn, hay in our hair.
> It's not just music.
> It's a way of life.

Justin Morris, another senior, took the stereotypes about black people and used them in his celebration. His poem demonstrated an in-your-face love for all aspects of his heritage. (One night I was at a local copy store making huge posters of these poems to hang around the school. Several African American men from the community were copying on a machine close to my oversize machine. They laughed when they read Justin's poem and took one of the copies to hang in their office.) This is Justin's poem:

> For My People
> This is for my people
> who are "colored"
> who are proud.
>
> For my people
> who cause white women to clutch
>   their purses
> who white men look down on
> who drank from different
>   fountains

who fought prejudice.

For my people
with kinky afros
and jheri curls.

For my people
with big lips
and wide noses.

For my people
with black power
fingertips drenched with barbecue
     sauce.

For the people
with pink hearts
and brown/black skins.
For my people:
Stay strong.

    The woman who feared for her life each time she walked Jefferson's halls "confessed" her racism—which is perhaps the first step toward change. I will bring her my students' poems. I want her to see beyond the baggy pants and sweatshirts to the whetstone that sharpened their minds. I hope that by reading their words, she'll see the "pink hearts" inside the "brown/ black" skin, she'll hear the intelligence that ricochets off Jefferson's walls and know she doesn't have to be afraid.

Linda Christensen (lmc@lclark.edu) is director of the Oregon Writing Project at Lewis & Clark College in Portland, Oregon, and a Rethinking Schools *editor. She is author, most recently, of* Reading, Writing, and Rising Up: Teaching About Social Justice and the Power of the Written Word *(2nd edition).*

Resources

Giovanni, N. (2001). Legacies. In B. Rochelle (ed.) *Words with Wings: A Treasury of African-American Poetry and Art.* Singapore: HarperCollins.

Hughes, L. (2001). My people. In B. Rochelle (ed.) *Words with Wings: A Treasury of African-American Poetry and Art.* Singapore: HarperCollins.

Walker, A. (2001). Women. In B. Rochelle (ed.) *Words with Wings: A Treasury of African-American Poetry and Art.* Singapore: HarperCollins.

Walker, M. (1989). *For My People. This Is My Century: New and Collected Poems.* Athens: University of Ga. Press.

Chapter Forty-Six

THE OTHER INTERNMENT
Teaching the hidden story of Japanese Latin Americans during WWII

By Moé Yonamine

My unit on the largely unknown history of the internment of Japanese Latin Americans began more than a decade ago. I was on a bus from Portland, Ore., to Tule Lake, Calif., site of one of the largest Japanese American incarceration camps during World War II. "I am from Japan," the elder sitting next to me said in Japanese. "But I am originally from Peru." For me, it was an honorable coincidence to find myself next to this elder.

JORDIN ISIP

An elder sitting in front of us turned around and said in English, "He looks very familiar." As I translated their conversation, it came out that they were both young boys interned at Tule Lake. "I know him!" said the Japanese American elder. "He was my friend!" Grabbing the Peruvian man's hand and shaking it firmly, he explained that they played baseball together often but that one day his friend just disappeared. His friend had only spoken Spanish, so he could never ask him what he was doing in the camp. He had wondered all of these years what had happened to him. The Peruvian Japanese elder's face beamed with joy as the two continued to shake hands, not letting go. "I am so glad you are safe," he said. They had reunited after more than 50 years.

Among those who attended the Tule Lake Pilgrimage were children and grandchildren of internees who hoped to learn from the oral stories of the elders. Many have since joined the Campaign for Justice, seeking redress from the U.S. government for orchestrating and financing the forcible deportation and incarceration of Japanese Latin Americans (JLAs) during World War II.

This is the little-known background to the unit that I decided to teach my 8th-grade U.S. history students: Even before Pearl Harbor, in October 1941, the U.S. government initiated plans to construct an internment camp near the Panama Canal Zone for JLAs. The United States targeted JLAs it deemed security threats and pressured Latin American governments to round them up and turn them over, prompting Peru to engage in the mass arrest of Japanese descendents it sought to expel. Beginning in 1942, 13 Latin American governments arrested more than 2,300 JLAs in their countries (more than 80 percent from Peru), including teachers, farmers, barbers, and businessmen. The U.S. government transported the JLAs from Panama to internment camps in the United States, confiscating passports and visas. Two prisoner exchanges with Japan took place in 1942 and 1943 of at least 800 JLAs—many of whom had never been to Japan. Fourteen hundred JLAs remained in U.S. internment camps until the end of the war, when the government deemed them "illegal aliens." Meanwhile, the Peruvian government refused to readmit any of its citizens of Japanese origin. With nowhere to go, more than 900 Japanese Peruvians were deported to Japan in December 1945. Some JLA survivors are now telling their stories for the first time; new information is still being uncovered.

The Campaign for Justice seeks redress from the U.S. government for the forcible deportation and incarceration of Japanese Latin Americans during World War II.

As an Okinawan, this history hit close to my heart. In *The Japanese in Latin America,* I learned that large waves of Okinawans migrated to South America beginning in the late 1800s as the once sovereign Ryukyu island chain was brought under Japanese control. By the time WWII began, the majority of immigrants to Peru were Okinawan. There was also a large group in Brazil. Many families in Okinawa today have relatives from South America including my own, but stories of their migration and their lives thereafter remain largely untold.

My own questions turned into my inquiry as a history teacher. How can I teach 8th graders to imagine the experiences of people from another time in history and make connections to today? How can I teach them about social injustice in a way that will make them feel empowered and not cynical? How can I encourage students to visualize what a just world would look like to them?

Teaching Internment

"Are those refugee houses?"

"It looks like people are being treated like animals."

"It looks hot. Is it World War II? Are they Asian? Are they Jewish?"

"I think of boot camp and prison."

My students had just walked through a photo gallery showing the forced removal and incarceration of JLAs. Our overcrowded room (40 students!) included many immigrants—Mexican, Vietnamese, Filipino, Pacific Islander, Russian—along with Chicana/os, African Americans, and white students. They wrote their impressions of the black-and-white pictures, trying to make sense of a story none had ever heard.

Then I wrote on the board:

> **How can I teach my students about social injustice in a way that will make them feel empowered and not cynical?**

> Rounded up in the sweltering yard.
> Unable to endure any longer
> Standing in line
> Some collapse.

This is one of 13 poems etched in the stones of the Japanese American Historical Plaza of Portland, which honors the internment stories of local Japanese Americans. I read the poem aloud to the class and asked students to write what they thought the poem was about. It brought up more questions than answers. One student wrote: "In trouble? Military thing? Why is she there? What did she do to deserve this?" I read a few more of the poems and students continued to write.

One Mexican American student wrote: "Like any group working in the camp, they can't take the heat anymore because they've been working all day. Standing outside ready to be transported to a new place like the Asian people in the pictures." Throughout the unit students wrote regularly in journals. This particular student often wrote about his family's experience as migrant workers and connected their experiences to those of the internees.

When I showed the class a map of the detention centers and incarceration camps, Ashley shouted, "That's Oregon!" I explained that many people from Portland were affected and told the story of the Portland Expo Center (now used for large community events and cultural festivals), which was a detention center used to round up Japanese American families from our area. "You mean the racetracks up there in North Portland?" one student asked. "I grew up there!"

My students had learned little about the incarceration of local families. I explained that many people left Japan for the mainland United States, Hawaii, and Latin America, beginning in the late 1800s, to look for work. "Like the Mexicans now," Javier said. "We come over here because there's no work, you know. There's no money. Our parents just want to do something so they can make sure there's food and stuff." A few other Mexican American students in the room nodded, listening attentively.

"Well, it's like that for Filipinos, too," Addel chimed in. "I know my family came over for a better life. I think it's like that for a lot of people." Javier looked at Addel and nodded from across the room. I had never seen Javier and Addel interact with each other before.

I introduced President Franklin Roosevelt's Executive Order 9066, ordering the internment of Japanese Americans along the West Coast in 1942. I explained that more than 110,000 Japanese Americans were incarcerated. But there were also Japanese Latin Americans. I pointed to the photo gallery and a student let out a gasp from the back of the room.

We read excerpts from "Latin Americans," an appendix to *Personal Justice Denied,* a report by the Commission on Wartime Relocation and Internment of Civilians. Students immediately jumped in with questions:

"How could they get away with that?"

"That's messed up. How can people just sit there and let this happen?"

Sam, an immigrant from Liberia, interjected passionately, halfway out of his seat, "Why couldn't we [the United States] just let everyone live here?" Since Sam had never before participated in class discussion, his excitement brought smiles from classmates.

Reparations Role Play

I didn't tell too much of the history because I wanted the role play I had developed to spark the students' curiosity. I based my role play on the format of Wayne Au's "Addressing Redress," which focuses on the issue of Japanese American redress. Au's activity appealed to me because it is structured so that students are empowered to imagine a different conversation among groups and a different outcome in providing justice.

I introduced the role play by telling the class that, since there is not enough information on this history, a committee has been appointed to hold hearings and to make decisions on the issue of redress: "We are going to imagine what the outcome should be. You are each going to represent someone who has something to say about this." I explained that they would share their character's experiences and different perspectives with the committee.

When the students walked into class the next day, the group assignments were written on the board. Even before the bell rang, all of the students had circled their desks into groups and seated themselves. I handed each group a placard to write their group's name. The groups represented: Japanese Latin Americans interned in the United States who stayed here; those who were deported to Japan; the governments of Latin American countries that gave up their Japanese descendents to the United States; Latin American vegetable growers who lobbied against the return of Japanese farmers; and contemporary U.S. citizens opposed to reparations. A final group of students were the judiciary committee that would have to make the ultimate decision on redress.

As I walked around the room introducing the groups to each other, the vibe was good-spirited and eager. There were some high fives and smiles of "What?!" when students learned what their role would be. Then I gave each group their full role play description to read together (available at http://www.rethinkingschools.org/static/archive/25_01/Yonamine_roleplays.pdf).

As part of their regular journal writing, I asked students to introduce themselves to me in character to help them internalize the information.

After students wrote, they proceeded to discuss with their group—staying in character—the following questions:

Was the removal and internment of Japanese Latin Americans just or unjust? Why or why not?

If unjust, what kind of redress should there be? No redress at all, government apology only, commitment to public education campaign, or money?

Meanwhile, I gave the judiciary committee members copies of the role play descriptions of the other groups and asked them to predict what each group would propose.

The following day, students again were in their grouped seats before class began. Sam raised his hand and said, "This is for the whole class." He turned to the class and said: "Guys, I am really, really sorry for what I'm about to say today. I'm not trying to offend anybody. This isn't me. I know I'm going to make some of you guys mad. And I'm really sorry about that." Sam was about to speak on behalf of Americans opposed to reparations. I was blown away at his gesture of respect and solidarity. The class fell into silence, surprised by Sam's comments. I told him that I appreciated what he had said.

"Good job, man!" Addel said.

John, a Russian American student, nodded to Sam from across the room, "Yeah, that was tight."

I reinforced to the class that we were taking the roles of people who may have very different views from our own, saying: "The issues that we'll address in our conversations are themes we find throughout history. In order to understand how such events can occur and how different people were affected, we have to learn from the perspectives of others."

I opened the forum with a welcoming statement as the facilitator of this judicial hearing and reviewed the decision that the judiciary committee would need to make in the end.

The JLA group that volunteered to go first had studied a narrative taken in great part from the memoirs of JLA survivor Seiichi Higashide in *Adios to Tears*. "Nobody had the right to take us like that," Cesar explained. "We had a family, a home, and a country. We were taken just like that and put in the internment camp." They went on to recommend restitution for the JLAs, but didn't think any amount of money was enough to repay the survivors for what they went through.

Addel spoke for the JLAs who were sent to Japan. "We were kidnapped. Nobody gave us a choice of where we were going to go. And we were just there [in Peru] to work. But then, you guys made us prisoners and sent us to Japan. I had my wife and child. And you took that away from me because you sent me to Japan. That's not even where I'm really from." This group also wanted redress, but they demanded the right to live in the United States or go back to Peru.

Sam represented Americans against reparations. "We don't believe that any of this even happened," he said. As Sam counted the reasons on his fingers he said, "There's no proof, no evidence of these camps, and we don't think the Japanese people would've been fooled." He meant that the Japanese government would not have taken the JLAs in exchange for U.S. prisoners when some of them did not even speak Japanese. Sam continued, "And besides that, if the U.S. government did do all of these things, they probably had a good reason." Sam sat down. I asked him for their recommendation on redress, and several of the kids in the group called out "None!"

I was delighted to see students connecting their personal experiences to those of people more than 60 years ago.

Ashley presented the thoughts of Latin American vegetable growers. After explaining why they created their organization of small businesses, she said, "We feel that the Japanese are a competition for our business." She described how Japanese farmers came to dominate the agricultural market in Peru and said: "We don't want them to come back and take our jobs. We've worked hard to get to where we are, and they're just going to take it back again."

Last, the group representing the governments of Latin America said, "We feel bad for them [JLAs] but it wasn't like we had a choice." Tiffany explained, "If it wasn't for the U.S. asking us to gather and remove JLAs, we probably wouldn't have done it." Another student added, "And at the same time, we didn't want them [JLAs] in our country either because they were causing a lot of problems for us." She was referring to the anti-Japanese rioting and looting of businesses and homes in Peru. "We feel bad but it wasn't really our fault. The U.S. made us because we're scared of them," they concluded.

When I offered all of the groups a chance to add additional arguments, Maria, from the first JLA group, spoke up. She said that people need to have immigration documents and to feel secure knowing that they won't be deported. In the discussion, Maria, who is from Oaxaca, Mexico, expressed her feelings as a young immigrant in today's anti-immigrant climate. Cesar added that interning the JLAs was similar to treating immigrants as terrorists. "We are not terrorists," Cesar said.

"Don't treat us like that. That's racist." He was full of emotion and the entire class listened quietly. "This is like the cops harassing us and stuff. I don't know what the word is. . ."

Pedro looked up and said, "Profiling! Racial profiling!"

"Yeah," continued Cesar. "That's what I'm talking about."

Although Maria and Cesar stepped out of character, I was delighted to see students connecting their personal experiences to those of people more than 60 years ago.

'They Weren't Criminals'

From the energy in the room, I knew that students needed an outlet to express their own feelings on this issue. I asked them to write in their journals again, this time talking back in their *own* voices to their character or another group in the room. A number of students wrote that the forced removal and internment of Japanese Latin Americans was based on racism. Rumel, who had portrayed an American against reparations, wrote to his group: "They weren't criminals. They didn't do anything wrong. How can you say it's OK to treat people like this? It's just straight racist. Is this what we want to tell future generations?"

Ben, from the Latin American vegetable growers' group, reflected on his experiences growing up in Portland as a Vietnamese immigrant: "I used to feel invisible because I didn't belong anywhere. . . . I don't know what I'd do if someone told me I can't be here [in the United States] anymore just because of my race."

Jenny, who had struggled to stay in her character as the governments of Latin America during the role play, disagreed strongly with her group. She wrote, "It's just an excuse to say that the U.S. made us [the governments of Latin America] do it [the forced removal and internment of JLAs] because we didn't want them here in the first place. . . . I think everyone's trying to blame somebody else."

As the other students wrote, the judiciary committee had the job of deciding what would be a just response of the U.S. government. Students in the group felt heavyhearted with this responsibility. "This is a lot of pressure," Jasmine remarked.

Nick agreed. "How do we decide what's fair for these people?"

I encouraged the group to think about what they thought was the "messed-up-ness," a term coined by the class to describe social injustice. "Why do you think what happened was messed up or not messed up? Does the U.S. government need to do something to make that wrong right? And what does that right thing look like to you?" Finally, the committee began discussing their thoughts with each other.

The next day, the committee was eager to give its decision. Tina spoke on behalf of the group. She explained that they decided "yes" on redress. "What we [the United States] did to them was wrong and we're responsible to fix it." She said that since the JLAs were forced from their homes, they added their own type of reparation, which was "to help them reunite with their families." The committee

U.S. ARMY SIGNAL CORPS PHOTOGRAPH, NATIONAL ARCHIVE. COURTESY OF NATIONAL JAPANESE AMERICAN HISTORICAL SOCIETY

concluded that the U.S. government should also issue a formal apology and public education, but no money. "We should apologize because we know it was wrong," Tina explained. "We should have public education so this never happens again."

Nick added that they recommend that this story be taught in U.S. history classes "so that everybody knows." However, they did not want to give money because "our economy is in bad shape right now. . . . People are losing jobs and there's just no money. We're sorry, but we just can't pay them." This was an interesting conclusion and reflected the students' recognition of the economic difficulties of families in the neighborhood and nationally. Many students in the class were experiencing harsh living conditions as the economic crisis disproportionately affected families of color and immigrants. During the winter I taught this unit, I worried about whether students were going home to heated places. In addition, they had seen their classroom size explode and understood that a lack of money was the underlying factor. All of this had led students to assume that the U.S. government has no money, rather than that the money is distributed unequally or that the government is spending money on things that it thinks are more important, like the war in Afghanistan.

'What Really Happened?'

The next day, Sam walked into the room asking, "Ms. Yonamine, *now* are you going to tell us what really happened?" I told the students about the actual bill seeking redress and showed them a timeline of the bill's development and current status. As I shared information, students listened attentively. Addel jumped in, disturbed that all of the surviving JLAs had not yet received reparations, "So there's no decision yet whatsoever by us [the United States]?" I explained that we are still waiting for an official study by a congressional committee on wartime violations by the U.S. government against JLAs.

"What would you recommend to this committee based on what you have learned?" I asked. "Write them a letter." The class fell into silence as they busily went to work. This was the most effort I had seen students put into any written assignment all year. The responses showed their ideals and empathy.

"How would we feel if this happened to us?" asked Beto. "We did it. Now it is time to fix it. . . . They should especially include public education. That way in the future it won't happen again."

Sarah agreed. "They deserve to have their lives back. . . . Americans should provide apologies and money toward building their lives or whatever we took from them. . . . We need to help put all of the elders' minds at ease! So many of the elders have not given up in court yet and are still fighting to get back what they lost. We would want the same to be done for us."

By the time our unit was complete, something important had developed in our class. Students showed more courage to call out race and racism as they analyzed both history and current events. Students began to explore how race has been a fundamental factor in the history of U.S. foreign and domestic policy.

Most importantly, through their discussions and writing, students began to reflect on how race affects their own lives, often incorporating the history of their own families. They began to see how racism is not just an issue for some groups, but is an issue of human rights for all people.

Throughout this unit, my 8th-grade class inspired me with their compassion. Later in the year, students wrote reflections on their learning from this unit. Many suggested that it be taught each year.

"I can use the way we learned to talk to each other for the rest of my life," said Rumel.

"It challenged us to think like different people, and it gave us power to make the decision," said Nick.

And finally, Sam, after sitting silently for several minutes carefully pondering what to write, left me one line: "We listened to each other."

Moé Yonamine teaches social studies at Roosevelt High School in Portland, Oregon.

NOTE There is discussion among Asian American scholars and activists about whether to call what happened to Japanese Americans (and Japanese Latin Americans) during World War II "internment" or "incarceration." In this article, both terms are used interchangeably

Resources

Au, Wayne. "Addressing Redress." *Teaching About Asian Pacific Americans: Effective Activities, Strategies, and Assignments for Classrooms and Communities.* Lanham, Md.: Rowman & Littlefield, 2006.

United States. Personal Justice Denied—Report of the Commission on Wartime Relocation and Internment of Civilians. Washington, D.C.: U.S. Government Printing Office, 1982.

Higashide, Seiichi. *Adios to Tears—The Memoirs of a Japanese-Peruvian Internee in U.S. Concentration Camps.* Seattle: University of Washington Press, 1993.

Masterson, Daniel and Sayaka Funada-Classen. *The Japanese in Latin America.* Champaign, Ill.: University of Illinois Press, 2004.

Campaign for Justice. www.campaignforjustice.org ["History" and "Resources" tabs].

Japanese American Citizens League. www.jacl.org ["Education" tabs].

Map of internment camps is found at: www.jacl.org/edu/MapofConcentrationCamps.pdf.

Chapter Forty-Seven

BRINGING THE CIVIL RIGHTS MOVEMENT INTO THE CLASSROOM

By Larry Miller

When I taught a freshman citizenship class to all entering students at Metropolitan High School, a predominantly African American high school in Milwaukee, I included a five-week introduction to the history of the Civil Rights Movement. I felt strongly that students of every race should have an understanding of the rich history of struggle for equality in this country. We examined the tactics of the Southern Civil Rights Movement, the Black Power Movement as exemplified by the Black Panthers, and government repression against African Americans. We concluded the unit with a debate that represents the spectrum of opinion of 20th-century African American leaders.

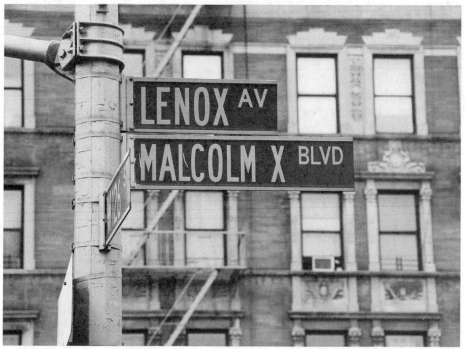

ISTOCKPHOTO

Southern Struggles

I started by introducing students to some of the key battles in the South in the 1950s and 1960s. An invaluable resource throughout the unit was the *Eyes on the Prize* series, a two-part film documentary that begins with the Emmett Till murder in 1955 (see below) and goes through 1985. The first, *Eyes on the Prize: America's Civil Rights Years 1954–1965,* is a six-segment documentary that first aired on PBS. *Eyes on the Prize II: America at the Racial Crossroads,* 1965–1985 is broken into eight parts of roughly one hour each. Both documentaries have extensive accompanying material in print.

I also used *Free at Last: A History of the Civil Rights Movement and Those Who Died in the Struggle,* a 104-page magazine-sized booklet that begins with a section on slavery and ends in the 1960s. It tells the history of the movement by focusing on individuals who gave their lives to the struggles in the 1950s and 1960s.

I edited selections from *Eyes on the Prize,* and kept the length of each segment between 10 and 20 minutes. I then followed with a reading from the booklet *Free at Last* that has a short description of each of the events just covered in the documentary.

Each day after showing the video segment and doing the reading, I held a discussion where I asked for students' impressions and thoughts. Then I had students write in their journals, giving their thoughts about what they just viewed, read, and discussed. I repeated my instructions for writing in journals each day, and I also wrote them on the board: "Don't just describe what you see or hear. Include your reactions and emotional responses, the questions the video and reading raise for you, and your thoughts on how you might have responded if you were there at the time." While students did this I walked around class and read their reactions as they finished.

Then at the beginning of class the next day I read from three or four of the journals, both to sum up discussions and spark new lines of inquiry. Here I talked to students about the tactics used in the particular struggles we are observing and studying.

One student, after seeing the brutality toward students sitting in at a lunch counter in Nashville, Tenn., said, "I could never be nonviolent, turn the other cheek, and not hit back. It makes me mad just to hear about this. No way would I put up with it." This comment gave us a chance to discuss the philosophies of nonviolence of Gandhi and Martin Luther King Jr., and the role of nonviolent civil disobedience in the Civil Rights Movement. It also led to a discussion on anger. One Latina student said she felt angry when she heard about what happened to African Americans during that era. We talked about how all of us, no matter what our race, should be angry about injustices in our history.

The historical events we have studied in this unit so far are:
- The murder of 14-year-old Emmett Till in 1955 in Money, Miss. Till, who was from Chicago, violated the white supremacist codes of the

time by—acting on a dare from another teenager—flippantly saying "Bye Baby" to a white store clerk as he left a country store. That weekend he was beaten, shot in the head, and dumped into the Tallahatchie River because, as the clerk's husband later said, "He thought he was as good as any white man." An all-white jury found the murderers "not guilty." (Shown in the "Awakenings 1954–1956" segment of *Eyes on the Prize* and on pages 40–41 of *Free at Last*.)

One Latina student said she felt angry when she heard about what happened to African Americans during that era.

- The Montgomery bus boycott in 1955, in which Rosa Parks, the young Martin Luther King Jr., and many others joined a growing movement to end the Southern Jim Crow rule that blacks had to sit at the back of the bus. I use this section in particular to highlight the courage and resourcefulness of black communities. (Shown in the "Awakenings 1954–1956" segment of *Eyes on the Prize* and on pages 14–15 of *Free at Last*.)

- The lunch counter sit-ins in Nashville to demand that public accommodations such as restaurants and restrooms be open to African Americans. In one year alone, 70,000 people—mostly young people and college students—participated in sit-ins at public accommodations, and 3,600 were arrested. This section is especially useful to talk about the bravery of young activists and to explain the philosophy of nonviolence that was characteristic of many in the Civil Rights Movement. (Shown in the "Ain't Scared of Your Jails 1960–1961" segment of *Eyes on the Prize* and on pages 18–19 of *Free at Last*.)

- The Freedom Rides in 1961, in which journalists reported on the bus rides of whites and blacks who set off from Washington in a heroic action to test compliance with a court ruling outlawing the segregation of buses and terminals. Angry white mobs attacked the Freedom Riders as they disembarked from buses. The Freedom Rides, organized primarily by the Congress of Racial Equality (CORE), were one of the first times in which the Civil Rights Movement consciously used the power of the media, in this case mostly print journalists, to win people over to their cause. (Shown in the "Ain't Scared of Your Jails 1960–1961" segment of *Eyes on the Prize* and on pages 20–21 of *Free at Last*.)

- The Birmingham struggle in 1963 demanding jobs for blacks and an end to segregation in this key Southern city. Protesters led by the Rev. Martin Luther King Jr. and the Southern Christian Leadership Conference were attacked by dogs and fire hoses under the orders of Police Chief Bull Connor. I note the movement's use of the television media, which brought the reality of Southern bigotry directly into the living rooms of households across America. (Shown in the "No Easy Walk 1961–1963" segment of *Eyes on the Prize* and on pages 22–23 of *Free at Last*.)

- "Freedom Summer" in 1964, which highlights the work of the Student Nonviolent Coordinating Committee (SNCC) in Mississippi, pointing out the blatant and widespread violation of the voting rights of African Americans. The section brings us into the issue of voting rights and also focuses on the role of young organizers. (Shown in the "Mississippi: Is This America? 1962–1964" segment of *Eyes on the Prize* and on pages 26–30 of *Free at Last.*)
- The Selma march in 1965 that united SNCC, CORE, and the SCLC in the demand for voting rights and was instrumental in the passage of the Federal Voting Rights Act of that year. (Shown in the "Bridge to Freedom 1965" segment of *Eyes on the Prize* and on pages 30–31 of *Free at Last.*)

More on Southern Battles

I then showed the movie *Murder in Mississippi,* a made-for-TV movie that re-enacts the 1964 murders of three civil rights organizers who were preparing for Freedom Summer. (This movie should not be confused with the Hollywood version of these murders, *Mississippi Burning,* which glorifies and distorts the role of the FBI in the Civil Rights Movement, transforming it from a tool of government repression into the "white saviors" of embattled blacks.)

In this section, because it highlights voting rights and "Freedom Summer," I also had students take the 10-minute Louisiana Literacy Test, used to prevent African Americans from voting. I write on the chalkboard, "Spell backwards, forwards" and "Print the word vote upside down, but in the correct order." Students always respond with dismay, asking, "Why?" I explained that these are the types of questions African Americans were asked in Louisiana on literacy tests as they attempted to vote. By actually taking the test, the students were able to see how hard the state of Louisiana worked to stop the black community from voting.

The Black Panthers and Government Repression

Here I focused on the Black Panther Party. The Panthers were the target of a coordinated attack from police departments and the FBI. By looking at the Black Panther Party experience, students saw the extent to which local and federal government agencies were willing to go to suppress a militant urban movement of African Americans.

We started with a discussion of the Panther Ten Point Program (see www.blackpanther.org). Students then wrote reflections on each of the 10 points. I asked students to do this as homework because of the length of the 10 points. The following day students discussed their reflections and answer for each of the 10 points,

"Does it have meaning today?"

Students generally agreed with the 10 points. But in one class, Naquandra expressed reservations about Panther point number 9, which calls for the release of all black men from jail because of the racist justice system. She stated, "The 10 points have a lot of meaning, even today. All black men have faced racism, but some are in jail for murder and rape. Some of them I don't want on the streets."

We then watched the section on the Panthers from *Eyes on the Prize,* which explains the origins of the Black Panther Party in Oakland and its focus on issues of police brutality and the creation of community programs to "serve the people." (Shown in "Power! 1966–1968" of *Eyes on the Prize II.*)

By looking at the Black Panther Party experience, students saw the extent to which local and federal government agencies were willing to go to suppress a militant urban movement of African Americans.

From here we watched the *Eyes on the Prize* section on the Chicago Panthers and the assassination of Fred Hampton by the FBI and Chicago police in 1969. The fact that the FBI played an open and direct role in Fred Hampton's death startled a number of students. This sets the stage to study the activity of the FBI and U.S. government toward black liberation leaders and organizations. (Shown in "A Nation of Law? 1968–1971" of *Eyes on the Prize II.*)

We looked at the FBI's infiltration, surveillance, and disruption of black leaders and organizations. Students read the article "J. Edgar Hoover and the Infiltration of Black Activists: A Comparison of FBI Surveillance of Marcus Garvey, Paul Robeson, and Martin Luther King,"[1] which shows how the FBI paid people to disrupt organizations and spread derogatory information about peoples' personal lives to try to destroy the freedom struggle of African Americans. Included with it are biographies of the three leaders and primary documents from FBI records. Students, in groups, gave biographies of the three men discussed in the articles and the ways in which the FBI harassed them.

I then had students brainstorm responses to the question "What are the ways that enemies of freedom movements can try to undermine them?" The list of responses always included buying people off, brutality, murdering leaders, jailing people, sabotage, subversion, lies, cowardice, denigration, complacency, eroding the base of support through the introduction of drugs, and the spreading of propaganda. I then went through the brainstorm list and asked students to give examples from our study.

Finally, I had students study the perspectives of a selection of African American leaders representing a spectrum of those who organized from as early as the turn of century through the 1960s. They debated each other representing those historical figures.

As the unit concluded, my students felt they had a more realistic picture of the history of this country. One white student stated, "I was surprised to see that this country was not completely built on the Constitution. I realized that there is a lot of U.S. history to be angry about."

"This knowledge will help me with perseverance," wrote Shawanda. "I know I will have to overcome racism and prejudice. But instead of focusing on people's negatives I am going to focus on what I am going to be as a black woman. Right now I am using my education and hopefully someday I will be able to speak out for freedom as someone who is respected and strong. I don't think anybody can take that away from me."

As the unit concluded, my students felt they had a more realistic picture of the history of this country.

Larry Miller taught for more than 17 years in Milwaukee Public Schools. For many years, he served on the school board for Milwaukee Public Schools. He is an editor of Rethinking Schools.

Endnote

1. "J. Edgar Hoover and the Infiltration of Black Activists: a Comparison of FBI Surveillance of Marcus Garvey, Paul Robeson and Martin Luther King," by Mary Lou Brewer, Eleanor Griffis, Mary Jane Colwell, Michael Furmanovsky, and Dorothy Logan, in *History from the Bottom Up*, produced by the Woodrow Wilson National Fellowship Foundation History Institute and The DeWitt Wallace-Reader's Digest Fund. (1990)

Resources

Sara Bullard, *At Last: A History of the Civil Rights Movement and Those Who Died in the Struggle* (Montgomery, Ala: Teaching Tolerance, 1989). Still available on Amazon.

Eyes on the Prize: America's Civil Rights Years 1954-1965. Available as a DVD at www.shoppbs.org. Also available in most urban public libraries.

Download a pdf of the Louisiana Literacy Test at http://www.rethinkingschools.org/static/img/archive/17_02/Vote_test.pdf

Chapter Forty-Eight

'WE NEED TO KNOW THIS!'
Student power and curriculum

By Jody Sokolower

Five minutes into the period, as I was explaining the industrialization project to my 10th-grade world history class, Tiffany had her hand in the air.

"It's almost the end of February and we haven't done anything about black history! Why don't we ever do anything about black people?" she demanded. A chorus of voices, all African American, backed her up.

"But we just finished studying Haiti," I protested. "Doesn't that count?"

"No!" they shouted. "This class is racist!"

As a white teacher, this accusation always hits me in the gut. My initial reaction was defensive—hadn't I started the year with a section on medieval Africa? Didn't I expand the curriculum to include more on the transatlantic slave trade and the Haitian revolution?

ISTOCKPHOTO

My mind was a jumble. On one hand, I could see my plans for the next months and my relationship with my history teaching partner shattering before my eyes. On the other hand, I knew they were getting at something really important—and that I needed to acknowledge the justice of their demand. I took a deep breath and promised to come back with a plan for discussing the issue.

"I can see three different approaches to adding more black content to the curriculum," I explained to both world history classes the next day. "We can look at what was happening to African Americans at each point in world history; we can focus more on African history; or we can look at what African American and African leaders were saying about world events. What do you think would be best?"

> **My mind was a jumble. On one hand, I could see my plans for the next months and my relationship with my history teaching partner shattering before my eyes. On the other hand, I knew they were getting at something really important.**

I was amazed at the discussions that resulted. No one asked which alternative would be less work, or more points. Students took the question seriously, listened to each other, and shared their frustration at their previous experiences with African history.

"I don't want to learn about slavery any more," said Rachelle, a conscientious and high-achieving African American student. "Every time we learn about black people, it's just about us being victims and it makes me feel terrible."

"What about Haiti?" I asked. "We learned about how Toussaint L'Ouverture led a successful revolution that created an independent country."

"I only remember the part about slavery," she responded.

"Every year we learn the same stuff about Rosa Parks and Martin Luther King—that's it," added another student.

After much discussion, the classes agreed that they wanted to focus on African history.

"We know less about Africa than anywhere else in the world," Emily, a white student, explained.

"OK," I agreed. "The next unit is on imperialism—that's the fight over land and resources before World War I. I'll look for information on the fight over Africa from an African perspective."

"I don't want to read a bunch of stuff that's just going to make me feel worse," Rachelle warned as the bell rang.

Rethinking History Teaching

As a college student in the late 1960s, discovering the historical truth behind the lies in my history books was a liberating and empowering experience. But most of my students see things differently. In the 1960s and '70s, revolutions around the world and boundless activism in the United States reinforced the connection between real history and social change. In the absence of that exciting tumult, many youth today experience the bitter truths of U.S. history as depressing—it only feeds their feelings of powerlessness and alienation. My African American students often express anger at a history where their ancestors are overwhelmingly portrayed as victims, relieved by a few pasteboard heroes.

I hoped that this unit, demanded by my students, would have a different effect. Their energy helped soothe my anxiety about falling even further behind in our race to finish all of world history by June. I revised my goals for the unit. To my original goal:

Students will demonstrate understanding of the Era of Imperialism in Africa, I added the following:

> Students will begin to explore their stereotypes, thoughts, and feelings about Africa. (I hoped this would free students like Rachelle to look at the positive and negative aspects of African history.)
>
> Students will analyze historical sources for point of view, including "bias by omission." (I wanted them to see that no historical source is neutral—textbook authors, like all historians, express a point of view.)
>
> Students will recognize the power of articulating their own questions about history. (All students have "enduring questions" about the world and how it got to be this way—I hoped to validate those questions and bring them into the classroom.)

I started my research by looking for something to read that would enable us to talk about Africa—about the images of Africa in the media, and about the complicated relationship between African Americans and Africa. I chose the first chapter of *Mandela, Mobutu and Me,* by Lynne Duke, a young African American journalist covering Africa in the 1990s. In the first chapter, she talks about her feelings of connection and pride at Africa's beauty and strength, her angst about the level of brutality and corruption, her hope for the future.

> **My African American students often express anger at a history where their ancestors are overwhelmingly portrayed as victims, relieved by a few pasteboard heroes.**

As we read the chapter aloud, I asked students to keep a dialogue journal—noting quotes and images on one side of the paper, their reflections on the other. Almost every student in both classes completed the dialogue journal, including Ida, an English language learner from Brazil, who hadn't turned in a piece of written work all year, and Kyla, an African American student who had just transferred into my class and up to that point had kept her head buried in a book. Here are a few excerpts from Kyla's reflections:

> Lynne Duke and her co-workers were hecka brave to go to Africa. It was sad to read about the chaos that was going on there. I could tell how

frustrated Lynne was getting from the blackouts, the food shortages, the violence that went on in the streets and just to see how Africa was in ruins. . . . I didn't think that Africa was still in wars and stuff. I thought that Africa was like peaceful and full of fun and beauty. I didn't know about all the struggle and violence. . . . I think she finished the chapters with the drummers on the boat because it was like symbolism. She said with each beat she was further away from despair and she called it her rhythm of salvation.

Maria, a white student, quoted Duke: "I thought of all the people, so many, many people, who had every reason, every right, to lose hope in Africa but did not" and then reflected: "These kinds of people amaze me. To some degree, I strive to be one of these people. Believing in something is what gets people through things. I want that."

Through African Eyes

Meanwhile, I began a search for Afrocentric (written from an African perspective) histories of African conflict with Europe from 1880 to 1918. I was appalled at how difficult it was to find anything at all. There were lots of histories of Africa, many of them anticolonial, but all of them quoted European historians and discussed the period from a European perspective. Eventually I found a brief section in Pan-African scholar John Henrik Clarke's *Africans at the Crossroads: Notes for an African World Revolution* that described the fierce resistance mounted by dozens of African cultures against European intrusions.

> **There were lots of histories of Africa, many of them anticolonial, but all of them quoted European historians and discussed the period from a European perspective.**

Before we read Clarke, I had my students read the section on "The Age of Imperialism" in their McDougal Littell textbook, *Modern World History: Patterns of Interaction*. "Make a list of what you consider the most important facts," I told them. They compared their lists in small groups and we came up with a class list of main events and concepts.

Then we turned to the Clarke reading. I had the students keep three running lists as we read the chapter aloud: important facts, personal reflections, and questions generated by the text.

I put the students into small groups and had them compare the two texts by answering the following questions:

What differences do you see between the two texts?

What are the strengths and weaknesses of the textbook?

What are the strengths and weaknesses of the Clarke book?

What examples of point of view do you see in each text?

What questions do you have now?

"Look at this," a usually alienated white student named Eric shouted. "Clarke says Europeans always called African leaders chiefs instead of kings because they didn't want them compared to European kings. Right here in our textbook they call Shaka a Zulu chief!"

"I don't know," Molly, also white, said. "Clarke seems awfully biased. How do we know what he says is true?"

"Clarke has so many examples of resistance movements and Europe didn't really control African land for that long," reasoned Elijah, one of the African American students who was angriest with me that first day. "But in the textbook it subtitles that whole section 'Unsuccessful Movements.' That's cold."

Our discussion comparing the two texts was one of the most engaged and thoughtful of the whole year, and the quality and quantity of work I received was exceptional. It was the high point of the year for most of us.

Same Curriculum, Different Results

This year I taught world history again. At the appropriate point in the curriculum, I explained what happened in my class last year, and we studied the same texts in the same way. But the results were very different. Some students were interested in the readings, and students who were good at critical analysis wrote thoughtfully about the differences in perspectives and information. But the excitement was gone. It was an educational experience, but not an empowering one. Most importantly, it did nothing to support African American leadership in the class. The student demand to learn something that they needed to know was an essential part of the equation.

The student demand to learn something that they needed to know was an essential part of the equation.

I have realized more and more as I teach history that progressive content is not enough. Teaching accurate, multicultural history doesn't necessarily have the impact on students that we, as progressive teachers, hope it will. If it's disconnected from students experiencing themselves as architects of their own education and makers of history, it often reinforces their feelings of cynicism and hopelessness about social change.

Being receptive to student need and allowing space for students to think about and express what they want to learn is critical to education as a liberating experience, as a component of social justice. It's more than offering a choice—would you rather create a diary or a graphic novel? It's creating an environment in the classroom where students will make demands. And it's listening, really listening, so we hear the demands and separate them out from the idle complaints.

The more substantive the choices we offer students, the more likely they are to articulate their ideas. (For example, "What should we do with the information we've learned about immigration—take a field trip to the capitol to lobby legislators or write letters to the editor? What ideas do you have?" And then, "What else do we need to learn before we do that?") But some of it I experience as a kind of letting go, of being open to what they have to say, being open to messing up my plans for something exciting and unscripted.

Being receptive to student need and allowing space for students to think about and express what they want to learn is critical to education as a liberating experience, as a component of social justice.

This is not an argument for spontaneity or against the importance of planning and perfecting curriculum over time. Developing strong curriculum takes an enormous amount of time and energy. The first few times I teach material, I realize the problems, try to fill the holes and inject more scaffolding. Carefully constructed units that have been honed through trial and error remain the backbone of effective teaching.

Finally, there are clear trade-offs to this approach. We never did get past Vietnam that year, and student demands probably won't dovetail with state standards or the upcoming standardized test. But we each have to ask ourselves—in the final analysis, who are we answerable to? If we can help our students see that knowledge is power and that they have the right and the responsibility to demand the knowledge they need, it's a good day at school.

Jody Sokolower is currently managing editor of Rethinking Schools. *Previously she taught social studies and English to middle and high school students in the California Bay Area.*

Resources

Clarke, John Henrik. *Africans at the Crossroads: Notes for an African World Revolution.* Trenton, NJ: *Africa World Press,* 1991.

Duke, Lynne. *Mandela, Mobutu and Me: A Newswoman's African Journey.* New York: Doubleday, 2003.

Chapter Forty-Nine

BURNED OUT OF HOMES AND HISTORY

Unearthing the silenced voices of the Tulsa Race Massacre

By Linda Christensen

In this chapter, Rethinking Schools editor and language arts teacher Linda Christensen describes a section of Stealing Home, a unit she created about ways the homes of people of color have been stolen through "race riots" and "urban renewal" in Tulsa, Oklahoma; Los Angeles' Chavez Ravine; and Portland, Oregon's Albina neighborhood.

I teach language arts, so why would I teach my students about the 1921 Tulsa Race Massacre? In language arts circles, we discuss reading as a window to the world, but in a country plagued with foreclosures and homelessness, we need to question the world we're gazing at: How are contemporary evictions a historical reach from the past? What has happened to Black and brown communities? Why

THE RESEARCH DIVISION OF OKLAHOMA HISTORICAL SOCIETY

THE RESEARCH DIVISION OF OKLAHOMA HISTORICAL SOCIETY

do people of color have less inherited wealth than whites? The untold history—the buried stories—reveals patterns that affect our students' current lives, from eviction notices to the hunger of deep poverty. I can wax poetic about the importance of story in students' lives, but reading literature of poverty and despair without offering a historical explanation leaves students with little understanding about how things came to be the way they are. And that's worth reading and writing about.

Jefferson High School, where I co-teach a junior language arts class with Dianne Leahy—a wonderful teacher who allows me to keep my teaching chops alive by creating and teaching curriculum with her—is located in a gentrifying neighborhood that once was the heart of the African American community in Portland. Families were pushed out of their homes because of urban renewal beginning in the 1960s and again, more recently, because of gentrification. As the price of homes rises in what is now called the "Alberta Arts Neighborhood," most of our students' families can no longer afford to live in our school's neighborhood. They live in apartments on the outskirts of the city, and a number ride buses or the commuter train to come to school at Jefferson.

For me, learning about the history of the Tulsa Race Masssacre coincided with the current economic crisis that has led to epic foreclosures and evictions. I realized that, like many people, the majority of my family "wealth" is tied up in our home. We drew on that wealth to send our daughters to college. They will inherit the house, and the wealth it represents, when my husband and I pass on. The story of Tulsa may be an extreme instance of violent dispossession, but it highlights a pattern of historical expulsions and exclusions that explains the lack of inherited wealth in Black and brown communities. According to historian Hannibal B. Johnson, "The Tulsa Race Riot of 1921 was set against a backdrop of a multitude of race riots in America. 1919 was known as 'red summer' because blood was flowing in the streets. There were over 25 major riots in 1919 in America." (See Elliot Jaspin's book *Buried in the Bitter Waters: The Hidden History of Racial Cleansing in America* for more on this topic.) The complicit silence of textbooks about the history of race riots and racial exclusions that pushed Black people off their lands and out of their homes keeps our students ignorant about the reasons for the lack of economic resources in the Black community. Instead students must imagine why their people lack wealth.

The term "race riot" does not adequately describe the events of May 31–June 1, 1921, in Tulsa. Though some sources labeled the episode a "race riot" or a "race war," implying that both Blacks and whites might be equally to blame for law-lessness and violence, the historical record documents that what occurred was a sustained and murderous assault on Black lives and property. This assault was met by a brave but unsuccessful armed defense of their community by some Black World War I veterans and others. During the night and day of the massacre, dep-utized whites killed more than 300 African Americans; they looted and burned to the ground 40 square blocks, including 1,265 African American homes, hospitals, schools, churches, and 150 businesses. White deputies and members of the Na-tional Guard arrested and detained 6,000 Black Tulsans who were released only upon being vouched for by a white employer or other white citizen; 9,000 African Americans were left homeless and living in tents well into the winter of 1921.

Building Background Knowledge and Interest

In class, before we began the unit, I briefly discussed the arc of our upcoming study. "We are starting this unit because I want you to think about wealth in this country. Who has it? Who doesn't? An important study just discovered that whites have 20 times the wealth of blacks. Why is that? When there's a question that puzzles you, you have to investigate. For many people, including me, our wealth is tied up in our homes. So what happens when you lose your home?"

Students frequently bring up the gentrification of the neighborhood, which has rapidly transformed from mom-and-pop grocery stores to chic restaurants and upscale boutiques. Rather than describe the problem of gentrification at this early stage of the study, I move them into the history, keeping the question of homes and wealth in front of them as we move forward.

To stimulate our students' interest in resurrecting this silenced history of Tul-sa, I created a tea party/mixer about the night of the invasion of Greenwood, as the African American section of Tulsa was called. Using sources from historians John Hope Franklin, Scott Ellsworth, and others, I wrote roles for students that gave them each a slice of what happened that night: the arrest of Dick Rowland, a young African American shoe shiner, who allegedly raped Sarah Page, a white elevator operator, in broad daylight (later, students learn that authorities dropped all charges); the newspaper article that incited whites and blacks to gather at the courthouse; the gathering of armed Black World War I veterans to prevent a lynch-ing; the deputizing and arming of whites, many of whom were in the KKK; the internment of Blacks; the death of more than 300 African American men, women, and children; the burning and looting of their homes and businesses. Because not all white Tulsans shared the racial views of the white rioters, I included roles of a few whites and a recent immigrant from Mexico who provided safety in the midst of death and chaos. These roles allowed students to understand that, even in moments of violence, people stood up and reached across race and class borders to help. I invented one role, Thelma Booker, as a compilation of people I'd read about; the others were individuals whose stories I found in Ellsworth's book, *Death in a Promised Land: The Tulsa Race Riot of 1921,* and other materials. Three of the roles give a sense of the information students learned through the tea party/mixer:

Mrs. Jackson: A mob attacked my home and killed my husband on the night of June 1, 1921. My husband was a surgeon. The Mayo brothers said he was the best surgeon in the country. My husband fought off the mob that attacked our house. An officer who knew my husband came up to the house and assured him that if he would surrender he would be protected. This my husband did. The officer sent him under guard to the Convention Hall, where Black people were kept for "protection" from the mob. While my husband was on his way to the detention center, he was shot and killed in cold blood. The officer who had assured my husband of protection told Walter White, the *Nation* journalist, "Dr. Jackson was an able, clean-cut man. He did only what any red-blooded man would have done under similar circumstances in defending his home. Dr. Jackson was murdered by white ruffians."

Thelma Booker: The National Guard came knocking on our door and told us we had to leave our homes. They said it wasn't safe and they were going to protect us. We didn't feel too comfortable about that. Then they marched us through the white area of Tulsa, made us raise our hands in the air as we walked through as if we were going to attack someone with our house slippers. First, we were taken to the Convention Hall, then to the ball field, and finally to the fairgrounds, like we were prize cattle. You know, they even went and rounded up Black folks who worked as domestics in white people's homes. Oh sure, they fed us and gave us medical attention. And while our homes and businesses were looted and burned behind us, they made us stay until a white person came and vouched for us. Anyone who was vouched for received a card. Anyone without a card on the streets could be arrested. Of course, we had to pay for our food and all while we were being "protected." We were sent out to clean up the city. We were paid standard laborers' wages. It was by no means an easy existence, but some whites soon complained that we were being "spoiled" at the fairgrounds and by the attention given us by the Red Cross and other charitable organizations.

Ruth Phelps: Honestly, I couldn't believe what was happening. We lived outside of the city along the road to Sand Springs, about a day's walk north from Tulsa. We helped out the Black folks running away from Tulsa. We hid and fed about 20 Black massacre victims in the basement of our home for most of a week. We believed that the Golden Rule applied whether people were white, Black, or Native American. So when terrified and hungry Black people came to our door, we hid them in our basement. I put an extra pot of beans and sow belly on the stove. Our house became a "safe house" for Black Tulsans who were not imprisoned by the white authorities. Just like the Underground Railroad, Blacks walked through the woods and along creek beds at night. Then we hid them during the day until it was safe for them to move on.

We didn't ask what happened that night in Tulsa. We knew by watching them huddle and cry in the basement that it was terrible. When we drove to Greenwood later and saw the burned down remains of their homes, we were glad that we offered sanctuary, so they knew that God lived in some white folks.

I briefly discussed the event before launching into the tea party. "You are going to become people who were involved in what is called the Tulsa Race Massacre on the night of May 31, 1921." I told them that Tulsa was divided into two sections—the white section and Greenwood, where most African Americans lived. We had studied Jim Crow, so they understood segregation. "I want you to figure out what happened that night. First, read over your role. Underline or highlight key pieces of information. You will need to be able to tell others about what happened to you and what you witnessed. Once you have read your role, turn over your paper and write down the key events, so you can retell them to your classmates."

After students read their roles, I handed out a series of questions to help them elicit information from each other's roles. We read over the questions, which included: "Find someone who suffered a loss during the massacre. What did they lose? What happened?" Students found one or more questions that they could answer based on their role. Before I turned them loose, I added, "You are entering the roles of people whose lives may have been shattered on that night. Take their lives seriously. Give them the dignity they deserve."

Students circulated through the room, talking in pairs, finding out bits and pieces of what happened that night. Because this was an introduction to the unit, not the full story, they ended the activity with information, but also with questions. I asked them to write down key facts they learned about the Tulsa Race Massacre and what they still wanted to know. Their questions filled the class: What really started the massacre? Did Black people rebuild their houses? Why didn't we learn about this before? (When I guest-taught this lesson in a history class at Jefferson a few years ago, a couple of students spontaneously pulled out their history textbooks and searched for an entry on Tulsa, but didn't find one.)

History and Poetry

Rather than answer their questions in a lecture, I discovered several accessible readings and YouTube clips (*The Night Tulsa Burned*, Parts 1–4, youtube.com/

watch?v=LD3aw4-RJpE&feature=relmfu). Four short related videos, narrated by historians Scott Ellsworth and Hannibal B. Johnson and Tulsa Historical Society director Robert Powers, tell the story, using historical photographs from the night of the massacre. These clips also feature interviews with three survivors: Juanita Burnett Arnold, George Monroe, and Ernestine Alpha Gibbs. I asked students to take notes that answer the questions they raised in class, but also to record details and stories that resonated for them. "You will write a poem, a piece of historical fiction, and an essay about this time period. I want you to absorb the era as well as the facts. Write down the names of people, buildings, streets, parks. Grab people's stories, their faces, and their lives. I want you to know what happened, but I also want you to try to understand how people felt about that night. As you learn about this history, make connections to what's happening today. How does this history echo in your life?"

How does what happened in Tulsa connect to the question of black wealth?

After watching each 10-minute video clip, we stopped and debriefed: "What questions got answered for you? What images stuck with you? Whose stories will you carry with you?"

Then I asked: "When we began this unit, I said that we were going to ask about wealth in our country: Who has it, who doesn't, and why? How does the history of Tulsa help us begin to answer these questions? How does what happened in Tulsa connect to the question of Black wealth?" As students talked, I listed their observations on the board as a reference they could return to during our writing.

Once we had images and names, I discussed two ways to write poems about the event—as a persona poem or an image poem: "For a persona poem, write from the point of view of a person or object. Use the word 'I'. For an image poem, describe what you see. Form a picture for the reader with your words." Christina wrote a persona poem from the perspective of a burned wall; she called it "The Last One Standing":

> I am the last one standing.
> Nothing lives within me.
> Nothing remains.
> All around me are ashes of what used to be.
> I am just a memory of what this
> town was before the riot.
> I felt the others burning down
> on my left and right.
> I saw the glowing flames in the midst
> of this dark night and the leftover embers
> of the morning.
> Bodies scattered about,
> blood on my stoop.

I am the last one standing.
I am the remains of this race riot,
never written in a textbook,
I hold one of history's lost truths.

Reading and Writing Historical Fiction

As we pursued the Stealing Home unit, Dianne and I discovered *If We Must Die: A Novel of Tulsa's 1921 Greenwood Riot* by Pat Carr. We wanted students to tap into the ways that literature can deepen history by bringing to life the mind-numbing numbers of loss through the stories of individuals. The novel tells the story of 1921 Tulsa through the character of Berneen O'Brien, a woman of "Black Irish" descent, who accepts a job at a Black school in Greenwood. She "passes" for Black during the day and returns home to her uncle, who is a member of the KKK. The reader discovers the racial tensions and the eruption of the massacre from Berneen's perspective.

Students kept track of historical events in their dialogue journal, but they also took notes on the author's craft: the way Pat Carr showed how characters felt through the use of interior monologue, actions, and dialogue, as well as the strategies she used to mix historical fact and fiction. After students read a chunk of the book, they gathered in groups and created posters about the difference between history and fiction, using notes from their dialogue journals. The poster had three sections:

1. Quotes that referenced history.
2. Quotes that illustrated the qualities of fiction.
3. Their analysis of the differences.

For the third section, one group wrote:

> In the novel, fiction is often very detailed and elaborated, for example, "The shoulder of his white shirt suddenly blossomed red as if he'd run headlong into a sack of crimson paint." Fact is usually subtle, using the names of people and place and events—Greenwood Avenue, Dreamland Theatre, the Drexel Building. Most events in the novel were factual—the shooting, the looting, the internment—but most of the characters and their personalities were fabricated. There are things that the author says to describe a character that couldn't be known—their body language, their speech patterns, their interior monologue.

As I teach social justice lessons, I am also always teaching students how to read and write with greater clarity. We don't have to parse out the language arts skills and teach them as stand-alone lessons; they are part of the daily classroom work.

We asked students to write a piece of fiction based on their knowledge of the events, modeled on Carr's work. Writing historical fiction pushes students to learn more about the past and to more fully understand the events and the time period. Students had to go back to the documents and videos to get down the sequence of events; they had to get inside people's heads to understand why the African American World War I veterans stood up for Dick Rawlins, why they were adamant that there would be no more lynchings. But they also had to learn about people's daily lives—where they lived, where they shopped, where they worked, and details like the fact that no one watched television in 1921.

Writing historical fiction pushes students to learn more about the past and to more fully understand the events and the time period.

To prime students for the assignment, we distributed a newspaper article written in 2009 that describes interviews with three survivors of the Tulsa massacre—Beulah Smith, Ruth Avery, and Kenny Booker. The article reviews the events and contains quotes from the survivors:

> Beulah Smith was 14 years old the night of the riot. A neighbor named Frenchie came pounding on her family's door in a Tulsa neighborhood known as "Little Africa" that also went up in flames. Get your families out of here because they're killing [Black people] uptown," she remembers Frenchie saying. "We hid in the weeds in the hog pen," Smith told CNN. . . . Booker, then a teenager, hid with his family in their attic until the home was torched. "When we got downstairs, things were burning. My sister asked me, 'Kenny, is the world on fire?' I said, 'I don't know, but we're in a heck of a lot of trouble, baby.'"

Many students used these specific incidents in their stories. Some even used the dialogue from the article, then invented the rest of the story.

Dianne and I developed a graphic organizer for students to get them started (see Resources). Then we spent part of a period listing potential characters and scenes that students could use in their stories: Kenny Booker, Sarah Page, Beulah Smith, Walter White, the NAACP journalist, Ruth Phelps. I also encouraged them to use pieces of their own lives in their stories. I told them, "In the novel I'm writing about women organizing for change on the Mexican border, I have the main character bake desserts when she's stressed. I also tap into my own desire for justice, my work organizing. I found that when I use pieces of my life, the characters come to life." Students who have experienced homelessness or evictions used their feelings of loss as they wrote. Desi, who is biracial, wrote her story from the points of view of two characters—an African American boy caught with his younger sister in the masssacre and fire, and the white girl who loves him. Jalean recreated his family—an older brother who lives with his mother and two younger siblings he adores. He also created a character modeled on the security guard at Jefferson, who has been a wise elder in Jalean's life.

The student writing was stunning. Students invented backstories to help read-

THE RESEARCH DIVISION OF OKLAHOMA HISTORICAL SOCIETY

ers understand their characters' histories and motivation. They used the tools of fiction writers—character development, dialogue, interior monologue, setting descriptions. Desiree DuBoise's story illustrates how students used the scenes from the photos of the city's destruction, the voices of the people we studied, and the history of the time period to create their stories:

The sky rained down rivers of flame. I had always been the man of the house, but now Mama was probably long gone, too. She had gone into Greenwood to her floral shop that morning, and never came back home. I was alone in the attic except for Billy Mae. I looked down into her round brown eyes and saw fear that reflected my own. Her thick black lashes were coated with tears, and the only noise that came from her was a soft keening. She was so young, younger than I had been when the Klan took Pop away. I watched as they strung him up like an animal and beat him till every inch of his tall frame was coated with crimson blood. That was years ago. Now my sister had to watch her own city burn, the only place she'd ever known. She could hear the screams coming up from the streets just as well as I could. The floorboards of the attic creaked as I shifted my weight. My sister looked at me then.

"Kenny?" she said my name quietly. "Is the world on fire?"

I looked away. Outside, a thick black fog hung in the air, rising noxiously from thick fingers of smoke that danced and clawed their way towards the sky.

"I don't know, Billy. But we're in a heck of a lot of trouble."

I looked to the window again. The last thing I would try to do in this world was protect my only sister.

"Billy, when we hit the street, if I fall, you run. No matter what, you keep running, OK?"

She nodded at me, tears streaming down her round, ebony-hued cheeks.

I grabbed her up and took the stairs two at a time. Around me, the world was aflame. Pictures of my family burned. My mother, a stunning shot of her in her white wedding dress was torched black, an eerie sight. I turned toward the front door, felt the hot breeze gusting through its gaping frame.

Dianne and I took our students to the band room, the only room big enough to comfortably accommodate all 42 of us, and students read their stories from the podium. The read-around took two days. As students read, those who were stuck or who couldn't get started figured out a storyline; others were prompted to revise after hearing their peers' details, flashbacks, and interior monologues. Although the students didn't directly address the loss of economic wealth through their stories, they wrote about the impact of the devastation: the deaths, the loss of photos, pianos, houses, neighborhoods. Jalean said, "I felt proud to know that there were thriving African American communities. I feel cheated that I never got to live in one."

> **'I felt proud to know that there were thriving African American communities. I feel cheated that I never got to live in one.'**

Reparations Role Play

To inject hope and justice into the unit, Dianne and I created a role play about the efforts to obtain restitution for the deaths and damages suffered by the Black population of Greenwood. We needed to return more directly to our theme of wealth inequality, to reinforce the idea that the injustices of the past affect the present, and that it's never too late for justice—even many years after an event like the Tulsa Race Massacre.

In 1997, the Oklahoma State Legislature authorized a commission to study the riot. After three and a half years of research, the commission delivered its report. Rather than just reading about the results of those proceedings and a 2003 lawsuit initiated on behalf of the survivors and their descendants, we wanted students to think about what "fair" compensation for the loss might mean. We put students in the position of commission members. We asked them to determine what reparations, if any, should be made to the survivors of the Tulsa Race Massacre and their descendants.

Before we started the activity, we reviewed the losses from that night—the deaths and the number of homes, schools, and businesses burned and looted. We gave students three choices to initiate their conversations:

1. Do nothing.
2. Repay individuals and their descendants for their losses.

3. Create reparations for the Greenwood community.

Students had passionate arguments about what should happen. Students' understanding of the long-term impact of the loss of inherited wealth through the destruction of homes and community echoed throughout their discussions. A number of students repeated Aaron's statement, "We can't change what happened in the past, but we can compensate the offspring for the loss of their property and inheritance. At least give the descendants scholarships." Some students felt that wasn't enough. Desiree said, "Who suffered the most? Which was worse—death or property loss? The entire community suffered. We should choose a mixture of compensations: There should be scholarships as well as compensation for the survivors and their descendants. There should be a memorial day and a reburial of the mass graves."

Sarah was afraid that bringing up the past would open old wounds and restart the racism that initiated the massacre. Skylar said, "Who cares if it makes people uncomfortable? They are going to have to deal with it. These things happened, and we have to address them." Vince and many others agreed. "This is not just the past. Racial inequality is still a problem. Forgetting about what happened and burying it without dealing with it is why we still have problems today."

And this was exactly what we wanted kids to see: The past is not dead. We didn't want to get lost in the history of Tulsa, though it needs to be remembered; we wanted students to recognize the historical patterns of stolen wealth in Black, brown, and poor communities. We wanted them to connect the current economic struggle of people of color to dynamics from the past. We wanted them to see that in many ways Tulsa and other historically Black communities are still burning, still being looted. We wanted to bring the story home.

Linda Christensen (lmc@lclark.edu) is director of the Oregon Writing Project at Lewis & Clark College in Portland, Oregon, and a Rethinking Schools editor. She is author, most recently, of Reading, Writing, and Rising Up: Teaching About Social Justice and the Power of the Written Word (2nd edition).

Resources

Download tea party roles at http://www.rethinkingschools.org/static/archive/27_01/Christensen-TulsaRoles.pdf

Download a graphic organizer at http://www.rethinkingschools.org/static/archive/27_01/ChristensenGraphic.pdf

Download tea party/mixer questions at http://www.rethinkingschools.org/static/archive/27_01/ChristensenTulsaQuestions.pdf

INDEX

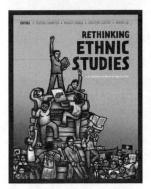

Teaching a People's History of Abolition and the Civil War

Edited by Adam Sanchez

A collection of 10 classroom-tested lessons on one of the most transformative periods in U.S. history. They encourage students to take a critical look at the popular narrative that centers Abraham Lincoln as the Great Emancipator and ignores the resistance of abolitionists and enslaved people. Students can understand how ordinary citizens — with ideas that seem radical and idealistic — can challenge unjust laws, take action together, and fundamentally change society.

2019 • Paperback • 181 pages • ISBN: 978-0-942961-05-8
Print $19.95*

Teacher Unions and Social Justice
Organizing for the schools and communities our students deserve

Edited By Michael Charney, Jesse Hagopian, and Bob Peterson

An anthology of over 60 articles documenting the history and the how-tos of social justice unionism. Together, they describe the growing movement to forge multiracial alliances with communities to defend and transform public education.

Paperback • 448 pages • ISBN: 978-0-942961-09-6
$29.95

Rethinking Sexism, Gender, and Sexuality

Edited by Kim Cosier, Rachel Harper, Jeff Sapp, Jody Sokolower, and Melissa Bollow Tempel

There has never been a more important time for students to understand sexism, gender, and sexuality—or to make schools nurturing places for all of us. The thought-provoking articles and curriculum in this life-changing book will be invaluable to everyone who wants to address these issues in their classroom, school, home, and community.

2015 • 476 pages • ISBN: 978-0-942961-59-1
Print: $24.95*
Ebook/Kindle version: $9.95 Digital and print bundle: $29.95

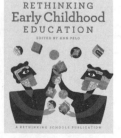

Rethinking Early Childhood Education

Edited by Ann Pelo

Inspiring stories about social justice teaching with young children. This anthology shows how educators can nurture empathy, an ecological consciousness, curiosity, collaboration, and activism in young children.

Paperback • 256 pages • ISBN: 978-0-942961-41-6
Print: $18.95*